Diplomatic
International Relations

Diplomacy does not take place simply between states but wherever people live in different groups. Paul Sharp argues that the demand for diplomacy, and the need for the insights of diplomatic theory, are on the rise. In contrast to conventional texts which use international relations theories to make sense of what diplomacy and diplomats do, this book explores what diplomacy and diplomats can contribute to the big theoretical and practical debates in international relations today. Paul Sharp identifies a diplomatic tradition of international thought premised on the way people live in groups, the differences between intra- and inter-group relations, and the perspectives which those who handle inter-group relations develop about the sorts of international disputes which occur. He argues that the lessons of diplomacy are that we should be reluctant to judge, ready to appease, and alert to the partial grounds on which most universal claims about human beings are made.

PAUL SHARP is Professor and Head of Political Science at the University of Minnesota, Duluth.

3/ Elements of DIPLOMACY
54/ Functions of DIPLOMACY
187/ DIPLOMACY emphasizes opportunities for talking & conversation even in the worst possible situations.

Cambridge Studies in International Relations: 111

Diplomatic Theory of International Relations

EDITORS
Christian Reus-Smit
Nicholas J. Wheeler

EDITORIAL BOARD
James Der Derian, Martha Finnemore, Lene Hansen, Robert Keohane,
Rachel Kerr, Colin McInnes, Jan Aart Scholte, Peter Vale,
Kees Van Der Pijl, Jutta Weldes, Jennifer Welsh, William Wohlforth

Cambridge Studies in International Relations is a joint initiative of Cambridge University Press and the British International Studies Association (BISA). The series will include a wide range of material, from undergraduate textbooks and surveys to research-based monographs and collaborative volumes. The aim of the series is to publish the best new scholarship in International Studies from Europe, North America and the rest of the world.

Cambridge Studies in International Relations

110 John A. Vasquez
   The war puzzle revisited
109 Rodney Bruce Hall
   Central banking as global governance
   Constructing Financial Credibility
108 Milja Kurki
   Causation in international relations
   Reclaiming causal analysis
107 Richard M. Price
   Moral limit and possibility in world politics
106 Emma Haddad
   The refugee in international society
   Between sovereigns
105 Ken Booth
   Theory of world security
104 Benjamin Miller
   States, nations and the great powers
   The sources of regional war and peace
103 Beate Jahn (ed.)
   Classical theory in international relations
102 Andrew Linklater and Hidemi Suganami
   The English School of international relations
   A contemporary reassessment
101 Colin Wight
   Agents, structures and international relations
   Politics as ontology
100 Michael C. Williams
   The realist tradition and the limits of international relations
99 Ivan Arreguín-Toft
   How the weak win wars
   A theory of asymmetric conflict

Series list continued after index

Diplomatic Theory of International Relations

PAUL SHARP
University of Minnesota, Duluth

CAMBRIDGE UNIVERSITY PRESS
Cambridge, New York, Melbourne, Madrid, Cape Town, Singapore, São Paulo, Delhi

Cambridge University Press
The Edinburgh Building, Cambridge CB2 8RU, UK

Published in the United States of America by Cambridge University Press, New York

www.cambridge.org
Information on this title: www.cambridge.org/9780521757553

© Paul Sharp 2009

This publication is in copyright. Subject to statutory exception
and to the provisions of relevant collective licensing agreements,
no reproduction of any part may take place without
the written permission of Cambridge University Press.

First published 2009

Printed in the United Kingdom at the University Press, Cambridge

A catalogue record for this publication is available from the British Library

ISBN 978-0-521-76026-3 hardback
ISBN 978-0-521-75755-3 paperback

Cambridge University Press has no responsibility for the persistence or
accuracy of URLs for external or third-party Internet websites referred to
in this publication, and does not guarantee that any content on such
websites is, or will remain, accurate or appropriate.

To Janny, Patrick and Caroline

I am suggesting that after many of the more incidental features of the case have been peeled away, we shall find at the heart of everything a kernel of difficulty which is essentially a problem of diplomacy as such.

Herbert Butterfield, "*The Tragic Element in Modern International Conflict*," in Herbert Butterfield, *History and Human Relations*, p. 26

Contents

Acknowledgements	page xi
Introduction	1

Part I Traditions of international thought and the disappointments of diplomacy ... 15

1. Diplomacy and diplomats in the radical tradition ... 17
2. Diplomacy and diplomats in the rational tradition ... 39
3. Diplomacy and diplomats in the realist tradition ... 53

Part II Elements of a diplomatic tradition of international thought ... 73

4. The diplomatic tradition: Conditions and relations of separateness ... 75
5. The diplomatic tradition: Diplomacy; diplomats and international relations ... 93

Part III Diplomatic understanding and international societies ... 111

6. Using the international society idea ... 113
7. Integration–disintegration ... 123
8. Expansion–contraction ... 149
9. Concentration–diffusion ... 169

Part IV	**Thinking diplomatically about international issues**	193
10	Rogue state diplomacy	195
11	Greedy company diplomacy	222
12	Crazy religion diplomacy	243
13	Dumb public diplomacy	266
Conclusion		293
Bibliography		312
Index		334

Acknowledgements

This book has had a long gestation and I owe a debt of gratitude to many people who have had to listen to parts of the argument over several years. I am particularly grateful to the following. Raymond Cohen and Geoffrey Berridge, though in their different ways they may regard this work as heresy, always provided reliable guides to what it is possible to say about diplomacy. Iver Neumann constantly reminded me that it is important not to keep saying the same old things in the same old ways and that, even in diplomacy, it is possible to say things of import without losing track of how profoundly funny life can be. Costas Constantinou encouraged me to see how emancipating to diplomacy and diplomatic thought it can be to see the Modern in historical terms. His insight that diplomacy can tell us about the world drives my argument, although not always in directions with which he would agree, I am sure.

James Mayall and Richard Langhorne read chapters and provided critical advice and encouragement at important moments. And to the anonymous external reviewers all I can say is thank you very much. Finally, I have benefited a great deal from the intellectual legacies of Herbert Butterfield and Martin Wight. Therefore, it follows that I should also acknowledge the work of Barry Buzan and Richard Little in reviving the English School as an intellectual project.

DIPLOMACY

1/ "it is a way in which countries talk to and negotiate with one another".

2/ '...diplomacy acquires the character of a magical balm-like "political goo"'

3/ ' It [diplomacy] consists merely of people doing the normal things like bargaining, representing, lobbying and, of course, communicating we find in all walks of life'

13/ 'Diplomacy is, first and last, a set of assumptions, institutions and processes — a practice — for handling certain kinds of relations between human beings'.

Introduction

When things go wrong in international affairs, we frequently find people talking about a failure of diplomacy. When something difficult needs to be accomplished, or when a settlement or general improvement in international relations is in prospect, more and better diplomacy is often called for. Newspaper and television editorials, in particular, assure us that the elements of this or that particular international problem are quite clear, as is the range of possible solutions. Governments have committed. Peoples are supportive. It is now, they assert, up to the diplomats. Not only are diplomacy and diplomats important, however, after the best part of a century of apparent decline, the demand for both of them is currently on the rise. It is so in the senses outlined above. It is often asserted, for example, that foreign policy failures, especially those of the United States (US) in the Middle East and in the "War on Terror," were in some sense caused, or at least made worse, by a lack of effective diplomacy. We even find those closely associated with these failures almost penitently declaring their determination to try more diplomacy in the future. However, this rise is also evidenced in a number of other ways. Both new countries and aspirant ones work hard to obtain diplomatic recognition and build new diplomatic services. New international actors seek changes in the practices of international relations that will permit them to acquire similar sorts of recognition and representation. Even individual people can join in some diplomatic conversations on the Internet and create a virtual diplomatic presence as impressive as those created by the foreign ministries and embassies of states.

While diplomacy and diplomats are regarded as important, however, and the demand for both is currently on the rise, quite what diplomacy is remains a mystery. To be sure, we have a sense that it is a way in which countries talk to and negotiate with one other. We also have images of embassies and ambassadors, consulates and consuls, and the presence of diplomats on a variety of public and private occasions, seated at tables with colleagues, walking with (or slightly behind) their political

1

masters, caught by journalists in airport arrivals and departures, or giving careful interviews on television. However, the distinguishing characteristics of diplomatic practice (if there are any) remain unspecified except for a general sense that they lie outside what is regarded as the normal range of human interactions. In the absence of this specification, therefore, diplomacy acquires the character of a magical balm-like "political will" which, when called for and applied to a problem in sufficient quantities, will in some mysterious way get things moving and make things right.[1]

Magic and mystery or, more properly, a belief in the former and an acceptance of the latter, certainly play a part in diplomacy's effectiveness, and the term has a talismanic quality. We consecrate attempts to negotiate an important agreement, achieve an interest or obtain recognition, for example, as diplomacy in the hope that this will help to secure what we want and avert what we fear. We may also identify developments that we do not want or do not like as the fruits of diplomacy as a black art, since a talisman can be used for good and bad purposes. In both its good and its bad applications, however, we use the term diplomacy in the hope that it may help convince others and possibly ourselves that a mysterious power is at work. The question arises, therefore, is there any more to diplomacy and diplomats than this? To say they have a talismanic quality is surely to imply that there is, for there must be some reason why people think them powerful. Even magicians have their own rules and magic its accounts of how and why it works. Yet here mystery is compounded by a puzzle, for neither the diplomats nor those who study them provide much insight into how and why diplomacy works.

In this regard, the former may be forgiven. One does not ask conjurors how they perform their tricks. Those who study them do not get off so easily. They certainly provide corroborative expert testimony for the talismanic qualities of diplomacy and diplomats. Beyond this, however, students of diplomacy tend to differ only over whether its sustaining myths should be protected or exposed. The minority position, taken by diplomatic historians, for example, is less interested in explaining diplomacy's mysteries as in charting the exploits of those who are said to

---

[1] An example of the use of "political will" in this sense may be found in Raymond Tanter, *Rogue Regimes: Terrorism and Proliferation* (New York: St. Martin's Griffin, 1999), p. 202.

Introduction

understand them without explanation. Unlike Dean Acheson, many students of diplomacy, particularly the historically inclined, accept the idea that the special skills of the diplomat involve a "mysterious wisdom, too arcane for the layman" which is derived from the sovereign character of those they represent.[2] In contrast, the majority position taken by those who have escaped the archives and embraced the international world beyond the Vienna *règlement* approaches the mysteries of diplomacy in a different way. The thrust of their work is to say that the more closely one looks at diplomacy – at its history, its sociology and its psychology – the more one comes to realize that, like fog, it cannot properly be said to exist in the way it appears from a distance. It consists merely of people doing the normal things like bargaining, representing, lobbying and, of course, communicating we find in all walks of life.

Neither buttressing diplomacy's mysteries nor seeking to normalize the activities of diplomats is a good idea in my view. The former involves viewing diplomacy as exclusively a state practice and diplomats through the prism of how three centuries of modern European interstate relations were presented, and it is now both impossible and wrong. It is impossible because it inexorably forces students of diplomacy in the minority position to defend claims at odds with a flood of material and social facts growing stronger every day. It is wrong because they can only manage this by ignoring more and more of the international relations we must and ought to talk about. The majority position in contrast, that of normalizing diplomacy, is quite possible but still wrong. It is possible because it does involve encountering and engaging these developments. It lets us see, for example, how more and more people are involved in the sorts of activities which used to be the exclusive preserve of state diplomats, and it lets us see the great changes which have taken place in what even state diplomats actually do. It is wrong, however, in that it suggests that diplomats are now simply operatives, like other operatives, in the great transnational social networks of power and influence which function both between and within countries. Insofar as this position is adhered to, it may

---

[2] Acheson's reaction described in Robert D. Schulzinger, *The Making of the Diplomatic Mind: The Training, Outlook, and Style of United States Foreign Service Officers: 1908–1931* (Middletown: Wesleyan University Press, 1975), p. 142.

contribute to the processes by which we see and produce more people whom we call diplomats in the world. Insofar as it denies that there is anything particular and distinctive to diplomatic practice, however, these diplomats will be far less effective than they might otherwise be at delivering the sort of magic for which expert opinion calls and which common wisdom hopes when things get difficult.

Of course, the mystery of diplomacy and source of its effectiveness do not reside in any magical powers that people may believe it to have. Rather, they are to be found in the distinctive ordering of familiar understandings, values and priorities that is particular to diplomacy as a social practice. What follows, therefore, is my attempt to make explicit what common wisdom hopes for, namely that there is something called diplomacy that can produce desirable effects when other ways of conducting human relations are regarded as inappropriate or have failed. Indeed, I shall argue that it is possible to identify a specifically diplomatic tradition of international thought from which the generation of diplomatic theory which can say interesting and useful things about international relations and human relations in general is possible.

Theory and international relations

To say that I am attempting diplomatic theory of international relations requires that I say something about social theory in general and international theory in particular. What do we understand ourselves to be doing when we engage in theorizing of this sort? There are no universal criteria as to what constitutes good social theory. Thus, there is no single answer to this question with which everyone will agree. In principle, as students of international relations, we seek to understand and, perhaps, explain the occurrence of significant phenomena in our field with the intention of having what we have found out and what we think about it used, more or less directly, to make the world a better place for some or all its people. Knowledge about international relations is accumulated by discoveries, while understanding is deepened by the interpretation and discussion of their possible significances. In practice, however, the processes by which theories are generated and considered are not straightforward. No general agreement exists among those who study international relations about what we are studying or how it should be studied, and when attempts are made to secure general agreement in this

Introduction

regard, they often produce a counter-reaction or are simply ignored. Indeed it sometimes seems as though, beyond sub-groups of the like-minded, we barely listen to each other. As for the wider world, it takes notice of a few of us only when we have something useful or relevant to say to projects, or on grounds, which should often make us feel distinctly uneasy.

The implications of these observations for the question, "what are we doing when we do International Relations (IR)?" may be captured by imagining a social gathering of members of the attentive public in an early fifth-century Roman provincial town.[3] They are considering a response to the barbarians soon to be at the gates. The discussion is led off by the more policy-relevant types polarized between those who call for more legions and those who maintain that legions are never the answer. It soon becomes derailed, however, by someone pointing out that, as a result of imbalances between imperial revenues and expenditures which are probably structural, more legions are simply not an option. To which someone else adds that even if they were, it would be no good because few people are willing to serve as soldiers anymore, and those who do won't fight. With the benefit of distance we can see how vital their deliberations must have seemed to the participants, and how the proto-political economist and proto-sociologist might have had a deeper, but not necessarily more useful, understanding of what was going on. We can also see how little these deliberations mattered in terms of the outcome to the crisis that prompted them (although, since this is a book about diplomacy, the story ends with a successful parlay which allows the barbarians to enter the town without burning it or killing everybody). Finally, we can see whose problems attract my attention, not, for example, the deliberations held in what I imagine to be the gloomy, brutal encampments soon to be established outside the town.

All this is going on when we "do IR." We are always involved in the world of international relations (ir/IR), whether by choice or implication. We may be influential in it, but rarely for the right reasons or in the way that we would wish, and never decisively because ir/IR is an

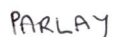

---

[3] I shall follow the convention of putting the academic discipline of field of study in upper case and the practice studied in lower case. Thus, International Relations is the study of international relations. The same convention will be followed for abbreviations, thus IR. Abbreviations will not be used in denoting the practice in question.

open-ended process. As to the debates one can have about which theoretical and methodological approaches to take, therefore, I have little to say beyond declaring that I am an adherent of Smithsonian pluralism rather than de Mesquita monism.⁴ There may be a best way to get at different kinds of truths about international relations, although I am not even sure about that, since people may differ on even how the same sort of thing is best apprehended. I am sure, however, that there is no single best way of getting at all of the things in which we are interested.

My own point of departure is to paraphrase one of Hedley Bull's attempts to identify international theory. Diplomatic theory may be understood simply as the leading ideas of diplomats and those who study them that have contributed to our thinking about diplomacy and international relations.⁵ Thus, and although they would have made better titles, I am not offering *a* diplomatic theory of international relations, still less *the* diplomatic theory of international relations by which all significant international phenomena can be explained in a few sparse and tightly related causal propositions. To be sure, my diplomatic theory attempts to generate some related propositions from these leading thoughts about diplomacy and diplomats, but it does not seek to capture and explain the whole world of international phenomena in terms of these propositions. It merely asks us to explore how these propositions might affect our view of that world and how to live in it. For all of its apparent simplicity, however, my adaptation of Bull's leading-thoughts-and-thinkers approach to diplomatic theory requires further clarification. It does so because it invites us to consider at least three types of thinking about diplomacy, in only two of which I am interested.

---

⁴ Former ISA Presidents Bruce Bueno de Mesquita and Steve Smith used the opportunity provided by the bully pulpit of their presidential addresses to lay out their sense of how the field ought to progress, the former claiming that scientific methods generated better knowledge in terms of both yielding truths and practical utility, the latter claiming that different approaches yielded different forms of knowledge and that claims for the inherent superiority of one form of knowledge over all others should be treated with great caution. See "Presidential Address by President-Elect Bruce Bueno De Mesquita," *ISA Convention*, Chicago, February 22, 2001 and "Presidential Address by President-Elect Steve Smith," *ISA Convention*, Portland, Oregon, February 27, 2003.

⁵ Hedley Bull, "Theory and Practice of International Relations, 1648–1789, Introduction," in Brunello Vigezzi, *The British Committee on the Theory of International Politics (1954–1985)* (Milan: Unicopli, 2005), p. 310.

Introduction

First, there is what a number of people, already on the brink of closing this book in disappointment, take to be diplomatic theory – namely the relatively narrow and applied body of knowledge pertaining to the right conduct of professional diplomats in their relations with one another and other servants of the states to which they are accredited.[6] Of diplomatic theory in the narrow sense, I have nothing else to say other than it is derived from reconciling general diplomatic assumptions with the historically specific circumstances of the modern state system. It sets out one way of doing diplomacy and, under certain conditions, a very good way at that. Secondly, there is what international theorists in Bull's sense have had to say about international relations and the place of diplomacy and diplomats within them, that is to say diplomatic theory as a subset of international theory. I am very interested in this, of course, but principally as a target of criticism. International theory provides or, at least, implies theories of diplomacy, whereas what I develop is diplomatic theory of international relations and, as it turns out, diplomatic theory of international theory too. Thirdly, my paraphrasing of Bull implies diplomatic theory in the sense of what diplomats themselves have had to say about international relations. They have had a great deal to say. However, because of their circumstances and priorities, this often appears in forms – autobiographies, diaries and histories, for example – which do not lend themselves well to the conversations and debates of theoretical discourse. It is my contention, nevertheless, that a coherent and distinctive set of propositions about international relations – diplomatic theory in this third sense – can be derived if not from the utterances of diplomats always, then from the place which is distinctively theirs in international relations.

Outline of the argument

I begin by critiquing what the academic study of International Relations (IR) has had to say about diplomacy and diplomats. To do so, I borrow heavily on the English School and, in particular, on the idea of traditions

---

[6] See, e.g., John Wood and Jean Serres, *Diplomatic Ceremonial and Protocol: Principles, Procedures and Practices* (New York: Columbia University Press, 1970), Elmer Plischke (ed.), *Modern Diplomacy: The Art and the Artisans* (Washington: American Enterprise Institute for Public Policy, 1979), and, of course, Earnest Satow, *Guide to Diplomatic Practice*, 2 vols. (London: Longman, 1979). From this point, I shall not use "diplomatic theory" in this narrow sense.

of international thought associated with Martin Wight.[7] This approach assumes that when we examine inquiry and debate over time, those engaged in it can be grouped on the basis of shared sets of assumptions about important questions, ways of answering them, and significant findings. It is not unproblematic for, while these traditions seem to take on a life of their own as patterned and distinctive ways of thinking with their own histories, this is not the case. They are always identified as such by someone and, as such, they are always shaped by the identifier's own priorities and way of seeing. Even Wight's own organization of the traditions, for example, operates like one of those tilting maze games where all movement seems complex but the slope carries you steadily in one particular direction. Thus, traditions of thought are always contestable, often contested and significant only to the extent that they secure a consensus from others about their usefulness and reasonableness. While each particular tradition may be challenged, however, people do seem drawn to the general activity of identifying traditions because doing so and maintaining that such traditions exist seems more useful than maintaining that they do not.

This being so, I employ Wight's schema from his essay in *Diplomatic Investigations*. In this, he suggests that Western thought about international relations can be broadly organized into three great traditions.[8] The first, which he identifies as a Machiavellian or realist tradition, presents the world in terms of interests and power. Its focus is on explaining why the world is the way it is, why this must be so, and how to survive and prosper in it. The second, which Wight calls the Grotian or rationalist tradition, presents the world in terms of interests and rights. Its focus is on exploring attempts to reform and improve international relations by the application of reason to the problems in which their conduct results. And the third, which he calls the Kantian or revolutionary tradition,

---

[7] For useful histories of the English School see Timothy Dunne, *Inventing International Society: A history of the English School* (Basingstoke: Palgrave-Macmillan, 1998) and Vigezzi, *The British Committee on the Theory of International Politics (1954–1985)*. For an extensive bibliography of English School research and much more see *The English School* website at www.leeds.ac.uk/polis/englishschool/.

[8] Martin Wight, "Western Values in International Relations," in Herbert Butterfield and Martin Wight (eds.), *Diplomatic Investigations* (Cambridge: Cambridge University Press, 1966), pp. 89–131 and Martin Wight (Brian Porter and Gabriele Wright, eds.), *International Theory: The Three Traditions* (Leicester: Leicester University Press/Royal Institute of International Affairs, 1991).

presents the world in terms of power and right. It proceeds from the assumptions that the existing arrangement of relations is itself the source of most problems, and its focus is upon how people, as moral beings or agents of a historical process, might overthrow or transform these relations.[9] In successive chapters of the first section I examine how diplomacy and diplomats appear in the theory and practice of each of these traditions. I argue that they play important parts in all three, but ones for which each tradition cannot fully account in its own terms. Instead, a common theme emerges. Not only do the operations of diplomacy and diplomats remain mysterious in all three traditions, they are also presented as disappointing, albeit in very different ways.

In the second section, I examine how diplomats look back at this world of competing traditions of international thought making their own sense of how it works, what may reasonably expected of it and, thus, what may be expected of them. Again, I use the traditions of thought idea as presented by the English School. This time, however, I rely on what may be termed Richard Little's corollary to Wight's exposition.[10] It is tempting to regard the traditions presented above as competing or contending approaches to International Relations which are, in principle at least, mutually exclusive. Something like the trinity appears in many college texts, for example, as a menu from which, at some point in the future if we are to be serious about IR, difficult choices will have to be made.[11] In Wight's approach, however, the three traditions are not presented as contending approaches to capturing some essential truth about international relations and the people who undertake them, nor even as watertight intellectual traditions in themselves. As Little makes clear, the traditions co-exist in more-or-less permanent tension with one another as the markers of a space within which international conversations and actions are undertaken and undergo further interpretation by theorists, practitioners and ordinary people alike.[12]

---

[9] I will refer to these as the realist, rationalist and radical traditions from this point.
[10] Richard Little, "The English School's Contribution to the Study of International Relations," *European Journal of International Relations*, 6, 3 (2000), pp. 395–422.
[11] See, e.g., Paul R. Viotti and Mark V. Kauppi, *International Relations Theory: Realism, Pluralism, Globalism* (2nd edn.) (New York: Macmillan, 1993) and James E. Dougherty and Robert L. Pfaltzgraff, Jr., *Contending Theories of International Relations: A Comprehensive Survey* (2nd edn.) (Cambridge, MA: Harper Row, 1981).
[12] Little, "The English School's Contribution to the Study of International Relations," pp. 395–422.

Little's corollary, I argue, makes it possible to identify a distinctive diplomatic tradition of thought from which diplomatic theory of international relations can be developed. It does so by implying a place to stand from which to make diplomatic sense of a world populated by people who think about international relations and conduct them in terms of any or all of the three traditions outlined above. At the heart of the diplomatic tradition lies the assumption that people live not as such, but as peoples in various sorts of groups. This *plural fact* both engenders and is engendered by a value placed on living separately. The diplomatic tradition thus presents peoples as living in *conditions of separateness* from one another, and even where they are not physically separated, a sense of separateness remains a dimension of their relationships. These conditions give rise to a distinctive form of human relations – *relations of separateness*, and diplomacy develops to manage these relations. Those whom we regard as diplomats occupy positions between human communities that make possible a specifically *diplomatic understanding* of the world. It is an understanding that privileges the plural character of human existence, the plural character of the ideas and arguments by which people make sense of their lives both to themselves and to others, and it treats as axiomatic the proposition that relations between groups are different from those within them.

This *diplomatic understanding* of human relations, in its turn, makes possible *thinking diplomatically* about their content, and especially about the sorts of arguments that people get into about the world, how it should be, and their places in it. Between groups of people, arguments cannot be definitively settled and the balance of virtue cannot be definitively determined in the senses in which both of these are usually understood, nor do they need to be. *Thinking diplomatically*, therefore, privileges the maintenance of relations – peaceful relations at that – over whatever those relations are purportedly about. The existence of this commitment to *raison de système* – keeping the whole show going – in addition to or above *raison d'état*, *raison de souverain* or even *raison de peuple* is extraordinarily difficult to establish. We get intimations of it, however, in the paradox by which actual diplomats are often criticized both for going against the grain of what everybody really wants and taking the line of least resistance instead of doing the right thing. What they are actually doing, I will argue, is attempting to manage three sorts of diplomatic relations: *encounter relations* between peoples meeting for the first time; *discovery relations* between peoples

Introduction

seeking to find out more about, and enjoy closer relations with, each other; and *re-encounter relations* where peoples stay in touch, yet keep one another at arm's length.

I then put this diplomatic theory to work. In the third section, I explore the possible relationships between diplomacy and diplomats, on the one hand, and international relations and international societies on the other. Do international relations, broadly defined, require or, indeed, presuppose diplomacy and diplomats? They do not, I argue, but the social character of all but the most brutal and simple of relations between groups very quickly brings diplomacy, if not diplomats, into existence. We should be glad that this is so because, and *pace* the English School's view of diplomacy as an institution of international society, it is diplomacy which constitutes, and diplomats (in the sense of those who act diplomatically) who produce, the international societies which put relations between separate groups on a more stable and peaceful footing than they otherwise would be.[13] It is perhaps in this sense that we can finally understand Wight's striking claim made long ago that the diplomatic system should be regarded as the master-institution of international relations[14] (a claim which, as Iver Neumann notes, neither Wight nor anyone else did much).[15]

I then examine what diplomatic theory can tell us about how international relations are, and might be, conducted in a variety of

---

[13] The international society idea is also closely associated with the English School on international theory. See, e.g., Hedley Bull, "Society and Anarchy in International Relations," in Butterfield and Wight (eds.), *Diplomatic Investigations*, pp. 35–50, Hedley Bull, *The Anarchical Society: a Study of Order in World Politics* (London: Macmillan, 1977), Hedley Bull and Adam Watson (eds.), *The Expansion of International Society* (Oxford: Oxford University Press, 1984), Barry Buzan and Richard Little, *International Systems in World History* (Oxford: Oxford University Press, 2000) and Barry Buzan, *From International to World Society? English School Theory and the Social Structure of Globalization* (Cambridge: Cambridge University Press, 2004).

[14] Martin Wight (Hedley Bull and Carsten Holbraad, eds.), *Power Politics* (Harmondsworth: Penguin, 1979), p. 113. See Martin Wight, "The States-System of Hellas," in Martin Wight (Hedley Bull, ed.), *Systems of States* (Leicester: Leicester University Press, 1977), p. 53 for an alternative formulation of the "master-institution" idea, "The master-institution of the modern Western states-system is the diplomatic network of resident embassies, reciprocally exchanged."

[15] Iver B. Neumann, "The English School on Diplomacy: Scholarly Promise Unfulfilled," *International Relations*, 17, 3(2003), pp. 341–69. His argument is foreshadowed by Alan James, "Diplomacy and Foreign Policy," *Review of International Studies*, 19, 1 (1993), pp. 94–9.

international society settings. To this end, I employ continua of the sort suggested by Adam Watson: the integration-disintegration of structures; the contraction-expansion of boundaries; and the concentration-diffusion of power within and between international societies.[16] Over time we can chart the movements of international societies along each of these dimensions, and at any given point in time we can identify the clash of claims, views and interpretations of what is and ought to be going on in these terms. What can diplomatic theory tell us about different sorts of international societies, specifically their conduciveness to the successful and peaceful conduct of relations between separate groups? What can it tell us about the dynamic properties of such societies as they undergo both quantitative and qualitative changes that have consequences for their character and identity? I argue that a *diplomatic understanding* can make an interesting contribution to our arguments about the sorts of international societies there can be, the sort we should want, and what is happening to the ones we have. It suggests, however, that, except in moments when it is generally agreed that a crisis exists or that a catastrophe has occurred, the forces shaping, moving and transforming international societies run to their own multiple imperatives that are almost beyond apprehending, let alone control. If this is so, then a *diplomatic understanding* suggests quietism, and possibly even quiet subversion, as the best response of us all to great projects based on the great images of the world and how it should be which are held by many of those whom diplomats represent.

In the final section, I move from what a *diplomatic understanding* has to say about the geology of international societies – the big questions of international theory – to the light which *thinking diplomatically* sheds on what people take to be the big issues of international relations and foreign policy at any given time or place. Diplomats pride themselves on being able to avoid or solve problems when given the chance because they have a better grasp of how to handle what is going on than do governments, experts, interested parties and ordinary people. I identify four big issues which currently bother governments and people alike: rogue states; greedy companies; crazy religions; and dumb publics, and ask what *thinking diplomatically* can tell us about how each of them might be handled. I intentionally frame these issues in terms that do not sit well

---

[16] Adam Watson, *The Evolution of International Society: A Comparative and Historical Analysis* (London: Routledge, 1992).

Introduction

with how the business of diplomacy is traditionally conceived to suggest they are tough cases. I also intentionally depict them in terms of agents, actors or people, rather than problems or issues. Diplomacy is, first and last, a set of assumptions, institutions and processes – a practice – for handling certain kinds of relations between human beings. Thus, personalizing these issues in this way is intended to make them subjects of diplomacy in a way in which, for example, terrorism, exploitation, intolerance and inclusive participation can never fully be.

Nevertheless, the pejorative terms in which these agents are identified signal the extent to which each one's right and ability to participate fully in international life are regarded as problematic by someone. Therefore, each subject considered here, and the problems associated with them, leads us quickly back into core arguments about international relations that are unlikely to be settled by the application of force, reason or revolution. However, this does not prevent human beings from trying and, in the course of their efforts, inflicting a great deal of harm on one another. In the conclusion, therefore, I suggest that core arguments especially can often be handled better if they can be classed as diplomatic arguments. I examine some objections to this claim – what happens when we avoid making moral judgments in disputes, appease the wicked and treat all claims as partial – and consider the limits they suggest for what diplomatic theory can accomplish. Finally, since professional diplomats can no longer be given a monopoly over handling such arguments, I call for the expansion of diplomatic education to match the contemporary trend of more people at all levels of society becoming directly involved in international relations.

PART I
Traditions of international thought and the disappointments of diplomacy

Diplomats are often misunderstood and unappreciated.
> James Lee Ray and Juliet Kaarbo, *Global Politics*, p. 251

1 | *Diplomacy and diplomats in the radical tradition*

What sort of places do diplomacy and diplomats occupy in each of Wight's three traditions of international thought? I am interested particularly in the accounts they provide of what diplomats do and the explanations they offer for how they accomplish it. I begin with the radical tradition partly because it is customary to leave it until last. More importantly, it is easy to suppose that resistance to the plural "fact" of human existence upon which my characterization of diplomacy rests will be strongest within this tradition. Why so? Our stories of the origins of diplomacy and, indeed, international relations often start with imagined encounters between groups of people who, until that point, did not merely regard themselves as separate, but were not even aware of each other's existence. As in Harold Nicolson's version, the first moment in international relations occurs at the point of contact between different groups. The second occurs when they institute an exception to the general injunction to kill and eat all outsiders in the form of immunity for heralds and messengers.[1] This is a plausible origin myth. It may capture aspects of what actually happened on numerous occasions, and I shall make use of it below. Nevertheless, both anthropological research into prehistoric societies and a modest exercise of the imagination suggest that this is not the only possible point of departure for a story about the origins of international relations.

The anthropological record of human development, for example, lends credence to stories of ruptured unities and the drawing apart

---

[1] Harold Nicolson, *Diplomacy* (Oxford: Oxford University Press, 3rd edn, 1969), p. 6, Harold Nicolson, *The Evolution of the Diplomatic Method* (Leicester, Diplomatic Studies Programme, University of Leicester, 1998), p. 2. A storehouse of anthropological examples of diplomacy in simple and early human systems may be found in Ragnar Numelin, *The Beginnings of Diplomacy: A Sociological Study of Intertribal and International Relations* (London: Oxford University Press and Copenhagen: Ejnar Munksgaard, 1950).

of human groups, as much as it does to stories of isolated groups encountering and entering into relations with each other. And individual experience indicates that the first encounters of actual human beings with others of their kind are always with members of "us," parents, siblings and relations, for example, rather than "others." The primary separation which each of us experiences is between me and the rest. The rest can be mapped out from the individual in concentric circles encapsulating increasing distance in some sense, but it is by no means clear why or how the notion of "otherness" necessarily begins to grow stronger and develops into a sense of us and them. Why, on the evidence from their encounters, don't people simply recognize each other as more of us? In fact we quite often do. We tend to assume, for example, that other people are more-or-less like us until we are given a reason, or acquire a motive, to think otherwise.

This is illustrated when someone who has not had occasion to think much about international relations is offered a brief explication of how the contemporary international society is organized, the institutions which provide it with some structure, the conventions and understandings which make these institutions possible, and the dynamics which both make them necessary and yet constrain them. As anyone who has taught an introduction to international relations will confirm, the reaction of their more thoughtful novitiates is often one of disbelief. Whether they have previously assumed the world to be a broadly peaceful place marred by only the occasional aggressor, or as some sort of racket run for the benefit of a few at the expense of the many, the system as it is presented to them will seem anything but natural. Rather, it may appear as a contrived and foolish obstacle to the happiness of ordinary people or as a sinister way of maintaining relations of oppression and exploitation over them.

Nor are such reactions the exclusive preserve of those who have not thought much about international relations. Some who pay a great deal of attention to international relations are driven by what they see as the willed and contrived awfulness of existing arrangements to argue and work for something better. Indeed, all of us, when the logic of the states system and the reasons of states seem to have driven us into corners with painful consequences which no one really wants, will at least wonder about the plural arrangements under which we live and the price we pay for so doing. In short, and the plural fact of our existence notwithstanding, the possibility of living otherwise, arguments to that effect, and people acting on the consequences of those arguments all exert a continuous presence in the world of international relations. They are part of it, and only the intensity of their presence and its effects fluctuates over time and space. It is this collection of possibilities, arguments and actions that constitute the elements of a radical tradition in international thought and practice.[2]

Diplomacy and diplomats as the enemy

Between diplomacy and diplomats, on the one hand, and the practical and political components of the radical tradition, on the other, it is both conventional and easy to pose an antagonistic relationship. The former seek to hold the existing world together at almost any price, while the latter seek to tear it apart and replace it with a new one. The Irish socialist revolutionary James Connolly, writing on diplomacy and diplomats for *The Workers' Republic* in 1915, gives fine expression to a strong current of suspicion and, indeed, contempt which exists in the radical tradition. Speaking of British diplomacy in particular, he refers to it as "hypocrisy incarnate." He continues,

Diplomacy has a code of honour of its own, has a standard by which it tests all things. That code has no necessary relation to the moral code, that standard has nothing to do with the righteousness of any cause … The diplomat holds all acts honourable which bring him success, all things are righteous which serve his ends. If cheating is necessary, he will cheat; if lying is useful, he will lie; if bribery helps, he will bribe; if murder serves, he will order murder; if burglary, seduction, arson or forgery brings success nearer, all and each of

---

[2] It is, perhaps, worth distinguishing here between the sorts of arguments in which the question of whether the real or underlying "human condition" is really a plural one or one of solidity and, indeed, solidarity, and those which use the plural "fact" suggested by the historical record and its consequences as reasons for making arguments and encouraging developments which emphasize the sense in which people exist or ought to exist as a single human community. Pushed too far, of course, the pluralism/solidarism distinction collapses, for solidarist sentiments at one level of social organization can strengthen pluralism at another and plural sentiments at one level can strengthen solidarist ones at another. For discussions of these themes, see John Williams, "Pluralism, Solidarism and the Emergence of World Society in English School Theory," *International Relations*, 19, 1(2005), pp. 19–38 and Nicholas J. Wheeler and Timothy Dunne, "Hedley Bull's Pluralism of the Intellect and Solidarism of the Will," *International Affairs*, 72, 1 (1996), pp. 91–107.

these will be done ... And through it all the diplomat will remain the soul of honour – a perfect English gentleman.³

Diplomats, in this view, are defenders and beneficiaries of the present international arrangements. It is they who, day by day, undertake the work, practice the deceptions and create the spectacle of a world divided into sovereign states by which the divisions or apparent divisions between peoples and between people and their real interests are maintained. They are the enemy in two senses. First, and most obviously, ambassadors and envoys are regarded as servants of those with power and influence. As such, they either support or take no position on the internal arrangements and processes by which their principals become and remain powerful and influential. Secondly, while diplomats may seek to advance the interests of their sovereigns at the expense of others, and may even help prepare the ground for violence to be used to serve these interests, they do so in such a way as to safeguard and perpetuate the understandings and conventions which make relations between the powerful and influential possible.

The only question then is whether or not they are important enemies. One response is to regard them as mere ciphers, or even ornaments, of established power, objects of resentment and subjects for kidnapping and assassination, but little else. Another is to assign special significance to them at particular historical moments, for example, during crises, or to see particular diplomats exerting undue influence like favorites at court. It is then that they will tempt their principals into taking terrible risks or shirking great moral responsibilities in order to serve the needs of some dark conception of domestic or international order. While they may be "enemies" of revolution, however, the overall view is that diplomats are symptoms, not causes, of what the revolutionary is up against, and servants of the real enemy, however the latter is viewed.

The enemy conception is often confirmed by the historical record. We can see diplomacy playing the part suggested by it on occasions, especially in the hands of the great powers, and we can see diplomats whose personal qualities conform to the unflattering picture Connolly paints

---

³ See James Connolly, "Diplomacy," *The Workers' Republic*, November 6, 1915 at www.marxists.org/archive/connolly/1915/11/diplmacy.htm. Connolly's quote would require little modification to serve as a conventional presentation of the contemporary international terrorist.

of them. However, the enemy conception presents an incomplete picture for, on occasions, we can hear the diplomatic representatives of great powers sounding like revolutionaries while, sometimes, we can see revolutionary movements represented by people who look and sound like diplomats, even to the point of manifesting some of the vices associated with them from within the enemy conception. I am referring, of course, to the phenomenon of revolutionary diplomats and to the idea of revolutionary diplomacy.[4] These pose problems for the way in which diplomacy and diplomats are presented in all three traditions of international thought but, in particular, for the radical tradition with its enemy conception of both.

This is so, because the characteristic *modus operandi* within that tradition is to present a series of characterizations of how the world is now, contrasted unfavorably with a series of characterizations of how it might be. Getting from the former to the latter involves big changes, an uprooting of the established ways in which we think and act. Revolutionary ideas and movements, nevertheless, find their expression in organizations of human beings who are condemned to live in and negotiate the world as it is presently organized and understood by the people with power around them. To advance their causes and maintain themselves these organizations require what anyone else would need to engage in effective political or military action, whether this is material assistance in the form of guns and money or ideational acceptance in the form of recognition. Accordingly, revolutionary movements, most obviously those which have been successful in seizing state power, find they need diplomacy, and those who conduct it quickly begin to act and sound like diplomats. From within the radical tradition, this development prompts three questions. Can those engaged in revolutionary diplomacy avoid the pressures to accommodate with and be co-opted by the existing order of things? Can they be used successfully to subvert

---

[4] For discussions of revolutionary diplomacy (although not from revolutionary perspectives) see David Armstrong, "Revolutionary Diplomacy," *Diplomatic Studies Programme Discussion Paper (DSPDP)* (Leicester: Centre for the Study of Diplomacy, November 1996), David Armstrong, *Revolution and World Order: The Revolutionary State in International Society* (Oxford: Clarendon Press, 1993) pp. 244–72, Wight, *Power Politics* pp. 88–9 and 117–21, and Wight, *International Theory: The Three Traditions*, pp. 154–8, 173–9 and 196–205. Wight presents revolutionary diplomacy as a perversion, but his use of Kant to signify the revolutionary or radical tradition makes this difficult for him to sustain.

and undermine that same order? And, most importantly of all, can revolutionary diplomats and diplomacy play a part in creating a new and radically different social order?

The radical tradition, revolutionary diplomacy and the problems of accommodation and co-option

Diplomats are conventionally not trusted by many of those they represent. Do they serve their Princes, themselves, or intricate and secret schemes of their collective concocting that they dignify with terms like stability, order and peace? The problem of trust is even worse for revolutionary diplomats. To begin with, those they represent are, generally speaking, a tense, suspicious and, above all, untrusting crowd. After all, they have already rejected the conventional appearance of things that the rest of us allow to regulate our lives. Much more importantly, however, they are aware of how those who represent them have to circulate in, and to a certain extent embrace, the world they have rejected and whose roots they are committed to tearing up. This does not matter so much for the sort of bargaining required to negotiate the exchange of hostages and the acquisition of supplies from friends and enemies alike. The skills required for this sort of horse-trading are not particular, or even particularly germane, to diplomacy. Sooner or later, however, all but the most nihilistic of revolutionary movements seeks recognition from others in the world in which they operate. Recognition and acceptance improve one's chances of guns and money, to be sure, but they also provide conduits by which new ideas and principles have a chance of becoming effective in international life.

This, for revolutionary diplomats, is where the troubles begin. To serve their principals well in this regard, they must operate effectively in the prevailing diplomatic system amidst the material temptations and norms of accommodation and compromise such systems usually exhibit. Conventional diplomats have to strike a balance between *raison d'état* and *raison de système*, which they often do, with more or less success, by maintaining a rhetorical consistency between them both and what their principals want them to do. Revolutionary diplomats, in contrast, have to maintain a balance between the requirements of their movements as actors in an international society, the requirements of those societies that make relations between their members possible, and a revolutionary *telos* committed to the destruction or transformation of both. It is a difficult juggling act, and it is also one they do not perform very well. At least, this is the conclusion to which we are drawn if we accept at face value the powerful story, often told, of revolutionary movements – even those with avowedly international and transnational objectives – being tamed and made ordinary by their engagement with the modern international society of states which they had originally set out to transform or overthrow.[5]

In the first flush of revolutionary victory, foreign ministries are declared closed, ambassadors recalled, sacked and shot, while the secret dealings of the old regime are exposed by a new army of direct representatives: citizen soldiers, polpreds, and people's bureaux who ransack the archives. All this, it is declared, will put the nation and, indeed, the world on a new course in which the conduct of international relations will be transformed. In the end, however, it is the transformers who are transformed or, at least, forced to conform with both the power political necessities and the diplomatic requirements of the international society of states.[6] The implication is that revolutionary movements either fail or become state-like because, in the end, full independence can only be achieved and exercised in a state-like manner, and a system of states implies or dictates a very narrow range of ways of relating to one another. If this is so, then revolutionary diplomats are simply in the vanguard of those who come to this realization, for they work at the interface between the revolutionary movement and the world in which it exists, and are exposed to the full force of the latter's degenerative effects upon their revolutionary health.

This revolutionary diplomat's version of "going native," as it were, is a source of considerable satisfaction for those in the realist or rationalist traditions who regard the resilience of international societies as a fact, a

---

[5] David Armstrong, *Revolution and World Order*, develops the theme of socialization of diplomats and those they represent into the existing order of things. Fred Halliday, *Rethinking International Relations* (Vancouver: University of British Columbia Press, 1995) provides a useful account of how socialization is not unidirectional.

[6] The terms "transformative" and "transformational" have considerable currency in contemporary social theory. The use of the latter term in connection with diplomacy by the US Secretary of State, Condoleezza Rice, however, nicely illustrates the problem of co-option under consideration here. See Condoleezza Rice, *Transformational Diplomacy*, speech given at Georgetown University, January 18, 2006, www.state.gov/secretary/rm/2006/59306.htm.

good, or both.[7] By the same measure, it is a source of dissatisfaction to some in the radical tradition, confirming the weakness of mere mortals in the face of the rewards and punishments the status quo has at its disposal for getting its way. After all, what kind of revolutionary could be tempted away from the privations and dangers of challenging the existing scheme of things by the carriages, limousines and high society of diplomatic life? Surely only one whose heart was not in it in the first place. This is a harsh, if understandable judgment. Certainly some revolutionary diplomats have wined and dined in the service of social transformation with more enthusiasm than others, and some have been corrupted by it. Not all of them have, however, and the choice which revolutionary diplomats face is not always a stark one between venal corruption and revolutionary purity. This is so because, as those in the radical tradition are quick to point out, there are many different types of revolutions for many different types of objectives.

Most of those in the last two centuries, for example, have been primarily nationalist in character, seeking not the overthrow of international society as such but "a place among the nations" for those they represent.[8] To this end, it is not merely for tactical reasons that representatives of the Palestinian Authority today, just like the representatives of Irish nationalism in the early part of the last century, seek to present themselves as the "normal" agents of a "normal" country. This is what they want to be, and it is not surprising that their diplomats should seek to act normally, even before the normal status of those they represent has been accepted by other members of the international society they seek to join. The revolution in these cases consists in their being accepted, not in the transformation of the world they seek to join, except perhaps in some of the consequences of their being accepted into it.

---

[7] "Going native" is a term from European experience with colonial officers adopting the ways of the local peoples whom they administered. It is applied in diplomatic life and sometimes elsewhere to those who are judged to have become overly sympathetic to the outlook and interests of those to whom they are accredited to the detriment of the interests of those they represent.

[8] Patrick Keatinge, *A Place Among the Nations: Issues of Irish Foreign Policy* (Dublin: Institute of Public Administration, 1978) is named after a common formulation of one of the objectives of the Irish nationalist movement. This phrase occurs elsewhere including a book about Israel by Benjamin Netanyahu, *A Place Among the Nations: Israel and the World* (New York: Bantam, 1993).

Less convincingly, perhaps, a similar argument can be advanced for presenting as unsurprising the fate of more radical and avowedly internationalist movements like the Bolsheviks in Russia or their imitators in China. Neither originally sought a respectable place among the nations, seeing themselves rather as the agents of a broader process of social transformation through revolution. However, they sought transformation through the exercise of a particular kind of power that the idea of the modern European state expressed. Seeing power in primarily statist terms, exponents of the Marxist-Leninist version of revolutionary communism fairly quickly accommodated themselves to many aspects of the external exercise and representation of state power, even as they kept their revolutionary fingers putatively crossed behind their backs. Then, as the tides of international and transnational politics turned against them, they became some of the strongest defenders of conventional state practices and privileges to protect their respective revolutionary spaces. What is a little surprising, perhaps, is that they also often became strident, if inconsistent, defenders of all, including the most superficial, forms and conventions of modern diplomacy.[9]

From a standpoint within the radical tradition, however, we are not encouraged to look at the fate of revolutionary movements purely in terms of their own frames of reference, and thus absorbed by the very things they were originally against. Instead, our attention is drawn to two themes. The first is the persistence of attempts to transform the world – the latter's structures may appear to stand, but the battering of transformational waves against them seems to continue unabated. People keep trying because the problems that bother them do not go away, but also because previous efforts have not been without results. While these efforts may have failed in their own terms to transform international relations, they have had a profound impact on aspects of their content. Accommodation has always taken place on what the terminology of contemporary negotiations calls a "two-way street." The fact that it has brings us to the second theme, the complexities to

---

[9] See, e.g., Keith Hamilton and Richard Langhorne, *The Practice of Modern Diplomacy: Its Evolution, Theory and Administration* (London: Routledge, 1995) pp. 148–53, and Armstrong, *Revolution and World Order*, pp. 244–72. The Soviet and Communist Chinese attitudes to the observation of conventional diplomatic forms are usefully contrasted and a different learning or socialization curve into an incomplete diplomatic respectability for each of them may be usefully postulated.

be discovered by unpacking the idea of accommodation and the part it plays in the activities of revolutionary diplomats and diplomacy. For while the latter may have been centrally involved in the efforts to demonstrate that those they represent are "normal" to the rest of the world, they have also been centrally involved in managing and representing the consequences of the fact that, in many respects, they are not.

Consider again in this regard the diplomatic representation of the Bolsheviks and the Soviet state. Initially after the revolution, the Bolsheviks were able to maintain three missions – in Sweden, Germany and Switzerland. Much of their work – local and regional agitation and propaganda – remained unchanged after the revolution, while they also assumed many of the consular functions of their Tsarist predecessors, working with displaced persons and on repatriation issues in particular.[10] While Bolshevik cadres slid into the places, figuratively if not always physically, of the former Tsarist missions, they all continued to effect a delicate balance between seeking out political allies and supporters in society at large and keeping their official hosts happy. Madame Kollontai and Karl Radek, however, had very different conceptions of accommodation from those of their colleagues who had been members of the old Tsarist service and retained by the Bolsheviks. And, of course, both had a very different conception from, for example, Mr. Dobrynin, who represented the Soviet Union in Washington in the heyday of Soviet power. Kollontai and Radek both regarded themselves as revolutionaries. Radek, in particular, performed a political role at the Berlin embassy in what was initially a highly revolutionary situation, whilst his Tsarist colleagues elsewhere sought to reconcile directives from Petrograd with their own conception of whatever Russian foreign interests and relations might be salvaged from the upheaval. Dobrynin, in contrast, served an apparently established state, and presented himself at times in the classical mode, an old diplomat damping down the passions of successive generations of political leaders whom he represented to one another and reducing the tensions between them.[11]

It may be objected that these differences simply reflect the passage of time during which the Bolsheviks evolved from a Russian revolutionary

---

[10] Alfred Erich Senn, *Diplomacy and Revolution: The Soviet Mission to Switzerland, 1918* (Notre Dame: University of Notre Dame Press, 1974).

[11] Anatoly Dobrynin, *In Confidence: Moscow's Ambassador to America's Six Cold War Presidents* (New York: Times Books, 1995).

movement with international characteristics, through a brash and insecure revisionist phase when they struggled for survival, into the established and, in diplomatic terms at least, highly conventional great power noted above. Such an evolutionary model over-simplifies the conduct of Soviet diplomacy, however. At times, the bourgeois formalism of Soviet diplomatic protocol co-existed with a radical approach to intervening in the internal affairs of other countries, whilst at others, the doctrines of, for example, socialist and proletarian internationalism were tailored to the power political requirements of the Soviet, Russian, state. As the final appeals of the Soviet leadership to their peoples to follow them down the road to Mikhail Gorbachev's "new political thinking" – a course which involved them in a full-frontal assault on the pillars of their own domestic and international standing – demonstrate, no full transition from revolutionary or revisionist to status quo power was ever completed. Now it is perfectly possible to view the Soviet diplomatic experience with accommodation either in developmental terms – the maturation/degeneration of a successful revolutionary movement into an established power – or in operational terms, as one tactic among many by which power is acquired and interests advanced. Plumping for one or the other, however, involves either forcing a great deal of evidence into frames it does not properly fit or discounting it completely. In point of fact, the Soviet Union was a complex entity with multiple personalities formed by Russian historical narratives of nation-building, modern ideologies and technologies of state-building, and a collective understanding of itself as being at the center of an enduring revolutionary project with international and civilizational significance. It was all this, not simply one dimension of it, which Soviet diplomats had to represent.

Far from being unusual, this sort of complexity is, in fact, the norm for most diplomats in the contemporary international society. All of them represent entities with multiple personalities and nearly all of them represent entities that, for one reason or another, wish to be seen as agents of change, challenging aspects of the existing state of affairs. An Indian diplomat, for example, simultaneously represents a regional great power with vast potential, a national idea built upon the secular unity of diverse religious and ethnic identities, and a set of principles by which a political movement sought to lead an escape from the dilemmas and horrors of a Western-inspired international politics. We can imagine how these cross-currents of identity operate in different contexts when Indian ambassadors talk, for example, with their American colleagues in New York, are talked to by their British hosts in London, or talk to their guests from Kathmandu or Dacca.[12]

To push the point beyond context to more basic elements of personal identity, we may wonder what was going on in the mind of the Taliban ambassador to Islamabad as he attempted to represent his movement and its ideas to the agents of the architects of a sinful world, and talked with them about heretical matters in heretical terms.[13] And we may reflect on how his experience compares to that of Mr. Mohammed al-Douri, Iraq's permanent representative to the UN in 2003, when he was summoned to the Security Council to hear its deliberations on his country's fate.[14] In the case of the Taliban ambassador, we might seek evidence of accommodation to new conventions and expectations about which he had previously barely thought. In the case of the Iraqi, in contrast, we can only speculate on the radicalizing effects of seeing his country treated as a rogue and he as its representative as such, on a man whose job had been to epitomize respectability and propriety in the service of Saddam Hussein.

Thus we may say that the experience of representing revolutionary regimes or movements may pull their diplomats in multiple directions at the same time. Sometimes they will feel pressures and, indeed, be tempted to let themselves be co-opted into serving and reproducing the existing scheme of things. Always they will be required to engage in some measure of accommodation. This may amount to little more than co-option but from within the radical tradition, we are encouraged to think of accommodation in more complex terms. It may involve representing the multiple and, at times, unstable personalities of a revolution to the outside world, providing a normal exterior within which a revolutionary vortex continues to spin, or acting normally at one level of international society while continuing to serve the vortex at another.

---

[12] Useful in this regard is Kishan S. Rana, *Inside Diplomacy* (New Delhi: Manas Publications, 2000).

[13] See Paul Sharp, "Mullah Zaeef and Taliban Diplomacy," *Review of International Studies*, 29, October (2003), pp. 481–98.

[14] For a summary of events leading to the second US-led war against Iraq and culminating in the presentation by US Secretary of State Colin Powell to the UN Security Council, February 5, 2003, see "International Developments, November 15 2002–February 1 2003," *News Review Special Edition* at www.acronym.org.uk/textonly/dd/dd69/69nr01.htm#summ. Al-Douri's modest part is well-captured.

The modern historical record may lead us to expect a secular trend towards co-option, but snapshots of more recent Iranian, Taliban and even Libyan diplomacy show all these forces in play and suggest that the socialization of religious radicalism in the Middle East and South Asia into the prevailing norms of contemporary international society is far from complete. Indeed at this point, it is hard to imagine roles into which movements like al Qaeda and Islamic Jihad could be socialized by the present international society, even if they wanted to be. Until revolutions have run their course, therefore, and there is much to suggest that they never completely do, the accommodation practiced by those who represent them will be tactical, rather than strategic or existential in its scope. Indeed, as they seek to carve out a place in an international society and conduct relations with its members, revolutionary diplomats may also seek to undermine the foundations on which it rests and weaken the sinews that hold it together. In multiple ways, they will play their part in undertaking its subversion. This brings us to the second question posed by revolutionary diplomacy and revolutionary diplomats from within the radical tradition of international thought. How effective can they be at subverting the existing order of things? It is a difficult question for within the tradition, the idea of subversion is almost as problematic as those of revolutionary diplomacy and revolutionary diplomats.

The radical tradition, revolutionary diplomacy and the idea of subversion

The idea of the revolutionary diplomat as a subversive is a familiar one. It conjures up images of the abuse of diplomatic pouches for running guns, drugs, money and even people on occasions, the presence of such diplomats at demonstrations and riots, and their secret meetings with their local sympathizers. All this is interwoven with their more conventional diplomatic life of representing, negotiating and reporting. Thus, revolutionary diplomats are held to be subversive in two senses, in what they actually do and how they present themselves. They are not what they appear to be. From within the radical traditions of international thought, however, the idea of subversion is troubling, and these troubles are not eased, as they were in the case of accommodation, by unpacking the idea. This is because the word subversion is seen as a politically loaded term which privileges a particular conception of existing social arrangements as *the* social order and, in so doing, confers an element of legitimacy on that conception. It is a term more readily used by defenders and supporters of the established order than by those who seek to overthrow it. This difficulty can be eased, however, by maintaining a distinction between the sociological use of the term legitimacy to say something about the extent to which people accept the social arrangements under which they live as being good and right, and the philosophical use of the term to make judgments about the claims of particular regimes in this regard. With all but the most repressive and unrepresentative of domestic political regimes, it seems reasonable to concede that they must enjoy a measure of legitimacy among their people in the sociological sense and that, hence, we may speak of aspects of an attack on this legitimacy in terms of subversion.

However, the extent to which we may apply the idea of legitimacy, even in the sociological sense above, to international societies is not clear. Even in their stronger forms, the latter are characterized by rules and conventions that are permissive by domestic standards and seem anchored by contractual commitments rather than rooted in the unchosen obligations of membership and belonging. As a consequence, international societies do not present big targets in terms of legitimacy to be undermined by subversion. This point may be illustrated by examining the activities of some of those who would clearly appear to qualify as subversive diplomats. In so doing, I shall develop the distinction made above between diplomats who engage in subversive acts and those who conduct the affairs of their missions in a largely correct and appropriate manner on behalf of states or movements that are, nevertheless, intent on overturning the existing order of an international society. Joachim von Ribbentrop's term as ambassador to Britain, for example, while marked by a number of professional lapses was, nevertheless, intended to present the respectable, if robust, face of Nazi Germany to this important member of the international society and rival great power.[15] Similarly, there is little to suggest that Mr. al-Douri above did anything other than conform to the highest standards of diplomatic propriety (the same cannot be said of his staff). Indeed, it was of vital importance to the regime of Saddam Hussein that he should

---

[15] John Weitz, *Hitler's Diplomat: The Life and Times of Joachim von Ribbentrop* (New York: Ticknor and Fields, 1992).

do so, as part of its effort to present itself as a respectable and wronged Islamic, Arab country.

Actively subversive diplomats, in contrast, conduct themselves in ways that are grossly inconsistent with their status as diplomats under agreements like the Vienna Convention. Missions may orchestrate and serve as centers of support for revolutionary political and propaganda activity or terrorism. As we have seen, Russian embassies were used by the Bolsheviks to hand out money and instructions to local Communists. Chinese diplomats during the Great Cultural Revolution gained notoriety by launching direct attacks on their colleagues from other countries and, when abroad, on the police officers of the receiving state providing security for their missions.[16] More recently, Iranian consulates have been involved in the distribution of arms and money to their religious and political allies in the Lebanon, Afghanistan and Muslim republics of the former Soviet Union.

These may all be regarded as examples of subversive activity, but the difficult question is "subversive of what?" We have two possible answers. The first is the organizing principles of the international society in which they are operating and the integrity of the processes by which its affairs are conducted. The second is the ordering principles and processes of the state to which they are accredited (and, hence, perhaps, the existing international order). It is very hard to identify unambiguous examples of the former. Propaganda tracts on the station platform at Brest Litovsk, readings from the Little Red Book in Portland Place, classes on classical Arabic and the teachings of the Ayatollah Khomeini in Herat might all seem to qualify. However, they may be just as easily read as attempts to advance primarily state interests by weakening the ordering principles and community bonds of rivals. The Bolsheviks may have been seeking to undermine the idea of a world of states by their direct approach at Brest, but they were also trying to influence the Germans in particular and sell themselves as a political force of a new type.[17] The Iranians may be trying to undermine the idea

---

[16] For useful accounts of this period in China see Kishan S. Rana, "Representing India in the Diplomatic Corps" and J. E. Hoare, "Diplomacy in the East," both in Paul Sharp and Geoffrey Wiseman (eds.), *The Diplomatic Corps as an Institution of International Society* (Basingstoke: Palgrave Macmillan, 2007), pp. 125–41 and 105–24 respectively.

[17] For differences in emphasis between Lenin and Trotsky regarding the scope of Bolshevik diplomacy and especially the latter's attempt to withdraw Russia

of a world of broadly secular powers by their assistance to a myriad of groups and tendencies, but they have also been trying to advance the interests of particular co-religionists by helping them in the hope that they become allies or even instruments of Iranian policy. There may be subversive consequences for an international society and its processes from the abuse of privileges like diplomatic immunity and non-intervention, but these consequences have not clearly been the primary intentions of those who undertake such actions.

Moreover, the argument that subversive diplomacy directed at particular states also contributes to a general decline in diplomatic standards and thus weakens international society is undermined by the fact that all sorts of states may use their diplomats in this way if they judge the need to be sufficiently pressing. Most embassies engage in gathering intelligence by methods other than those sanctioned by convention, international law or the expectations of the receiving state. As the activities of the US embassy in Tehran have illustrated on several occasions, the embassies of the great powers in their clients may take on vice-regal characteristics in their relationship to their host governments, and when the latter are judged to be failing may become active sources of support and guidance for political opponents of the regime. Indeed, on occasions coordinated efforts emerge from diplomatic corps to advise and assist the opposition to governments collectively deemed troublesome.[18]

In short, and as the popular conception of diplomats as complex, subtle and not entirely open characters would suggest, there is a great deal of subversive diplomacy and a great many diplomats acting as

unilaterally from the war, see John W. Wheeler-Bennett, *Brest Litovsk – The Forgotten Peace, March 1919* (London: Macmillan, 1966), especially p. 191, "Primary Documents: Lenin's Decree on Peace, 26 October 1917" on *First World War.com*, www.firstworldwar.com/source/decreeonpeace.htm and Leon Trotsky, "Official Government Documents for the People's Commissar for Foreign Affairs," November 1917 to March 1918, Brian Bagson, *History of the Soviet Government Documents website*, www.marxist.org/archive/trotsky/works/1918/gov.htm.

[18] Consider, for example, the role of the diplomatic corps in the Macedonian political crisis of 2002, the Nepalese crisis of 2005–2006, and the Paraguayan crises of 1996 and 2002. For Macedonia see Paul Sharp, "The Skopje Diplomatic Corps and the Macedonian Political Crisis of 2001" and for Nepal see M. Humayun Kabir, "The Kathmandu Diplomatic Corps in Search of a Role in Times of Transformation," both in Sharp and Wiseman (eds.), *The Diplomatic Corps*, pp. 197–219 and pp. 145–67 respectively.

subversives in an international society. They engage in such activities to widely disparate ends, however. Some, but not many, may seek to subvert international society and its processes, while others seek to subvert the power of rivals for reasons of state or even in the name of maintaining the particular order which exists in an international society at any given moment. A few diplomats – revolutionary and ordinary alike – of the more heavily co-opted variety may even present themselves as working with their colleagues to subvert the more radical projects of their own regimes. Insofar as diplomats engage in subversion, therefore, it is probably wise to consider such activities in terms of a vulgar Machiavellian preoccupation with power, rather than through the radical tradition's frame of investigating the dimensions of social transformation and advancing specific efforts in this regard.

The radical tradition and diplomats as revolutionaries

From within the radical tradition of international thought we can see how the accommodation practiced both by revolutionary diplomats and their more orthodox colleagues is neither simple nor unidirectional, how subversion is not the exclusive preserve of the former, and that how the intent to subvert entire international societies, as opposed to their members, is very hard to identify. These insights entail a reformulation of the third question suggested by the tradition concerning the part played by revolutionary diplomats and diplomacy in creating new and radically different social orders. Instead, they encourage us to ask can diplomats act as revolutionaries, as opposed to representing revolutionaries, and can diplomacy be seen as a revolutionary force in international affairs, rather than a means by which revolutionaries, among others, obtain representation and conduct some of their relations?

In both empirical and theoretical terms, the answer is yes. Nearly all contemporary diplomats, not just revolutionary ones, sometimes engage in a great deal of talk which would seem to have revolutionary implications for the arrangements of the present international society. In conferences on the environment, trade, international finance, arms control, disarmament, genocide and war crimes, for example, diplomats are often to be found at the forefront of those calling for global solutions to global problems. In regional organizations like the European Union they are centrally involved in the effort to present what were once issues requiring diplomacy between interest-driven actors as ordinary matters of public policy to be collectively managed. In short, they engage in a solidarist discourse and sound like agents of the various processes of globalization said to be dissolving both our ability to live in separate political communities and our reasons for so doing. Much of what diplomats say in these respects may be regarded as examples of *ketman*, bogus pieties expressed to serve a greater good, and such pieties have always been a feature of diplomatic discourse.[19] Insofar as they mask the role of power, passion, interest and relative gain in the conduct of international affairs, both skepticism about them and gratitude for them is in order. Even pieties insincerely expressed may have radical consequences, however, for they present new points of reference and new channels in which the old games have to be played. Insofar as they do, they deserve more attention.

Indeed, in this sense, it may be claimed that diplomacy and diplomats have been at the heart of every profound transformation in the structures and processes of international relations that has ever taken place. As the radical tradition makes us aware, not all revolutions are discreet events taking place over a relatively short period of time. Indeed, even "classic" revolutions such as those in America, Russia and China were climaxes in processes that began long before and continued long afterwards. And some revolutions – those regarding gender, race and slavery, for example, occur over extended periods without their subjects being fully aware of what is going on. International societies, like other societies, may appear as settled affairs waiting from some great exogenous shock to unsettle and transform them. They are, however, sites of continual arguments about how life is and ought to be organized. Even when things look relatively settled, we must view them, in Butterfield's striking image, like the arches of a great medieval cathedral – their solid, static qualities made possible by the stresses and strains of counterpoised powerful forces which may, in this view, become unbalanced at any moment.[20]

Thus, the first great "international" revolution in this broader sense, establishing the immunity of messengers from customary rules regarding

---

[19] For discussions of *ketman* see Sir Arthur H. Hardinge, *Diplomacy in the East* (London: Jonathan Cape, 1928), p. 273, and Christopher Hitchens, "The Persian Version," in *The Atlantic Online* (July/August 2006), at www.theatlantic.com/doc/prem/200607/hitchens-persian.

[20] For a different conception of a similar idea see Harold Garfinkel, *Studies in Ethnomethodology* (Englewood Cliffs: Prentice Hall, 1967).

foreigners, may be told as a story about diplomats, as may the story of how "continuous relations" of sovereigns emerged between the fourteenth and the seventeenth centuries in Europe, through the establishment of resident embassies and the conversations of their diplomats. A similar claim can be made about all the great international settlements of the modern period. Sovereigns might seek to impart general direction to their representatives, but it was the latter who were directly and creatively engaged in ongoing negotiations. Even if sovereigns retained direct involvement, the nature of the negotiations arguably drew them into behaving more like diplomats than like sovereigns. Thus, the Treaty of Westphalia, iconically presented as a foundation agreement for the modern state system, was actually conducted as an extended argument about who was entitled to what sort of representation.[21] Rather than showing up as unambiguous entities merely needing to work out the modalities of how to conduct relations with each other, modern states emerged from negotiations conducted primarily by diplomats at Westphalia and other conferences.[22] Not all great international settlements have transformative purposes to be sure. The Congress of Vienna and the Treaty of Paris at the end of the Napoleonic and Cold Wars, respectively, could be said to have been primarily restorative in their intent. Versailles, San Francisco and the various treaties of the European Union, however, all aspired to look forward and to deliver new international or regional political dispensations.

To the extent that diplomats are centrally involved in the processes by which such agreements are created, framed and implemented, therefore, it may be said that neither revolutionary diplomacy nor revolutionary diplomats are aberrations. Revolution may be presented as the enemy of diplomacy and diplomats as the enemy of revolution in the radical tradition of international thought but, in fact, diplomats have acted as agents of some of the most profound revolutions in human history. We may reasonably expect them to be at the center of the next one. The

---

[21] See Abraham de Wicquefort, *L'Ambassadeur et ses Fonctions* in Maurice Keens Soper, "Abraham de Wicquefort and Diplomatic Theory," *DSPDP* (Leicester: Diplomatic Studies Programme, 14, February 1996), p. 7.

[22] Richard Langhorne, "The Development of International Conferences, 1648–1830," *Studies in History and Politics/Etudes d'Histoire et de Politique: Special Issue, Diplomatic Thought 1648–1815*, 2 (1981/1982), pp. 61–91. See also Andreas Osiander, *The States System of Europe, 1640–1990* (Oxford: Clarendon Press, 1994).

implication of some recent studies of diplomacy undertaken by theorists working in the radical tradition is that we should not be surprised by this. Constantinou's etymological recovery of the relationship between the ideas of embassy and theory in journeys of discovery both of others and self arguably puts diplomacy at the heart of projects for human emancipation. More prosaically, perhaps, Davis-Cross suggests that diplomatic corps may constitute epistemic communities with their own way of seeing the world and their own solutions to problems which, when implemented, are capable of having a profound effect on the broader sets of relations within which they are situated.[23] Diplomats, it seems, must invariably be involved in revolutions because they work on the boundaries of, and between, human communities which appear settled and "natural," and because they are engaged in producing and representing the outer aspects of those communities in such a way as to make them appear so. They are at the smoke and mirrors end of the international business, working to maintain the illusions which help the world go round and, like all good illusionists, they cannot abide one which is beginning to fail, and will always be receptive to the possibility of new ones.

Even if the radical tradition in international thought allows us to see diplomacy and diplomats as bound up with revolution and the fates of revolutions, however, from within it they continue to puzzle and disappoint. They do so because the activity of diplomacy involves a certain kind of compromise and orientation to compromise in general. As we shall see, this charge can be made from standpoints within all three traditions. Within the radical tradition, however, it rests on two observations, one about the content of the change in which revolutionary diplomacy has been involved, the other about the means by which these changes have been effected.

First then, the content of the transformation in which diplomacy has been involved is, quite simply, context-dependent. Transformation at the time of Westphalia, for example, involved the replacement of a single, fading political community to which ideas of empire and Christendom had given expression with multiple political communities

---

[23] Costas Constantinou, *On the Way to Diplomacy* (Minneapolis: University of Minnesota Press, 1996) and Mai'a K. Davis Cross, *The European Diplomatic Corps: Diplomats and International Cooperation from Westphalia to Maastricht* (Basingstoke: Palgrave Macmillan, 2007).

of sovereign states. Transformation in the nineteenth century involved deepening the divisions in, or the plural condition of, humanity, by insisting on the existence of nations which were authentic, natural and, if they were to realize their potential fully, in need of their own sovereign states. Transformation today, in contrast, is widely presented as involving a flow in the opposite direction; that is, from a fragmented world of sovereign parts towards solidarist conceptions of humankind in some emerging single political community, whether this is conceived in imperial or civil society terms. This pendulum effect implied by the shift from seeing revolutionary progress in pluralist terms to solidarist terms, and possibly back again, is at odds with the progressive strain within the radical tradition. If one is engaged with effecting changes directed at emancipating human beings, as opposed to studying and understanding the processes by which these changes occur, it cannot be the case that what was wrong and unjust under one set of conditions can be right and just under another. If one is committed to the construction of a global, inclusive, egalitarian civil society, for example, then one can only understand how at one point people saw the creation of national sovereign states in emancipatory terms, one cannot agree with them.

It may be objected that counter-currents to these trends have always existed and continue to exist today. The architects of Westphalia and the new Europe, alike, were countered by arguments for political communities below or between states which would somehow avoid the requirements of sovereignty, and the pluralism of national states was countered by claims about class and, eventually, human solidarity. However, diplomacy and diplomats, even in their revolutionary articulations, always appear to have been on the side of the big battalions or, at least, sailing with the prevailing winds and currents of world politics. If the revolution moved in a pluralist direction yesterday, then so did diplomacy and diplomats. If it takes on a more solidarist character today then so too do they. Who knows what they will do tomorrow other than follow the trend? Diplomacy and diplomats may be more open to radical change than is generally supposed. They may serve as its agents on occasions, but it is not what they are about in the driving sense that those within the radical tradition are interested.

Secondly, a relationship between the context-dependent character of the changes in which revolutionary diplomacy has been involved and the means by which revolutionary diplomats have contributed to them can be identified. They may work in social conditions of great indeterminacy and ambiguity, and they may be highly involved in giving a revolutionary new shape and sense to those conditions. However, they appear to do so, and certainly like to present themselves as doing so, by the pragmatic application of reason to negotiations in which existing realities are allowed to condition future possibilities. We are neither friends nor enemies of revolutions and transformations, they seem to say. We merely aspire to work through their consequences in as civilized and reasonable ways as we can.

This may not be saying much. The historical record suggests that it is perfectly possible for diplomats to facilitate murder and mayhem by appearing civilized and applying reason and tact. And reason may be as easily devoted to revolt as to any other ends. However, reasoning, and particularly diplomatic reasoning, from a posited state of affairs, as opposed to first principles, constitutes thin gruel within the radical tradition of international thought. Whatever its potentials in theory, in practice it is seen to encourage accommodation of the worst sort – speaking one way and acting another – with the existing state of affairs. At the most in this view, diplomatic reasoning can deliver modest improvements that may only serve to put off the wholesale redevelopment required. It is for these reasons that, within the radical tradition, diplomacy and diplomats are more easily associated with the other two traditions. Diplomats appear to offer pleasantries, rather than speak truth, to power and they appear to engage in what is presented as conventional reasoning to define and address problems in conventional ways. While they may conform to the requirements of revolution, war and power when they must, it is when talking is allowed that the diplomats come into their own. Thus, diplomacy and diplomats are more easily associated with the second great current of international thought identified by Wight: the rational or Grotian tradition. Indeed, some are tempted to argue that diplomacy is nothing less than reason made manifest on the international stage and that its pedigree is intrinsically and indelibly liberal.[24]

---

[24] Maurice Keens-Soper, "The Liberal Pedigree of Diplomacy," Butterfield Papers, University Library Cambridge (BPULC) Box 332, paper for the British Committee on the Theory of International Politics (BCTIP) 1974.

2 | *Diplomacy and diplomats in the rational tradition*

Wight's rational tradition identifies approaches to international thought which assume individual human beings are its proper subjects, and that their affairs are best addressed by the application of reason, both to the challenges and opportunities which they face, and to the processes by which arguments over what to do about them are settled. Put thus, it is a broad and attractive church, for who would openly disagree with putting individuals first, and who would not prefer reason to other methods, even of merely getting one's own way? Ask diplomats, of course, and they will tell you that, when it comes to international relations in particular, a great many people, leaders and followers alike, subscribe to neither principle, but that they, the diplomats, are among the strongest supporters of reason in both respects.

This claim has considerable purchase. There is certainly overlap between the habits of mind and vocabulary of the rational tradition and the diplomatic tradition of international thought. Both are interested in dampening passions and moderating egos by reducing ignorance and elevating reason, and both are interested in the resolution of conflicts by procedures that encourage fair compromises. The overlaps, however, are apt to lead to more confusion than clarity, for the differences between the two are considerable, especially on the question of procedures for resolving disagreements and how they are to be established and operate. Indeed, and notwithstanding the close links between the rational tradition and diplomacy claimed by theorists and practitioners alike, a good case can be made for saying that of the three established traditions, it is the rational one that has the least to say about diplomacy *per se*. Its proponents simply assume diplomacy, or good diplomacy, to be an expression of the sort of conduct they regard as wise and virtuous. The result is much misunderstanding and unhappiness on both sides when the rational tradition and diplomacy part company, especially as they seem to have now over the extent to which the plural condition of humanity may be regarded as natural, necessary or desirable.

The rational tradition and the growth of reason and reasonableness

As with the radical tradition, it is helpful to employ the anthropological fiction of the first encounter between human groups to establish its key assumptions regarding diplomacy and diplomats. In the rational tradition, the significant moment does not occur when people develop, or have imposed upon them, a notion of otherness. Given the empirical and moral primacy accorded to individuals, the notion of separateness, if not otherness exactly, is taken as a given. The significant moment occurs, therefore, when one or both the parties to such encounters recognizes that, even though they value their freedom, they must communicate with the other to get what they want. This realization implies a rational calculation about the limits to what one's own will and power can achieve in an external world of multiple powerful wills, and from it a great deal of wisdom is said to flow. The reasoning behind the decision to communicate with others gives rise to relations with them. These relations, in their turn, somehow open the door to the growth of a civilized reasonableness which recognizes that one's own will may not be the only one worthy of consideration, and that the exercise of brute force may not be the best or most reasonable way to achieve outcomes, even when one is in a position to get one's own way. This reasonableness of valuing others and cooperation with them then leads to the establishment of understandings, conventions and rules for putting these new relations between people on a more stable footing. People progress from having relations to being in relationships with one another.

Presented thus, it may be seen that the calculations by which groups enter into relations and relationships with each other are the same as those that are held to account for how and why individuals within groups enter into relations. To be sure, those laboring in the rational tradition note that the process by which such wisdom is applied to relations between groups, and to the conduct of international relations in particular, has been neither smooth nor constant. However, they offer no particular account of why this is so which is consistent with the tradition's own terms. They note, rather, that in relations between groups, other forces besides reason and reasonableness are at play, and that circumstances make it less easy to be rational, let alone reasonable. Despite difficulties, however, a progressive sense of historical direction

Diplomacy and diplomats in the rational tradition

is present in rationalist accounts of international relations. Things will improve if people are smart. The historical record suggests that they can be, and historical experience has moved people, or some of them, to become smarter. On the whole, today's international relations are more rational and more reasonable than yesterday's, and the international relations of tomorrow promise to be more rational and more reasonable than today's.

A great deal is packed into this brief argument about the growth of reason and reasonableness in the world. While this growth consists of reasoning undertaken by individuals, as a social or historical process it proceeds by a series of jumps – crises, formative experiences and realizations – rather than by logical steps. It proceeds unevenly, in the sense that growth may occur in one part of the world before it does in another. And it may lead in multiple directions in terms of the social relations to which it gives rise. Within the rational tradition, however, these differences are usually presented as local in their origins and arising from exogenous preferences – cricket instead of baseball, driving on the right instead of the left, and coffee instead of tea, for example. One variation cannot be presented as better than the other in either moral or practical terms, and all of them are less important than certain common features of social relations that emerge everywhere when reason and reasonableness are allowed to grow.

There is no particular reason why the application of rationality to a relationship should necessarily privilege cooperation, nor why cooperation should necessarily lead to imbuing the identity and interests of others with moral significance. Nevertheless, proponents of the rational tradition tell stories of a growing international order in which this can happen and is happening. They regard themselves as contributing to this growth, and they operate in a world in which their view of how things happen enjoys great currency.[1] It is a world to which good diplomacy and good diplomats make their own contribution in three distinctive ways. They do so, first, by acting as civilizing influences encouraging their principals to engage in rational cooperation; secondly, by developing and guarding the institutions and processes which help keep those they represent civilized; and thirdly, by contributing to the

---

[1] David Long and Peter Wilson (eds.), *Thinkers of the Twenty Years' Crisis: Inter-War Idealism Reassessed* (Oxford: Clarendon Press, 1995) provides a useful collection of essays on the liberal international thought of the period.

construction of a civilized international or world order by which the scope of individual human freedom will be maximized.

Civilizing diplomats and rational cooperation

Within the rational tradition, individual human beings are seen as moral agents exercising their free will in the service of their interests and what they regard as good. They can behave wisely and well or foolishly and badly, and by so doing, they can either help or harm themselves and others. In this regard, kings and emperors, presidents and prime ministers differ from the rest of us only in terms of the potentially greater consequences of their encounters with what Wight called "the same old melodramas" of international life.[2] Like us, however, they exercise their free will in circumstances that make it more or less easy to be wise and good. Therefore, the role of diplomats is, quite simply, to help those they represent to be wise, good and engage in civilized international conduct. They are presented as doing this in several ways. They perform as moral tutors like Jiminy Cricket to Pinocchio, providing advice and serving as consciences. Their principal message is that peace is generally good and best maintained by the exercise of restraint in the pursuit of interests. It is based on a moral, epistemological and practical humility that encourages a sympathetic and charitable understanding of the interests and beliefs of others. Others are worth as much as you. We cannot be sure of what they want or why. We can be sure that they and their wants can pose both challenges and opportunities for us.

Good diplomats as civilizers, advocating restraint and charity, are not the simple appeasers of common imagination who, in the popular jibe, serve the interests of every country but their own. They may be, in Berridge's words, "less enthusiastic servants of a strong national policy."[3] However, in the rational tradition, their role as advocates of restraint also shapes the character of the discourse between themselves and with those to whom they are accredited. They establish a way of talking which presses on others to act with restraint too, not just their

---

[2] Martin Wight, "Why Is There No International Relations Theory," in Butterfield and Wight, *Diplomatic Investigations*, p. 26.
[3] See G. R. Berridge on the characteristics of "old" diplomacy and diplomats in *Diplomacy: Theory and Practice* (London: Prentice Hall/Wheatsheaf, 1995), p. 13.

own masters. We can see this in the way they transform crude bargaining about objects of interest and desire into discussions about the moral and rational bases for particular claims and policies, and how they make those whose claims and policies are said to be inconsistent with any notion of restraint into shared problems. We can also see it in the way their shared discourse of restraint encourages diplomats to work for conditions in which it is easier for their principals to be well behaved, and less likely that they will succumb to the temptations of willfulness and self-righteousness.

Thus, the rational tradition presents diplomats as architects and builders contributing towards the construction of more civilized conditions for the conduct of international relations. Beyond their consequences, however, it is not always clear what these more civilized conditions are. Certainly, they involve securing arrangements that make diplomats' own jobs possible and easier. Grant us our immunities, recognize our privileges, and put us to work, the diplomats seem to say. Then you shall see the growth of reason and reasonableness in the relations between those we represent. Even this sparse set of conventions and understandings opens the door to something of potentially greater significance, however. Some sort of international system or society is implied, with its own logic or reason, and thus its own requirements that, to the extent that they are satisfied, will allow it to function more effectively. In such a system, restraint, charity and understanding towards others may be regarded as right, not merely because they advance the prospects for better relations between particular states. They also enhance the operations of the system as a whole and this makes better relations between everybody possible.[4]

Civilizing diplomats and international societies of reasonableness

Of course, the outline above is abstracted from a real historical process in which, between the seventeenth and eighteenth centuries in Europe,

---

[4] Adam Watson's *Diplomacy: The Dialogue Between the States* (New York: McGraw Hill/New Press, 1983) and *The Evolution of International Society* both capture this account of a growth of practical cooperation into something more very well. In a very different form, so too does the international regime literature epitomized by Richard Keohane's and James Nye's *Power and Interdependence: World Politics in Transition* (Boston: Little, Brown, 1979).

there emerged the sense of *raison de système* noted above. Formalizing the privileges and immunities of diplomats, constituting the diplomats accredited to the same capital as a corps, and establishing the idea of continuous relations between sovereigns who recognized one another were all elements of a system that imposed restraints on the conduct of the sovereigns themselves. If one wished to be part of a refined system of "dialogue between the states," as Watson calls it, then one had to put up with one's own diplomatic guests conducting heretical religious services, talking to each other about you, seeking to talk to you as if you were merely their equal, and reporting to their own masters what you were up to. Reason or rational calculation got you into it, and the growth of reasonableness helped keep you there. This society of diplomats, however, was but one aspect of a broader international society that developed at the same time. International law, the great powers, the balance of power and war itself were all interpreted in the rational tradition as elements of a society of states that made an international, and eventually world, order possible and sustained it.[5]

This international society was said to work because it was a rational and reasonable outcome of a collective meditation on the interests of its members and their sense of what was possible and what was right. Positivists emphasized what was possible, while adherents to conceptions of natural law saw the international society of states as reflecting some deeper sense of moral reason and order in human affairs.[6] Dominating both currents was an assumption that the limits to what is possible and desirable are conditioned by the fact that people live as peoples and nations in states, and probably always will. If this pluralist "fact," were so, then Europe's international society could be presented as a design for placing relations between all peoples in a civilized setting where reason and reasonableness had their best chance of prospering. Even arguments about how this design might be, or ought to be,

---

[5] This claim is, of course, based on reading Hedley Bull's *The Anarchical Society: A Study of World Order* as a liberal text.

[6] See the essays in Kai Anderson and Andrew Hurrell (eds.), *Hedley Bull on International Society* (Basingstoke: Macmillan, 2000) together with Bull's own "The Grotian Conception of International Society," in Butterfield and Wight, *Diplomatic Investigations*, pp. 51–73 and Herbert Butterfield's "Comments on Hedley Bull's Paper on the Grotian Conception of International Society," BPULC 330, July 1962, also in Karl Schweizer and Paul Sharp (eds.), *The International Thought of Herbert Butterfield* (Basingstoke: Palgrave Macmillan, 2007), pp. 198–206.

improved by setting up conferences, congresses and assemblies enjoying rules of procedure and membership assumed (as many still do), that any international society must be a society of people living as peoples and nations in states.

However, a third current within the rational tradition of international thought distinct from positivist and naturalist understandings of the state system emphasized the extent to which the international society of states was but one of many possible outcomes of reflections on international relations. As such, it was crucially dependent on the extent to which people continued to believe in it. As with Tinker Bell, if experience, reason or willfulness led people to stop believing, then the arrangements of this particular form of international society would lose their power, fade and die. The great upheavals of the nineteenth and twentieth centuries, in the form of domestic revolutions, world wars and the collapse of empires, all supercharged by developments in science and technology, posed huge challenges to the place of this plural "fact" in the rational tradition of international thought. Particularly after the First World War, the old argument that sovereign states, far from being the building blocks of the best possible international order to which we might reasonably aspire, were themselves the principal obstacle to reasoned and reasonable relations between people, received a tremendous boost. A gap was identified between the requirements for reasoned and reasonable relations between peoples and the requirements for reasoned and reasonable relations between states, giving renewed voice to other, more cosmopolitan and solidarist, currents within the rational tradition. Diplomacy, as a primary institution of an international society widely seen as having failed in 1914, became one of the targets of these currents, and questions from within them began to echo those emanating from the radical tradition. Given all that had happened and diplomacy's part in it, what, if anything, did the future hold for diplomacy and what ought good diplomats now be trying to accomplish?

Civilizing diplomats, world society and individual freedom

The crisis precipitated by the First World War in the partnership between the rational tradition of international thought and diplomacy added a new tension to the old one between serving the Prince and serving Peace. Now, there also existed a tension between serving *la raison de système* by maintaining the requirements of a civilized system of states, and serving the cause of humanity by helping it move beyond the state system to some other sort of international or world society in which the freedom of individuals could be better sustained and their potentials fully realized.[7] Confronted by such a tension, the duty of good diplomacy and diplomats within the tradition became and remains clear. They should facilitate the process of transition, playing pluralist tunes on the piano, as it were, while at the same time moving the instrument upstairs to a more solidarist location. State and state relations might be privileged only so long as they offer the best chance for the growth of reason and reasonableness in human relations generally. If they do not, then good diplomats have no business maintaining them, and bad diplomats risk becoming part of the problem.

It is a measure of the close relationship between the rational tradition and diplomacy's own understanding of itself that when the former issued its challenges in these terms, the "liberal pedigree" of the diplomats entailed that they attempted to respond in kind and continue to do so. The ascendance of the view of war as a problem after 1918 provided a great boost to seeing other issues as problems to be solved or, at least, managed, on behalf of people as a whole by the creation of new institutional arrangements. Political, economic, social and, latterly, environmental issues between states have been increasingly re-presented as global problems which are said to affect all people and require global solutions on behalf of all people. Thus, conferences gave way to standing conferences which, in turn, have mutated into the new institutions and processes by which the power of individual states can be curbed, while their collective efforts are enhanced in a new, more solidarist political dispensation.[8] A new sort of diplomacy practiced by a new

---

[7] The limitations of the traditions-of-thought approach are evident here. The rational tradition has never been the exclusive preserve of statist and pluralist approaches. I would argue, however, that they dominated it prior to the First World War. Only after that catastrophe is it possible to identify a rational, as opposed to radical, problematizing of both the desirability and the necessity of people living as peoples and in states.

[8] Richard Langhorne, *The Coming of Globalization: Its Evolution and Contemporary Consequences* (Basingstoke, Palgrave Macmillan, 2001) provides a good general account of globalization in these terms although with considerable uncertainty about eventual destinations. Ian Clark, *Globalization and Fragmentation* (Oxford: Oxford University Press, 1997) and *Globalization and International Relations Theory* (Oxford: Oxford University Press, 1999) provide accounts which emphasize the extent to which globalization remains a state-directed and shaped project.

sort of diplomat is customarily presented as accomplishing all these changes. It is perhaps more accurate to say, however, that new sorts of people with new priorities have become directly involved in diplomacy: technical experts, people from other professions and branches of government and, latterly, private citizens. These new diplomats are not primarily concerned with maintaining and improving the institutions and processes by which relations between states are conducted. They are more likely to see themselves as lobbyists for particular interests and causes for which they seek to influence, outmaneuver and even subvert the state system; as the architects and agents of a new global civil society in which the actions of governments will be constrained and channeled.

To these sorts of changes in thinking about international relations, even most conventional diplomats have adjusted. The experience of attending problem-solving conferences as their new colleagues' minders and watchdogs for official conceptions of their delegations' briefs leaves its mark upon them, just as serving abroad opens up the possibility of their "going native." Even if they might not absorb the sense of being engaged in constructing a new and better order, they experience the novelty of looking out for national or state interests in such negotiations as just one stakeholder in their outcomes among many. In a world in which the revolution in communications technologies can be seen to be undermining the hierarchical social structures and information scarcity which is traditionally associated with diplomacy and diplomats, it is often argued, they have no choice but to adjust or perish. The hard boundaries that historically have made it appear that the achievement of rational and reasonable relations between states is an important precondition of similar relations between people in general are melting. Even governments, to judge by the new emphasis being placed on public diplomacy not just as government-to-people, but also people-to-people, contacts, appear to be taking these changes in international relations seriously.[9]

In short, it is possible to identify a solidarist turn in both the conduct of international relations and reflections on them that gathered pace

---

[9] These themes are dealt with in more detail in the chapter on Public Diplomacy below. Mark Leonard and Vidhya Alakeson provide an arresting account of the new international relations in which, they maintain, people and peoples figure prominently in *Going Public: Diplomacy for the Information Society* (London: The Foreign Policy Centre, 2000) and Leonard again in *Why Europe Will Run the 21st Century* (London: Fourth Estate, 2005).

throughout the twentieth century and continues today. As a consequence, the reasoned and reasonable relations by which the scope of individual freedom is to be broadened are now said to spill across boundaries in networks involving new and fluctuating centers of power. Within and across these, shifting coalitions seek to influence one another on a multiplicity of issues by engaging in popular and democratic discourse which has shed the representative character of traditional politics and diplomacy in favor of direct involvement.[10] No matter what positions different people actually occupy in the world, they all now seem to be looking in a solidarist direction and engaging in a discourse embedded in this current of the rational tradition, even the diplomats.

Diplomatic irrationality and unreasonableness

Yet diplomacy and diplomats remain nearly as disappointing and puzzling in the rational tradition of international thought as they do to its radical counterpart. They do so for two reasons. First, even in the assessment of the rational tradition, the evidence that international relations are undergoing a qualitative change, as opposed to standing in need of such a change, can still be viewed as inconclusive. Each of the great shifts in twentieth-century international practices, for example, may be viewed as a response to old-fashioned crises that reoccur, rather than as steps in an escape away from anarchy to a more constructed international order. Every step forward, if such it is, is accompanied, if not always by a step back, then by resistance which delays and diverts progress into new and unanticipated directions. International organizations, for example, far from eroding or short-circuiting old obstacles, pose new versions of old ones and new ones of their own. The same may be said for the emerging regional entities. Far from finessing,

[10] This view of contemporary international relations and foreign policy is well captured by Brian Hocking, "Foreign Ministries: Redefining the Gatekeeper Role," in Brian Hocking (ed.), *Foreign Ministries: Change and Adaptation* (Basingstoke: Macmillan, 1999), pp. 1–16, "Introduction: Gatekeepers and Boundary-Spanners – Thinking About Foreign Ministries in the European Union," in Brian Hocking and David Spence (eds.), *Foreign Ministries in the European Union* (Basingstoke: Palgrave Macmillan, 2005), pp. 1–17, and regarding diplomacy especially, "Beyond 'Newness' and 'Decline': The Development of Catalytic Diplomacy," *DSPDP* (Leicester: Diplomatic Studies Programme, 10, October 1995).

for example, the economic "irrationalities" of political communities formed earlier with narrower and smaller terms of reference, they begin to acquire the character of *blocs* and states. Even the virtuous, liberal great powers, espousing both reason and reasonableness in their foreign policy rhetoric, fall short of expectations when their own short-term interests pull against arrangements which are said to be in the long-term interests of all.

Secondly, in all the disappointments and uncertainties of this uneven or questionable progress, whatever their causes may be, diplomacy and diplomats appear to be deeply implicated. It is they who hold up good economic or environmental agreements for bad political reasons, for example, insisting on a pace of forward momentum so slow that it is possible to suspect that no movement is occurring at all. Accordingly, from within the rational tradition of international thought emerges its own version of the enemy conception of diplomacy. Diplomats cannot be trusted for we can no longer be sure that they buy into what reason and reasonableness now dictate that international relations require and that new technologies, political freedoms and understandings have made possible. Therefore, to declare a problem to be one of diplomacy, in this view, is to admit the failure of reason and to consign it to a mysterious and often sordid regime in which the irrationalities of people are pandered to and haggled over with little prospect of genuine success. If the diplomats succeed, it will probably be for the wrong sort of reasons and they will probably have achieved a bad agreement. However, they are more likely to fail by making negotiations more complicated than they need to be and getting in the way of the real movers and shakers in contemporary international life.[11] Except in high political crises of a traditional kind whose causes, in the rational tradition, are no less stupid, wicked and tragic than those of daily international life, but whose potentially appalling consequences must

---

[11] At a conference in Suriname, I once heard a presentation on the theme of the "ideal" ambassador by a very successful local businessman. He painted a picture of a man who was in the office before eight in the morning, made his own coffee, knew the local business scene, was proactive in developing useful contacts, and did not let the dignity of his office get in the way of making himself generally useful to the business people of his country. Real ambassadors, by implication, fell far short of this ideal, did not work hard, focused on the wrong sorts of things, and made life more complicated. Presentation at workshop on diplomacy, Hans Limapo Institute, Paramaribo, Suriname, October 2002.

be feared, diplomats may be regarded as obstacles to be negated, irrelevancies which can be dispensed with, or as a combination of both.

Many people, including some diplomats and those who train them, subscribe to the thesis that their professional orientation leaves them singularly unprepared to deal effectively with contemporary international relations.[12] They are often said to be too slow to act, too circumspect in their thinking, too close with information, and too concerned with pronouncing, rather than with conversation or merely listening, in an era when everyone, including their colleagues in other departments of government, is beginning to conduct their own diplomacy. As a consequence, they are becoming people "of no real power engaged in activities which, in reality have no effect upon world events."[13] Certainly, in the public eye, diplomats often seem unsure of themselves or ineffective, as if their priority is to avoid making mistakes. They may try to convey the impression that they are not being left behind, engaging the general public, inviting elements of it into their own formerly secret and holy places, but their hearts, in this view, are not in it. And, even as they go public, some of them give the game away by asserting that even if diplomacy is no longer a world of elites, exclusivity and privilege, aspects of it might still run a great deal better if they were.[14]

No doubt there are many diplomats and aspirant diplomats to whom this observation applies, just as there are teachers, lawyers and doctors who have made an uneasy peace with what they understand the present in their own professions to be, while pining all the while for a remembered version of its past. Nevertheless, as a general characterization of contemporary diplomats, the claim that they act as they do because they do not realize, or do not care to realize, how much the world has changed is unconvincing. It is so not least because many highly conventional diplomats have foresworn their loyalty to the national state, narrowly and traditionally conceived. Instead, they have jumped ship

---

[12] Comments off the record, particularly about senior and older diplomats, from instructors involved in diplomatic training and also captured in Shawn S. Riordan, *The New Diplomacy* (Cambridge: Polity, 2003).

[13] Eric Clark, *Diplomat: The World of International Diplomacy* (New York: Taplinger Publishing Company, 1974), p. 264. It is a view with which he did not agree.

[14] This position is approached in Nicholas Henderson, *Mandarin: The Diaries of Nicholas Henderson* (London: Weidenfeld and Nicolson, 1995). See also Nicholas Henderson, "Foreword," in Grant V. McClanahan, *Diplomatic Immunity: Principles, Practices, Problems* (New York: St. Martin's Press, 1989), p. xi.

in favor of working for the very organizations, both public and private, which are viewed as narrowing and undermining the sovereignty of their former principals in the cause of various iterations of a broader human solidarity. The UN and its related agencies, the various foreign offices of the EU, the more established humanitarian organizations and, increasingly, transnational business corporations experience no difficulty in recruiting diplomats and former diplomats to represent their interests and their views on how the world might best be organized. If some diplomats are confused, from the standpoint of the rational tradition's sense of how international relations are changing, then clearly others are not.

However, transfers of loyalty such as these are easily understood in terms of a long tradition of diplomatic ship-jumping, rather than as manifestations of a new, post-state international society. In the European system of the eighteenth century, it was not unusual for people who were good at diplomacy and knew the right people to transfer their services and their loyalty from one sovereign to another, in much the same way that successful corporate executives move between large companies today. In the following century, popular ideologies anchored diplomatic loyalties more tightly to particular countries. Even so diplomatists like Talleyrand were able to survive the apparently most radical internal regime changes and remain as advisors to new governments. And in the twentieth century, mass diplomatic desertions occurred from the services of failing states in the Soviet Union and Yugoslavia to the new services of their successors. Clearly, diplomats are capable of manifesting great elasticity of mind and flexibility of commitment, the consequences of only some of which are consistent with the rational tradition's understanding of the growth of reason and reasonableness in international relations.

However, an alternative explanation with which all such examples are arguably consistent may be found in the diplomatic equivalent of Willie Sutton's explanation for robbing banks. Diplomats fall short as agents of reason and reasonableness because, from within the rational tradition, they appear more as agents attracted to power, not holding it or wielding it necessarily but as Neumann suggests, simply being close to it.[15] If this is so, then diplomats will serve particular states, regimes or

---

[15] Iver Neumann, "To Be a Diplomat," *International Studies Perspectives*, 6, 1 (2005), pp. 72–93.

organizations, because that, in their judgments, is where the power lies. If the power moves, and if the opportunity for them to move presents itself, then that is what we may expect the diplomats to do also. In such a conception, reasonableness vanishes and reason shrinks into the rationality of self-interest in a very narrow sense. International Relations may not be, or ought not to be, all about power and interests, therefore, but diplomats and diplomacy are. Why, especially, given everything they say about themselves and their profession, is this so? Both the radical and rational traditions in international thought frame their answers to this question in terms of their sense of the sorts of men and women who would be diplomats. To put it bluntly, they are second raters exhibiting venality to various degrees, but uniformly interested in having some of the power and prestige of their principals rub off on them.[16] Wight's third tradition, in contrast, frames its answers in terms of neither the diplomats themselves nor the particular entities which they seek to serve, but in terms of its understanding of the very nature of international relations. According to the Machiavellian, power political or realist tradition, those relations are, and must be, about power. This is why diplomats should be interested in power, and they serve states because that is where, in the main, power continues to reside. As we shall see, however, so far as many realists are concerned, diplomats are not nearly so interested in power as they ought to be.

---

[16] In fairness to diplomats, it may be worth noting Lord Vansittart's observation at this point that "If you want someone really artful, look in a University, rather than an Embassy," in *The Lessons of My Life* (London: Hutchinson, 1943), p. 17.

3 Diplomacy and diplomats in the realist tradition

Introduction

The intuitive attractiveness of the power political, or realist, tradition in international thought is very strong. It is said to dominate the way in which both practitioners and students of international relations think about international relations. In their different ways both struggle with varying degrees of success against the gravitational forces political realism is said to exert. The practitioners try to be good but are overwhelmed. The academics assert, and have been asserting for at least the last forty years, that the realist hegemony over their field has been recently overthrown, yet their stories still seem to orbit the power political account of international politics, whether as commentaries or critiques. It is something of a puzzle and a shock, therefore, to realize that the salience of the realist tradition is matched by the difficulty of specifying exactly what is being claimed within it and why. It is certainly no clearer than the other two traditions and, in some respects, less so. People are said to want power, but what power is and why they want it are both very difficult questions to answer. It is useful to start by thinking in terms of people with material needs and psychological wants living in a resistant environment populated by other people with needs and wants. This, at least, seems reasonable. Quite how one gets from this to the various accounts of international politics as occurring between interest-driven states for which the accumulation and retention of power overrides all other concerns, however, is by no means clear. Or, more accurately and, as in the case of the other two traditions, we can see how the axiomatic claims from which the realist tradition seems to proceed *could* send us to Morgenthau's politics among nations or Waltz's international system. We just cannot see why they *must* do so nor, indeed, why we must accept those claims.[1]

---

[1] Hans J. Morgenthau, *Politics Among Nations* (New York: Alfred A. Knopf, 1948) and Kenneth Waltz, *Theory of International Politics* (Reading: Addison Wesley, 1979).

Wight's own work is emblematic of this difficulty. The term "power politics" resonates with connotations in both expert and popular use, and Wight himself associates the tradition with Machiavellianism. In his essay "power politics," however, he says he refers merely to politics among the powers, by which he means states.[2] We are back to an old conundrum. To what extent do power politics arise from the fact that we are organized into a system of interest-driven sovereign states, and to what extent does that system reflect and arise out of who we are as power political people? Wisely, Wight avoids descending decisively from the fence between these two, to one side or the other, for any length of time. However, others, especially those clearly laboring in the tradition, are less cautious. I will follow their lead, therefore, to reconstruct the place of diplomacy in the realist tradition by examining first, systemic or macro-conceptions of power and international relations and second, individual or micro-conceptions of power and people. In so doing, I will argue that the partnership between diplomacy and power politics implied by the other two traditions to solve their difficulties with it is by no means as straightforward as they suggest. Indeed, those in the realist tradition "throw" diplomacy and diplomats back to the other two to solve the tradition's own problems with them.

Diplomacy in systemic and statist conceptions of power politics

The role of diplomacy in systemic understandings of power in international relations is akin to the means by which an aircraft's wings are kept attached to the fuselage. That is to say, the fact that the wings stay attached is important, but the manner in which they do so is uninteresting except to a few aeronautical engineers and metallurgists. Diplomats, like those they represent, act in accordance with the logic said to inhere in an anarchical system of power distributed between self-interested, self-helping, power-maximizers. To be sure, diplomacy fulfils an essential function as a neutral medium for the conduct of international relations. Someone has to gather and disseminate information. Someone has to communicate threats, promises and bargaining positions. And, less certainly, someone has to perform the tasks associated with the more concrete aspects of representation such as negotiation. These functions occur automatically, however, and we

[2] Martin Wight, "Powers," in Wight (Bull and Holbraad, eds.), *Power Politics*, p. 23.

lump them together as "diplomacy" for convenience. That term does not convey any sense that these functions, taken together, make an independent contribution to what happens, or explaining what happens, in international relations at the system level. The tendency for a balance of power to emerge, for example, does not depend on people who have a commitment to the idea as an institution of international relations making sure it operates. To be sure, changes in interaction capacity brought about by changes in the technologies of travel or communication may be of interest, for they will affect the quantity of information available in a system and the speed at which it flows.[3] These are viewed, however, as systemic properties, not diplomatic ones and, it may be noted, they are not specific to power political or realist conceptions of the international system. If diplomacy matters in systemic theories, therefore, it does so only occasionally as one of those contingent factors about which it is neither possible nor necessary to theorize.[4]

In contrast, the place of diplomacy in those parts of the power political or realist tradition whose focus is upon the state level is much more developed. In addition to providing a necessary medium for the conduct of international relations, diplomacy and, more particularly, diplomats are viewed as instruments of foreign policy. As such, they may be characterized as reflections of their sovereigns. Not only do they represent them, they are like them, playing their parts as lesser team-members in the same game. The game metaphor is useful here because it suggests that the game (foreign policy or state-behavior) can be more or less well played. One determinant of how good states are, in this respect, will be the effectiveness of their diplomacy and diplomats. It is one thing to decide to threaten someone, for example, but it is another to have that threat delivered effectively. Consider the consequences, in this regard, of the performances of Ambassadors Glaspie in Iraq and Henderson in Nazi Germany, as these have been popularly understood.[5] A similar point can

---

[3] For a discussion of material and social technologies and their consequences for the character of international relations, see Buzan and Little, *International Systems in World History*, especially pp. 190–215 and 276–99.

[4] See Waltz, *Theory of International Politics*, for a strenuous view of factors which may be important on occasions, but about which it is impossible and undesirable to theorize.

[5] Andrew I. Killgore, "Tales of the Foreign Service: In Defense of April Glaspie," *Washington Report on Middle East Affairs*, digital document from the American Education Trust (August 1, 2002), at www.wrmea.com/archives/august2002/0208049.html, Stephen Twigge and Len Scott, "Twisting in the wind? Ambassador April Glaspie and the Persian Gulf Crisis (update)," Kennedy School of Government

be made about the respective effectiveness of US diplomacy under President Bush senior and President Bush junior in coalition-building before their respective wars against Iraq. The former is widely judged to have been good at it, partly because of his previous experiences in government and, indeed, diplomatic service. The latter is judged less effective, partly out of disinclination and partly out of lack of ability.

In state-level conceptions of the power political or realist tradition, therefore, diplomacy and diplomats may be viewed as another element of power, like armed forces, wealth and population. Countries can enjoy a reputation for being strong in diplomacy – Canada, Ireland and Britain are often cited as examples in this regard – just as countries can be strong in other elements of power.[6] It remains, nevertheless, a peculiar or second-order sort of lever or instrument, for it is primarily used to communicate the promise or threat to deploy other instruments of policy. To put it another way, the advantages diplomacy confers are more likely to come from being good at it, rather than possessing a lot of it. Diplomacy, in short, is to be regarded as what economists and strategists call a multiplier, not an element of power in itself. Revealingly, countries good at it are sometimes said to be "punching above their weight."[7] This is an interesting metaphor. Insofar as the focus is on "punching" as the ability to get what states want, then the conception of diplomacy as an instrument holds up. Insofar as the focus is on "… above their weight," however, then the implication is that effective diplomacy and diplomats can deliver more to a country than its material or "real" power would lead us to expect. It can enhance a good policy and even, on occasions, rescue a bad one. In other words, good diplomacy and good diplomats can be seen, not just as elements of power and instruments of policy, but as somehow capable of finessing

---

Case Program (Cambridge, MA: Harvard University Press, 1992), Peter Neville, *Appeasing Hitler: The Diplomacy of Sir Neville Henderson 1937–1939* (Basingstoke: Palgrave Macmillan, 1999) and Sir Neville Henderson, *Failure of a Mission: Berlin 1937–39* (London: Putnam, 1940).

[6] See, e.g., David B. DeWitt and John W. Kirton, *Canada as a Principal Power: A Study in Foreign Policy and International Relations* (Toronto: John Wiley and Sons, 1983), Ben Tonra, *Global Citizen and European Republic: Irish Foreign Policy in Transitions (Reappraising the Political)* (Manchester: Manchester University Press, 2007), Douglas Hurd, *Memoirs* (London: Abacus, 2004).

[7] Douglas Hurd, Chatham House Lecture reported in "UK's World Role: Punching above our weight," BBC News, Open University, *Open Politics* at http://news.bbc.co.uk/hi/english/static/in_depth/uk_politics/2001/open_politics/foreign_policy/uks_world_role.stm.

both. Writers in the realist tradition would claim that this is not saying much. Everyone likes to finesse power if they can. Even a Hitler, it is often maintained, would prefer to achieve his objectives without the use of force, for it is always risky, expensive and painful. Diplomacy's opportunities in this regard, however, are, according to realists, necessarily limited in both scope and duration. As Phil Silvers used to say, the fight may not always go to the strong nor the race to the fleet of foot, but that is still the way to bet.

This may be so, and clearly there is no such thing as "pure diplomacy" detached completely from the marshaling of resources and arguments in particular circumstances.[8] This still leaves unexplained, however, what this force multiplier, policy instrument, or power override actually is. How does it work, and when does it get its opportunity to become effective? To answer these sorts of questions, power political or realist approaches generally go "out of area" and borrow from the rationalist tradition. Mere talking, they note, will serve on some, less vital, issues, and even on some more important ones between those whose coincidence of interest allows them to regard one another as friends. It may also be conceded that the discourse of bargaining has its own repertoire of psychological and organizational skills that can come into play when clubs are held back from being trumps. One may out-talk the powerful, at least for as long as they are prepared to let you do so. These are important concessions from within the realist tradition, but they come with few pointers as to when and why the discourse of diplomacy gets its chance on some occasions and not others. If we shift from systems and states to focus on individuals as interest-driven power-seekers, however, the picture becomes somewhat clearer. By making this shift, we can see the multiple ways in which human beings acquire power and seek to influence one another. With this focus, we get a rather different view of the significance of diplomacy and diplomats in the power political or realist tradition. Diplomacy changes from a more-or-less neutral medium by which more material forms of power and influence are communicated or technique by which force is

---

[8] José Calvet De Magalhães, *The Pure Concept of Diplomacy* (New York: Greenwood Press, 1988). Wight also writes of "pure diplomacy, negotiation abstracted from coercion and bribery," *International Theory: The Three Traditions*, p. 203. The term is also used by Charles O. Lerche and Abdul A. Said, "Diplomacy – Political Technique for Implementing Foreign Policy," in Elmer Plischke (ed.), *Modern Diplomacy: The Art and the Artisans*, p. 19.

multiplied, into a form of power itself. Indeed, it begins to appear as a form of power that, in some sense, makes the other forms possible.

Diplomats in individual-based accounts of power politics

If individuals are to be charged with interest-driven power-seeking, then diplomats are easily presented as evidence for the prosecution. Diplomacy puts people in touch with power. It does so, however, in a complex and paradoxical way. For people who actually expect to hold and wield power, all diplomatic missions are hardship postings where reputations can always be damaged but rarely strengthened. The correspondence of ambassadors from the early modern European period is full of complaints about their being exiled from court where the real opportunities for power and advancement resided.[9] More recently, Galbraith's memoirs of his time in India record a similar frustration with being sent abroad when he had expected to be one of Kennedy's key advisors on economic policy.[10] No one expecting or aspiring to exercise power directly, therefore, would take the diplomatic route to success from choice. Indeed, being sent abroad often represents a decline in one's political fortunes.

In addition, the power to which diplomats are supposedly attracted in power political views of the world is not diplomacy's own power of persuasion and value promotion, so much as the hard power of the state. They are regarded as providing the silken glove over the iron fist, enjoying the delicate, almost exquisite, contrast between the refined sensibilities of their own intercourse and the coarse and potentially brutal character of what is often communicated by it. Thus, diplomats, especially in international political fiction, are often presented as courtiers, groupies or even voyeurs, fascinated by, egging on, but not engaging in, the real action.[11] One might paraphrase the old Shavian dig at

---

[9] Garret Mattingly, *Renaissance Diplomacy* (London: Jonathan Cape, 1955), pp. 231–2.
[10] See Kenneth Galbraith, *A Life in Our Times: Memoirs of John Kenneth Galbraith* (Boston: Houghton Mifflin, 1981).
[11] Compare, for example, the presentation of diplomats and intelligence officers in Lawrence Durrell's *The Alexandra Quartet* (London: EP Dutton, 1957–1960). The former observe and evaluate while the latter act, albeit ineffectively much of the time. Consider also the roles of Wurmt and Vladimir in moving Verloc to action in Joseph Conrad, *The Secret Agent* (London: Penguin, 1963, first published 1907).

teaching by claiming that those who can achieve power do so, while those who cannot, represent it. Of course, most people either do not want, or realize they have no chance of acquiring, the sort of power to which a frustrated aristocrat parked in some distant posting might have originally aspired. For those living with less great expectations, however, diplomacy promises its own attractions and the possibility of acquiring power and influence within its admittedly more modest terms of reference. If such people are driven by their own quest for a lesser kind of personal power, then diplomacy may be said to provide three sources of it: the symbolic role conferred upon diplomats; the opportunities provided by interactions with their colleagues; and the advantages conferred by positions as expert advisors to those with the real power, their political masters.

Personal power and diplomats' symbolic role

The realist tradition is often criticized for over-emphasizing the material aspect of power and neglecting its ideational element. This is unfair. In the classical version of realism that rests, in part, on a characterization of human nature, power is presented as a psychological relationship, and ideas and their symbolic expression are both regarded as important elements of power. Morgenthau's account of foreign policy, for example, incorporates prestige as an element of power and his account of diplomacy reaches back into the history of the subject to demonstrate the importance of symbolism in diplomatic practice.[12] The power of diplomats is generally seen to reside in their representative character and functions, with the extent of that power dependent on prevailing conceptions of what representation involves. In medieval Europe, for example, ambassadors did not merely represent the interests of their sovereigns in the way modern lawyers are said to represent the interests of their clients. Rather, they literally stood for or in the place of those being represented.[13] In early modern European diplomacy this sense of correspondence was strengthened by attempts to

[12] Morgenthau, *Politics Among Nations*, p. 522.
[13] Mattingly, *Renaissance Diplomacy*, p. 250. Michel Foucault, *The Order of Things: An Archaeology of Human Science* (New York: Random House, 1970) is also very useful on different conceptions of the relationship between symbols and that which is represented which are possible and have existed at different times and places.

address the problem posed by the presence of non-subjects at court. Since one was either a sovereign or a subject, it was established that ambassadors enjoyed the right to be treated as if they were their respective sovereigns, entitled to all their rights and privileges. Remaining covered in the presence of the sovereign to which you were accredited or enjoying right of chapel may have been small compensations to senior noblemen and politicians who believed they ought to be playing powerful roles at home. For others, however, the chance of exercising such rights, albeit temporarily, and enjoying the privileges associated with them provided some sort of breakthrough into the magic circle of status and power.

Representation is understood less literally at the present, at least in modern, Western countries. When a French ambassador, for example, explains the policy of his country at a UN press conference, very few of us will regard him as "France," in quite the way his predecessors were so regarded by the courts of fifteenth- and sixteenth-century Europe. We know that he is not France and yet, since we regard France as existing in some sense and seek to have its position on matters of interest to us authoritatively stated, we still have no better device than to regard the ambassador as "France" for some purposes.[14] Thus, when we invite diplomats to public events, interrogate them at press conferences, or kidnap them and hold them hostage, we recognize their considerable significance as representatives. Somehow these people have acquired the role of standing for their country for certain purposes in certain circumstances, and this affects both our expectations of them and our responses to them. The aura that generates both may not survive any sustained personal contact, but that is another matter. Suffice to say that the idea of the diplomat in general and the ambassador in particular carries a certain weight from its representational significance which we may presume is attractive to the power-seekers writ small who covet it.

It may be attractive not only as a means to some power, but also as an end in itself. Consider, for example, how ambassadorships, especially those of, and in, not particularly important countries, are regarded as second prizes which reward and recognize a fairly successful career or services rendered. Holding such positions may actually be regarded as more important than undertaking the associated tasks, especially if

---

[14] Grant V. McClanahan, *Diplomatic Immunity: Principles, Practices, Problems*, p. 28.

there is very little to do. Indeed, success in such postings may depend on attempting very little of substance lest this disturbs existing and satisfactory arrangements. Such a rationale, it may be supposed, is less attractive to those who see diplomacy as their career and still hope that they are accomplishing something rather more than maintaining a state of affairs. Even such officers, however, derive at least some satisfaction from the fact that whatever they are doing, they do on behalf of their country and their compatriots. And beyond that, it is reasonable to suppose that just as the members of other professions enjoy the idea that they have managed to become, for example, a doctor, a lawyer or even a university professor, diplomats too take comfort from their profession as a measure of their achievement and their status in the scheme of things.

Personal power and diplomats' interactions with colleagues

Diplomats, then, value their symbolic status as an end in itself worth pursuing and as a source of power and influence. The latter, of course, raises the questions – a source of power and influence in what and with whom? The answer lies in what they spend most of their time doing, that is, talking to other diplomats and government officials. It is here, paradoxically, with the concrete activity of talking, that the realist tradition begins to run into difficulty making sense of diplomats. How does one establish lines of causation between all the talk and the great patterns of influence and strategic moves the tradition identifies as being important in international relations? Obviously, a great deal of diplomatic talk is not important in these terms. Where good relations or few issues exist, for example, diplomats may justify their existence primarily in terms of being, rather than doing. This is not to say that they are not busy, but their busyness will be directed primarily at maintaining a state of affairs and, thus, will not attract the attention of those who are interested in how specific power political causes produce specific power political effects. Nevertheless, we do have a popular image of diplomats involved in the sort of talking consistent with the image of interest-driven power-seekers which we are considering here. At home, we may suppose that ambitious diplomats behave like ambitious members of any other hierarchical organization, who seek to advance by gaining control of more resources, and whose purpose in advancing is to gain more control. Abroad, however, the route to advancement has historically been, and remains, quite different and more difficult. Diplomats abroad cannot belong to the local hierarchy or aspire to exercise control (formal or legitimate control, at any rate) over its resources. And their own society in a capital, the diplomatic corps, exhibits hierarchy in only the most symbolic of ways and usually offers only the most mundane and feeble of resources to be controlled. Rather than acquire resources, therefore, ambitious diplomats abroad seek to make themselves personally influential within their society and among their receivers and senders or, failing that, they work to be regarded as such.

For much of the history of modern diplomacy, this amounted to acquiring the skills of court politics, and particularly the skills associated with those who enjoyed no formal office of state and its attendant powers. In a sense, ambassadors possessed the informal status of favorites, although since they had acquired it by different means, they did not necessarily have to be liked by the sovereign. They were also quite likely to be treated with suspicion and, if they were effective, resentment by other members of court. Thus, they built their influence by the usual measures of court politics – knowledgeable and upright behavior where possible, intrigue, bribery and flattery where necessary. Once they possessed colleagues (other ambassadors) and their collective sense of a common identity and interest began to develop, then court politics could be extended to relations within the diplomatic corps.

It is from this process that our image of the ambitious diplomat as a virtuoso capable of controlling and manipulating the expectations of others in his or her own interest emerges. He or she is a Machiavel in the popular sense of that term, playing a game whose relationship to the interests of anyone but themselves is by no means clear. In many respects, this image is highly context-dependent. The Amarna record suggests, for example, that the ambassadors of great kings would have enjoyed few opportunities for playing such a part, even if they were sometimes detained at the pleasure of their receivers for years at a time.[15] There were neither enough people to talk with nor enough business to talk about. The courts of Renaissance Italy, in contrast, or

---

[15] Pinas Artzi, "The Diplomatic Service in Action: The Mittani File," in Raymond Cohen and Raymond Westbrook, *Amarna Diplomacy: The Beginnings of International Relations* (Baltimore: Johns Hopkins, 2000), pp. 205–11. See also Mario Liverani, *International Relations in the Ancient Near East, 1600–1100 BC* (Basingstoke: Palgrave Macmillan, 2007).

perhaps, more accurately, the dramatic representations of those courts with which we remain familiar, would lend themselves very well to such activity.

It might also be reasonable to assume that this diplomacy of court politics would be squeezed out by the professionalization of diplomacy and the bureaucratic rationalization of government policy-making and decision-taking which gathered pace in modern Europe. We see virtuosos, the charismatic heroes of Balkan diplomacy for example, at work late into the nineteenth century and even enjoying short-term successes.[16] However, they are increasingly regarded as working against the grain and providing an element of unpredictability that is no longer valued. Surely, it might be supposed, there is no place for such virtuosos in the dense networks of problem-solving diplomatic intercourse characterizing relations between developed industrial and post-industrial societies today? It is difficult to imagine a Guicciardini or an Aerenthal, for example, prospering in the staff of the European presidency or even on the present UN Security Council.[17]

[16] See Harold Nicolson, *Diplomacy*, p. 78 for the heroic element in the German style of diplomacy as he frames the latter. Diplomacy and statecraft in the Balkans, both by the great powers and by the leaders of newly independent states, was often characterized by grand démarches and a heroic character in the latter half of the nineteenth century. The term "charismatic diplomacy" is used by Dobrescu to distinguish the diplomacy of romantic nationalism and culture from the "egghead" and "no-nonsense" diplomacy of the more recent Communist past. Caius Dobrescu, "Charismatic, Egg-Head and No-Nonsense Diplomacy: Conflicting Models Within the Work-In-Progress of Contemporary Central European Diplomacy," in "The Role of Diplomacy in Countries in Transition With Special Emphasis on Education and Training," *Diplomatic Academy Year Book* 1, 1 (Zagreb: 1999), pp. 35–9.

[17] Francesco Guicciardini (b. 1483), who represented Florence to Spain and served a number of popes, is remembered for his writings on policy and diplomacy which are often favorably contrasted with those of Machiavelli and the "Italian method" as this is presented by Harold Nicolson, for their practical and flexible character. Guicciardini assigned a major and potentially decisive role to the well-timed interventions of diplomats in the quarrels of their masters. See G. R. Berridge, "Guicciardini," in G. R. Berridge, Maurice Keens-Soper and T. G. Otte, *Diplomatic Theory from Machiavelli to Kissinger* (Basingstoke: Palgrave MacMillan, 2001), pp. 33–49. Aloys, Count Lexa von Aerenthal (1854–1912), was the Austro-Hungarian foreign minister responsible for the annexation of Bosnia-Herzegovina in 1908 in what was supposed to be a masterstroke of timing and maneuver exploiting what he took to be a momentary commitment from Russia, the momentary isolation of Germany, and the momentary hesitation of the rest of the great powers. Useful accounts of the consequences of his misjudgments in these regards are to be found in

In fact, the opportunities for such characters are limited only to the extent that contemporary government and governance structures do not exhibit features of court politics. This should give us pause for thought for, of course, all governments exhibit some of these features some of the time, and the politics of a great deal of the world remain close to court politics. Perhaps the most we can safely say is that to the extent that government consists of complex and rationalized procedures, the likelihood of court politics and hence the diplomacy of court politics having a decisive impact is diminished. However, there are better grounds for suspecting the image of diplomats as pure intriguers or manipulators working in their own, individual interests. It is difficult, although not impossible, to imagine a completely self-interested representative of a completely non-consequential country securing anyone's ear, let alone that of the Prince, on the basis of his persuasive charm and manipulative skills alone. The power and influence of even the most Machiavellian diplomats, it is reasonable to suppose, must be grounded in at least two other things: the aggregation of power, wealth and legitimacy which they represent, and the extent to which they perform the tasks they are supposed to be performing well.

Good performances in this regard are generally seen, not in terms of the diplomats' ability to build up their personal power *per se*, but in terms of their ability to secure and exercise sustained influence with their colleagues and with those who receive and send them. Indeed, diplomats who enjoy neither may scarcely be regarded as such. They acquire such influence by not only knowing what is going on, but also being able to make a persuasive assessment of its significance based on their knowledge and understanding of the world. Thus, the third and most important way in which diplomats are associated with power is as the discreet purveyors of expert advice on statecraft to those who practice it. Such advice can bring them closer to the centers of power, so close in fact that diplomats may, on occasions, become *de facto* statesmen themselves and, thus, primary objects of interest in the power political or realist tradition.

A. J. P. Taylor, *The Struggle for Mastery In Europe: 1848–1914* (Oxford: Oxford University Press, 1954, paperback 1971), pp. 450–6, and Harold Nicolson, *Sir Arthur Nicolson, Bart. First Lord Carnock: A Study in the Old Diplomacy* (London: Constable and Co., 1930), pp. 279 and 300.

Personal power and diplomats' roles as advisors to their sovereigns

Ambitious diplomats begin as go-betweens who aspire to be courtiers. They advise those who advise the decision-makers, principally by providing their superiors with information and analysis. They are doubly cursed, both by distance from power and by their profession's taboo on having a direct role in policy-making, as opposed to advising and implementation. However, the situation is not always as bad as it appears. The effects of distance are neither simple nor constant. Prior to the development of modern communications, for example, distance from home might permit ambassadors so much autonomy that they could be said to make their country's foreign policy with respect to their hosts.[18] And the general taboo on policy-making, fond of citing it though diplomats often are, is not as strong in practice as it is in principle. It is probably more useful for resolving questions of political and legal responsibility than for providing an insight into how policy is actually made and implemented. Thus, diplomats may be drawn towards the centers of decision and, hence, power, in a number of ways. The most obvious is as special advisors, of which there are two sorts. There are those who are brought home to participate in policy deliberations at the highest level when a crisis has developed in the country to which they are accredited.[19] Their masters may simply feel uncertain about how to proceed, needing a combination of expert help and cover. It is also true to say, however, that representatives may be brought home for political and symbolic reasons, not all of which signify that they are being drawn into the center of power. Their recall, itself, may be the

---

[18] The autonomy of ambassadors and ministers in residence, and their ability to commit their countries to courses of action, before the advent of the telegraph, steamships and railways is well covered in the literature. The role of the British ambassador to the Sultan, Stratford Canning (Stratford de Redcliffe) in the run-up to the Crimean War is often presented as iconic, albeit controversially so, in this regard. Nevertheless, his competition with the Russian minister, Menshikov, for influence in Constantinople in 1853 provides a glimpse of the extent to which, whether ambition drove them to act as they did or not, these men often acted alone, making and responding to démarches as best they could. See, e.g., Stanley Lane-Poole, *The Life of Lord Stratford de Redcliffe* (Whitefish, Montana: Kessinger, 2006).

[19] See, e.g., Stephen Bosworth, "Political Transition in the Philippines," in Robert Hopkins Miller, *Inside an Embassy: The Political Role of Diplomats Abroad* (Washington: Institute for the Study of Diplomacy, 1992), pp. 66–72.

foreign policy or they may simply be brought home because confidence in their abilities is absent. The second type of special advisor has a more permanent situation and may primarily serve either abroad or at home. It is an American practice, for example, to appoint a special representative of the president on particular issues, for example trade, or to troubled regions like the Middle East and, in recent years, the Balkans.[20] As these two examples suggest, however, such an appointment in itself does not guarantee a personal boost in either internal or external influence. Indeed, the Middle East example provides evidence to suggest that the reverse can be a distinct possibility.[21]

Special advisors who serve at home are better defined by their relationship with their masters than by their remit in terms of policy issues, for they usually provide advice on foreign policy in general. It was British practice in recent years, for example, to request that someone be seconded from the Foreign Office to work for the Prime Minister as their personal advisor on foreign policy. One might expect this to present senior diplomats with a far more promising road to power and influence, but the picture is mixed. What happens largely depends on the chemistry of the personal relations between those involved, especially if the senior diplomats in question are asked to help their new boss balance and counter the influence of their former associates. By all accounts, for example, the experience of Sir Anthony Parsons, a proper career diplomat in every sense of the word, as advisor to Margaret Thatcher was an unhappy one, principally because he persisted in giving a diplomatic perspective on political questions. This was precisely what his prime minister did not want, although what she did want was by no means always clear. In contrast, Charles Powell, seconded from the Foreign Office in the same capacity, developed the position into one of considerable personal influence on the general thrust of both foreign and domestic policy.[22]

---

[20] Richard Holbrooke, *To End a War* (New York: Modern Library, 1999).

[21] See, e.g., Dennis Ross, *The Missing Peace: The Inside Story of the Fight for Middle East Peace* (New York: Farrar, Strauss and Giroux, 2005). Arguably, the duration of Ross's missions made him anything but special, whatever successes he may have achieved.

[22] Sir Anthony Parsons served a year as Mrs. Thatcher's special advisor in 1983 following his success in representing and protecting her policy at the UN Security Council during the Falklands War. Only his latter service is mentioned in Margaret Thatcher, *The Downing Street Years* (London: Harper Collins, 1993). Powell's experience in a similar position was far more successful, if not primarily in foreign

Of course, what the Powell example, in particular, indicates is the presence of court politics. We should not be surprised that this is so. In even the most hyper-rationalized state, masters and servants would remain people and, as such, their political relationships and human relationships would be inextricably bound up with one another and have both political and personal consequences. The United States provides an obvious yet paradoxical, given its constitutional arrangements and the principles on which they rest, example in this regard. Court politics are given life by the need to secure and retain access to the President. Henry Kissinger became America's "chief diplomat" by playing court politics effectively, and a lively, if narrow, story of American foreign policy may be told in terms of the struggles of others to emulate his success in this regard.[23]

The presence of court politics also helps to explain another route to power and influence for ambitious diplomats. They may be far from home and the power of their own masters, but they can be close, informally at least, to the center of power to which they are accredited. To be effective, diplomats have to gain the confidence of their hosts, and some are so successful in this regard that they secure special access and even participate in policy making. Sometimes this is because their respective countries enjoy a quasi-imperial relationship in which the ambassador takes on some of the characteristics of a pro-consul. The advice of Soviet ambassadors in Eastern Europe and American ambassadors in Central America and, more recently, Iraq, was closely attended to, and those ambassadors, it was widely assumed, expected to wield considerable influence in even the domestic affairs of their respective hosts.[24] One imagines that such power and influence is very much a second prize for ambitious diplomats for it is wielded amongst those who are, by definition, lesser gods in the diplomatic pantheon. Far more satisfying are those circumstances in which ambitious diplomats secure

---

policy or diplomatic matters. See G. R. Urban, *Diplomacy and Disillusion at the Court of Margaret Thatcher: An Insider's View* (London: I. B. Taurus, 1996).

[23] Alexander Haig's attempts to control US foreign policy under Reagan, for example. Alexander M. Haig Jr., *Caveat: Realism, Reagan and Foreign Policy* (New York: Scribner, 1984).

[24] While not an ambassador, former State Department official Paul Bremer performed something very like a proconsular role in Iraq, as too have his ambassadorial successors from the US. L. Paul Bremer and Malcolm McConnell, *My Year in Iraq: The Struggle to Build a Future of Hope* (New York: Simon and Schuster, 2006).

access to the deliberations of a greater or rival power. Ormsby-Gore, the British ambassador to the United States at the time of the Cuban missile crisis, provided the benchmark for his successors with regard to the former. He was consulted by Kennedy not just with regard to Britain's position, but also on how the crisis might be handled.[25] Less certainly, Anatoly Dobrynin, the Soviet Union's ambassador to the US during the Cold War, provides an example of influence in the heart of a rival that is unlikely to be emulated by his Russian successors in the foreseeable future. The example is less certain, however, because, as both Dobrynin's and Kissinger's memoirs make clear, the line between being included for substantive reasons and for instrumental ones is very hard to draw.[26] The Americans have a record of pulling foreigners into their deliberations not for advice, but as added ballast for their positions in internal fights over policy.[27] And, of course, foreigners have provided records of how intensely flattered and pleased they are to be so "buttered up," a state of affairs of which their American hosts, their reputations as poor diplomats notwithstanding, are well aware.

Court politics, therefore, provide opportunities for ambitious diplomats both at home and away. Unsurprisingly, however, they provide the best opportunities when something like a formal court with power and authority residing in a single person actually exists. Heads of the foreign service bureaucracy may wield great administrative power, for example, but one of the most influential permanent undersecretaries in the British service, Lord Hardinge, was so because of his close personal relationship with his king.[28] Those who have enjoyed the confidence of their sovereign in this way have been able to wield considerable influence at the nexus of policy and diplomacy, but it may be noted that the road to preferment for statesmen-diplomats generally proceeds up the ladder of domestic influence and then out into the wider world. The great kings of the ancient world sent forth trusted ministers who had established themselves on matters of state, that is questions of power

---

[25] See Stephen Twigge and Len Scott, "The Other Missiles of October: The Thor IRBMs and the Cuban Missile Crisis," *Electronic Journal of History* (June 2000) at www.history.ac.uk/ejournal/art3.html.
[26] Dobrynin, *In Confidence*, and Henry A. Kissinger, *The White House Years* (New York: Little, Brown and Co., 1979) and *Years of Renewal* (New York: Simon and Schuster, 2000).
[27] James A. Baker, *The Politics of Diplomacy* (New York: Putnam, 1995), pp. 94–6.
[28] Lord Hardinge of Penshurst, *Old Diplomacy* (London: John Murray, 1947).

and control in which the internal and the external were blurred by a continuum running from subjects through tributaries to foreigners.[29] The influence of such people possibly reached its apogee in early modern Europe. Mazarin and Richelieu climbed domestic ladders, but then developed diplomatic systems that would advance the interests of their sovereigns. In so doing, they began the shift of sovereignty from the person of the Prince to the idea of the state, for it was not the sovereigns themselves who conducted continuous relations in this new system, but those who represented them.[30] By comparison, Metternich and Bismarck merely remade the political order of Europe, not its constitutive principles. And, while their respective achievements provide testimony to the autonomy European departments of state had achieved from their monarchs by the nineteenth century, their subsequent fates, one undone from below, the other from above, underlined how vulnerable the statesman diplomat continued to be.

The disappointments of diplomacy

Stories of diplomacy and diplomats seem more easily told from within the realist tradition than the other two. The narratives of experience and the examples from practice seem to confirm the realist logic of international affairs, whatever the participants or observers may think of that logic. This is so, however, not because the realist tradition captures best the universal truths about international politics in which all diplomats find themselves immersed. It is because the stories of diplomacy with which we are familiar are bound up with the modern state system that emerged in Europe, the problems its participants encountered, their priorities, and the terms in which they envisaged helpful answers.

This becomes clear when the realist *telos* of power and interest is applied to the diplomats themselves as individuals or as a profession, rather than as the unquestioning servants of those they represent. Certainly, we can see the parts they play in securing the interests and advancing the power of the states they serve. We can see them also attempting to amass personal power and influence from their symbolic

---

[29] Cohen and Westbrook, "Introduction," in *Amarna Diplomacy: The Beginnings of International Relations*, pp. 1–14.
[30] Herbert Butterfield, "Raison d'Etat," First Martin Wight Memorial Lecture BPULC 111 (Brighton: University of Sussex, April 23, 1975).

standing, the skill with which they conduct relations with dear colleagues, and from their roles as courtiers and expert advisors. At all levels from within their missions to amongst the corps and at the courts of both their own government and those to which they are accredited, they can achieve considerable success in this regard. Diplomats can make a difference to the effectiveness of foreign policies and change the terms on which their principals engage in relations with one another, arguably with consequences for the character of the principals themselves. In short, in its presentation of the idea of diplomats as power-seekers in their own right, the realist tradition provides an opening to understanding diplomats in their own terms, but it takes us no further. Diplomats working for themselves may serve the interests and help to extend the power of those they represent, or they may merely get in the way of the game well played by "going wobbly," advocating appeasement, or doing anything which ensures a quiet life and does not upset the apple cart.[31] However, which they are likely to do and why remain mysteries. Therefore, albeit for different reasons, the sense of disappointment with diplomacy and diplomats extends across all three traditions of international thought. Both may appear to be on your side for a while, serving what you think is important, but ultimately both will let you down. Radical diplomats will become co-opted by established power and subvert the revolution, rational diplomats will defend the unreasonable and promote irrationality, and realist diplomats will obstruct or finesse state power and the national interests which it serves. Thus, from a standpoint within each tradition, diplomacy and diplomats seem to act in ways consistent with expectations and preferences of the other traditions. A number of explanations for this baby-passing phenomenon are possible. The most obvious, of course, is that all three traditions are interested in things to which diplomacy and diplomats are peripheral. Hence, they do not need good – in the sense of consistent with the key assumptions of each tradition – understandings or explanations. In this view, diplomacy and diplomats can be assigned to the realm of ad hoc interpretation without doing great damage to intellectual projects that are more important. They never come into proper focus, but this does not matter.

---

[31] See, e.g., Con Coughlin, "John Bolton thinks diplomats are dangerous," *The Daily Telegraph* (November 30, 2007) at www.telegraph.co.uk/opinion/main.jhtml?xml=/opinion/2007/11/30/do3002.xml.

However, an alternative explanation for this baby-passing, and the one for which I am about to make the argument of this book, is that diplomacy and diplomats have an existence outside the senses which can be made of them within the three traditions. Specifically, diplomats provide their own sense of what they are doing when they conduct relations between those they represent, and their own sense of what it is important to achieve in the conduct of those relations. Both are manifestations of what we may term a diplomatic tradition of international thought built on the experience of those engaged in diplomacy and reflections on it. These two explanations do not necessarily contradict one another. It may be that diplomats have their own understanding of what is going on and that it does not matter that they do. Indeed, I shall argue that the tradition to which this understanding gives rise does not stand in direct competition to Wight's three, even in the sense in which they are conventionally regarded as antagonistic. As we shall see, it is silent, or establishes no consistent position, on a great many things rightly regarded as important. What it does do, however, is focus on the "inter" in international relations, as opposed to the entities between which those relations are conducted, their preoccupations, or the specific contexts in which those relations exist. This focus, I shall argue, makes possible a better understanding of why diplomacy and diplomats persistently disappoint, yet why the sense endures that they are, or ought to be, important. It does so by offering a more complete account of what international relations are, and can be, about at any given moment. And this account provides the basis for diplomatic theory of international relations that sheds new insights on how international systems or societies operate, what we can expect from them, and how certain important issues might be handled within them.

PART II

Elements of a diplomatic tradition of international thought

Vain are the thousand creeds which move men's hearts: unutterably vain.
Emily Brontë, "Last Lines (No Coward Soul Is Mine)"

- **Diplomacy as MEDIATION M**
  a) M as catalytic brokerage
  b) M as representation & communication necessary for international life
  c) M as practice of building bridges

- **HUMAN RELATIONS AS DIPLOMACY**
  We spend our lives making REPRESENTATIONS of ourselves to others

  necessarily / sometimes willfully
  INCOMPLETE / PARTIAL

- **DIPLOMACY's own terms I: Conditions of separateness**

  SEPARATENESS is/of the condition of living
  in ISOLATION or APART from others
  either individually or collectively

  SEPARATION is (external, observable condition
                 (internal (emotional, psychological) in (collective) condition

  SEPARATION Continuum
  Complete ————————— Complete
  Isolation   Integration

  separateness as impulse existing in every social situation.

- **DIPLOMACY'S OWN TERMS II: relations of separateness**

- **PRACTICAL & MORAL PROBLEMS regarding relations of separateness**
  all people are of EQUAL WORTH

- **RELATIONS of SEPARATENESS from within the Diplomatic Tradition**
  1) ENCOUNTERED Rels
  2) DISCOVERY Rels
  3) RE-ENCOUNTER Rels

4 | *The diplomatic tradition: Conditions and relations of separateness*

What, then, are the elements of a diplomatic tradition of international thought? As noted above, identifying them is difficult because the balance between thinkers and doers within it has been historically skewed towards the latter.[1] There exists no great canon of diplomatic thought about international relations with its broadly settled structure of knowledge, and familiar pathways for debate and argument. As a consequence, the task of recovering such a tradition involves an even greater exercise of the imagination and creative faculties than usual. It is made even more difficult by the fundamental disagreements that exist among those who study diplomacy and diplomats about what they should be studying. We can find an uneasy consensus around the idea that diplomacy is whatever diplomats do, but it quickly falls apart again around the question of who are the diplomats. Are we to stick with the modern diplomacy's narrow insistence that only states are entitled to diplomatic representation or are we to adopt the sort of broader approach to which a flood of new hyphenated diplomacies – public, field, track two and, even, internal – attests?[2]

In the quest for a diplomatic tradition of international thought, one can start with either, so long as one does not ignore the other. Here,

---

[1] For this point see Brian Hocking and Donna Lee, "The Diplomacy of Proximity and Specialness: Enhancing Canada's Representation in the United States," *The Hague Journal of Diplomacy*, 1, 1 (2006), pp. 29–52.

[2] For a state-anchored conception of diplomacy see Berridge, *Diplomacy: Theory and Practice*. For treatments of diplomacy not so anchored see Costas Constantinou, *On the Way to Diplomacy*, James Der Derian, *On Diplomacy* (Oxford: Blackwell, 1987), and Luc Reychler, "Beyond Traditional Diplomacy," *DSPDP* (Leicester: Diplomatic Studies Programme, 17, May 1996), p. 12. For different attempts to avoid this choice see Hamilton and Langhorne, *The Practice of Modern Diplomacy: Its Evolution, Theory and Administration*, and Geoffrey Wiseman, "Polylateralism and New Modes of Global Dialogue," *DSPDP* (Leicester: Diplomatic Studies Programme, 59, November 1999) p. 26. Both, but the former in particular, take as the point of departure the diplomacy of the states system and then attempt to develop new dimensions to diplomacy.

however, I will adopt the broad conception of diplomacy because my intention is to tease out when it is that people begin to recognize aspects of their relations as diplomatic, why they do so, and with what consequences. In this regard, we do get some help from theorists interested in diplomacy: those who see it in terms of mediation; and those who see it as opening the door to a number of ways of thinking about human relations in general.

Diplomacy as mediation

Mediation is conventionally thought of as an activity by which third parties help other people communicate with each other and, in particular, resolve their disputes.[3] It involves people adopting a position between the parties from which they exercise a series of skills. Therefore, diplomatic relations, it can be argued, are those human relations which require mediation, and those who mediate may be recognized as diplomats or, at least, to be acting diplomatically. This insight has been put to use effectively by several students of diplomacy. In Hocking's account of the transnational networks of relations that increasingly overlay old patterns of interstate diplomacy, for example, contemporary diplomats, and ambassadors in particular, occupy key nodal points.[4] Cultural norms about the standing of diplomats, combined with their traditional skills, allow them to exploit these positions to construct the sort of issue-specific coalitions which are important in post-modern politics, both international and domestic. To the established conception of diplomats mediating between antagonists, therefore, we can add, in Hocking's view, the idea of mediation as a form of catalytic brokerage. That is to say, diplomats mediate between stakeholders in any particular issue, and between stakeholders and others, on behalf of the people, the interests and the ideas they represent.

---

[3] Chester A. Crocker, Fen Osler Hampson and Pamela Aall, *Herding Cats: Multiparty Mediation in a Complex World* (Washington: United States Institute of Peace, 1999). General principles of mediation plus a sense of the extent to which it has become a public, private and commercially organized practice may be obtained at *Mediate.com: The World's Dispute Resolution Channel* at www.mediate.com/index.cfm.

[4] Brian Hocking, "Beyond 'Newness' and 'Decline': The Development of Catalytic Diplomacy."

Jönsson and Hall, in contrast, emphasize a rather different and more philosophical conception of mediation in their attempt to capture what they call diplomacy's "essence."[5] Diplomacy and diplomats provide the representation and engage in the communication without which international life could be neither produced nor reproduced. In addition, however, Jönsson and Hall maintain, diplomacy mediates between the universal and the particular in human affairs.[6] Political, economic, cultural and legal relations between individuals and groups, groups and other groups, both and global conceptions of humanity as a whole all present themselves as a series of tensions. How am I to live as myself and as a citizen of my country? How is my country to live as itself and as one among many countries? And how are all of these to live as themselves and as iterations and subsystems of humanity taken as a whole? Mediation takes place not so much between people, therefore, as between the various ways in which people experience social life. And it falls to diplomacy to undertake this mediation between people and the many ways in which they experience international life.

This more philosophical orientation towards mediation also appears in Der Derian's work. However, he uses it in a distinctive and troubling way. In both the previous works, as in most conventional accounts, the world and the way in which people live are presented as given states of affairs which require diplomacy to help them function more smoothly. In contrast, for Der Derian, diplomacy does not merely act as a go-between for people, ideas and interests. It also maintains the conditions that seem to require it as a go-between.[7] Der Derian refers to this condition as one in which people experience a sense of estrangement, both from one another and from themselves. This is not a natural condition or, more accurately, it should not be regarded as natural even though it may present itself as such. It is also neither a very healthy nor, in a moral sense, good condition. Estrangement allows us to think ill of others and ourselves, to treat equals as unequals and, by so doing, it can provide sanction for relations of domination and exploitation. In contrast to Jönsson's and Hall's

---

[5] Christer Jönsson and Martin Hall, *Essence of Diplomacy* (Basingstoke: Palgrave Macmillan, 2005).
[6] Jönsson and Hall, *Essence of Diplomacy*, pp. 33–37.
[7] James Der Derian, *On Diplomacy*, p. 6. I am not clear if this condition of estrangement implies "an 'original' state of human solidarity" in Der Derian's argument or if his intention is to develop the ideas about alienation and estrangement of those who did posit such an original condition: p. 5.

notion of diplomacy easing the tensions between two highly abstracted conceptions of how people live and want to live, therefore, Der Derian implicates it in the creation of those conditions conventionally said to call for diplomacy. In his view, a practice which is presented as dealing with strangers creates them by estranging people, and a practice which is presented as building bridges between peoples, in so doing, creates and maintains the gulf between them which it claims to span.

All three approaches provide valuable insights on aspects of diplomacy. All three improve upon conventional accounts of what diplomats do. And all three set us well on the road to identifying what is diplomatic about the diplomatic dimension to international relations. They do so by directing our focus away from the familiar agents and structures of international relations and towards the interstitial character of diplomatic activity. Whatever is going on – the brokering of coalitions, the resolution of tensions, the creation and maintenance of estrangement – is going on in the spaces between the agents and structures of social worlds as these are conventionally understood. The great liberating consequence of this shift of focus is that it allows us to unhook our understandings of diplomacy *per se* from the diplomatic systems of particular times and places, most notably that of modern Europe. Whatever understanding of diplomacy is offered or implied by each of the three works considered above, none of them depends upon the existence of a system of sovereign, territorial states to give it meaning and significance.

While their focus on mediation is fruitful, however, it does not provide us with the basis for a distinctively diplomatic tradition of international thought. This is so because mediation, while an important diplomatic function, is not exclusive to those relations we identify as being diplomatic. The network settings in which Hocking's contemporary ambassadors, for example, find themselves share the properties of any complex organization under modern communication conditions. Thus, the ambassador's traditional skills and status are presented almost as legacy features which, as luck would have it, turn out to be transferable to the sorts of worlds in which diplomats now often find themselves. Similarly, the need to mediate between the universal and the particular that Jönsson and Hall identify as an element of diplomacy's essence, would seem to crop up all over the place, not just in the realm of international relations. Finally, in presenting both estrangement and its mediation as bad things, Der Derian shifts attention back to the moral character of the agents whose relationship is being mediated – exploiters and victims or dominators and dominated. Like Jönsson and Hall, therefore, Der Derian provides valuable insights into a certain type of diplomacy, but not all diplomacy, and his insights are derived from other narratives and subjects which are assumed to determine or, at least, over-determine, the scope of diplomacy.

In short, all three accounts of diplomacy actually see it as an instance of something else and derive their explanatory force from outside diplomacy. Despite their shared focus on mediating and the interstitial position implied for diplomats by this focus, all three may be located as rooted in Wight's three traditions of international thought. Hocking offers a new conception, part power political and part institutional liberal, of the setting in which diplomacy is undertaken, and suggests the kind of interest-driven behavior which will prosper in it. Jönsson and Hall employ a humane and soft version of rationalism to present diplomacy as engaged in both conventional and transformational problem-solving under distinctive constraints. And Der Derian's view of diplomacy as an obstacle to emancipation, or as part of that from which we need to be emancipated, places his account in the radical tradition of international thought. None of the three tells the story of diplomacy on its own terms, nor attempts to interpret the world from the standpoints of diplomacy and diplomats, that is from within a diplomatic tradition of international thought.

Human relations as diplomacy

More fruitful in this regard are Constantinou's explorations of the various ideas people have about diplomacy. In his earlier work, he is interested in how we have come to associate deception, ambiguity and the manipulation of ambiguous identities with the practice of diplomacy.[8] He suggests that elements of this Machiavellian understanding of diplomacy are far more present in our own lives than we care to admit. Ambassadors may be involved in negotiating "frame-ups" when it comes to the presentation and reproduction of international life.[9]

---

[8] Constantinou, *On The Way To Diplomacy*.
[9] Costas Constantinou, "Diplomatic Representation ... Or Who Framed the Ambassadors?" *Millennium*, 23, 1, Spring 1994, p. 19. Harold Nicolson's inquiry into the etymology of "prestige" is also useful in this regard. He notes the connotations of blinding as in the sense of dazzling and in the sense of deceiving, as in the tricks of jugglers and conjurers. *The Meaning of Prestige* (Cambridge: Cambridge University Press, 1937), p. 7.

However, all social life, and not just those parts of it that take place around international conference tables and on used car lots (in the US at least), can be viewed as a negotiation, not just of interests but of meanings and identities too.[10] Understanding human relations as diplomacy yields powerful insights. We spend much of our lives making representations of ourselves to others that are necessarily incomplete, and sometimes willfully partial. If social life in general may be read as diplomacy, however, this is by no means all bad news. Merely acknowledging the murky side of our representations allows us both to ease up on the truth claims about identities and relations and to be open to other ways of seeing what they are and might be. More importantly, in his later works Constantinou shows how terms like embassy and ambassador have their etymological roots in ideas about an open-ended journey of intellectual and moral discovery of the self and others.[11] Diplomacy, in these terms, points the way out of the conceptual and practical boxes in which we are imprisoned and from which we do harm to others and to ourselves.

A world populated by people guided by this insight would be calmer, more peaceful and possibly more just than the one we currently inhabit. Indeed, when people reach successful agreements an element of this sort of diplomacy is always in play. Constantinou's approaches, however, leave us with two big problems. First, they bring us no closer to understanding what is meant by diplomacy. To put it another way, why should human relations involving deception and ambiguity, intellectual and moral discovery or combinations thereof be regarded as diplomatic relations? Secondly, and following from this, what are we to make of all those relations which are not essays in ambiguity and deception, still less open-ended explorations and embassies of discovery which are, nonetheless, widely regarded as diplomatic? Constantinou's own response to these concerns is based on his sense of the intimate connection between the way in which people experience the world and the language in which

---

[10] For the notion of diplomacy and international relations in general as a species or sub-set of bargaining see Roger Fisher, Andrea Kupfer Schneider, Elizabeth Borgwardt and Brian Ganson, *Coping With International Conflict: A Systematic Approach to Influence in International Negotiation* (Upper Saddle River: Prentice Hall, 1997).

[11] Costas Constantinou, "Human Diplomacy and Sprituality," *Clingendael Discussion Papers in Diplomacy* (*CDPD*), Clingendael, Netherlands, No. 103, April 2006, p. 20.

they express their apprehension and understanding of it. People cannot call anything diplomacy, but we should not underestimate the wide variety of uses to which they put the word nor worry too much about the fact that they do so. Instead, we should identify the different uses, account for them, and creatively explore their consequences for the users, ourselves and other people. One consequence of such investigations, however, is the discovery that it is easier to see some sorts of relations as more diplomatic than others. While people at very different times and places may have very different understandings of what is meant by diplomacy (or their broadly equivalent term), the fact that some relations are more easily identified as such suggests that they have something in common which transcends time and space. What might these common terms of reference be, and do they provide the basis for identifying a diplomatic tradition of international thought?

Diplomacy's own terms I: conditions of separateness

The common terms of reference for how diplomats – as diplomats – see the world are the mutually constitutive ideas of conditions and relations of separateness. We have to be careful here. I say "as diplomats" for, as Neumann points out, diplomats are merely human beings and, as such and like the rest of us, they live multiple narratives or, to use the language of an older sociology, they perform multiple roles.[12] As lovers, parents, careerists, civil servants, they do many things that contribute to complex identities. As diplomats, however, they encounter a plural world in which people and peoples believe themselves to be living in conditions of separateness. They encounter this world from positions in the spaces they occupy between these people and peoples, and they are responsible for conducting the distinctive relations that exist between them. For most people, international relations involve the parties they are between and the issues they are about. How they see and order these shapes their ways of seeing international relations. For diplomats, in contrast, it is the conditions of separateness that provide the distinctive site or space from which diplomats see the world, and from which a diplomatic tradition of international thought emerges to make its own distinctive sense of the resulting relations.

[12] Neumann, "To Be a Diplomat," pp. 72–93.

By separateness, I mean the condition of living, either individually or collectively, in isolation or apart from others. This is a complex notion. It can take the form of a physical or social fact, or some combination of both.[13] Before the great European voyages of discovery, for example, Americans and Europeans were physically separate because of distance and oceans. The peoples of New Zealand and Great Britain today are separated by a combination of physical distance and political arrangements (although the trends in each respect may be said to be pulling in opposite directions). The people of Belgium and the Netherlands are kept apart almost solely by social facts, although even some of these collaborate with the absence of physical distance to undermine this separation in both sub-state and supra-national ways.

The condition of separation is to be found within any, all or combinations of the sectors into which human relations can be usefully divided, for example: social; cultural; political; economic; legal and sexual. One or more sectors may be thought of in terms of exercising a controlling role over the others. In the modern state system, for example, all other separations are presented as subordinate to those generated by political and legal borders. Thus in the notions of American men and women, on the one hand, and Mexican men and women on the other, for example, it is the adjective which is regarded as ruling. In contrast, in a gendered understanding of social reality, in this example, it is the noun on which this significance is conferred. The question of which dominates is, of course, itself a political one in some, but crucially not all, respects. As these examples suggest, separation may also be viewed in both horizontal and vertical terms, with the former conveying notions of equality while the latter conveys notions of hierarchy, and social hierarchy in particular. Hierarchy also implies the notion of subsystems of separation that are illustrated by the way in which, for example, the membership of a family separates one from those who are not members, even though we may all attend the same church and live in the same city.

However, separation is not merely an observable, external condition. It also finds its expression in the emotional, psychological and

---

[13] See Alexander Wendt, *Social Theory of International Politics* (Cambridge: Cambridge University Press, 1999), pp. 47–190 for a useful discussion of the distinction between social and material facts and forces and, of course, his argument about the usefulness of seeing social reality as constructed by thought and action.

intellectual internal states of human beings. They feel separate and, indeed, they often want to be alone as a way of creating, reproducing, affirming, stabilizing, or just plain hanging on to who they think they are. This internal or experiential aspect of the idea greatly complicates the task of setting out a framework for analysis of the external dimensions of separation. It is the more valuable of the two aspects for our purposes, however, for it allows us to think of separation in terms of a continuum between complete isolation and complete integration, rather than as an either-or state of affairs. Poor Ben Gun on Treasure Island and the science fiction *genre* of communities isolated by nuclear or climactic catastrophes provide examples of extreme isolation and the sense of separation likely to accompany it. Fiction also provides examples of the opposite. The *Matrix* films and the Borg in *Star Trek*, in their different ways, portray beings whose individuality is radically submerged, ant-like, in the consciousness and physical needs of vast collective projects. As we can see from these examples, however, even in the world of fiction the extremes of isolation and integration are not absolute. Ben Gun still likes cheese. That is to say, he keeps with him a notional world of people, culture and values, which orients him to his circumstances and permits him to recognize and accept the opportunity for rescue when it presents itself. And the fictional presentations of suffocating families and identity-absorbing totalitarian societies are often merely setups for rebellions by which individuals and groups assert themselves.

The world lies, or moves at variable speeds, between these two extremes of isolation and integration. One can certainly observe long-term secular trends in the technologies of travel and communication that have reduced the possibility of complete separation exemplified by the New World and the Old World noted above. The ability of most peoples to be unaware of the existence of most other peoples has been virtually eliminated, and a statesman would find it far harder today than Chamberlain did in the 1930s to speak of quarrels in "a faraway country between people of whom we know nothing."[14] One might

---

[14] Neville Chamberlain, 1938, speaking of the clashes between the Czechoslovak Government and the German minority of the Sudetenland. "How horrible, how fantastic, how incredible it is that we should be digging trenches and trying on gas masks here because of a quarrel in a faraway country between people of whom we know nothing." www.secondworldwarhistory.com/quotes_neville_chamberlain.asp.

suspect that these same secular trends have opened up the possibility of something approaching the complete integration of human communities and, hence, their members with one another. Thus, in terms of international history, it is perfectly possible to maintain, for example, that the ancient empires of the great kings of the Middle East were more separate from one another than were China and Rome. Both of these were more separate from one another than were the countries of the modern, European international society of states, and the members of that society were more separate from one another than are the members of the present European Union (EU).

At the same time, however, we can see separateness, or the desire for it, as an impulse existing in every social situation. We live with each other, well aware of each other, but we feel various degrees of separation from, or wanting to feel separate from, each other for much of the time. The fact that what Chamberlain said was not true, even as he said it, is an indicator of this impulse. And it is this internal dimension of the notion, rather than its external referents, that provides the starting point for diplomacy and diplomats. After all, there can be no diplomacy when people are completely separate and, hence, unaware of one another. It is when they know each other exists that relations become possible. It is when people want those relations with one another, but also want to keep apart, that the conditions of separateness are created. And these conditions provide the space in which diplomacy and diplomats work.

Diplomacy's own terms II: relations of separateness

What then is distinctive about relations under conditions of separateness, and why do they require diplomacy and diplomats? All human relationships may be said to impose restrictions on the ego, interests and wills of those involved. If one sees relationships in terms of exchange, then these impositions are the price one pays in terms of giving for what one takes. I put up with her and her wants, so that she will put up with me and mine. Even if one has a richer conception of relationships in terms of, for example, of their constituting at least part of one's own identity in which the giving is not seen as a loss, the daily negotiation of these relationships still involves impositions, even if they are more willingly and, indeed, joyfully accepted. In loving relationships, for example, accepting these impositions and having one's own happily accepted is a big part of the fun. Love provides just one of several reasons and motives, however, for why people accept the claims of others on them. A whole set of prompts ranging from biological and apparently natural to social and conventional, play their part in getting us to accept, whether for reasons of interest or right, or with very little reason but a great deal of feeling, that we and some people belong together in a way that we and others do not.

Relations of separateness exist, therefore, where people believe or feel that the claims of others upon them have less emotional pull, legal force or moral weight. We owe more to our own, and they to us, than we do to strangers. Thus, a family puts up with one another around the home on a more-or-less permanent basis, receives friends and treats them well for a defined amount of time; and accepts complete strangers on highly circumscribed terms or not at all. Citizens can work and vote. Resident aliens can work. Foreigners can do neither and better leave when their time is up. Here we can see a clear set of boundaries that delineates what sort of impositions "we," who belong, are prepared to accept from "they," who do not. Not only are they clear, they are boundaries which most of us accept as natural and reasonable so long, at least, as we avoid the misfortune of becoming "they" in a particular situation. A great deal lies behind these clear boundaries appearing natural, and the mapping of concentric circles around the individual or collective personality provides some help in understanding what it is. Meeting obligations takes a great deal out of us, and we are finite beings while the demand upon us in terms of other's needs is, in principle, infinite and certainly inexhaustible. Thus, we may give up our lives for the inner circle of family, pay taxes to help the middle ring of fellow citizens, and give charity to those at the outer limits so long as there is no external obligation to do so and it does not cost too much. Working back the other way, we may kill those in the outer circle, engage in rule-bound competition with those in the middle, and regard ourselves as not competing with those whom we regard as fully our own.

This schema is only useful in a suggestive sense, however. It does not provide a completely accurate map of where relationships of separateness are to be found. They may not, for example, be always relegated to the periphery. The most intimate of human relationships may involve a measure of separateness on certain matters. Indeed it is generally regarded as healthy that they do, and separateness can come to dominate intimate relationships when things go wrong to the point where violence and murder become distinct prospects. Conversely, people have been known to die for complete strangers, and a sense of separateness itself can permit certain kinds of intimacy in some circumstances. We may share with a stranger what we could never share with a partner. Over time, the sense of separateness and its consequences can shift locations. Until fairly recently, for example, European peoples believed it to be right and fitting to die and kill in large numbers for their respective countries, their countries' interests and the ideals they were supposed to be upholding. This is no longer clearly the case. Arguably, their sense that other Europeans, and possibly all foreigners seen as humanity as a whole, are less strange and less separate is growing. Economic, social and, latterly, environmental policies may all give expression to this changing sense of who is separate from whom and should be treated accordingly. Therefore, it may be that the further people are away from us in terms of distance, community or family, the more likely it is that the normal bonds of human relations will be weaker. However, we cannot say with certainty where and when relations of separateness will be found, only that where they are people will feel under less obligation to one another. Europeans may feel closer to foreigners abroad at the moment, for example, but with those whom they regard as foreigners among them, familiar patterns of distancing are growing more pronounced. We owe less to immigrants and minorities than we have been told that we should, the cultural and racial majority in many European states appears to say. And they seem to owe less to us than we had previously assumed.

Practical and moral problems regarding relations of separateness

In addition to the complexities and uncertainties that make it difficult to map where and when relations of separateness occur, an important objection to the notion must also be considered. It can be maintained that once one has inquired into how relations of separateness are produced, one can no longer accept the way they are presented as a given, an unavoidable and irreducible social, and possibly biological, fact of life. Instead, one should reject all attempts to present relations of separateness in these terms and demonstrate the follies and evils that flow from people so doing. It is the case that relations of separateness, just like relations of togetherness, are always, in an important sense, produced. We often attempt to create fellow feeling by setting out role expectations, for example those of fatherhood for young men who are shortly to become parents, into which people should grow. These expectations concern what they should do, but also what they should feel. Thus, a great deal of emotion and uncertainty may be channeled by suggesting that it would not be inappropriate for a father-to-be to feel like he would die for his baby and to say so. By similar processes, we may also attempt to socialize people away from old conceptions of associations and towards new ones. Thus, we may say, for example, that we should not treat strangers in the ways we have in the past or, grasping the other end of the stick, we may say that this or that people should no longer be treated as strangers, or even that there are no moral or empirical grounds for declaring anybody to be strangers anymore. Strangers, we may say, do not, or ought not to, exist.

Indeed, a great deal of moral reasoning in the West and elsewhere has been drawn to the conclusion that, as human beings, all people are of equal worth and that no or few moral grounds can be established for treating them unfairly or, less certainly, unequally. All should have a right to life, for example, and all should be free and have an equal opportunity to pursue their own conception of what is worthwhile and the happiness said to flow from that. This being so, we have a uniform obligation, perhaps to help, and certainly not to hinder, one another in these regards. The fact that people act otherwise, privileging themselves and those they care about to the neglect, and sometimes at the expense, of others is, thus, regarded as a great problem. It is the acceptance of differential treatment in these terms that puts us all on the slippery slope to oppressing, dominating, enslaving and exterminating one another. Whatever the practical obstacles, therefore, we should at least try to treat everybody fairly and equally.

The ubiquity of such themes, and the entrenched character of their presence in our thinking, is no better illustrated by the academic study of International Relations. It is often regarded as even more dismal and questionable a science than Economics, yet its modern history as an academic study may be presented as beginning with a foundation agreement that conditions of separateness and the relations to which they give rise are bad things. It then proceeds to arguments about the causes of both which, in turn, give rise to arguments about what we ought to do as a consequence. These bring us to the present high ground of arguing about how bad separateness is relative to other bad things in international relations, which now have come to include some of those things – economic development, interdependence and legal regimes with universal application, for example – that might plausibly be regarded as reducing our sense of separateness from one another.[15]

IR's preoccupation with separateness as a problem and what to do about it helps account for its uneasiness with diplomacy and diplomats. For the latter's position on these conceptual problems, empirical difficulties and moral objections, is broadly one of saying "and yet." We may be uncertain as to when relations of separateness are likely to occur, and we may be clearer that they are produced and that they do not simply naturally occur, yet at any given moment, they *are* occurring and they *are* being produced. As to whether they are a good thing or not, for diplomats, the question is almost as meaningless as asking the same about the weather. One can have good and bad weather, but weather as such is simply there. As to what to do about relations of separateness, therefore, the diplomats, as diplomats, advocate neither "jailbreaks" from the conditions giving rise to them nor a *sauve qui peut* for surviving and prospering in a prison regime.[16] Indeed, insofar as they may be regarded as pathological, relations of separateness require the care of the hospice rather than the curative approaches once proclaimed by hospitals. And the real challenge is to head off the development of pathologies in the first place. As to the causes of conditions and relations of separateness, this is of interest to diplomats only insofar as different conditions give rise to different kinds of relations. Accordingly, the initial focus of a diplomatic tradition of international thought is on identifying these different types.

---

[15] A useful history of IR in terms of sequenced debates – the liberal critique of international relations, the realist critique of liberal IR, the neo-liberal critique of realist IR, the neo-realist critique of neo-liberal IR, and the assertion of a neo-neo synthesis, primarily for the purpose of post-positivist critiques of the whole ensemble of IR – is provided by Chris Brown and Kirsten Ainley, *Understanding International Relations* (Basingstoke: Palgrave Macmillan, 3rd edn., 2005), especially pp. 1–62. A more direct treatment of the issue raised here may be found in Nicholas Wheeler, *Saving Strangers: Humanitarian Intervention in International Societies* (Oxford: Oxford University Press, 2001).
[16] The term "conceptual jailbreak" is used by James Rosenau, *Turbulence in World Politics: A Theory of Change and Continuity in World Politics* (Hemel Hempstead: Harvester Wheatsheaf, 1990).

Relations of separateness from within the diplomatic tradition

What sorts of relations of separateness can we identify? The diplomatic tradition suggests three. First, we may speak of **encounter relations** similar to those suggested by the anthropological fictions of the origins of diplomacy where peoples, actually or figuratively, run into each other for the first time. Such encounters between people occur all the time in ordinary life, but they do so usually in social contexts in which language and meanings are to a great extent shared. Of interest here are the ones we imagine taking place between prehistoric peoples and those we know took place between the explorers, traders and soldiers of European empires and some of the people they ran into on their expeditions. Though we have examples of such encounters from history and pre-history, they are far fewer than might be imagined. Peoples generally seem to have known of each other before they made contact, although there are some cases where the encounter has taken one or both parties completely by surprise. The initial problem in such encounters is how, once a relationship has been decided upon, to establish communications between people whose languages and whose very understanding of the world and what is important within it are not known to each other. As we shall see, this is not as difficult as might be supposed. We have no records of encounters which failed simply because people could not communicate sufficiently. Hence, actual examples of encounter relations are generally of short duration, and their use within the diplomatic tradition is generally as counterfactuals to illustrate points about other types of relations of separateness.

Since some sort of relationship is usually established without great difficulty, encounter relations quickly merge with the second type of relations identified in the tradition, **discovery relations**. The use of "discovery" here may appear unfortunate, since it connotes explorations which find people and things for the first time. Anchored by its noun, however, it suggests those relations by which peoples attempt to render their respective and independently developed cultures mutually intelligible. For a wide variety of reasons, people are curious about one another, and once the simple questions of "what are you doing; what are you saying?" are answered, the question "why?" quickly follows. Encounter relations give way to discovery relations, therefore, but these are not the only circumstances in which the latter are found. Cultures develop and change like living things, and it is impossible to know absolutely everything about a particular culture. Therefore, discovery relations persist, and, unlike encounter relations, they are a permanent feature of any system or society comprised of multiple peoples with their respective cultures.

Thirdly, and most importantly, re-encounter relations are identified from within the diplomatic tradition. It might be supposed that encounters and discoveries narrow, or should narrow, relations of separateness by eroding the sense of difference from one another experienced by people. It is a commonplace of ordinary life, for example, to say that we discover that strangers and foreigners are "just like us." This is often the case, but so is the opposite. That is to say contacts with others give rise to a sense of both similarities and differences, sometimes with complicating consequences for people's sense of who they are and the security of that sense. The questions "should we be more like them?" and "will we become more like them?" together with their obverse, "should they be more like us?" and "will they become more like us?" may be asked in anticipation of danger or opportunity. Either way, such questions place a great strain on existing patterns of relations and the established identities between which they are conducted. Re-encounter relations, therefore, attempt to keep others who are known, and possibly very well known, at arm's length by reproducing and emphasizing difference. They may do so to a variety of degrees, to maintain pre-existing identities completely intact, for example, or to maintain them in some sectors and not others. At a minimum, however, they involve managing the pace at which a controlled docking and final merger of identities might occur, while at a maximum they may emphasize and extend existing differences, creating some where none existed before, in processes which estrange those who were formerly familiar to each other or even regarded each other as one.

This is beginning to sound sinister. It is important to note, however, that these three types of relations of separateness do not, in themselves, imply enmity or friendship. Nor do they imply the policies by which conventionally good and bad diplomatic relations are manifested or created.[17] This point may be illustrated by re-considering the favorite

---

[17] For a useful typology of relationships in terms of enmity, rivalry, and friendships and their respective consequences for the "logics of anarchy" see Wendt, *Social Theory of International Politics*, pp. 246–312. For an attempt to apply them to exploring possibilities for continuity and change in contemporary international relations see Barry Buzan, *The United States and the Great Powers: World Politics in the Twenty-First Century* (Cambridge: Polity, 2004).

metaphor of diplomacy, noted earlier, that of its service as a bridge between peoples. This is widely, and rightly, regarded as a sign of good relations or the desire for them. A bridge brings people together. It was noted, however, that the idea of a bridge implies two sides and a divide and, thus, its use as a metaphor can be viewed as an instrument or conduit of estrangement. The existence of bridges may be asserted or the need for them proposed as a way of maintaining or producing distance. Notions of separation and bringing together can co-exist, therefore. The important thing to note here, however, is that the notion of bridges may join people or keep them apart, and it may do so in the context of either good or bad relations. This open or neutral character applies to all relations of separateness, as they are understood from within the diplomatic tradition. Thus, encounters can lead to marriage and trade, segregation and massacre, and all points in between. Discovery can lead to friendship born out of similarities or complimentary differences, or it can lead to hostility born out of differences or uncomplimentary similarities. Both friends and enemies can be kept at arm's length, and maintained as such, by re-encounter relations.

However, this simple typology of relations of separateness, implying neither enmity nor friendship, merely limited liability and commitment, is greatly complicated by political, economic and cultural forces at play in what for the associated diplomacy, at least, is the background. By this, and following Watson, I mean that at any given time, relations of separateness are being conducted in the midst of great swells pushing peoples together and/or pulling them apart along different dimensions of their relations.[18] Thus, in political terms, we may talk of a historical tendency for the distribution of power to swing between the concentrations of empire and hegemony at one end, and plural centers and fragmentation at the other. Economically, we can chart historical processes of integration drawing peoples into the same organization of production and distribution, while casting out others or leaving them behind. Culturally, we can chart the emergence, triumph and decline of ideas about the "real" community of humankind and attempt to map their complex relationships with the political and economic processes which they seek to explain, sanction, or critique. In short, relations of separateness are conducted on shifting sands and tidal waters which may, in different times and at different places, make their conduct,

---

[18] Watson, *The Evolution of International Society*.

and hence the task of diplomacy, easier or harder and more or less important. That this is so provides the beginnings of an answer to the next question focused upon from within the diplomatic tradition of international thought. Why does the conduct of relations of separateness become the task of diplomacy and diplomats?

5 | *The diplomatic tradition: Diplomacy; diplomats and international relations*

Relations of separateness do not have to be conducted by diplomacy and diplomats. War and soldiers, trade and merchants, slavery and slavers, extermination and criminals can also serve, sometimes concurrently with diplomacy, but more often driving it out. However, when peoples must have relations, but do not want, or believe that they cannot have, relations like those just listed, something recognizable as diplomacy quickly emerges. That is to say there is very little in the way of peaceful relations of separateness without diplomacy. Law and lawyers and politics and politicians, for example, may provide peaceful relations, but not relations of separateness. To explain why this is so and, indeed, what I mean by it, I will return to the anthropological fictions about the beginnings of diplomacy and employ my own version of them.

The emergence of diplomacy within the diplomatic tradition

Recall that most of these postulate a first encounter between peoples who were previously unaware of each other's existence. The waterhole meeting between ape-like humans in the film *2001: A Space Odyssey* is emblematic in this regard, although unfortunate in that it leads to the discovery of how a jawbone may be used as a weapon. We may imagine things turning out more fortuitously. Since both parties need access to the waterhole, and neither seems capable of overwhelming the other, one imagines multiple violent encounters until one or both parties wish to stop fighting but stay in contact and both parties find a way of communicating with each other. Then, they must find a way of circumventing the taboo on contact with strangers we assume them to have, and they accomplish this by developing the idea of heralds who are exempt or immune from its application. The problem with this sort of account is that we know from real anthropology that peoples did not or, at least, did not always encounter one another in this way. They might know of each other's existence long before they entered into relations of the sort suggested above (the taboo on strangers above implies as much). Indeed, indirect and unofficial relations for trading, breeding and religious purposes might be quite highly developed without anything like the imagined, heraldic diplomacy of anthropological fictions developing.[1]

This being so, it is helpful to consider a different kind of encounter built around the indirect exchange of gifts which sometimes takes place between simple societies and also, on occasions, between soldiers of opposing sides in times of war.[2] Instead of meeting up directly, groups of people commence a relationship by sequentially leaving goods in a common place. One group leaves something there and, after a decent interval, returns to the place anticipating that their good will be gone and something else will be there in its place. If the good is accepted and properly reciprocated, then a relationship may be said to be in the process of coming into being. What is going on can be presented in at least three ways. The first is a rational choice account involving one of both groups' desires for gain, calculations of risks, and expectations of behavior. Initially, at least, the story can be told in entirely subjective terms. Even the socialized expectations of exchange and reciprocity which surround gift-giving are initially experienced subjectively within one or both groups. With indirect contact through a successful exchange the situation changes, but even so, a rational choice story can still be told about the generation of expectations by reciprocal behavior re-enforcement. The groups may simply continue to leave goods at the common place when mood takes them or need dictates, knowing that the chances of something they want appearing their in their place are higher than normal. The ideas of gift giving and exchange, together with the relationships implied by these, do not need to be present, merely the sense that there is a place at which goods may be left, taken and replaced by something else. It is important that both groups designate the same place for this to happen, but they do not even need an inter-subjective agreement on where this place is.

---

[1] Buzan and Little, *International Systems in World History*. See also Jared Diamond, *Germs, Guns and Steel: The Fates of Human Societies* (New York: W. W. Norton, 1997).

[2] Bronislav Malinowski, *Magic, Science and Other Essays* (Westport: Greenwood Press, 1992) and Marcel Maus (translated by W. D. Hallis), *The Gift: The Form and Reason for Exchange in Archaic Societies* (London: Routledge, 1990).

It is highly likely, however, that conditions develop about which a second and much richer story can be told once the process of exchange gets under way. After all, the replacement gifts have to come from somewhere and someone, and it stretches credulity to suggest that both groups can maintain such a process without getting some sort of sense of each other's existence. As they do, it may be claimed that the two groups are in the process of constituting themselves into a single society of exchange linked by a common understanding of the gift-giving which is going on, common expectations based on the idea of reciprocity about what will happen and what ought to happen, and a shared sense that all the above is the case. However, to infer that whatever it is the two groups share is a society in the same sense that each may be regarded as a society seems, at least, premature. They may constitute a simple society of sorts to the outside observer equipped with a checklist of the features required to qualify as such. It is highly doubtful that they regard themselves as such, however. Indeed, the processes of exchange may underline the differences and separate identities of the parties to it and, in some respects, be designed to do so. We are the providers of pelts, for example, and they of obsidian.

A third story, therefore, suggests itself about two groups groping towards each other on the basis of their respective understandings of how the world works and what is important in it, but with little sense of rule-based liabilities, moral commitments or emotional fellow-feeling towards each other. In this story, those among the first group who suggest leaving a gift and those among the second group who suggest that it be reciprocated rather than just taken, may be said to be thinking in equal part as diplomats and commercial risk analysts. They are thinking as risk analysts in that they are proposing scarce goods and those who bear them be exposed to the unknown. A total loss may result. They are thinking diplomatically in the sense that they are proposing the possibility of a relationship with others to whom their people believe they are under none of the usual emotional, moral or legal obligations with which they bind themselves to one another. If those who propose such adventures may be regarded as thinking diplomatically, in part at least, then those who carry the gifts may be said to be acting in equal part as diplomats and traders. And those who reflect upon how this process of exchange might be put on a firmer and more predictable footing may be said to be contributing equally to the diplomatic tradition of international thought and the economic tradition of thought about international exchange.

In short, diplomacy can enter into stories of simple relations between peoples at a very early stage. It does so after rational calculations have produced attempts to establish peaceful contacts. Diplomacy may even quickly come to supply the dominant narrative for such contacts if, for example, the pursuit of gifts becomes less important than maintaining and developing the relations originally established to secure them. This being so, it is tempting to think in terms of diplomatic relations constituting a way station or half-way house between groups conducting relations with one another in a social vacuum and those same groups developing a common society within which to conduct their relations. Indeed, this sense of common society might grow in such a way that the sense of separateness between its members shrinks concomitantly. There is plenty of evidence to suggest that diplomatic relations might be viewed as proto-social relations in this sense. However, there is also plenty of evidence to suggest that this is not always the case. Diplomacy can be conducted between established groups that seek to maintain their distance from one another, and between the new groups emerging as old societies fade and fall apart, as much as between the members of new societies in the process of coming together and merging. The primary concern of diplomacy, therefore, is with neither constructing new societies nor dismantling old ones. It is with the conduct relations between people who, whatever the underlying trends in these terms, at the given moment do not believe or feel themselves to be bound to one another by conventional familial, community, or societal links and yet who want to, or believe that they have to, have relations with each other. If we can see how relations of separateness quickly give rise to diplomacy, however, it still remains unclear why diplomats, in any sense other than people who are given immunity from the usual rules about strangers, are needed. What is so special about diplomats? This is an important question for practical reasons, but also because it is only once diplomats emerge from people acting diplomatically that the diplomatic tradition's understanding of international relations starts to become clear.

The emergence of diplomats in the diplomatic tradition

The early emergence of diplomacy in all sorts of settings characterized by relations of separateness is not matched by the appearance of diplomats as we would recognize them, or they would recognize themselves, today. In the conventional literature, diplomats emerge in a story that takes us from proto-diplomats such as heralds and *proxenoi* of ancient Greece, through *legati* and envoys of Rome, to the resident ambassadors and their professional staffs of the early modern period in northern Italy. Successively we see the problems of alien status and immunity, who may represent, whether or not to confer plenipotentiary powers, and permanent presence being addressed.[3] However, the first and last concerns on this list are presented as the most significant. Alien status and immunity give those who act diplomatically the grounds for having a collective sense of themselves as such, but it is lying abroad together with dear colleagues in some foreign capital centuries later that provides the opportunity and means for actually developing and sharing this sense. The emphasis in the story is upon the end, and what is often presented as the final product, not least because it is of the end in these terms that we possess good historical records. Watson, for example, suggests that when "the design for ordering the affairs of a system which is implicit in a diplomatic dialogue becomes visible to its practitioners, when it breaks surface so to speak, then diplomacy can achieve its full stature." And he suggests that the modern European diplomatic system deserves our attention in these terms because "it was the most developed, the most self-aware and the most imaginative that we know," and its institutions and practices "expanded beyond the society which evolved them."[4] However, the center of gravity of the story can easily be moved back to its first element, the problem of alien status and the consequences for those involved. If we do so, it becomes possible to see that the situation or, better, predicament in which diplomats find themselves and come to know themselves as such is far older than the histories of modern diplomacy would suggest. It also becomes possible to see what the predicament demands of diplomats in terms of their distinctive outlook and actions, and how both become valuable and useful to those amongst whom they work.

This investigation of the predicament in which diplomats find themselves has been attempted in a number of ways within the diplomatic tradition of international thought. The most prominent, noted earlier, is the literary *genre* emerging from early modern Europe in which authors

---

[3] Mattingly, *Renaissance Diplomacy*, Hamilton and Langhorne, *The Practice of Modern Diplomacy* and Linda S. Frey and Marsha L. Frey, *The History of Diplomatic Immunity* (Columbus: Ohio State University Press, 1999).
[4] Watson, *Diplomacy*, p. 93.

reflected on the qualities of a good ambassador or envoy and thus, by implication, the circumstances in which all diplomats found themselves.[5] This *genre* has been criticized on several grounds. Much of it, but by no means all, is focused on the appropriate conduct for gentlemen at court. Much of it, but again by no means all, can be faulted for having the quality of the sort of advice Polonius provides his son Laertes.[6] Calling for the qualities required in all human relations – common qualifications but on which special calls are made, in one rendition – may be viewed as unhelpful or even mischievous.[7] It is all very well to say that people in general, and diplomats in particular, ought to be good, but often they are not, runs the objection. Therefore, we should be seeking to explain and understand why this is so, rather than painting a picture of diplomats which may embellish their reputations, but which is at odds with the far less attractive facts. Both objections have been overplayed. As noted earlier, it remains important to know how to talk to egotistical people who possess a great deal of power, whether they are your own sovereign, the one to whom you are accredited, or not a sovereign at all. Further, promoting virtue cannot be entirely without merit. The advice of Polonius is, after all, quite good, and even the academic study of International Relations has re-opened its doors to inquiry which explicitly considers how things might be and ought to be.[8] One suspects, indeed, that it is unease at the association of virtue with diplomacy, *per se*, rather than with discussions of virtue in

---

[5] See, e.g., Abraham de Wicquefort, *L'Ambassadeur et ses Fonctions* and François de Callières, *De la manière de négocier avec les souverains, de l'utilité des négociations, du choix des ambassadeurs et des envoys, et des qualitez nécessaires pour réussir dans ces employs* (Paris: Brunet, 1717). Excellent examples of the writings of these authors and other early moderns or theorists of old diplomacy, plus commentaries upon them, may be found in the following: G. R. Berridge (ed.), *Diplomatic Classics: Selected Texts from Commynes to Vattel* (Basingstoke: Palgrave Macmillan, 2004), Berridge, Keens-Soper and Otte, *Diplomatic Theory from Machiavelli to Kissinger*, and H. M. A. Keens-Soper and Karl W. Schweizer (eds.), *The Art of Diplomacy: François de Callières* (New York: University Press of America, 1983).
[6] William Shakespeare, *Hamlet, Prince of Denmark*, I, iii.
[7] Montague Bernard, *Four Lectures On Subjects Connected With Diplomacy* (London: Macmillan, 1868), p. 148.
[8] See Chris Brown, *International Relations Theory: New Normative Approaches* (Hemel Hempstead: Harvester Wheatsheaf, 1992) for a general discussion of the revival of explicitly normative IR theorizing.

general, which fuels the devaluation of the qualities-of-diplomats literature on these grounds.

For the purposes of the argument being advanced here, the most important weakness of the *genre* is not that what it says is inappropriate, trite or unimportant. It is our old objection, namely that it provides no insight into those aspects of the diplomats' predicament which might be said to be particular to diplomacy. For this, we must look to more imaginative accounts that focus on what I shall refer to as the subjective and objective articulations of this predicament. By subjective, I mean how diplomats appear both to themselves and others from vantage points within the societies sending them and receiving them. By objective, I mean how their predicament appears when they look at each other, or we see them, as a class of people situated between those they represent.

Why diplomacy gives rise to diplomats I: the subjective articulation of diplomats as strangers

In the subjective articulation diplomats appear, both to themselves and others, as strangers. We may assume that this was as true for the first, prehistoric heralds, as it must have been for the ministers sent by Great Kings to the courts of those they recognized as their brothers in the ancient world, and as it is for diplomats today. Sasson Sofer's work on "the diplomat as stranger" is exemplary in this regard.[9] It draws on sources in anthropology, sociology, literature and theatre to imagine how diplomats will act as a consequence. Strangers, by definition, feel less informed about their circumstances than those who belong and, as a practical matter, also feel less secure. Unless they are powerful, they are likely to be curious to find out more about their circumstances, cautious in their actions and judgments, and polite, so as not to give unnecessary or unintended offence, in their communications. This is the strangers' part in ensuring good relations with their hosts. In return, the latter, once they have decided to accept a visit, offer hospitality, the warmth and intensity of which go beyond what is normally expected. Both parties are aware, however, that the good relations which may obtain from such conduct are fragile, shallow, and possibly of short duration.

---

[9] Sasson Sofer, "The Diplomat as Stranger," *Diplomacy and Statecraft*, 8, 3 (November 1997), pp. 179–86.

Misunderstandings may occur, unwelcome intentions may be revealed and, above all, guests, although well treated whilst visiting, are expected and expect to go home.

Diplomats, however, are examples of a particular kind of stranger. Like other strangers, they seek to become familiar with and to those with whom they have relations. Unlike them, however, they also work to maintain a distance. This is not just the distance that all professionals – doctors, lawyers, teachers – need to prevent personal relations getting in the way of what they sometimes must do. It is a distance bound up with their professional identity. They are, as it were, professional strangers and need to remain so to do their job. The value of the Pharaoh's minister in Hatti, just like Our Man In Havana, resides in their being seen as such by all concerned, as much as it does in anything particular they might do. The idea of diplomats-as-strangers is useful, therefore, in that it focuses on their "lying abroad" (in the less pejorative sense) or, more accurately, their status as outsiders placed within another society of which they are not members.[10] It directs our attention to the old tongue-in-cheek notion of diplomatic progress as a transition from the convention of eating strangers to that of inviting them as honored guests to dinner.[11] It also directs our attention to the sort of problems diplomats face. The need to establish their immunity from normal conventions about both members and non-members, the need to stabilize their standings as neither fish nor fowl, and the danger of their over-identifying with local cultures are all long-standing examples of specifically diplomatic predicaments arising out of diplomats' standing as professional strangers.

The notion of diplomats-as-strangers sheds light on their predicament. It also provides the beginnings of an answer to why the rest of us find them useful. They can do some things more effectively than the rest of us because of the skills and priorities their predicament encourages them to develop. What, however, does it tell us about how diplomats see

---

[10] Sir Henry Wotton (1604), "An ambassador is an honest man sent to lie abroad for the commonwealth," cited in Robert Wolfe, "Still Lying Abroad? On the Institution of the Resident Ambassador," *DSPDP* (Leicester, Diplomatic Studies Programme, 33, September 1997), p. 1. The pun on "lie" exists only in the English translation, not in the original Latin ("mentiendum") as is made clear in Hamilton and Langhorne, *The Practice of Diplomacy*, p. 255.

[11] Richard Langhorne, *Diplomacy and Governance* (Moscow: MGIMO-University, 2004), p. 7.

international relations in general? If their caution, curiosity and politeness as strangers contribute to their security and effectiveness as diplomats, then it may be reasonably supposed that they wish those they represent to exhibit the same qualities. If princes were more like their envoys, just as if masters were more like their servants, then the world of diplomacy would be a better place. This, however, is the thin gruel common to all professions that involve representation. Lawyers, teachers and doctors all wish that their clients, students and patients were more like them, although self-interest dictates that they be so only up to a point. Diplomats, therefore, may hope for a world of international relations inhabited by cautious, curious and polite leaders (and followers), while knowing that they cannot, and should not, always be so.

Why diplomacy gives rise to diplomats II: the objective articulation of diplomats between worlds

To learn more, it is necessary to shift from the subjective articulation of the diplomats' predicament as strangers to the objective articulation of their occupying places between communities, societies, or organizations of peoples. As strangers, we see diplomats as belonging to one place but located in another. This makes them strange only up to a point, for while they are not citizens of here, they are presumably citizens of somewhere like here. Thus, we may see the ministers of the great kings of the ancient empires sent to each other's courts, the resident ambassadors of northern Italian states in one another's cities, or even the second secretaries of third-rate nations in New York, Geneva and Brussels, ensconced in their little pieces of home abroad. They may have arrived and are functioning "here," but they function in terms of, and have come from, back "there." Make no mistake, say diplomats when asked, we represent our sovereigns and serve their interest, whether the sovereign is said to be a God-King, the State, or the Nation.

In an important sense, however, when diplomats are sent, the boat is pushed out, they leave, but they do not fully arrive in the place where they are to be received. This is easy to imagine with early diplomats traveling far beyond the power of their own sovereigns even to avenge them, let alone secure them. It remains the case, however, even with contemporary diplomats networked into an almost instantaneous communication with, and no more than a two-hour shuttle away from, direct contact with their senders. The sense of being at home, within a culture, society or organization gives way to being between cultures, societies or organizations. This, in itself, should not be hard to grasp, for we all experience it as the spaces between the multiple roles we perform and the social contexts that give them their sense. Between home and work, between office and business trips, between listening to superiors and talking to subordinates, one experiences this sense of one set of priorities fading as others gain ground. The difference with diplomatic relations, however, and, hence, with diplomats, is that this point between becomes a resting place rather than a place to pass through, the site of operations, rather than a barrier to be negotiated before operations can commence. This sense of standing in-between manifests itself in a number of ways. While diplomats certainly do represent their principals and seek to advance their interests, the position from which they do so is different from that of those they represent. At a minimum this difference involves a far stronger sense of both the identities and interests of those who receive their representations. At a maximum, it can reduce those they represent to just one complex of identities and interests among several or many in the diplomats' busy world.

In addition, the distance diplomats experience from both home and abroad imbues them with a sense of distance from the issues and interests which their senders and receivers think that their international relations are about. Some of the manifestations of this distance have already been noted above. It is frequently read as cynicism as when, for example, diplomats are seen to accept great variations in the policy and, indeed, the character of the regimes they represent. Diplomats themselves, in contrast, note the senses of tragedy and resignation to which a career in professional diplomacy often seems to give rise. The world is full of fools and wicked men who lead us all into trouble by promising what we want. Thus diplomats find themselves caught up in their own near-tragedies when they are, like Satow's "patriotic and devoted public servant compelled to contend for a bad cause."[12] A deeper tragedy resides, however, in the fact that perfectly respectable regimes pursuing perfectly intelligible and reasonable objectives may, nevertheless, find themselves on collision courses. They may do so because their objectives and values, while reasonable, are genuinely mutually exclusive, or because relations between even reasonable people can get

---

[12] Sir Earnest Satow, *An Austrian Diplomatist in the Fifties* (Cambridge: Cambridge University Press, 1908), p. 56. The essay is on Count Joseph Alexander Hübner.

out of hand in conditions where the usual bonds of community and society are weaker or even absent. Then, the tragedy for diplomats is a double one, both in terms of the catastrophe that may result, and in the sense that this is precisely the sort of catastrophe – one born of misunderstanding – which successful diplomacy is supposed to head off.

Neither diplomatic cynicism nor a highly developed sense of the tragic may be much use to the rest of us, except in providing short-term gain or solace for its absence respectively. However, a third consequence of occupying places in between peoples and the sense of distance in which this results is both less well known and far more important. It is the disposition to believe that resolving most of the issues over which people argue, on the terms in which they argue about them, is impossible. While we all talk as if we are arguing towards the day when there will be no more arguments or, at least, far fewer of the big ones, the historical record and daily experiences to which diplomats refer suggest that this is not the case. So long as multiple perspectives on multiple issues are produced – as they have been in the past, are in the present, and show every promise of doing so in the future – then what is important for diplomats is the processes by which they are handled, not which position or perspective is in some sense the right one or has more merit. The challenge is to keep international relations going between people who may be willful and wicked, and who are certainly worried and apt to misunderstand one another, and who do not share the diplomats' sense of distance from the substance of these relations and the terms in which this substance is understood.

By keeping relations going, I mean generally peaceful relations and, at a minimum, relations not scarred by unwanted violence. On occasions, diplomats may work for war, participating in provocations or coalition-building to that end, for example, and diplomacy can continue in the midst of war. Diplomats would generally argue that it should. A core assumption within the tradition of diplomatic thought, however, is that wars should be avoided before they start and ended once they are underway for, in themselves, they negate diplomatic ends, and in their details they obstruct diplomatic means. By saying that the diplomatic tradition subordinates the content of international relations – in the sense of the arguments which the rest of us have about interests, fairness and what is right – I do not mean that no position on such matters has more merit than any other, even for diplomats. Many of the latter have strong views on the content of international relations, but not as diplomats. As diplomats, their priorities are different. Thus, to take an example which is often held up to demonstrate the moral poverty of diplomacy and the dangers of allowing it too much influence, there is nothing intrinsically wrong with appeasement, seeking to preserve peace by acceding to the demands of others. Even a peace in some sense unjust, yet sustainable, may be preferable to no peace or a peace that cannot be sustained. To make this point explicit, from within the diplomatic tradition, the Munich agreement, had it been acceptable to all the parties and had all the parties intended to keep their word, would have been just as good (and, of course, as bad) an agreement as, for example, those reached at Vienna and Versailles.[13]

Diplomats, therefore, as a consequence of their occupying spaces between communities, societies and organizations, see the world differently and with different priorities from those they represent. A corollary of this, of course, is that they see it in a similar way to other diplomats, not just those in the same service, but also their "colleagues" in the service of others. We have historical records of diplomats experiencing their predicament collectively, and it does not take a great deal of effort to imagine their prehistoric forebears doing likewise, present as rivals but united by a common estrangement from their hosts.[14] Where we find more than one foreign representative, therefore, we can begin to speak of a diplomatic community and, in the modern system, the diplomatic corps gives expression to a highly formalized version of this idea, a body held together by the importance it attaches to processes being properly conducted and a great deal of skepticism about what others take to be the content and substance of their international relations.[15] Once such a body is aware of itself operating in this sense, then the first great preoccupation of the diplomatic tradition of international

---

[13] By the Munich agreement of 1938, the great powers of Europe required Czechoslovakia to cede territory inhabited by its German minority to Germany in return for guaranteeing the integrity of its remaining territory. The agreement is widely seen as confirming the moral bankruptcy of great power politics in general and the Anglo-French policy of appeasing Hitler in particular. The Germans dismantled the rest of Czechoslovakia the following year and the guaranteeing powers did nothing. I shall return to this settlement below.

[14] See G. R. Berridge, "The Origins of the Diplomatic Corps: Rome to Constantinople," in Sharp and Wiseman (eds.), *The Diplomatic Corps as an Institution of International Society*.

[15] Antoine Pecquet (Aleksandra Gruzinska and Murray D. Sirkis, trans.), *Discours sur l'Art de Négocier* (Paris: Nyon, 1737) (Currents in Comparative Romance Languages and Literatures, Bern: Peter Lang, 2004).

thought, "what sort of outlook makes for good diplomats?" begins to merge into a second. Can good diplomats produce and constitute systems of their own which makes their work more effective and easy and, thus, themselves more useful to others? It is their answers to this question that give the diplomatic tradition its distinctive orientation to international relations in general and the relationship between diplomatic systems and international systems in particular.

Diplomats and diplomatic understandings of international systems, societies and communities

We commonly speak of diplomatic systems, diplomatic communities and, perhaps less easily, diplomatic societies. In so doing, however, we glide over two sets of problems. The first are generic problems of speaking in terms of systems, societies and communities. The second concern the relationship of any diplomatic system, society or community to the international system, society or community with which it is associated. Regarding the generic difficulties, most of these revolve around two themes: the extent to which their existence depends on our apprehending them as such; and the extent to which their effectiveness depends upon their members treating them as, and believing them to be, real and existing independently.[16] These difficulties sharpen as one moves up the ladders of conceptualization and imagination from mere systems of interrelated parts, through societies, the members of which are consciously tied by agreements and interests, to communities whose sense of collective self is experienced by their members as real to the point of being organic. Thus, we may assert the existence of social systems with little controversy, even where their participants may not be aware of them as such. One suspects, for example, that the native peoples of Africa were unaware of the great triangle of the slave trade in which they participated on a variety of terms. All that is needed to assert the existence of such a system are regular and frequent interactions between people or peoples

---

[16] There is an interesting debate on this theme regarding great powers. It is neatly, but not conclusively summed up by Wight. "The existence of what is recognized determines the act of recognition, and not the other way round." Martin Wight, "Powers," in Wight, *Power Politics*, pp. 45–6 cited in Buzan, *The United States and the Great Powers*, p. 62. Bull maintains the conventional position that to enjoy the rank of a great power, a country has to be recognized as such by its fellows: Bull, *The Anarchical Society*, p. 196.

with observable effects.[17] Those who fulfill these conditions are regarded as members of, or constituting, the system. However, when members are conscious of their membership, place a value on it, and work to reproduce their system of relations with conventions, rules and institutions, we begin to talk in terms of societies and communities. We say they exist when we can map patterns of people's behavior and record people's utterances that suggest that this is the case.

Yet it is here that the problems begin. The existence of social systems in these terms is reasonably easy to assert. Not so societies and communities. Some (the US and China, for example) clearly do, at least for most people. Regarding others (Europe and Greater Manchester, for example) it is less easy to say. And some (Yugoslavia, Northern Cyprus and, currently, Iraq) highlight the political dimension to, and indeed controversy implicit in, making such assertions. These problems with systems, societies and communities absolutely permeate the practice of international relations and, hence, its academic study. We can reasonably easily identify international systems according to conventional definitions of social systems. We may even be able to identify world systems of regular and frequent interactions, between some at least, with observable effects. Some people even speak as if international and world communities exist. However, given their anarchical quality – that is the absence of an overarching power and authority – the sense in which we may properly speak of the existence of international or world societies and communities has been sharply contested.[18] Indeed, in the way that Wight has set up his three traditions of international thought, arguments over their existence in fact or potential are central. International and world societies and communities may be said to exist in some sense, but in what sense and with what consequences are the questions on which distinctive and differing positions are adopted.

---

[17] Linear trading systems where participants are only aware of immediate neighbors rather than end-users provide another example of such a system.

[18] Bull is credited with developing and sharpening the distinction between system and society to make his arguments for the possibility of order within an anarchy: Bull, *The Anarchical Society*. See Alan James, "System or Society," *Review of International Studies*, 19, 3 (1993), pp 269–88 for a skeptical view of the value of the distinction. See also Buzan, *From International Society to World Society?*, pp. 99–100 for dropping the system-society distinction in favor of a continuum in which human relations exhibit more or less social qualities.

In contrast, there exists a broad agreement in all three established traditions about the relationship between diplomatic systems, on the one hand, and international or world systems, societies or communities, on the other. To begin with, diplomatic systems are usually presented as such, and not as diplomatic societies or diplomatic communities, except in the local sense of people involved with diplomacy in a capital city or at the headquarters of an international organization. This is so because diplomatic systems are nearly always presented as sub-systems of international or world systems, societies or communities, not functionally necessary to their operations, perhaps, but certainly very helpful. Thus, for example, the modern diplomatic system is regarded as derived from the modern state system. It takes on its priorities and reflects its character. And where there exists a sufficient consensus about how, and by whom, international relations should be handled, the international system, society or community and its diplomatic sub-system may appear to elide. That is to say, international relations and diplomacy may be spoken of as if they are the same thing.

The predicament of diplomats, however, allows the diplomatic tradition of international thought to present the relationship quite differently, and it differs in a number of ways. First, it makes it possible to speak of diplomatic systems, societies and communities in the sense that people doing diplomacy at different places and times may be differentiated like other groups by degrees of consensus about what they do and ought to be doing, and by the extent to which they have a sense of themselves as such. One can imagine a system of diplomacy between simple pre-historic communities, for example, with regular patterns of interaction made possible by various iterations of the immunity rule. We know that those responsible for conducting relations between the natives and the Europeans in colonial America saw themselves as a distinct society while, even amongst those forest negotiators who were of mixed race, their sense of community remained tribal, national and racial, if only in aspiration and not in acceptance by those to whom they saw themselves belonging.[19] And we also know that the diplomats of the modern system saw themselves in some respects as a distinct

---

[19] See, e.g., James H. Merrell, *Into the American Woods: Negotiators on the Pennsylvania Frontier* (New York: W. W. Norton and Company, 1999), Joseph S. Walton, *Conrad Weiser and the Indian Policy of Colonial Pennsylvania* (Philadelphia: George W. Jacobs, 1900) and Howard Lewin, "A Frontier Diplomat: Andrew Montour," *Pennsylvania History*, 23 (1966), pp. 153–86.

community, just as those who serve international and regional organizations today may be coming to do so.[20]

Secondly, notions of world systems, societies and communities appear fainter in the diplomatic tradition than do those of their international counterparts. We may live at a time in which it is plausibly claimed that the old plural world of states is being transformed, and that even the appearance of an elision between international relations and diplomacy is fading as diplomacy is squeezed out by new solidarist forces operating on a global scale. From within the diplomatic tradition, however, this is not how the world appears. It is not moving, as a whole, in any particular direction. Instead, at any given time, it consists of many people engaged in multiple types of revolutionary, rational and realist thought and action which fuel great and ongoing processes of coming together and pushing apart. Different processes may be locally dominant at a given time and place – thus, here the world is coming together where elsewhere it is coming apart. Yet these processes may also be seen to exist dialectically in the sense that a particular coming together, the ever closer union of the European Union, for example, may involve a particular coming apart, for example, the weakening of trans-Atlantic or pan-Slavic ties.

To put this another way, from within the diplomatic tradition, something like international systems, whether they have the character of societies or communities or neither, always exist and, thus, something like world societies or communities never do. Notions of world society are merely present, and their bearers are participants in affairs that remain resolutely plural in character. For diplomats, their work is like conducting relations in an earthquake zone where the interplay of different people's thoughts and actions – including those about how to moderate the effects of earthquakes or put an end to them altogether – are principal determinants of the frequency, duration and intensity of earthquakes. It is with this reading of history and human relations – namely that the specific comings together and pullings apart necessarily result in generally plural conditions and their associated relations of separateness – that the diplomatic tradition of international thought emerges from the predicament in which diplomats find themselves.

---

[20] See, e.g., Davis Cross, *The European Diplomatic Corps*.

This being so, the third and final difference is that from within the diplomatic tradition, diplomatic systems are not viewed as subsystems of their international counterparts. If plural conditions giving rise to relations of separateness are seen as permanent, then international systems, societies and communities are but iterations of this general condition. If this is so, then it becomes possible to make a rather striking inversion. The elision of diplomatic and international systems in the modern state system can be presented as taking place on the terms of the former rather than the latter. In this view, the modern state system did not call into being a complimentary subsystem of modern diplomacy. Rather, diplomacy and diplomats developed a refined system of relations of separateness, the international society of states, which facilitated their own effective operations. Stretching the argument, we might suggest that achieving an elision on these terms is an objective of diplomacy and diplomats, while exploring the requirements and conditions for achieving such elisions is a central problem in the diplomatic tradition of international thought. If limited liability relations of separateness are a constant, then stabilizing them remains a constant problem. The first set of important questions from within the tradition, therefore, concern the impact of different sorts of international systems, societies and communities as these emerge, expand, reproduce themselves, and decline, collapse or are transcended, upon the effective conduct of diplomacy. What can a *diplomatic understanding* tell us about how relations of separateness might best be conducted under these different and changing conditions? Are some conditions more suited than others to the effective conduct of such relations by diplomacy? And can diplomats do much to affect and shape the contours of systems, societies and communities in which they have to operate?

PART III
Diplomatic understanding and international societies

Diplomats do not represent their countries, but some international Society clique.

Adolf Hitler, cited in Hamilton and Langhorne,
The Practice of Diplomacy, p. 181

6 | Using the international society idea

Diplomacy is conventionally regarded as an aspect of an international system, society, or community, or as an institution necessary to their effective functioning. Within the diplomatic tradition, in contrast, international systems, societies and communities are seen as different ways in which the terrain is organized upon which relations of separateness are to be conducted. Before exploring some of the implications of this insight, however, I want to take another look at the international society idea and some of the arguments that lie behind it. This is useful for a number of reasons. First, doing so provides an opportunity to map out the terms in which international societies vary from one another and change within themselves. Secondly, such a mapping illuminates the shifting character of the terrain upon which diplomats operate and helps us identify the extent to which diplomacy is a trans-historical and ubiquitous practice. Last, but not least, re-visiting the international society idea will allow me to make a case for jettisoning the clumsy triumvirate of system, society and community, and for referring to all as international societies from there on.

International systems, societies and communities

The general distinctions between systems, societies and communities elaborated above apply in principle to their international equivalents. We can imagine international systems characterized only by frequent and regular contacts between their members but little else. We can see international societies whose members are bound by shared understandings of the rules about what is and ought to be going on. And we sometimes talk about the international community as a world whose member states or countries know and feel that they belong to one another. In the study of International Relations, however, these ideas and the relationship between them have a specific history. To begin with, the notion of an international community is rarely mentioned

113

except to illustrate the problems with it or to question the way it is used in ordinary life by governments, diplomats and people in the mass media. The main academic focus, therefore, has been on international systems, international societies, and how the use of the latter term modifies the conventional understandings of international relations implied by the former. It is possible, indeed probable, that even in the absence of a government or overarching authority, relations between peoples can develop a social character in the sense of shared understandings, conventions and rules about what is, and what is supposed to be, going on. They are not doomed to remain, and probably never have been, in the Hobbesian state of nature to which political realists appeal to derive their accounts of power politics and justify their foreign policy prescriptions.

Where such procedures and shared understandings about them do emerge, as Bull suggests, we may think in terms of an international society and when they do not, we may think in terms of an international system.[1] As Bull was well aware, however, this conceptual distinction breaks down in practice. It does so because almost all human relations seem to imply some social context, even if it is only one constituted by the relations themselves.[2] Only certain types of forced relations, and not even all these if they occur regularly and frequently, would seem to be exceptions to this observation. This difficulty probably did not matter much to Bull because, insofar as the distinction does collapse, it does so in the direction of the general point he wished to make, namely that there can be anarchical societies. If that is established, then we can abandon the stark conceptual contrast between systems and societies and, instead, look at sets of international relations in more empirical terms to evaluate the extent to which they exhibit a social character. Henceforth, therefore, I will generally discard the idea of an international system and use the term international society.

I will do so, however, with the important caveat that the extent and the character of the societal properties of the relations under consideration remains an open question. This caveat introduces the other purpose for which people use the term international societies, namely, to suggest that there are different ways in which international societies can be

---

[1] Bull, *The Anarchical Society*, pp. 3–21.
[2] James, "System or Society" and Buzan, *From International Society to World Society?*

organized which reflect different reasons and motives on the part of their members, together with the material and social facts which help shape these reasons and motives. However, that this is so introduces a second caveat, namely that the use of the adjective "international" does not restrict the term to societies of nations or, more accurately in terms of its usage, states, but also to arrangements in which other sorts of actors are or might be members. Bands, tribes, kingships and empires have also been members of "international" societies in the past.[3] Firms, religions, denominations thereof, social classes, and other aggregates of humanity have conducted international relations and aspired to membership of international society in the past and continue to do so.

To be sure, we live in an international society whose rules still insist on only one kind of full member – sovereign, territorial states recognized by each other as such. There is no reason in principle or history, however, which forecloses on the possibility of international societies with a different class of membership, for example, certain tribes or cities; different categories of membership, for example, states and protectorates; or even mixed membership, for example, kingdoms, dioceses, and merchant trading companies. Thus, we can see discussions, arguments and fights in the past and in different places about who should be the members of an international society and how their relations should be organized. These discussions, fights and arguments run on into the present about our own international society or societies, and it is entirely reasonable to suppose that they will result, are resulting, in considerable changes in existing arrangements and the ways these are viewed. What makes societies international, however, is that the groups within them see themselves as radically separate from one another. What separates them is more important to how they see themselves than what might bring them together, and most of them want this to be so, at least for certain purposes.

Mapping international societies

Viewed as such, international societies may be mapped and analyzed along three dimensional continua: integration–disintegration; expansion–contraction; and concentration–diffusion. By the first I mean the way in

---

[3] Watson, *The Evolution of International Society* and Buzan and Little, *International Systems in World History*.

which we think of international societies coming together and pulling apart along a continuum from complete separation and no contact to complete fusion and loss of member identity. This movement can be conceived of in horizontal terms. At various points in their respective histories, for example, we speak of the tribes of the Iroquois League, the colonies of the original English settlers in North America and the nations or states of the European Union moving closer together.[4] Similarly, during a distinct and extended period of history, we can see the kingdoms, principalities, duchies and republics of the Holy Roman Empire moving further apart. However, we can also think of movement along the integration-disintegration continuum in vertical terms. Thus we speak of a deepening process by which the internal relations of the members of an international society are increasingly coordinated or the political authority directing them is fused. Much of the history of the European Union may be told as a series of efforts to deepen its internal relations by coordinating policies and rendering practices uniform among its members.[5] The North American Free Trade Area and the Soviet-sponsored Council for Mutual Economic Assistance also provide examples of societies to which the language of deepening relations can be applied.[6]

We can also think of international societies in terms of shallowing, a process by which the internal relations of the members become less coordinated. Thus, we might chart the transformation of the British Empire from a fairly centralized imperial entity into a highly integrated international society, the British Commonwealth of Nations whose members enjoyed home rule, which, in turn, loosened to the point at

---

[4] Francis Jennings, "Iroquois Alliances in American History," in Francis Jennings, William N. Fenton, Mary A. Druke and David R. Miller (eds.), *The History and Culture of Iroquois Diplomacy: An Interdisciplinary Guide to the Treaties of the Six Nations and Their League* (Syracuse: Syracuse University Press, 1985). See also Daniel K. Richter, *The Ordeal of the Long-house: The Peoples of the Iroquois League in the Era of European Colonization* (Chapel Hill: University of North Carolina Press, 1992).

[5] For a useful general treatment see Desmond Dinan, *Europe Recast: A History of the European Union* (Boulder: Lynne Rienner, June 2004).

[6] See K. Fatemi and D. Salvatore (eds.), *The North American Free Trade Agreement* (London: Pergamon, 1994) and Adam Zwass, *The Council for Mutual Economic Assistance: The Thorny Path from Political to Economic Integration* (Armonk, NY: M. E. Sharpe, 1989).

which the sense of it as a world within a world has nearly vanished.[7] Similarly, the EU's principle of subsidiarity, by which it is asserted that political decisions should be taken at the lowest practical level, might be said to provide an example of a policy intended to deliver a measure of vertical disintegration.[8]

Secondly, international societies may be seen to expand and contract. We can think of this in terms of the way they gain and lose members. The Iroquois League, for example, added the Tuscaroras and the modern European state system added the Ottomans, while fifth-century Britain and eighth-century Japan were subtracted from the Roman and Chinese worlds respectively. We can also think of expansion and contraction in geographical terms. Thus, the European international society was extended by the movement of its peoples into hitherto "empty" lands and by the absorption of other peoples' territories through conquest, colonization and assimilation. Arguably, after over three centuries of the expansion of the global version of Europe's international society, we are witnessing its contraction, just as Greek, Roman and Islamic worlds contracted before it. While it is intuitively straightforward to maintain that international societies expand and contract, however, it is important to be clear about what we mean when we say so. It is probably not the case, for example, that the Roman and European international societies expanded when their soldiers, settlers and traders established their presence in most of their respective known worlds. It is more likely that they did so only as their respective habits of thought and understanding about how peoples should relate to each other first became operative among former outsiders and then accepted by them. Therefore, in the European case, at least, this presents us with the apparent paradox that its international society only really expanded as the ability of its established members to control directly what was happening actually declined.

I say apparent paradox, however, for it arises only from a confusion of our second continuum – between expansion and contraction – and the third. This is between the complete diffusion of power among multiple weak actors at one end, and its complete concentration in the

---

[7] The fading of the Commonwealth can be exaggerated, however. See Lorna Lloyd, *Diplomacy With A Difference: The Commonwealth Office of High Commissioner 1880–2006* (Leiden: Martinus Nijhoff, 2007).
[8] *Europa*, Glossary, "Subsidiarity," at http://europa.eu/scadplus/glossary/subsidiarity_en.htm.

hands of a few great powers or one imperial authority at the other. The ancient Eastern empires and China, Rome and, less certainly, its Holy Roman successor and the United States-dominated world of the late twentieth and early twenty-first centuries, may provide examples of international societies towards the concentrated end of the spectrum. The Chinese "Spring and Autumn" period, the post-Roman so-called "Dark Ages" and the era of the classical balance of power in Europe, may be seen as examples of international societies at the other end of the spectrum where power is very diffused.[9] Indeed, as Watson argues, it is useful to think of the history of international societies in terms of pendulum-like movements between the poles of diffusion and concentration. The velocity of the movement is not constant and a full traverse will not necessarily be completed but, at any given moment, he suggests, an international society will occupy a position between these points of complete diffusion and complete concentration.[10]

The dangers and difficulties revealed by mapping international societies

International society thinking can inject a measure of conceptual and practical order into the conduct of international relations by getting scholars and practitioners alike beyond the simple anarchy *problématique*. We ask how an international society is and might be organized. Mapping international societies, however, draws our attention in quite a different direction, raising questions about boundaries and identities. If international societies have boundaries then this raises the question of what lies beyond them. The old answer from within Europe where the international society idea first emerged in its current form was nothing, or nothing much any longer. It was this claim that allowed people to speak in terms of "*the* international society" or even "International Society" as if there were only one which was stable and unchanging. However, this proposition was never actually the case, always morally wrong, and has increasingly dangerous practical consequences. Wherever peoples

---

[9] K. J. Holsti, *International Politics: A Framework for Analysis*, 1st edn. (Englewood Cliffs: Prentice Hall, 1967) provides a well-known account of international systems in terms of cycles from concentrated to diffused power.

[10] Watson, *The Evolution of International Society*, pp. 13–18.

engaged in relations beyond the boundaries of the European society of states, there other international societies, more or less developed, existed. Further, we may speak of multiple international societies existing not only in the horizontal plane, but also in the vertical one, that is to say overlaying one another. This is perhaps most apparent today in parts of Africa where the cover provided by the international society of states has become thin to the point of threadbare.

The existence of multiple international societies at the same time or place raises the problem of how to think about relations between them. Can international societies have relations, or only their respective members? It is usually assumed that while Rome and China, Europe and the pre-Columbian civilizations of the Americas, for example, may have posed interesting questions in these terms, the expansion of the European society of states into a global international society has rendered them of historical interest only.[11] Is this the case, however? It may be, for example, that the current "civilizational" stresses and strains in international relations are related to the relative weakening and strengthening of different international societies that co-exist where this stress is most manifest. Thus, we might be wise to view the rhythms of international politics in what Fred Halliday calls "the arc of crisis," as not generated solely by attempts to stabilize and reform that part of the international society of states and the resistance which such efforts provoke.[12] They may also be generated by the efforts of some older worlds to protect themselves and others to re-surface, conducting their own arguments and fighting their own fights all the while as they do so.

If international societies can have relations, however, then this raises identity problems in regard to how both we and their members should

---

[11] Wight, "Hellas and Persia," in Wight, *Systems of States*, pp. 73–109 provides an analysis of relations between worlds. Bull and Watson (eds.), *The Expansion of International Society*, provides a strong sense of world history moving in the direction of a single international society. Herbert Butterfield, "Notes for a Discussion on the Theory of International Politics," BPULC 335 (January 1964) reflects the emphasis on learning from the internal workings of other international societies rather than relations between them. See also Arnold Toynbee, *A Study of History* (edited, revised and abridged by Arnold Toynbee and Jane Caplan) (Oxford: Oxford University Press 1972, Barnes and Noble, 1995), pp. 379–476.
[12] Fred Halliday, *Soviet Policy in the Arc of Crisis* (Washington DC: Institute for Policy Studies, 1981).

see them. Clearly, international societies are sites for action by their members. If they can have relations with each other, however, are they actors too? They may be viewed as both and, over time, they may make a transition from when one identity predominates to when the other one replaces it. The Holy Roman Empire and the United Nations, for example, may be read both as actors and sites for action, with the former making a transition from actor to arena over two centuries while the latter is arguably moving in the opposite direction. When we speak of "the Roman world" or "the Chinese world," the use of the term "world" flags this ambiguity. They were both empires simultaneously constituting their own international societies and acting in a wider world of which they might or might not regard themselves members. However, when Chinese and Romans came to know of each other, first indirectly and then by direct, but sparse, contacts, it is very difficult to say what was going on.[13] Should we speak of "international" relations between the two greatest empires in the world at the time and, if so, did the two of them constitute their own, albeit fragile and limited Sino-Roman international society? Or should we see them both as merely minor participants in a different international society constituted by the relations of peoples at the fringes of the Roman and Chinese worlds respectively whose local, more than their imperial, identities framed their actions?

As these questions imply, empires rarely have hard boundaries confirming their identities. Rather, they can be mapped in terms of their imperial cores, dominions, zones of hegemony and the world beyond.[14] In the core we find Romans. In the dominions we find people who wish to be Romans, try hard to be, but are not. In the zones of hegemony the Romans wish people to be Romans, but the people are unsure, and beyond reside the worlds of those seen as others who are content to be so seen. Thus "Rome" simultaneously signifies the Roman world as both a society and an empire, Rome itself (whether the city or the city plus the provinces of the Italian peninsula) as the key member of that world, and "Romanness" as a contested set of practices established, extended and maintained by Roman power. In precisely the same way, of course, we can interrogate the ideas conveyed by the EU, and Europe

---

[13] Wight, *Power Politics*, p. 24.
[14] For this sort of mapping see Watson, *The Evolution of International Society*, p. 14 and Toynbee, *A Study of History*.

and, perhaps more obviously, the *Pax Americana* and US hegemony, and explore the relationships between them.[15]

Mapping international societies, therefore, highlights the shortcomings of presenting international history only as a story of how the Roman world, the Chinese world and several others emerge, merge and eventually give rise to a universal international, now global, society in some Leninist or Toynbeean process of developmental stages.[16] It is even misleading to tell the story as one in which Europe, as a result of a short-lived technical edge and moral certainty, short-circuited the whole process, rose to the top and imposed itself and its world on the rest. Both, while they present themselves as stories about international relations in general, are still overly focused on one historical trajectory, the "rise of the West." As such, they may be a poor preparation for what is to come. In the longer view, of which this story is one part, we see international societies integrating and disintegrating, expanding and contracting, concentrating and diffusing. They do so in part as a consequence of impersonal processes like environmental changes, and what seem like impersonal processes arising from scientific and technical developments. As the "rise of the West" story effectively demonstrates, however, they also do so as a consequence of the export, promotion and imposition of norms and values that accompanies policies of expansion together with the resulting resistance.

In seeking to explain or justify our actions or to advocate a course of action as wise or right, we often appeal to the idea of an international society as a stable space in which shared understandings allow us to communicate and argue with one another as members about what needs to be done. In thinking about international societies themselves, however, we are struck by an indeterminacy that is both cause and consequence of the two questions about them we are most interested in having answered. First, what is the best, or best available, way in which

---

[15] See, e.g., Chalmers Johnson, *The Sorrows of Empire: Militarism, Secrecy and the End of the Republic* (New York: Henry Holt and Company, 2004), Noam Chomsky, *Hegemony or Survival: America's Quest for Global Dominance* (New York: Henry Holt and Company, 2004), Niall Ferguson, *Colossus: The Price of America's Empire* (New York: Penguin Press, 2004), and Thomas M. Magstadt, *An Empire if You Can Keep It: Power and Principle in American Foreign Policy* (Washington DC: Congressional Quarterly Press, 2004).

[16] V. I. Lenin, *Imperialism: The Highest Stage of Capitalism: A Popular Outline* (Peking: Foreign Languages Press, 1970) and Toynbee, *A Study of History*.

our international relations might be arranged? Second, how is this way to be best attained and sustained? From within the diplomatic tradition of international thought, however, international societies, both in their conception and in their operations, pose problems of a quite different order. How best are relations of separateness to be stabilized and conducted in the midst of the arguments which emerge as a result of people's attempts to answer the two questions above and to put their answers into practice? As we shall see, diplomatic thinking about this question continually pushes us away from the idea of international societies as existing along the three continua suggested by Watson, and reveals the usefulness of thinking about the three pairs of end points in dialectical terms. Thus, wherever we can identify the processes by which an international society is integrating, expanding or concentrating, we may well be able to see another international society disintegrating, contracting or diffusing. Wherever we see a particular separate identity fading or disappearing, we may well be seeing another separate identity emerging. The next three chapters of this section, therefore, will examine what diplomatic thinking can tell us about the problems which international societies, viewed in both senses, can pose for the conduct of encounter relations, discovery relations and re-encounter relations.

7 | Integration–disintegration

By international integration we generally refer to the processes by which states merge with one another to form a larger unit, although, more often, what we mean is the processes by which life within them, or aspects of that life, becomes merged with life in other states under a new and broader political dispensation. This complicates the idea by leaving "final" destinations open. EU experience, for example, suggests that states may integrate without any new entity, and certainly not a new state, emerging.[1] By international disintegration, we refer to the opposite of all this but, in fact, we rarely talk about it as such. This is partly because most processes of international disintegration are viewed as the antithesis or backwash of integrative processes pointing to the future and, thus, in which we are more interested. However, it is also because we see disintegration in terms of particular states coming apart, rather than the international societies of which they are members.

Even where, as in parts of Africa, for example, the incidence of failed and disintegrating states supports a case for talking about a failed and disintegrating society of states, most of our attention remains fixed on the particular states in question and how to put them back together again. This is so because we see both international integration and disintegration taking place within an international society whose broad outlines we assume are settled. Accordingly, we tend to think about both these processes in terms of their implications for the independence and power, wealth and efficiency, freedom and peace, of the countries in which we live and the welfare of those for whom we care, including ourselves. Integration is presented as a strategic choice (do we or don't we?), followed by a series of secondary questions about how far to go and

---

[1] Charles Pentland, *International Theory and European Integration* (New York: Free Press, 1973) still provides a good introduction to theoretical approaches to the idea of integration.

the extent to which the answers to those questions also remain a matter of choice.

Diplomats, as individuals, citizens and even as the servants of particular states, share these concerns. They may take different positions from one another regarding the merits of a particular instance of international integration and, indeed, whole foreign services have been understood to change their positions regarding particular integrations and disintegrations from being generally hostile, at one time, to generally favorable, at another.[2] As diplomats, however, they tend to be agnostics about the particular worries integration and disintegration present to the rest of us in terms of price and employment levels, rules and regulations, and what will happen to our ways of life. Indeed, they can even be agnostics about the problems these processes pose for the sovereignty and independence of those they represent. They see all through the prism of how it affects their ability to conduct relations of separateness. Thus diplomats sometimes strongly support and, indeed, attempt to orchestrate processes of integration, while on other occasions, they express concern and attempt to apply the brakes. The diplomatic tradition of international thought contains no position on the effects of integration and disintegration in general.

This is a surprise, for we would expect people charged with handling relations under difficult circumstances to value the stable set of expectations provided by international societies, and to see any movement along the integration–disintegration continuum as a potential threat to that stability. Certainly, diplomacy and diplomats play a major part in securing for international societies that solid, natural and timeless quality that enables all societies to work better. Consider, for example, the Vienna conventions on diplomatic and consular relations. The former begins with the claim that the status of diplomatic agents has been recognized by "peoples of all nations from ancient times." Similarly, the latter asserts that consular relations have "been established between peoples since ancient times."[3] To be sure, these may be statements of

---

[2] Consider, for example, the "bias" the British Foreign Office was said to have against joining the European Economic Community in the 1950s and the shift towards a bias in favor of joining over the next ten years.

[3] *Vienna Convention on Diplomatic Relations*, April 14, 1961, available at www.un.int/usa/host_dip.htm and *Vienna Convention on Consular Relations* (April 24, 1963) available at www.geocities.com/CapitolHill/5829/Vienna02.html.

general and background principles, and ones which are not necessarily of diplomatic provenance. Nevertheless, we can detect their presence in the daily operations of both diplomacy and international law. In presenting their countries' positions or policies in either formal settings or to the public, both good diplomats and good international lawyers seek to create a thick moral, legal and cultural rendition of the international society in which they and their countries are acting. There is, their arguments imply, a settled world out there of which all peoples are members, from which the meaning and moral significance of their actions is derived, and which provides sanction for the particular views of those we represent and what they want to do.

This diplomatic effort often intensifies as the prospect of change increases and becomes more obvious. Those responsible for the relations of Lombard and Frankish kings, Roman popes and Byzantine emperors in eighth-century Europe, for example, were desperate to maintain that they were being conducted in the context of an imperial international society, a claim at odds with all the material and most of the ideational facts of the actual situation.[4] Appeals to a ghostly imperial context continued in Europe until Napoleon put an end to the Holy Roman Empire at the start of the nineteenth century, and similar imperial ghosts may be seen providing contexts for international relations at various stages in Chinese and Japanese history. In contemporary international relations, it might be argued that references to a Europe of sovereign states by EU members, on the one hand, and an emerging global civil society governed by the principles of the UN Charter, on the other, provide evidence of the attractiveness of appealing to a more settled past and a more settled future, respectively, in preference to an uncertain present.

The reasons why diplomats are often involved in such efforts are straightforward. Most of them represent entities that have a great stake in the world, and their place within it, being accepted as presented. Sierra Leone wants to be taken as seriously as the United States in these terms, and both are served by the idea of a world of peoples and nations, such as themselves, having existed "since ancient times." It is also the case that this particular presentation does not do too much violence to the historical record. Peoples, certainly, and nations or something like

[4] David Jayne Hill, *A History of Diplomacy in the International Development of Europe, Vol. 1: The Struggle for Universal Empire* (New York: Longmans, 1905).

them, have existed since ancient times, even if they have not been the particular ones which seek to credential themselves today by having it pointed out that this is so. Thus, while integration and disintegration in international societies are probably best understood as evolutionary processes, we might expect diplomats to subscribe to a tipping point conception of how they should be handled. Resist the pressures for change or, more accurately, act like they are not occurring, until it becomes absolutely clear that they are irresistible, and then jump ship to take the lead in speedily building up the new arrangements as natural, reasonable, and maybe even more authentically in touch with a timeless or historic past than the arrangements which they have just replaced.

This can happen. As their conduct at the time of the collapse of the Soviet Union illustrates, eastern European diplomats were as capable of defending the Socialist Commonwealth to the last before hurriedly abandoning it, just as they did their respective Communist regimes.[5] As such situations of profound and sudden change are relatively rare, however, examples of diplomats resisting integration–disintegration before capitulating and racing to the front of the forces for change are not the norm. More typical is the high tolerance for ambiguity demonstrated by those responsible for diplomatic relations in the disintegrating international societies, fading post-imperial structures and emerging regional entities cited above. Diplomats seem to function well, and accept with equanimity, processes of integration and disintegration which unsettle the boundaries and rules about membership and interaction in international societies, even when, as in the case of the EU, these developments appear to threaten, for many of them, their own *raison d'être*. By this I mean they move smoothly between worlds, proclaiming the constancy of the one they happen to be in, while being prepared all the while to act in accordance with the logic of another.

They do this for three reasons. First, like the rest of us, they do not know how things are going to turn out and, therefore, hedge their bets to avoid being caught out by change. Secondly, while integration and disintegration can sometimes make their jobs more difficult, they are

---

[5] See, e.g., Vitaly Churkin, final spokesman for the Soviet Union's Foreign Ministry on the prospects of a revived Russian foreign service: "I think serving the foreign policy interests of Russia is a calling, maybe the dream of any Russian diplomat," Moscow Central Television First Programme Network, November 28, 1991 cited in *Foreign Broadcast Information Service* (November 29, 1991), pp. 23–5.

permanent features of the terrain on which diplomats operate. And thirdly, some processes of integration and disintegration, far from posing obstacles to the conduct of relations of separateness by diplomacy and diplomats, actually make diplomacy possible and diplomats more effective. To see how this is so, however, we must shift our attention from how we see diplomats operating within processes of integration and disintegration. Instead, we must examine how these processes appear to them as they manage relations of encounter, discovery and re-encounter.

Integration–disintegration and encounter relations

Encounter relations occur when peoples meet for the first time. They take place between people on behalf of peoples who are members of different international societies. Before contact, these peoples and their respective worlds did not know, or knew little, of each other and had no or few relations. As both modifiers suggest, there are several conceptual and practical problems with the idea of first encounters and when they may properly be said to take place and start. To begin with, first contacts rarely turn out to be so; somehow peoples seem to have known something of each other before they meet up.[6] The classic, formalized and, indeed, stylized first diplomatic contacts between the European powers on the one hand, and the Ottomans, Chinese and Japanese on the other, for example, took place within a rich context of previous relations.[7] Many of the first contact stories of early peoples are told as part of a process by which they separated and differentiated themselves from other peoples before meeting up again. North American Indians, for example, encountered each other in the new continent as distinct, self-conscious peoples, yet shared a pre-history of common geographical origins retained in the folk memories of at least some of

---

[6] Buzan and Little, *International Systems in World History*. See also Diamond, *Germs, Guns and Steel*.

[7] See, e.g., Lord Kinross, *The Ottoman Centuries* (New York, First Morrow Quill Paperback, 1979), Robert A. Bickers (ed.), *Ritual and Diplomacy: The Macartney Mission to China 1792–1794* (Port Murray: Wellsweep, 1993) and Thomas Naff, "The Ottoman Empire and the European States," Gerrit W. Gong, "China's Entry into International Society" and Hidemi Suganami, "Japan's Entry into International Society," all in Bull and Watson (eds.), *The Expansion of International Society*, pp. 143–69, 171–83 and 185–99 respectively.

them.⁸ Secondly, given what followed many historic first meetings, it may make us queasy to grace with the notion of an encounter what was often but a brief prelude to massacre, enslavement and extermination of the weaker party by the stronger. Thirdly, unless some disaster radically separates peoples again or we meet up with people from another world, encounter relations are examples of a historical phenomenon whose time has largely passed. As far as we know, all the peoples on the planet have gone beyond them to conducting relations of discovery and re-encounter. And finally, the notion of encounter relations, as I have set it up, would seem to preclude it shedding light on processes of integration and disintegration, for these take place within societies which presumably have already to exist.

However, the diplomatic tradition alerts us not only to how elements of integration are present, and elements of disintegration can be present, in encounters. It also alerts us to the kind of problems that these processes very quickly generate. Fortunately, we do have historical records of encounter relations broadly as I have defined them here – those between the peoples of Europe and the peoples from whom they were geographically remote in the Americas and on the islands of the Pacific.⁹ What these suggest is that the people concerned possessed a repertoire of behaviors capable of delivering or, more accurately, signaling simple messages. Dressing up and assembling before the others to make faces, dance, or demonstrate weaponry and fighting skills, for example, all indicated power and a potential for friendship or enmity without people even leaving their shores or the decks of their ships. There might be difficulties in terms of different signs used to signify a notion that would have been mutually understood.¹⁰ And some demonstrations might not have been as unambiguous as one or other party

---

[8] See Thomas Peacock and Marlene Wisuri, *Ojibwe Wasa Inaabidaa: We Look In All Directions* (Afton: Afton Historical Society Press, 2002), Guy Gibbon, *The Sioux: The Dakota and Lakota Nations* (Oxford: Blackwell, 2003), William W. Warren, *History of the Ojibway People* (St. Paul, Minnesota: Historical Society Press, 1984).

[9] See, e.g., Gavin Daws, *Shoal of Time: A History of the Hawaiian Islands* (Honolulu: University of Hawaii Press, 1974), Merrell, *Into the American Woods* and Richard White, *The Middle Ground: Indians, Empires, and Republics in the Great Lakes Region 1650–1815* (Cambridge: Cambridge University Press, 1991).

[10] The recent difficulties experienced by American troops and Iraqi civilians regarding different meanings given to hand signals familiar to both illustrates how this problem persists.

supposed. As William Bligh discovered, for example, the discharge of muskets and cannon might not, in itself, produce the desired effect. This was achieved only when they were used to harm people.[11] Whatever the particular problems of indicating potentials, however, the generic problem was that such demonstrations could not reliably convey intentions. To get beyond a general display of threat, respect and welcome required signals capable of carrying more complex and understandable information, and satisfying this need seems to have entailed physical interactions and material exchanges.

The most obvious of these were the gift-giving and exchange noted above; activities which seem to be universally understood. When American Indians brought fruits and vegetables into the camps of the Europeans or when Hawaiian islanders paddled out to Cook's ships, everybody seemed to know what was going on and what was expected of the other side. It is by no means clear that we should confer a commercial, as opposed to a sacred, social or even political, character on these initial exchanges. Indeed it might be wise to regard initial encounters as simply undifferentiated relations capable of being read in different ways (sometimes with disastrous consequences for the parties involved). What is clear, however, is that once signaling across the waters, the campfires, and the vast cultural divide which both embodied, was replaced by more direct contacts, then a measure of integration followed immediately. Both peoples, in their respective solitudes, might have a concept of gift-giving and exchange, but for the process to proceed, they had to learn what each other valued, for example, which fruits and plants, nails and hammers were available and which were manna or integral to the operations of the ship. And before this, they had to establish the proper times and ways for entering each other's camps and into commitments to one another. In short, even an encounter required that the two parties' respective understandings of the world, indeed their respective worlds, underwent a measure of integration.

The integration associated with such encounters was not restricted, however, to the construction of rudimentary international societies of inter-subjective understanding. Initially, at least, contacts often took place at all levels of societies along all the dimensions of human relationships, and some of these contacts could quickly lead to trouble, even

---

[11] Daws, *The Shoals of Time*, p. 10.

between people who did not want it. Thus the diplomatic tradition alerts us not only to the significance of the first great ceremonial encounters between peoples in establishing a measure of intersubjective meaning in which each party could be represented to the other. It also alerts us to the consequences of the less formal and uncontrolled integration whirling around them, creating misunderstandings, quarrels and worse. Hard on the heels of representative diplomacy, therefore, we can see following what we would recognize as consular diplomacy. So long as the objective of both peoples was to continue their relations, as opposed to massacring or driving each other off, then their relations would have to be structured and conducted in such a way that some were privileged and permitted to regulate and restrict others. Who might talk to one another, about what, and under what conditions were the key questions on which agreement had to be reached, and success in these regards required that diplomacy, or something very like it, would have to be master.

Behind the practical problems of how to communicate associated with encounters and the consular difficulties in which integration might quickly result, lay deeper worries about the consequences of such contacts for the psychological, social, political and moral integrity of the parties to them. The existential shock for one or both learning that they were not alone was considerable. It does not seem to have been an insurmountable one, however. While the sense of being "the people" or "the human beings" alone and at one with nature might have been fatally undermined by meeting others, the fact of their existence and its form could both serve, if properly handled, to confirm the distinctiveness of one's own people's identity. Indeed, some myths, for example about the arrival or return of visitors at a certain time, were confirmed, albeit at the price of shaking a people's sense of permanence and setting their historical clocks ticking.[12] At the level of ideas, people seem to have adjusted quickly to both the shock and integrative consequences of these initial encounters.

The material and practical aspects of such encounters were, however, another matter. One visit by a ship's crew infected with disease, for example, might pose disaster, and there was little that diplomacy could

---

[12] Miguel León Portilla, "Men of Maize," in Alvin M. Josephy Jr., *America in 1492: The World of the Indian Peoples Before the Arrival of Columbus* (New York: Vintage Books, 1993), p. 175.

do about this until it was too late. More importantly, while the diplomatic tradition alerts us to how the integrative requirements of encounter relations require diplomacy, it also makes clear the consequences of those we might recognize as diplomats being absent. Those who had to come up with answers to the problems generated by encounters were not primarily diplomats, but rather priests, courtiers, officers, traders and, of course, leaders themselves, acting in a more-or-less diplomatic capacity. They might work to organize peaceful relations between their peoples by demonstrations of respect and friendship based on the premise of equality (no matter what they actually thought of one another in these terms). They might struggle with the technical problems of trying to understand each other. Most importantly of all, they might try to explain to their own side the importance of allowing the other's understanding of what was going on to restrain and shape their own actions, and to demonstrate to the other side that this was happening. Unfortunately, they were sometimes not very good at it. Encounters were often highly volatile situations made worse by the fact that those trying to act diplomatically were composed of volatile material themselves. It is, after all, difficult to combine the qualities of a good diplomat on the one hand, and those of a god-king, soldier-adventurer, or servant of the one true faith on the other, especially if one party to an encounter is strong, both are scared, and neither likes the look of the other.

After the initial impulse to establish contact was successfully accomplished, therefore, relations often broke down. Whether what followed is best seen in terms of integration–disintegration, or that story is better told in terms of expansion and contraction, it moves us beyond the initial problem of encounter relations. Once peoples know of each other, have established a rudimentary shared understanding of their relations within which to communicate, and want to find out more about each other, they move from encounter relations to those of discovery. When they do, the challenge posed by integration and disintegration to relations of separateness becomes more pronounced, the activity of diplomacy more distinct, and the existence of diplomats more certain.

Integration–disintegration and discovery relations

Discovery relations are more complex than encounter relations and, whereas the former may be seen as discrete and episodic, discovery relations are dimensional and ongoing. By dimensional, I mean that there is a dimension of discovery involved in all human relations, in the way in which, for example, there is not an element of encounter present in established relationships. By ongoing, I mean that the process of discovery does not come to a halt, because people and peoples are complex and because they are, in important respects, ever-changing. Indeed, the process of having relations with others is one of the sources of this change. Relations of discovery involve coming to know and understand one another, albeit for vastly different purposes. We may hope to obtain wealth, security, friendship, intimacy and love from other people, and all these involve discovering who they are, what they want, and how their identities and interests, in turn, affect who you are and what you can have. Within the diplomatic tradition, however, discovery relations almost lose this instrumental character to become ends in themselves. The field reports of anthropologists, the political and economic appraisals to be found in the Venetian *relatzione*, and CIA country reports, for example, all result from relations entered into and conducted primarily to obtain information.[13] Indeed, as de Callières noted in his comments about "the freemasonry of diplomacy," what holds them together is that they worked "for the same end, namely to discover what is happening."[14]

Of course, it is perfectly possible for peoples to live without taking much interest in the affairs of others beyond their locales. Despite the great changes associated with developments in communication and

---

[13] The Venetian *relatzione* were reports provided by Venetian diplomats upon the conclusion of their missions. Unlike the reports of missions undertaken by other Italian states from the late fifteenth century, they were known for providing a full analysis of the political, social and geographical circumstances of their hosts. Hamilton and Langhorne, *The Practice of Diplomacy*, p. 53. See also Tessa Beverly, "Diplomacy and Elites: Venetian Ambassadors, 1454–1494," *DSPDP* (Leicester: Diplomatic Studies Programme, 51, March 1999). For the reports of the Central Intelligence Agency see *The Central Intelligence World Fact Book* available at www.cia.gov/library/publications/the-world-factbook/. The US State Department and other Foreign Ministries provide similar country analyses.

[14] "Since the whole diplomatic body works for the same end, namely to discover what is happening, there may arise – there often indeed does arise – a freemasonry of diplomacy by which one colleague informs another of coming events which a lucky chance has enabled him to discern," in De Callières, *On The Manner Of Negotiating With Princes* (South Bend: University of Notre Dame Press, 1963), p. 113.

information technologies suggesting a wholesale collapse of distance, a great deal of news remains local because this is what most people are interested in. Indeed, in some of the most developed and connected parts of the world, news organizations are re-directing their resources from abroad to back home, while presenting the international news on which they do report in increasingly local or "human interest" terms. Diplomats are criticized for showing insufficient interest in discovering what their hosts are like and, on occasions, can display an impressive lack of interest even in how their opposite numbers conduct diplomacy. The peoples of the Iroquois League and other north woods American Indians, for example, learned that a commitment from the Europeans was of little value unless they created and signed a document long before they learned to read and write the languages of the Europeans. The latter, in their turn, learned that lasting agreements with Iroquois required that they be read into message strings and wampum belts and frequently renewed through face-to-face meetings, although they never learned to read the former or to understand with sympathy why subsequent meetings were necessary.[15] Nevertheless, in all but the least-developed parts of the world, it is becoming progressively more difficult for people only to think and act locally, even if the capacity for discovering and communicating without understanding displayed by the Indians and the Europeans remains very much in evidence.

One reason why this is so is that discovery relations generate processes of integration within international societies and processes of disintegration within their members. By finding out more about each other, peoples' senses of difference and the material facts which support them may be diminished or increased. Indeed, from within the diplomatic tradition we can see how it is through relations of discovery that identities are constantly being formed and maintained, on the one hand, and eroded and dissolved, on the other. Within the other traditions of international thought, the extent to which this is so is consistently underestimated, albeit for very good practical reasons. In them, the identities of the principal participants, whether one likes them or not, are uniformly presented as stable and enduring, and evidence to the contrary is read as suggesting exceptional circumstances. The

---

[15] Michael K. Foster, "Another Look At the Function of Wampum in Iroquois-White Councils" in Jennings, Fenton, Druke and Miller (eds.), *The History and Culture of Iroquois Diplomacy*, pp. 99–114.

exceptional qualities accorded to processes of integration and disintegration are clearly in evidence in conventional presentations of events in the European Union. It is said to be an exception to, or new departure from, normal international relations by people who approve and disapprove of it, alike.

The diplomatic history of Europe, however, points to the dangers of making this assumption. Certainly, a latter-day Thucydides might present that history as a story about the rise to power of a series of popes, emperors and kings and the fear each ascent caused in others. And in such a story, the EU is more easily presented as a departure than as the latest contender for the domination of a European system whose organizing principles are presented as essentially unchanged. From other perspectives, however, an equally good story may be told about ongoing attempts to discover the new terms on which Europe's separate peoples might be integrated into a new European republic or re-integrated into a revived conception of Christendom. In this story, the EU is merely the latest chapter in a long story of how European peoples are drawn together and pulled apart by their discovery relations. Similar stories might be told about the Greek city-states or the American colonies with only the eventual (as it currently seems) outcome in each case determining which narrative is to be dominant. The Greeks' is a story of failed hegemonic bids and the disintegration of their world as a consequence; the Americans' a story of successful integration into a national project. The Greek story has changed again, of course, with EU membership and the portents, at least, of future changes in the American story can already be observed.

If the diplomatic tradition's presentation of international relations as the continual drawings together and comings apart of peoples resulting from their desire to discover one another is accepted, then the complex role of diplomats in processes of integration and disintegration can be better understood. They may be agnostic about integration and disintegration in general and they can work against it on some occasions. Even as the guardians and managers of relations of separateness, however, they can also be at the forefront of the sort of integrative projects to which relations of discovery give rise. Boniface's missionary work among the German tribes across the Rhine, Weiser's attempts to secure the chain of friendship between Mohawks, settlers and colonial governments, and the efforts of any number of diplomatic virtuosos in the peace processes following major European wars all provide evidence of diplomats' leading roles in attempting to stabilize international societies by initiating or accelerating processes of integration towards new political orders.[16] At all times and all places, we see diplomats supporting and working for the creation of leagues, associations, congresses, assemblies and other arrangements which promise order and predictability by pulling those they represent into shared and regularized ways of undertaking their relations. Indeed, it is difficult to identify discovery relations in which diplomats oppose the integrative impulses *per se* to which they give rise on the grounds that they make diplomacy more difficult.

Again, the contemporary conduct of diplomats representing members of the EU on questions of monetary, customs and, increasingly, political union is instructive in this regard.[17] They appear to be negotiating some of their number, if not out of a job, then out of a profession. As the efforts to which the representatives of sovereigns would go to negotiate suzerainties and vassalages in medieval Europe illustrate, however, neither the reasons for doing it, nor the consequences of having done so were always straightforward. On occasions, for example, a measure of formal integration on superior–inferior terms would be worked for by the inferior party. Thus, English kings would concede that they held certain French lands as vassals of the French crown. In so doing, they hoped to head off existential debates with the French about what was properly France and what was properly English and to weaken the challenge of third parties to their practical control of the territories in question. At least, that was the calculation, although it did not always work that way.[18] Perhaps the most compelling evidence of

---

[16] Hill, *A History of Diplomacy in the International Development of Europe*, Vol. 1, p. 77, Paul A. W. Wallace, *Conrad Weiser: Friend of Colonist and Mohawk* (Lewisburg: Wennawoods Publishing, 1996) and Henry A. Kissinger, *A World Restored: Metternich, Castlereagh and the Problems of Peace 1812–1822* (Boston: Houghton Mifflin, 1957).

[17] See, e.g., Brian Hocking and David Spence, "Towards a European Diplomatic System?" *Discussion Papers in Diplomacy* (The Hague: Netherlands Institute of International Relations Clingendael, 98, May 2005) and Simon Duke, "Diplomacy Without a Corps: Training for EU External Representation?" *DSPDP* (Leicester: Diplomatic Studies Programme, 76, April 2001).

[18] Hill, *A History of Diplomacy in the International Development of Europe*, Vol. 1, p. 383. Richard the Lionheart also accepted vassalage to the Holy Roman Empire to secure his freedom (p. 310). Venice accepted its formal status as a Byzantine province determined by the *Pax Nicephori* (811) to dilute the more proximate power of Charlemagne's empire. See John Julius Norwich, *A History of Venice* (New York: Random House, 1989), p. 25.

the equanimity with which diplomats deal with the consequences of integration comes from their own profession, however. Shared representations and missions, whether of medieval kingdoms to the Papacy, former Soviet republics to the other great powers (albeit temporarily), or EU members to the UN, for example, seem to have elicited no objections, on principle, from diplomats and have attracted their support. Through the integration of diplomatic services, diplomats themselves seem to discover that they like working with each other.

By drawing our attention to the dynamics of the relations of discovery, the diplomatic tradition of international thought allows us to see how diplomats have to work with the processes of integration and disintegration which these relations engender as part of the ebb and flow of international life. We may go further and say that the agnosticism of diplomats about the general idea of integration gives way to enthusiasm about particular iterations of it when these will allow relations of separateness within an international society to flow more smoothly and peacefully, and when they are attainable. These are nebulous criteria for analysts, but they provide important caveats for diplomats who represent particular peoples and serve particular principals as well as the requirements of effective diplomacy in general. Just as encounter relations may confirm a people's separate identity at precisely the same moment that they confirm they are not alone, so discovery relations may give rise to a backwash of reservations about integration. Just like the regrets of Hawaiian islanders about intimate liaisons with strangers the night before, the concerns of American consumers about what Chinese imports are doing to their job prospects even as they continue to buy them, and the Chinese government's sense that the success of the Chinese economy in attracting foreign investment is not all good news for its own political position are examples of how discovery relations and their consequences leave people feeling uneasy about themselves and who they are. Enough of discovery, they seem to say. If we must have, indeed want, relations with other peoples without feeling that we are losing ourselves in the process, then how is this to be achieved?

Integration–disintegration and re-encounter relations

The answer to which the diplomatic tradition points us is re-encounter relations. These share the dimensional quality of discovery relations and are also ongoing. Like discovery relations, their conduct presumes some sort of international society in which understandings and conventions have been established. Unlike discovery relations, however, re-encounter relations operate to reaffirm the current identities of those between whom they are conducted. As such, it might be supposed that processes of integration and disintegration would make re-encounter relations more difficult and possibly less necessary. How, after all, does one maintain a stable sense of oneself in a world which is constantly pulling together and coming apart and why does one need to? From the diplomatic tradition of international thought we obtain a sense of how these questions are wrongly formulated. The relationship between peoples' sense of identity and processes of integration and disintegration is more complex than is often assumed, and this has important consequences for the conduct of re-encounter relations by diplomacy and diplomats.

In simple international societies such as those that emerge from first encounters, re-encounter relations may simply be directed at restoring as much of the *status quo ante* as possible. Relations between different peoples may be restricted and reduced by, for example, re-affirming taboos on contacts with strangers. Indeed, the achievement of an initial shared understanding about who may speak to whom, how, about what and under what conditions, must always involve elements of a re-encounter in this sense. The Byzantines experience with their *Skrinrion Barbaron* for minding envoys, the seventeenth-century Japanese restriction on all foreign contacts to one ship a year and, more recently, the attempts to restrict contacts made by states like communist Albania, Burma/Myanmar and North Korea, all provide examples of explicit attempts to engage in contacts in such a way as not only to maintain separateness, but to reinforce it.[19] They also provide examples of how difficult it is to undertake this approach successfully. Contacts seem to grow and relations become more complex despite the best efforts of those with power to control them and keep them simple.

The more complex an international society becomes, the harder it becomes to maintain distance and difference by re-encounter relations designed to restrict contacts. However, once there is no prospect of

---

[19] See Nicolson, *The Evolution Of The Diplomatic Method*, p. 25 and Hamilton and Langhorne, *The Practice of Diplomacy*, p. 19.

putting back the clock in this sense, relations can develop in such a way that they, themselves, serve and are used to emphasize the distinctiveness and separateness of peoples. As noted earlier, inter-communal conflicts provide an example of how close relations between "objectively" similar peoples can be used to keep them apart. They are forced, figuratively and sometimes literally, to re-encounter one another on a daily basis through heavily scripted patterns of routine interaction that confirm their differences. As examples from Northern Ireland, the former Yugoslavia and Sri Lanka, among others, demonstrate, it is perfectly possible for peoples whose relations with each other are highly integrated in most respects, to maintain strong senses of their separate identities. Unintegrated sectors, for example, separate education systems or forms of religious observation, may contribute to this, but actual relations – the terms on which these peoples live with each other – play a major role in confirming separate identities.[20] Nor is this observation restricted to the malign relations of inter and intra-communal conflict. Participation in, for example, religious celebrations and sporting events has long been used by peoples to emphasize both their membership of a common international society and the terms of their memberships as separate and distinct peoples.[21] We are all Hellenes here, but you are Athenians and we are Spartans.

Accordingly, it cannot be said that high levels of integration within international societies automatically render the conduct of re-encounter relations more difficult. Nor can it be said that they may make a separate sense of identity less necessary, for they can be implicated in actually creating and reinforcing those identities, rather than eroding them. This is so even when processes of integration have taken on a dynamic and intense character and have developed institutional expressions of their own. Even then, other factors shape the ability of diplomats to conduct re-encounter relations and the likelihood of their success. Consider, for example, the mix of objective and subjective factors which have shaped Canadian diplomats' experiences with the

---

[20] See, e.g., Anthony D. Buckley and Mary Catherine Kenny, *Negotiating Identity: Rhetoric, Metaphor and Social Drama in Northern Ireland* (Washington: Smithsonian Institute Press, 1995) and Biljana Vankovska, *Current Perspectives on Macedonia*: No. 1, "The Path From 'Oasis of Peace' to 'Powder Keg' of the Balkans," Heinrich Böll Foundation (undated).

[21] See Wight, "The states-system of Hellas," in Wight (Hedley Bull, ed.), *Systems of States*, pp. 46–72.

North American Free Trade Agreement (NAFTA), on the one hand, and Irish and British diplomats' experiences with EU membership, on the other. Membership of NAFTA, it is generally agreed, has narrowed the areas of public policy over which the Canadian government exercises exclusive, formal control. It may be claimed, however, that this loss has been offset by the new opportunities provided by NAFTA's regime politics for Canadian diplomats (broadly defined) to assert Canadian identities and viewpoints before their US and Mexican colleagues.[22] This may be so. However, the balance of power between Canada and the United States, the sorts of American foreign policy which this permits, and Canadians' own sense of their country as well-endowed, but underachieving, all encourage continued skepticism about the idea that a positive relationship exists between the exercise of these new diplomatic opportunities provided by NAFTA and Canada's ability to be itself and advance its interests.

Canadian diplomats may have seen the need for membership of NAFTA as arising from a sober recognition of the economic realities of being wealthy and remaining so. Their Irish colleagues, however, have always been advocates of an ever-closer European Union, partly on economic grounds, but also as a way by which their national identity and political independence might be asserted. Their historical standard, direct and indirect domination by Britain, allowed them to view a similarly tight relationship, only with multiple European states similarly bound, far more favorably.[23] Even if Ireland remained small and dependent (but no longer poor as it turned out) nevertheless it would get out from under Britain's thumb. The British experience of membership, in contrast, was more like that of the Canadians, at least until the prospects of their country continuing to act as an independent great power faded. British diplomats worried about the constraining effects of membership on their freedom of action, even though they mostly regarded the economic case as clear. Eventually, however, they were also able to enjoy the benefits, denied to Canadian diplomats by NAFTA's simpler and less balanced underlying structure, of working

---

[22] See Charles Doran, "Canada–US Relations: Personality, Pattern and Domestic Politics," in Patrick James, Nelson Michaud and Marc O'Reilly, *Handbook of Canadian Foreign Policy* (Lanham: Lexington Books, 2006).
[23] Brigid Laffan, "The European Union and Ireland," in Neill Collins (ed.), *Political Issues in Ireland Today* (Manchester: Manchester University Press, 1999), pp. 89–105.

in an association with multiple members and with several cards of their own to play.[24]

Participating as Europeans, members of the EU find it increasingly difficult to act out of concert with their fellows. Participating as separate national states, however, they can exploit precisely the same processes that make it harder to emphasize their separateness and distinctiveness through independent action, to emphasize them by performing the dissenter's role in discussions about collective action. Even mechanical approaches to finessing this negative form of self-assertion and affirmation, such as reforming and weighting voting procedures, can be exploited. Within Europe at least, the Papal and Imperial experiences both show that possessing a majority of the electors or votes is of little use when it fails to coincide with geographical and political concentrations of power.[25] Indeed, as recent EU experience suggests, mechanical measures of this sort provide another opportunity for the, often non-diplomatic, conduct of re-encounter relations which can actually threaten the whole process of integration. Voting "no" in European Union referenda on constitutional reform may be read, at least in part, as a startling example of citizen diplomacy engaged in the relations of re-encounter.

Nor is it only representatives and citizens of established states who are provided with opportunities by international integration to conduct re-encounter relations. Claims to a separate and distinct existence can also be made on behalf of historical peoples who do not enjoy a separate existence under the current political dispensation as well as apparently new combinations of peoples that never existed before. I say apparently new because in many of these cases, the peoples have enjoyed a previously independent or separate existence. This is particularly the case in the EU, where new regional political structures, avowedly responding to the imperatives of economic efficiency and democratic accountability, may be located on the territories of previous kingdoms, dukedoms, city states, leagues and associations. Claims made on behalf of Lombardy and Flanders to participate in international life on whatever the terms of

---

[24] See Duncan Watts and Colin Pilkington, *Britain in the European Union Today* (Manchester: Manchester University Press, 2005).

[25] Hill, *A History of Diplomacy in the International Development of Europe*, Vol. 1, pp. 180, 201, and Wight, *Power Politics*, p. 297.

full membership may come to be, rest on old grounds like those of Scotland and the Basque country, as much as they do on new ones.

One may be struck, therefore, by the apparent stability and unchanging character of the basic culture groups underlying the shifting territorial arrangements and political settlements of European history. The latter may be read as a series of superficial attempts to come to terms with problems arising from a distribution of peoples that has changed little since the time of the Roman Empire and possibly before. Thus, we see Lombards, Scots and Bavarians, for example, as well as Romans, English and Prussians, at various times independent, suzerain, enslaved, or democratically absorbed, sometimes highly conscious of themselves as such and sometimes less so, but all the while providing important boards in the stage on which European relations have been played out. European diplomatic history (in the orthodox sense of that term as international history), then, can be viewed in epiphenomenal or superstructural terms, sitting atop a relatively fixed distribution of European peoples and addressing the problems to which that distribution gives rise. This is probably unwise, however, and for a number of reasons. First, while the present distribution of culture groups in Europe has been stable for a long time, it has not always been so and will not always be so in the future. Secondly, even these stable culture groups have not always been self-conscious, nor have they always aspired to political independence. Italians, for example, have not always believed that they all ought to live together as Italians in a single political community. Thirdly, this stability cannot be taken to imply that a political dispensation satisfying the claims of all groups to separate representation is at least theoretically possible. All answers, both those that have sought to ignore this relatively fixed distribution of peoples and those that have sought to elevate some version of it to an organizing principle, have created their own problems.

From within the diplomatic tradition, therefore, the relationship between processes of integration and disintegration, on the one hand, and some posited authentic distribution of separate peoples, on the other, is not, in itself, important. Nor are whatever erosive consequences these processes are believed to have for the idea of separate identities maintained, in part, by re-encounter relations. Processes of integration and disintegration not only generate re-encounter relations between existing identities feeling the pressure. Since these processes create new identities, they also generate new re-encounter relations between these new identities. Most interesting of all, however, they also provide established identities with new opportunities for asserting their continued distinctive and separate existence.

Disintegration of international societies

A dialectical understanding of the process of integration and disintegration leads us to focus on the former, at the expense of the latter. In principle, it ought to be possible to examine the rise of Rome, the establishment of the modern society of states, or the emergence of the European Union with our attention firmly focused on what was disintegrating or being replaced. From within the established traditions of thought about international relations, however, we are rarely invited to do so. Like the problems posed by closing down businesses, arranging divorce settlements and disposing of estates, those associated with the international relations of disintegration are neglected by all but the specialist and, perhaps, the romantic for they belong to the losing side of life. In addition to being more fun, it is sometimes easier to think in terms of what is coming together, rather than what is coming apart. To what extent, for example, do successful successive stages of EU integration move its members away from previous iterations of the EU as opposed to moving it away from *l'Europe de pays*? Thus, it might be expected that the conceptual differentiation of relations of separateness offered here either does not apply, or that its insights are lost in the gathering gloom as relations, together with the now-disintegrating international societies which made them possible and necessary, fade away.

Yet, as the biographies and autobiographies of imperial governors-general, high commissioners, ambassadors of governments-in-exile, and delegates to sidelined international organizations make clear, the representation of disintegrating actors and the fading worlds they constitute are regarded as important tasks by diplomats. From within the diplomatic tradition we obtain a sense of why this is so, and a better sense from that in the other traditions of international thought as to why it is important to an understanding of international relations and what we want from them. Much of the diplomacy of disintegration consists of putting up a front, and whether this involves the skillful exercise of bluff and timing in the execution of a withdrawal or the drawn-out absurdities of claiming a state of affairs that is patently no longer the case, it is invariably treated with sympathy, if not always respect.[26] Keeping up appearances, for example, the fictions of one China or a Holy Roman Empire noted above, permits questions to which there are as yet no answers or only prohibitively costly ones, to be postponed or avoided. It may also preserve the peace by protecting the sensibilities of those, like post-Soviet Russia, who have experienced failure or decline. And, if appearances are maintained for long enough, they may even one day, as in the case of the Baltic republics, once again coincide with more material facts.

When international societies disintegrate, re-encounter relations come to the fore. Encounter relations would seem to be ruled out by definition, for disintegration presumes a society of peoples who already know each other. Discovery relations, if present, would belong to whatever new arrangements are coming into being. Re-encounter relations, however, are concerned with maintaining and possibly increasing the sense of separateness that presumably accompanies disintegration. Britain and India, for example, had to re-encounter one another outside the framework of Empire after 1947. If re-encounters constitute the dominant theme, however, it is still possible to imagine and, indeed, to obtain glimpses of other sorts of relations under conditions of disintegration which are both counter-intuitive and suggestive. We can conceive, for example, of encounters where people meet, establish communications, and then quickly separate again. We know that the Europeans and Chinese were supposed to have visited many places before their official "discovery," but can only imagine the sort of relations conducted between them and native inhabitants.[27] Julius Caesar's raid on Britain in 55 BC was accompanied by negotiations with the local inhabitants, we know. Whether a society of inter-subjective understandings was established in the sense discussed above, however, or whether the Romano-Celtic international society that already existed provided a context for relations is much harder to determine, as is the role of either

---

[26] For the insistence on a mirror by the Emperor's representative at the negotiations for the Treaty of Utrecht so he might sit opposite an equal see Langhorne, "The Development of International Conferences, 1648–1830," pp. 61–91. He also insisted on entering the negotiating room first.

[27] See Song Nan Zhang, *The Great Voyages of Zheng He* (Union City: Pan-Asian Publications, 2005) and Gavin Menzies, *1421: The Year China Discovered America* (New York: Harper Collins, 2003).

in making possible the Romans' withdrawal.[28] Terminated visits also raise a new variant of an old problem, the extent to which a break in communication can be viewed as a communication itself. Peoples and countries which stop talking to one another often continue to have a relationship, but the extent to which peoples who only know of each other's existence may be said to be in a relationship is not clear.

We can also see ways in which the disintegration of international societies can produce new discovery relations that do not belong to whatever new dispensation may be emerging. Thus, the same medieval kings who would accept the formal status of vassals to consolidate their effective control of territories might also concede the formal freedom of cities in return for promises of obedience. A similar calculation played a part in securing the acquiescence of European imperialists to decolonization. The direct control of formal empires that no longer enjoyed legitimacy might be replaced by the indirect control of the newly independent colonies by their former imperial masters. In both cases, disintegration would permit the discovery of new identities by which the substance of the old relations might be maintained and rendered more secure. The historical fate of both examples suggests, however, that new identities, once established, and the worlds they presuppose quickly sweep away, or at least submerge, the substance of old arrangements once the latter's form has disintegrated.

A different example of discovery relations operating in the midst of disintegration is provided by Rebecca West's account of the first visit of officials of the new Turkish republic to the former Ottoman territory of Bosnia in the 1920s.[29] The local Muslims, who have felt abandoned and neglected in the new Kingdom of the Serbs and Croats, turn out in force, dressed in the clothes and sporting the symbols of a vanished empire, to greet the successors to their former patrons. Neither they, nor the uneasy, quiet Turks in Western business suits who urge them to come to terms with their new circumstances, know what to make of each other. What had formerly held them together has vanished, but the new terms on which they might conduct their relationship have yet to be worked out.

---

[28] Of course, Caesar's raid took place within a context of developed commercial relations. See Thomas Lewin, *The Invasion of Britain by Julius Caesar* (Whitefish: Kessinger Publishing, 2005) [1859].

[29] Rebecca West, *Black Lamb and Grey Falcon: A Journey Through Yugoslavia* (Harmondsworth: Penguin, 1994) [1941] pp. 316–18.

West's story is a microcosm, not only for what was happening in the former imperial territories in Europe at the time, but also of the later dislocations in Yugoslavia and the Soviet Union. In both, peoples formerly (and formally) together have had to establish new terms on which to conduct relations with one another, essentially by discovering who each other is. In this regard, the peoples of Eastern Europe are under intense pressure to locate themselves either within or adjacent to the new integrative processes of the EU and NATO. The wealth, power and general attractiveness of both exert a pressure to integrate with them that, it is widely assumed, will eventually be irresistible. Like the gravitational forces of collapsed stars, however, the former Yugoslavia and former Soviet Union continue to exert their own pull to which diplomacy gives expression especially when the new forces become too ambitious. And the physical absence of these old constellations also permits other new and old ways of defining their respective peoples to be advanced, notably as independent national states seeking local security and possibly local dominance. Accordingly, the process of joining the great projects of European integration itself may acquire a status of some permanence. Whether, like Slovenia and the Baltic states, they are on the right side of the line, or like Serbia and Macedonia, they are on the wrong side, all may find themselves suspended in various orbits around Europe maintained, like all orbits, by countervailing forces. In this case, they are the pull of new integrative projects on the one hand, and the consequences of old projects disintegrating on the other. Governments, politicians, private companies, international organizations and academics may attempt to push them in one direction or another, but it is with this state of suspension that diplomats also have to deal for the foreseeable future.

Integration, disintegration and separateness

From within the established traditions of international thought, processes of integration and disintegration give rise to questions about why they are occurring, what drives them, and whether or not we should regard them as good things. It is also widely assumed that both pose headaches for diplomacy and diplomats. The former serves, and the latter's interests are said to be served, by representing, and possibly producing, the particular divisions that exist at any given time. The diplomatic tradition of international thought has very little to say about these concerns, and a diplomatic understanding sheds a different light on both processes and the role of diplomacy and diplomats within them. We see diplomats serving, if not as the designers usually, then as the planners and site managers for new international architectures, as the executors of holding orders on behalf of established residents now threatened by the new developments, and as advocates for the rights of squatters previously ignored but affected by the demolition and new construction. And we see the same diplomats acting in all three capacities, if not at once, then in quick succession.

How so? From the places between separate political communities, processes of integration and disintegration do not appear as disruptions to international societies which would otherwise be settled. They appear rather as permanently operating conditions of all international societies. It is a measure of integration that makes relations and their management by diplomacy and diplomats possible in the first place. Once relations are established between separate peoples, then the processes pushing them together on new terms and pulling apart the old ones are also set in train. These processes develop for a variety of reasons to solve particular problems, realize particular values and serve particular interests or conceptions of them. It follows that no particular process of integration can be regarded as settling all the problems of international relations about which we worry, and no particular process of disintegration can be the source of them. Integration does not put an end to relations of separateness. Disintegration does not make their orderly conduct impossible. What both do, however, is generate changes in the particular terms on which relations of separateness in a plural world are conducted.

A sense of what this orientation involves may be obtained by imagining diplomacy as one of those trades or crafts dominated by families in which the skill is passed from fathers to sons and (latterly) daughters. In Western Europe, a family still in business would have a history of representing a variety of political forms in a variety of different settings. Provinces and dioceses which sought favors from and demonstrated loyalty and obedience to Imperial and Papal courts respectively, gave way to vassals and suzerainties balancing old-style demonstrations of fealty with new attempts to pursue their own interests in relations of jealous equality with their fellows. These, in turn, gave rise to kingdoms and republics for which independence and sovereignty became matters of life and death, and for some of which at least, their own imperial projects became an ambition. And now, arguably, a measure of subordination to a higher order – the will and interest of humanity as a whole – as a way of achieving all that is important has returned to the fore. Our family of diplomats would have represented those for whom they were responsible through all these changes with very few constants. Sovereign status, for example, they might remember, not as an end of diplomacy, but as a condition of it to which people attached more or less importance at different times. As such, it might be helpful to the business of conducting relations between separate peoples, but not necessarily. Even (perhaps especially) between peoples who elevated sovereignty to the status of the highest good, our diplomatic family would have recognized its capacity for generating unwanted outcomes and worked to soften the rigor with which their governments and, sometimes, their peoples wanted its logic applied to the conduct of their relations. Between those who attached less importance to their independence and felt less separate from one another, however, they would have facilitated integration, sometimes to the point of rendering their own craft redundant and sometimes to the point when the second thoughts of those they represented kicked in.

It is from the standpoint of such a family, therefore, that we can see that processes of integration and disintegration are ever-present in international societies. What the diplomatic tradition of international thought suggests is that they might be best managed as such. In this, it enjoys an advantage over the other traditions. Insofar as the participants in those traditions become absorbed by, and take positions on, the particular arguments which at any given time are pulling peoples together or pushing them apart, and insofar as anyone pays attention to what they have to say, then they are part of that which requires diplomatic management. The diplomatic challenge is to manage these changes successfully, which usually means peacefully, and certainly without the unwanted or un-intentioned conflict to which such movements can give rise. Somehow, the world, or parts of it, has to be continually moved from what look like the old settled terms on which re-encounter relations were conducted to what promise to be the new settled terms. Sometimes the pace of change is glacial, in which case the task of diplomacy in this regard is relatively easy. Sometimes it is like an avalanche, in which case re-encounter relations are impossible until it is over. More often, however, it is something in between, and the image of diplomats as instructors with novice skiers is helpful. Once the latter actually manage to stand up, how is one to create and maintain conditions of dynamic stability as they begin to slide from one relatively level place to the next?

Generating and maintaining stable encounter relations under such conditions is a major challenge for diplomacy and diplomats. However, great changes in the identities of separate peoples and their relations also come from outside the international societies of which they are members. In particular, they do so when whole international societies rub up against one another through processes of expansion and contraction. Viewed from within the diplomatic tradition of international thought, a major purpose of international societies is to regulate and stabilize the conduct of relations of separateness. What happens, therefore, when two or more ways of accomplishing this come into contact with each other? The resulting challenges for diplomacy and diplomats would appear to be at least as great as those posed by processes of integration and disintegration within a single international society. At least they would if the question of how international societies relate to one another is not just one of historical interest only. As we shall see, the diplomatic tradition of thought strongly suggests that we should not think of it only in these terms. It also suggests, however, that we should not think of the current resurfacing of multiple international societies, if such is what is happening, as something new and unprecedented.

8 | Expansion–contraction

It remains very easy to think of the world as primarily constituted by a single international society of states. We may argue about aspects of this claim: who may properly be regarded as its members; the nature and strength of the ties with which it binds them together; and, above all, the part it plays in explaining what happens. Yet there it seems to be, everything of consequence within it and nothing much without. For academics, this ubiquitous quality and its historical provenance are definitively portrayed in Bull and Watson's edited work, *The Expansion of International Society*.[1] The editors' focus is on how the organizing principles of European relations became principles for the whole world. Through processes of conquest, colonization and, finally, a distinctive form of decolonization, a global international society of sovereign territorial states bound by international law, diplomacy, war, great powers and the balance of power principle emerged in Europe's image. The stories told in the Bull and Watson volume may be criticized on several grounds. The focus on Europe puts the rest of the world out of focus. It oversimplifies the story of the expansion. And, perhaps, in doing so, it implies – nothing stronger – that with the consolidation of the European society as a global international society, the history of international societies came to a full stop.[2]

However, these shortcomings are less significant than two contributions the volume made. The first was to see international societies as historical phenomena with life cycles of their own. These life cycles may be thought of principally in terms of expansion and contraction which can occur in a number of ways. Existing members of a society may

---

[1] Bull and Watson (eds.), *The Expansion of International Society*. For extensive commentary see also Vigezzi, *The British Committee on the Theory of International Politics (1954–1985)*.
[2] On this see Hedley Bull, "The European International Order (1980)," in Kai Anderson and Andrew Hurrell (eds.), *Hedley Bull On International Society* (Basingstoke: Macmillan, 2000), pp. 170–89.

acquire or lose peoples and territories from or to the world outside. Outside peoples and territories may join as members in their own right, now regulated by the same sorts of understandings and rules and enjoying the same sorts of relations as established members, or established peoples and territories may cease to be members and leave an international society. International societies as a whole may also be said to expand and contract in a horizontal plane. Thus, we can see the Roman and Arab-Islamic worlds, for example, expanding outwards and establishing their respective organizing principles in new territories. And we can see international societies contracting horizontally, as both worlds did in the fifth and eleventh centuries respectively when Romans and Arabs vacated territories they had formerly controlled. Finally, we can see expansion and contraction taking place in a vertical plane. Thus, using the same examples, we can see Roman and Arab understandings overlaying, permeating, or replacing the understandings of the worlds into which they are entering in ways usefully illustrated by metaphors from archaeology and geology about depth, layers and discontinuities. Less easily, we can see them fading, or retreating up the social structure to a point where they cease to exist. Latin and Arabic, for example, came into Britain and the Iberian peninsulas respectively but then disappeared with the international societies they mediated.

Bull's and Watson's second contribution involved looking at international societies in plural terms. As Wight had noted earlier, we can identify times in the past at which more than one international society existed as roughly equal worlds in terms of extent and power. We can also see subordinate societies within or adjacent to dominant ones and processes by which old societies pass away and are transformed into, or replaced by, new international societies with their own distinctive organizing principles.[3] Wight's examples, however, were largely from the ancient world and, as such, reinforced the modernist notion that multiple international societies were a thing of the past, while the European society of state was now dominant and would remain so for the foreseeable future.[4] The principal value in looking at other international societies, therefore, was to see if their operations might shed light

---

[3] For a discussion of secondary state systems see Wight, *Systems of States*, p. 24.

[4] The modern notion of human history drawing differences together into a single way of living is well captured by Harvey Wheeler's image of the contemporary world now reduced to a single, robust tree trunk from many roots. Harvey Wheeler, *Democracy in a Revolutionary Era* (New York: Praeger, 1968).

on the workings of our own. In its conception, Bull's and Watson's volume did little to undermine this. Their greatest worry was with how well an international society could perform with so many badly socialized members. However, the identification of international societies co-existing opens up the possibility of relations between them. If so, then to what extent may it be said that international societies, as opposed to their members, encounter and discover one another and, insofar as each maintains a measure of coherence in its own terms, engage in re-encounters of the sort suggested in the diplomatic tradition of international thought? And what insights may be obtained by employing a diplomatic understanding when looking at the processes by which international societies expand and contract?

Expansion–contraction and encounter relations

The most obvious objection to the idea of relations between international societies would seem to be apparent in standard encounter narratives. When the hydraulic civilizations of the Nile, the Tigris and the Euphrates met the agrarian and nomadic civilizations to the north, we assume it was as the Egyptian, Babylonian, Hittite and Assyrian empires respectively. When the worlds of Rome and China maintained a finger-tip contact with one another around the Caspian Sea and across the Gobi desert, we assume that it was as the Roman and Chinese empires. And when the *respublica Christiana* of Europe and the pre-Columbian societies of South America encountered each other on the shores of the Caribbean and Pacific, we see the resulting collisions as taking place between the Spanish Empire on the one hand, and the Aztec and Inca empires on the other. We assume, therefore, that it is not international societies that encounter one another, but their members. In an important sense this is so. *The Niña*, *The Pinta* and *The Santa Maria* were Spanish vessels and the *conquistadores* of Cortez were Spanish troops, not European ones, just as the armies of Montezuma were Aztec and not Mezo-American. However, more was usually going on.

The parties to such encounters often did see themselves as representing more than just their respective sovereigns, kingdoms and people. In their very different ways albeit, Aztec and Inca emperors, on the one hand, and *conquistadores*, on the other, saw themselves as manifestations of their respective gods at work in the world. The Spaniards, in particular, saw themselves as representing a community of Christian,

European and, latterly, civilized and civilizing peoples to the rest of the world. Moreover, people often also saw the other party as representing something larger. Nor was it only the weaker or more ignorant party that might see the other in these terms. More developed, and better informed peoples, the Greeks and Chinese for example, were quite capable of lumping together in a residual category like "barbarians," foreigners whom they knew to be differentiated. They might do so out of the hubris which flows from regarding oneself as the center of the universe, or because, by their rough conduct at least, foreigners were indistinguishable from one another, whether they came from Persia, the steppes and mountains beyond, or from what were to become England, France and Germany.

The possibility of relations between international societies being present in such encounters may also help us make better sense as to why they sometimes go well, and sometimes badly. We note, for example, that encounters have never proved impossible to undertake. There seems to be no record of peoples giving up on each other because it is too difficult for them to communicate. Given how the pattern by which normal rules of interaction are suspended, immunities established, and heralds appointed seems to be repeated over and over again, it is tempting to think in essentialist terms. All people seem to have a diplomacy gene guiding their actions on such occasions. If this is so, however, then why do things start to go wrong very shortly after encounters get underway? The diplomatic tradition suggests a possible answer in that when one or both parties are not members of international societies, then the simple protocols for treating individual strangers most peoples have will guide their actions. These can get you into communications, but not for long and not about a great deal.

What, therefore, might we suppose the influence of one or both parties belonging to its own international society would be on such encounters? One possibility might be that the members of international societies encountering one another for the first time would have an even harder time than parties living previously in some sort of isolation. To the difficulties generated by mutual incomprehension, suspicion and fear would be added those resulting from the fact that each international society would already have developed its own distinctive way of conducting relations of separateness. The encounters of simple peoples, and even the encounters of simple peoples with more developed ones, might consist of them simply working out ways of communicating with one another. The encounters of the members of different international societies, in contrast, would have to overcome each party's confidence that they already knew how to do this sort of thing.

At first glance, the famous difficulties generated by European attempts to gain access to the Ottoman and Chinese courts in the seventeenth and eighteenth centuries would seem to confirm this expectation. The Europeans refused to perform ceremonies that would acknowledge the inferior standing of their own courts, and the Ottomans and Chinese would grant them audiences on no other terms.[5] The difficulties were real and resulted in great tensions and long delays in the establishment of relationships. However, there is little evidence to suggest that one or both sides in each case could not understand what was going on. There is considerable evidence to suggest that everyone involved knew very well the sorts of games which were being played and what was at stake in them. This was so because, in an important sense, their respective worlds had already met and were in relations with each other. Between Europe and the pre-Columbian civilizations in the Americas, in contrast, the diplomatic ground was less well prepared with explosive consequences as encounters gave way to discovering who each other was and what each other wanted.

Expansion–contraction and discovery relations

The problems engendered by encounters between the members of different international societies were rarely insoluble. The same cannot be said of what happened when the members of different international societies engage in discovery relations. The historical record and all three established traditions of international thought strongly suggest that when this occurs, and interaction capacities permitting, one society will expand and the other will contract, and they will do so by processes which generally have a contested character. We assume, for example, that Rome and China did little about each other simply because they were in no position to do so. Neither could project its power a sufficient distance to even imagine a successful war against the other. Had they

---

[5] Bickers (ed.), *Ritual and Diplomacy*.

been able to so, they would have discovered a rough equivalence and found themselves in a stalemate, with or without an offensive catastrophe for the more aggressive of the two. At the other extreme, we have the impression of the Europeans walking all over North America, once they could get there in sufficient numbers, and imposing their ways simply because the native inhabitants were unable to stop them. Somewhere in between we see the boundaries of the Arab-Islamic and European-Christian worlds shifting from southern France in the west to Jerusalem in the east, reflecting the ebb and flow of military fortunes over centuries when a rough balance of power was disturbed by the achievement of local and temporary superiority by one side over the other. Once one society appears to deteriorate decisively, however, we see the processes of expansion, penetration and assimilation by the other proceed apace.

We see all this, of course, because, even though it is not all that happens when international societies engage in discovery relations, when it does happen, it does so strikingly and often with catastrophic consequences for someone. Thus, we may say that to the extent that discovery relations are characterized by a tendency to expand that is governed only by the capacities of the respective parties in any particular case, then the diplomatic tradition of international thought has little to tell us about them. Such relations, even if drawn-out, have a terminal character. In the past, they were conducted with peoples – infidels, barbarians and savages, for example – to whom less is owed than to the foreigners of one's own international society, with a view to their eventual conversion, assimilation or extermination. Those peoples in their turn either shared ambitions of the same order or were simply interested in survival. Thus, neither the practical imperative to stabilize relations with others nor the moral imperative to respect their independence exerted their usual force. One did not need to establish a reputation for honesty or straight-speaking with those who were variously regarded as less than human, bound for Hell or, at least, soon to be dispatched from this Earth. All that diplomats needed to do was help secure for their masters what they wanted at as little cost as possible. Work by any method to defeat and destroy the enemy while avoiding unnecessary wars and bringing necessary wars to a successful conclusion as soon as possible. The only real moral dilemma involved the extent to which it was possible to work with the outsiders to gain advantage over members of one's own society. Could one, for example, mobilize Guarani to gain advantage over the Portuguese or Pathans to hurt the Russians?[6]

The historical record certainly provides plenty of evidence of this sort of expansion and contraction and of the undistinguished parts diplomacy and diplomats played in both as the servants of power. However, when we approach the record from within the diplomatic tradition, it also provides evidence for a far more complex picture of what discovery relations between international societies can involve. The tendencies to expansion and contraction were not constant themes in the relations of all international societies at all times, and not merely because they were dependent on interaction capacities. Some societies were either not interested in expansion or deliberately turned their back on it. The Chinese and the Romans may have been unable to hurt each other, but there is little evidence to suggest that the former would have if they could (the same cannot be said with such confidence about the Romans). Even between international societies in close contact with one another a constant pressure to expand was not always exerted. As already noted, the frontier between Islam and Christianity, for example, remained stable for decades and sometimes centuries at a time.[7] Liberties in terms of piracy, raiding and kidnapping might be taken with each other to a degree and with a ferocity uncommon within each society, but other, more peaceful forms of exchange were also extensively developed. This might be the case even where boundaries were constantly shifting. Despite the steady Westward movement of Europeans across North America, for example, their daily relations with native peoples could take on a settled character, and a measure of co-existence between worlds could occur. And sometimes, even after a conquest, the patterns of the defeated society might hold up within the newly occupied territories. Thus, Hungarian landowners continued to extract rents from holdings that had come under Turkish control. In the Balkans and Spain, peoples from one side were allowed to live on the other side of the line, albeit tenuously. Indeed, they might come to fight

---

[6] Received opinion said one ought not, and those who ignored it were judged to have violated civilized standards of behavior. The fact that this collective opinion was violated on occasions does not, of course, provide grounds for concluding that it did not exert an influence, if rarely a decisive one, on the calculations of states and others in this regard.

[7] See, e.g., Noel Malcolm, *Bosnia: A Short History* (New York: New York University Press, 1994) and Kinross, *The Ottoman Centuries*.

for those on the other side of the line. And, even the Mongols kept still for years at a time between their great movements before they settled for imperial retirement.

In short, in even the most unpromising circumstances, the practical problems of maintaining settled relations, not just between peoples, but between the worlds their respective international societies constituted, presented themselves, if sometimes only for relatively short periods. Thus, if only for practical reasons of discovering what is happening and why, simple diplomatic virtues like honesty and clarity, and simple diplomatic devices like identifying who may, and who may not, speak on behalf of a people, were needed even in relations with peoples about whom one was unsure from worlds which seemed alien, blasphemous and, on occasions, revolting. Even in such cases, however, discovery relations undertaken for instrumental purposes yielded complex pictures of other international societies which, whether they liked it or not, posed difficult moral questions for everyone involved. The more peoples found out about each other, the more they had to wrestle with the problem of how others seemed both different from and similar to themselves. Mohammed instructed the Faithful on what they did and did not owe the infidels they discovered as Islam expanded, and as the Europeans discovered Americans, a whole literature developed on the extent to which they could be regarded as men and women and, thus, could be entitled to be treated as such. Could they, for example, be regarded as owning property and, if so, under what circumstances, particular and general, might they forfeit that right?[8] Christians and Muslims reflected on the fact that they were both, in the latter's phrase, "peoples of the book" as were, even more problematically for both, the Jews. Did this common root of their respective identities bring them closer together, therefore, or did the other party's different and, in their respective views, heretical development of the tradition place them even further beyond the Pale than savages? Similar questions confronted those who were on the receiving end of such expansions. Attempts to unite native peoples in both the Americas and India against the common enemy, for example, prompted reflections on the nature of the agreements and commitments into which separate tribes and peoples had

---

[8] See Martin C. Ortega, "Vitoria and the Universalist Conception of International Relations," in Ian Clark and Iver B. Neumann (eds.), *Classical Theories of International Relations* (Basingstoke: Macmillan, 1996), pp. 99–119.

already entered into with the Europeans. Were the Iroquois, for example, bound by their treaties with the English, people from another world, when the Huron, rivals and enemies from their own world, asked for help in making war on them?[9]

Thus, discovery relations between international societies tend to generate movement along the expansion–contraction continuum. The diplomatic tradition suggests, however, that they do so in ways that simple images of conquest, resistance and absorption do not always capture. In particular, when they are undertaken so as to take into account the differences of the peoples in the areas being entered, diplomacy and diplomats get a chance to play their parts, although both may easily become instruments of attempts to convert and assimilate. As a re-consideration of the world's experience with European expansion employing a diplomatic understanding illustrates, however, even an apparently successful exercise in this regard faces great difficulties with the consequences of which we continue to live.

European expansion and diplomacy

The role of the civilizing imperative in the expansion of Europe, and eventually the West, into the rest of the world is well-known and controversial. Missionaries, educators, administrators, commercial entrepreneurs and adventurers from Europe all played, and continue to play, their parts in making the rest of the world conform to their various conceptions of what a life which is good and right entails, principally by securing local converts. Governments were also involved in the processes of European expansion, chiefly through their armed forces and colonial administrators, but also through the service of their diplomats. The latter, it might be supposed, would have acted as something of a brake upon the way in which relations of discovery were seen to lead naturally to the need to civilize peoples who were sufficiently like the Europeans to make this possible. Diplomacy's foundation in the recognition of separateness as a fact and possibly a good, together with European diplomacy's own development on this, that non-interference

---

[9] The creation and transformation of Indian and European identities in the *pays d'en haut* (the lands beyond Iroquia and Huronia in the Old North-West) which posed difficult questions for Iroquois, Algonkian and European "tribes" alike is well captured in White, *The Middle Ground*.

in the affairs of others would reduce the sources of international conflict, both pointed diplomats in this direction. And to an extent, western diplomats, when acting as diplomats, advocated this sort of caution. At least, they often did so in regard to the internal affairs of particular peoples.[10] The idea of leaving the local people as much as one could to themselves while, perhaps, securing cooperation from, and skimming wealth off, the top was epitomized by Britain's indirect rule in West Africa and represented a coincidence of diplomatic and liberal, or lazy, imperial preferences.

Where the diplomats of the European powers with empires completely failed to advocate this indirect approach, in fact did just the reverse, was in regard to the way in which other international societies were configured and the different principles on which these configurations rested. While great differences in the way life might be organized inside separate political communities were tolerated, all communities had now to be organized as sovereign, territorial states or parts thereof. Diplomats advocated this partly because it aligned with the preferences of those they represented. Whatever variations they might allow within their colonies, the European powers wanted them to present as uniform and stable a front as possible to the outside world. Increasingly, in the latter half of the nineteenth century they attempted to exert the sort of control over their imperial territories which they enjoyed at home by incorporating them more closely and developing them. They did this in response to pressures from rivals to be sure. Often, however, they did so in response to the rising tide of doubts about whether empires, or empires with two standards of civic and economic life, at least, could be morally justified. In addition, where they could not, or did not want to, control territories and people themselves, governments advocated their independence as a way of denying them to their imperial rivals. Once Spain and Portugal had been driven from South America, for example, no one for a moment imagined that its peoples would be left

---

[10] Diplomats' enjoyment of their privileges and immunities has been historically linked to their fulfilling their duties and obligations, one of which is to refrain from interfering in the internal affairs of their host countries. This linking of privileges and immunities, on the one hand, and duties and obligations, on the other, appears in Article 41 of the Vienna Convention on Diplomatic Relations. As such it reflects a similar prohibition on those they represent interfering in each other's internal affairs that may be found in both the Covenant of the League of Nations and the Charter of the United Nations.

to re-establish or re-devise their own international society. Their only choice was to participate in the European one either as colonies or as sovereign, territorial states.

However, European diplomats also had their own reasons for replacing local arrangements by the European international society of states. The business of diplomacy was to stabilize relations of separateness and their own way of doing this, they believed, as the evolved product of advanced practice and refined reflection was the best way, indeed the only way.[11] One may sympathize with them, for it is hard to see what alternatives existed once the processes of discovery between the European society of states and other international societies got underway. Diplomatic relations could no longer be conducted on a non-reciprocal basis as in the manner of the Chinese and Ottoman empires, for example, once the existence of others whom they could not dominate, yet with whom they had to have relations, was a fact of ever-growing significance.[12] Nor could they be conducted on the basis of even only a formal assumption of human solidarity such as that of Christendom or the *Umma*, when these no longer appeared solid or could be said to constitute their own worlds. The only alternative appeared (especially to those who had the power to make their writ run) to be that all peoples, whatever their internal political arrangements, must eventually be given firm territorial boundaries within which to live and sovereign status as a way of circumscribing arguments. This is what Europe's experience with intensifying pluralism had taught its diplomats. There could be no international society but *the* international society if relations of separateness were to be stabilized and put on a firm basis between peoples so different and at such different levels of development. Everybody had to live in a state. That

---

[11] See Nicolson, *The Evolution Of The Diplomatic Method* and Sir Earnest Satow, *Guide to Diplomatic Practice*, 2nd edn. (London: Longman, Green and Company, 1922 (also 5th edn. 1979 revised)). See T. G. Otte, "Satow," in Berridge, Keens-Soper and Otte, *Diplomatic Theory From Machiavelli to Kissinger*, for a bibliographical note on Satow, pp. 149–50. See also Herbert Butterfield, "The New Diplomacy and Historical Diplomacy," in Butterfield and Wight (eds.), *Diplomatic Investigations*, pp. 181–92.

[12] Geoff Berridge drew my attention to how the Ottoman refusal to send its own permanent representatives abroad provides evidence that the dynamic of reciprocity did not always operate. It was, for centuries, possible to receive resident missions without sending them.

was the European diplomatic dispensation. Whether it would be their own state or someone else's was a political matter.

The expansion of the European society of states was a remarkable achievement. In a process lasting less than 500 years, the various international societies which had developed through thousands of years of human existence encountered one another, discovered what they held in common and what they did not, and on the basis of this their members apparently agreed to the establishment of a single international society based on the achievements of one of their number in this regard. No peoples and no significant territory were left outside its arrangements. Those representing new members seemed to welcome this development with great enthusiasm for it offered them, initially the promise, but eventually the fact, of their own exclusive territorial and political space in which to do what they wished. Certainly, there were those who were left out, indigenous peoples, for example, and those national and ethnic minorities whose independence, it was judged, would cause more problems than their continued bondage. And one might worry about some newcomers who seemed to pocket the privileges and rights of international society membership while ignoring the duties and responsibilities, either because they regarded that society as illegitimate or suffered from some sort of moral deficiency. With the right socialization and modest economic incentives, even they might learn in time. To be sure, guns, as well as money and technology, had played their parts in securing this state of affairs. The diplomatic tradition of international thought, however, allows us to see the extent to which it was primarily a diplomatic achievement, for guns, money and technology would have played their parts in any settlement. This one, however, reflected not the terms of whoever had the most of each, but the form of plural condition for which the Europeans had themselves reluctantly settled in the past and which most of them now had come to value.

Expansion–contraction and re-encounter relations

The world's experience with Europe's expansion suggested to its participants that the prospects for sustained and stable re-encounter between international societies were not good. They might be conducted for extended periods, albeit *sotto voce*, in the background, but they must be seen as truces pending some final settling of accounts in which the international society of the strongest drives out the rest. However, it also suggested, at least to the Europeans, that this was not particularly bad news because it is only first-order societies, not second-order societies of societies, which need to be represented to one another. Everybody needs international societies and, judging by the ease with which encounter relations are established, all peoples start from a very similar place in developing diplomacy. Presumably, then, they all evolve along the same diplomatic road, albeit at different speeds, and once a successful system for handling relations of separateness is developed in one place, it ought to be able to take care of them everywhere else. Other international societies would no longer be needed. They might either vanish, as did the societies of American Indians when their members joined the international society of states, or they might become subordinate members of that society reducing their own members to the status of confederated states or provinces like the states of India and the Malay Peninsula. This was good news, the Europeans concluded, for, even if the need for re-encounter relations between international societies is openly endorsed and promoted, as opposed to tacitly and temporarily conceded, it remains very hard to imagine what they would look like and how they would be undertaken. Once encounters were concluded and discoveries underway, how could relations between a society of states, self-described world empires, multiple tribal systems and communities of the faithful be put on anything approaching an equal footing? The European experience with Church, Empire and territorial states suggested that a hierarchy of types leading to a uniformity of type was the only durable answer.[13]

Remarkable though the establishment of a global international society on European terms was, however, it was also an incomplete achievement. How incomplete is revealed by a simple question. What happened to the international societies displaced by the expansion of the European society of states? They contracted, of course, but it is also widely assumed that they ceased to exist. They were said to have collapsed, as the Aztec and Inca worlds were supposed to have done or to have faded, as pre-colonial, tribal and clan relations in Africa were supposed to have done. Traces might remain as in the lip service new, westernized elites in South American states pay to older patterns of relations and the identities implied by them. They were judged,

---

[13] Neo-realists make a similar point but with far sparser conclusions about what an international system of independent political units must necessarily look like.

however, to be of greatly diminished importance. In some, but crucially not all, respects, this is the case. There no longer is an Aztec Empire, the Arab world has become many things besides that which it never quite was, and the established patterns of relations between the peoples of West Africa have been irreversibly disrupted. However, the distinction between ceasing to exist, on the one hand, and diminished importance, on the other, is becoming more important. Rather than ceasing to exist, altogether, these international societies were displaced vertically. They went underground into cold storage like ideas of the Caliphate and a Chinese civilization as the center of the universe, or they simply became invisible like the patterns which still, beneath the Western radar, hold together different American Indian and Arab tribes, or the peoples of Central and South West Asia respectively. These worlds are often just beneath the surface and sometimes they are all around us, even if, as inhabitants of the international society of states, we are slow to notice them.

The great achievement of European diplomacy in horizontal terms, therefore, was matched by much less success in vertical terms. As Raymond Cohen has demonstrated, the global diplomatic culture that emerged is by no means the effective medium of inter-cultural or transcultural communication which diplomats themselves often believed it to be.[14] This is so because the new, global international society it represents and has helped to construct is shallower than has previously been thought. Indeed, many of the people involved in it remain far more rooted in their own cultures and modes of understanding than they themselves realize. Submerged beneath the surface of the contemporary international society lie not only the compartmentalized cultural roots of the particular states which emerged and with which, to their credit, diplomats attempt to come to grips. There also lie the understandings, conventions and rules of displaced international societies regarding what international relations are, and ought to be, about, and how they might best be organized to secure a different conception of what is good and right. The diplomatic tradition as it emerged in Europe may still be right that re-encounter relations between international societies

---

[14] See Raymond Cohen, *Negotiating Across Cultures: Communication Obstacles in International Diplomacy* (Washington: United States Institute of Peace Press, 1991) and "Language and Negotiation: A Middle East Lexicon," in Jovan Kurbalija and Hannah Slavik (eds.), *Language and Diplomacy* (Malta: DiploProjects, 2001), pp. 67–92.

are very hard to conceptualize, let alone execute. Its assumption that these challenges no longer needed to be embraced, however, now looks far less secure.

Re-encounter relations and vertical diplomacy

We are currently witnessing the re-emergence of other constellations of international life, both old and new, and from both below and above the international society of states. Some of these constellations mesh with existing arrangements more easily than do others. Regional societies of states like those who find their expression in, for example, the EU, Mercosur and the Organization of South East Asian States, can be seen as sub-units of the international society of states for some purposes and take on actor-like qualities for others which allow them to be represented in state-like ways. It is assumed, however, that their dual identity as actors and societies will be, or needs to be, resolved over time in one direction or the other.[15] In contrast, it is not at all clear how others – the societies implied by the restored interest in civilizational and indigenous identities, for example, and some of those implied by liberating and solidarist conceptions of the consequences of globalization – could possibly be made to fit with current arrangements. Where, for example, would the worlds of a restored Caliphate, non-territorial yet sovereign tribes and virtual realities in which people participate on transnational terms, fit if they outgrow their present roles as descant choirs and pressure groups in national capitals and the headquarters of international organizations?

Three possibilities suggest themselves. The first, a renewed separation of the sort that existed between the Roman and Chinese worlds or Europe and the Americas, is all but impossible because of the interaction capacity that currently exists in the world. Only an environmental catastrophe or political disaster of systemic proportions could sufficiently weaken these

---

[15] Consider the debate on the future of Europe, for example, as this is to be seen in John Redwood, *Superpower Struggles: Mighty America, Faltering Europe, Rising China* (Basingstoke: Palgrave Macmillan, 2005) and Anthony Gamble, *Between Europe and America: The Future of British Politics* (Basingstoke: Palgrave Macmillan, 2003). While taking very different positions on which choice Britain should make between Europe and the United States, a strong sense of the European Union being on the road to a more conceptually and practically distinctive and state-like identity is present in both.

capacities to break the world apart. This being so, a second possibility is the successful maintenance of the current international society of states' monopoly position as the only international society, or its replacement by a challenger with similar monopolistic tendencies. After all, several of the alternative international societies suggested above simply present us with the familiar dimension of horizontal expansion and contraction and the dynamics of destruction, absorption and suppression only on their own terms. It is at least conceivable that the world might become Muslim or Chinese at some point in the future, in the same sense that it was European and potentially Communist in the past. Thirdly, what would look to us like a hybrid international society, but would eventually be a different sort of international society *sui generis*, might emerge with different types of members, serving different kinds of purposes, and engaging in both horizontal (with like) and vertical (with unlike) relations. In a sense, something between option two and option three already exists. We can see old anomalies from previous worlds that never completely went away and new sorts of actors all being stuffed into the existing international society of states like groceries into a string bag. And like a string bag, the international society of states has, informally at least, exhibited great flexibility and capacity for accommodation. All the discernible trends indicate, however, that the pressures and burdens placed upon it from a variety of sources are only going to increase.

It is likely, therefore, that we will witness the re-emergence of relations between international societies, that these will best be conceived of in terms of existing in a vertical plain and that, as such, they will impose considerable strain on our diplomatic resources, capacities and, above all, imaginations, as these presently exist. In particular, they will have a profound and discomforting effect upon the world of states because in any formally acknowledged vertical arrangement of international societies, states will no longer be able to claim sovereignty all the way up or all the way down. If, for example, a restored Caliphate co-existed with an international society of states, governments would not exercise control over certain aspects of some of their citizens' relations. Just as when the One Holy Catholic and Apostolic Church was a fact rather than an aspiration, however, this control would be absent not because states chose not to exercise it, but because they had renounced their right, and might even have lost their power, to do so. It would be beyond their remit, belong to another's remit, and be acknowledged as such. Thus, it would also be likely that the idea of a hierarchy implied by vertical relations between international societies, with that of states at its apex, would begin to erode. Indeed, in such a combination of worlds, a society of sovereign states as these have defined themselves to date as constituting the political and legal framework for all else could not exist.

This is not as big a claim as it sounds. Arguably, the universalist claims of the international society of states have already been undermined from below by civil society actors and from above by international organizations. Both have enjoyed some success, for example, in modifying sovereignty claims by seeking to attach them to the performance of duties defined by others.[16] Considerably more movement in this direction could occur without undermining the existence of a society of states that, although no longer sovereign in a formal sense, remained both powerful and effectively independent. And an end to sovereign states, of course, would not spell an end to diplomacy. The relations between international societies (as well as within some of them) would retain a diplomatic character so long as their respective members wished these societies to remain separate, yet in contact. They would also remain diplomatic because, while states would have lost their final say in the organization of all international life, they would not have lost it to anyone else in particular. The world of international societies would remain a plural one in which no one would be in a position to lay down the general law to others. Indeed, for both historical and conceptual reasons, the terms on which the international society of states engaged in vertical relations with other international societies would remain highly advantageous to it for the foreseeable future. Thus, while the prospect of vertical diplomacy and the concessions which it might imply to other international societies may seem daunting, we can already see how need, combined with a series of palliatives, is making it acceptable, even attractive, to states, whatever its eventual consequences for their formal sovereignty. The challenge these developments pose within the established traditions of thought is to think through the terms on which a world of multiple international societies could and ought to be organized. In addition to this, the challenge they pose within the diplomatic tradition is to establish how

---

[16] See Brown and Ainley, *Understanding International Relations* for a useful survey of state sovereignty and human rights debates plus a useful bibliographical essay, pp. 207–31. See Kofi Annan's Nobel Peace Prize lecture for an authoritative linking of sovereignty and human rights (December 10, 2001) at http://nobelprize.org/nobel_prizes/peace/laureates/2001/annan-lecture.html.

peoples can continue to conduct peaceful relations of separateness in the midst of these reflections, discussions and arguments.

In this regard, the tradition is helped by the fact that diplomats in the modern state system already engage in vertical diplomacy, at least on an informal basis, and are often quite good at it. Whenever political agents, district commissioners and soldiers of imperial powers sought to come to grips with the patterns of relations among the tribes with which they had to deal in the past, they might be said to have been conducting a form of vertical diplomacy, even if for distinctly horizontal ends.[17] The diplomatic challenges by the indigenous peoples of the Andes, the tribes along Pakistan's border with Afghanistan, or relations inside the EU taken as a world to itself, are not too different from those which faced their colonial forbears. Indeed, not only do diplomats engage in vertical diplomacy, they increasingly do so with the blessing of their respective governments in the activity known as public diplomacy.[18] When they believe that the substantive gains in terms of increased exports or political influence abroad, and increased investment, jobs and security from terrorism at home outweigh the ideational costs of undermining government-to-government relations, which is to say nearly always, governments push their diplomats to engage in this form of vertical diplomacy.[19] And, of course, the efforts of state diplomats upwards and downwards are mirrored by the attempts of representatives of those societies absorbed, suppressed, or submerged by the expansion of the international society of states to obtain recognition not only of their own particular people, but also of the wider worlds in which their lives and identities were originally, or might be at some time in the future, given meaning. They can be so successful, for example in parts of Africa, that governments abandon the challenge of trying to find state partners in troubled areas and even relinquish responsibility for their own attempts to help other actors from civil society.[20] We can see signs,

---

[17] See, e.g., Hardinge, *Diplomacy in the East*.
[18] See the essays in Jan Melissen (ed.), *The New Public Diplomacy: Soft Power in International Relations* (Basingstoke: Palgrave Macmillan, 2005).
[19] See Lars-Göran Larson, "Modernizing Foreign Services – Facing the Internal Challenge," in Kishan S. Rana and Jovan Kurbalija (eds.), *Foreign Ministries: Managing Diplomatic Networks and Optimizing Value* (Malta: Diplo, 2007), pp. 67–74. See also, for example, Cynthia P. Schneider, "Culture Communicates: US Diplomacy That Works," in Melissen (ed.), *The New Public Diplomacy*, pp. 147–68 and Chapter 13 below.
[20] See Langhorne, *Diplomacy and Governance*, pp. 117–18.

therefore, not only of what Susan Strange termed "the retreat of the state," but also of the retreat of the international society of states, led in part, and paradoxically, by the diplomacy of states themselves.[21]

From *la raison de système* to *la raison des systèmes*

We see states engaged in the vertical diplomacy by which different international societies may discover and re-encounter one another, because its long-term implications for their claims to be sovereign seem to be offset by a range of more instrumental and immediate benefits which their governments believe it can deliver. Herein lies a problem, however. Nearly all the vertical diplomacy we can identify is not conducted with a view to stabilizing relations of separateness between international societies, but with a view to narrow advantage, or to securing or advancing a particular conception of how a single international society should be organized. Thus, while states engage in public diplomacy for particular policy reasons with which we may or may not sympathize, in so doing they seek to reassert their control over peoples whose changing interests and identities are providing them with new ways of participating in international life. Participate, by all means, governments seem to be saying to everyone, but it is the society of our states in which you participate and it is our states that facilitate your participation. In a similar way, the representatives of other international societies engage in vertical diplomacy to open relations and conduct dialogues, but they do so with a view to expanding their worlds and securing, thereby, some contraction of the international society of states.

We have, in short, a situation in which a number of international societies and potential international societies increasingly contend with one another in terms of expansion and contraction, regarding how to organize the world. We have very little idea about whether our present international world will hold together or be replaced by another, and perhaps even less about which outcome we should prefer. We do know, however, that the achievement of either, or something in between, by diplomacy and diplomats is preferable to their achievement by other means. In relations between the members of an international society,

---

[21] Susan Strange, *The Retreat of the State: The Diffusion of Power in the World Economy* (Cambridge: Cambridge University Press, 1996).

diplomacy and diplomats are capable of reducing the duration, intensity and likelihood of violence, whatever the overall direction, if any, of these relations. They are helped in this regard when they enjoy a degree of freedom from the narrow subjectivisms of those they represent and a sense of professional solidarity with each other about their craft, what it values, and what it requires from the world. Thus, just as modern diplomats and those who reflected upon their activity developed a notion of *la raison de système* to which an international society of sovereign states could plausibly give rise, so might those who engage in and reflect upon the vertical diplomacy between layered international societies seek to develop *la raison des système*s by which their work might be facilitated.

Their prospects in this regard, however, will not depend on an exercise of the collective imagination alone. Just like the horizontal diplomacy of the international society of states, vertical diplomacy between international societies involves more than exchanges of views between reasonable people.[22] Bound up with these are considerations of power and interest. Indeed, while the arrangements of an international society reflect what its members think is important, right and good, they reflect disproportionately what those considered powerful in it believe to be important, right and good. As a creation of diplomacy and diplomats, the international society of states was built around these constellations of power, interest and thought about both as they existed in a particular time and place. It may be supposed, therefore, that the re-emergence of other international societies reflects shifts in the distribution of power or, perhaps more importantly, the terms in which power is now understood. A consideration of power, however, draws our attention to the third and final dimension along which international societies can be examined, the continuum between its complete concentration at one end and its complete diffusion at the other. What, then, does the diplomatic tradition of international thought have to tell us about the idea of power being distributed in international societies, what distribution we might desire and how shifts in that distribution might best be handled?

[22] Herbert Butterfield, "Diplomacy," in Ragnhild Hatton and M. S. Anderson, *Studies in Diplomatic History: Essays in honour of David Bayne Horn* (London: Archon Books, 1970), pp. 357–73.

9 Concentration–diffusion

International societies can be thought of in terms of the way anything we think is valuable or interesting in them is distributed, and the extent to which this distribution is concentrated or diffuse. Thus, we can describe the world in terms of concentrations of things like natural resources, products and money, or in terms of people like bankers, soldiers, doctors and children. Our interest in the way people and things are distributed in societies is usually tied to an interest in how those societies are organized and operate and how both shape the lives of their members. To this end, we often try to lump them, or some of them, together calling them power, and ask how this is distributed. This is a notoriously difficult activity to undertake, but the magnitude of the difficulty seems matched only by the magnitude of our compulsion to keep trying and the arguments that break out as a consequence.[1] We keep trying because we believe that an understanding of the distribution of power in any social setting will give us a better understanding of the way things are, what may be attempted, and what is likely to happen. Many of us also believe that such a better understanding will make us stronger, freer and more secure, and this is often, but not always, the case. Whether we are better or happier people because we are stronger, freer and more secure is, of course, another matter.

We think of international relations in terms of the distribution of power and international societies in terms of the extent to which power is concentrated within them. This is an important distinction. The former refers to the distribution of power in any particular situation and is, therefore, short-term, contested and context-dependent. When diplomats spend their days trying, in de Callières' phrase, to find out

---

[1] For an attempt to lump attributes of power together and generate a league table of countries' strengths in aggregated terms see Ray S. Cline, *World Power Assessment: A Calculus of Strategic Drift* (Washington DC: Center for Strategic and International Studies, 1975).

"what is happening," some of this, at least, involves assessments of the distribution of power in any particular situation. And when they act, it may be to influence this distribution in favor of those they represent. When we think in terms of the concentration of power in international societies, however, the suggestion is of a basic structure within which agents engage in international relations of the more transient sort above. This structure is seen as changing by a combination of slow evolution and episodic major crises. When diplomats speak in terms of being "present at the creation" or "a world transformed," usually after big peace conferences, they show a sensibility to this dimension.[2]

Watson's pendulum, referred to earlier, provides a useful starting point for thinking about this diffusion and concentration.[3] At one extreme, we may imagine power completely concentrated in an international society, at its top when viewed vertically, and at its center when viewed horizontally. At the other, we may imagine power completely diffused down to its base or out to its perimeter respectively. In the first case, it would be difficult to speak of an international society existing at all since a society requires multiple members and an international society presumes a developed condition of separateness and capacity for independent action among them. One would have, instead, a totalitarian society consisting of those at the top/center with power and the rest without. In the second case, it would be equally difficult to talk about an international society because the complete diffusion of power would render the idea of members with actor-like abilities, other than individual people, and, hence, relations between them, impossible.[4]

As a result, when discussing the degree of concentration or diffusion of power within actual international societies, we find ourselves describing intermediate stages, and using a mix of different approaches which generate considerable, but probably unavoidable, confusion. The simplest is to borrow from more positivist attempts to explain the dynamics of international systems in terms of poles of power. Thus we hear people speak of multi-polar, bi-polar and, latterly, unipolar worlds.[5] This

---

[2] Dean Acheson, *Present at the Creation: My Years in the State Department* (New York: W. W. Norton and Co., 1969) and George Bush and Brent Scowcroft, *A World Transformed* (New York: Vintage/Random House, 1998).
[3] Watson, *The Evolution of International Society*, p. 17.
[4] See, e.g., Watson, *The Evolution of International Society*, pp. 69–76.
[5] See Waltz, *Theory of International Politics* and Morton Kaplan, *System and Process in International Politics* (New York: Wiley, 1957).

immediately raises difficulties, however, for poles of power are always other things too. For most of the people just cited, for example, it is always a state. There are, however, different types of states or, more accurately, collective entities with state-like attributes or which remind us of states. Most obviously, there are empires, generally distinguished by their exercise of a claim to rule over others that states do not.[6] There are hegemons, distinguished by their capacity to set the rules by which others interact with one another without directly ruling over them. And there are states themselves, possessing authority over their own people, but exerting different amounts of power and influence over other states and people. Less obviously, there are combinations of states – alliances, leagues, associations, for example – that may be viewed for some purposes as concentrations of power themselves, and there are would-be or nearly states like mandates, suzerainties, protectorates and possibly provinces, colonies and territories. There are also political movements in the process of acquiring or losing statehood and, it could be maintained that there are or can be private enterprises which possess some of the features and undertake some of the functions associated with states. Finally, international societies – especially regional ones – may be read for some purposes as actors with state-like qualities.

It may be objected that all these variations are matters of historical interest or, from the point of view of explaining international relations in power terms, of no interest whatsoever. As the recent debate over whether or not the United States should now be viewed as an empire and the growing debate over the status of some private and civil actors in international life both illustrate, however, this is not the case.[7] The idea of empires, if not yet empires themselves, is reviving in discussions about both the centers and the peripheries of power in the contemporary international society. What these discussions allow us to see is how one pole may be viewed as a state, an empire, a hegemon, and all of the above or any combination thereof by different people. And we can extrapolate from this to the possibility of international societies consisting of multiple combinations of these types of actors making the

---

[6] This is a distinction with intensely political dimensions.
[7] See references above to Johnson, *The Sorrows of Empire*, Chomsky, *Hegemony or Survival*, Ferguson, *Colossus* and Magstadt, *An Empire if You Can Keep It*.

question of to what extent power is concentrated very difficult to answer. How, for example, would we say power is concentrated in an international society composed of a weak empire claiming authority over forty percent of the world's population, a strong hegemonic state exercising direct power over ten percent and underwriting the rules for everybody else's interactions, and another fifty states sharing what is left? The problem is not that questions such as these are unanswerable, but that they are capable of yielding multiple answers. And note, these difficulties have emerged before other forms of power – informal, private and ideational, for example, and power's dynamic properties – it may be increasing, decreasing or shifting – have been introduced into the discussion.

For these reasons alone, it might be supposed that diplomats are in the front ranks of those who depreciate power and steer well clear of discussing international relations in terms of its distribution. As noted above, diplomats do not refer to power much and, when they do, they talk about it as picnickers talk about the weather. It is always potentially a factor, one can never ignore it, but try not to let it spoil the day or get in the way of what we are all trying to accomplish. Unless, in their judgment, things are going seriously wrong or those they represent have no respect for one another, most of their conversations revolve around the assertion and interpretation of principles and claims about whether specific conduct, actual or potential, is or is not consistent with them. This is surprising, given how most of us imagine international relations and diplomacy, but the surprise is that diplomatic discourse is no more than a careful and, at times, stylized version of the way the rest of us talk about difficult things. Good diplomats skirt around power and interests for precisely the same reasons the rest of us do. Explicit reference to them is not conducive to good relationships and framing what is going on in terms of power can destroy them. Indeed, I have attempted to follow this convention so far, relegating power to the background in my examination of the diplomatic sense to be made of international societies. As with relationships, so too with analysis and reflection, the explicit introduction of the idea of power can have a terrible reducing effect, whether warranted or not. Nonetheless, and as the continuum between the concentration and diffusion of power in international societies suggests, it cannot be ignored. I shall let it out to prowl and cast its baleful stares, therefore, like a big cat at the circus before, like all lion tamers (and good diplomats), attempting to return it safely to its cage.

Concentration–diffusion and encounter relations

During prehistoric encounters, it seems reasonable to suppose that, in addition to developing the terms on which they could communicate with one another, the parties involved attempted some sort of assessment of each other's strength in terms of numbers, resources and qualities. However, we have no idea of the part played by proto-diplomats in making these assessments or what they had to say about them, nor do we know if anyone moved beyond a consideration in terms of "what we have and what they have." Historic encounters provide us with a little more information. They reveal, for example, the close relationship that often existed between assessments of strength and the likelihood of relations of separateness being conducted by diplomacy. The record, in this respect, is both well known and terrible. The Europeans, the Arabs, the Chinese and the Indians all, when they encountered simple peoples of stone-age cultures, might sweep them aside at the first signs of resistance and take what they wanted. However, historic encounters also reveal the complexity of the relationship that exists between assessments of the other peoples' power and the likelihood of treating them properly. Columbus's sailors might abuse the naked men and women they encountered because they could. They did so, however, because they believed it was all right. They extrapolated from the material inequality of strangers to a judgment about their moral inequality to an extent they did not with the weak among their own people.[8]

Diplomats, as diplomats, have had little to say about grossly unequal encounters of this kind. Objections to the resulting mistreatment were certainly raised, often by people serving in what we could call a diplomatic capacity. However, they were lodged, not on the grounds that peoples were different, separate and should be allowed to remain so, but that they were like us, or could be, once they enjoyed the benefits of civilization and had become assimilated. It is difficult to avoid the conclusion, therefore, that the diplomatic tradition instructs us to engage in diplomacy only when we need to, with need defined in terms of power and our inability to get what we want by other means. Kill or assimilate

---

[8] See N. Scott Momaday, "The Becoming of the Native: Man in America Before Columbus," in Josephy, *America in 1492*, pp. 13–19.

when we can. Negotiate when we must. If so, then this is one of the great limitations upon what diplomatic theory can tell us regarding what people want to know about international relations and believe to be important. However, this limitation is mitigated by the rarity of encounters in which the distribution of power was so lop-sided and apparent that even diplomats would say that diplomacy was not required. The distribution of power in the simple international societies created by encounter relations was rarely apparent, even if it became clearer later. Encounters initially made peoples, or their respective leaders at least, feel insecure, emphasizing their own weaknesses and the strengths, real and apparent, of the other side. One side typically enjoyed the advantages of home field: numbers; familiarity with the locale; and security of supplies. The visitors, in contrast, whatever advantages they might possess in technical means and whatever confidence they might obtain from comparing the new world with the one they had come from, were often far from home at the end of long and tenuous lines of supply.[9] Under such conditions, when neither party could be sure it might prevail in a test of arms, diplomacy could establish a toehold and, once it did, there was always a chance that relations developed out of calculations of necessity might grow into something more.

Thus, while encounter relations generate simple international societies in which it is possible, at least in principle, to talk about how power is concentrated, the historical record and common sense both suggest that this was not done by the participants and would have been very difficult to accomplish. There exists insufficient structure for power to be thought of in terms of the way its concentration or diffusion in an international society affects the interests, opportunities and action of its members. Instead, the parties to encounters made assessments of the distribution of power between them in terms of their daily interactions, the immediate circumstances that shaped them, and the calculations that underpinned them. Very quickly, however, this changed as encounter relations gave way to relations of discovery, for one of the principal

---

[9] See Francis Jennings, "Iroquois Alliances in American History" and "The proceedings recorded by Father Barthelemy Vimont S. J., of the 'Treaty of Brotherhood Between the French, the Iroquois and the Other Nations'," in Reuben Gold Thwaites (ed.), *The Jesuit Relations and Allied Documents*, 73 vols. (Cleveland: Burrows Brothers Co., 1896–1901) and reproduced in Jennings, Fenton, Druke and Miller (eds.), *The History and Culture of Iroquois Diplomacy*, pp. 37–65 and 137–53 respectively.

objectives of these is to map out the contours of the wider world in which peoples find both themselves and other peoples. Then, the shape of the world in terms of power begins to matter much more. Indeed, it is the process by which encounters with the fact of other's existence grows into the discovery that they are different, and sustainably so, that opens the door to thinking systemically in general about international relations. It also opens the door to a particular set of ideas in these terms often associated with diplomacy and diplomats, namely, the theory of the balance of power.

Concentration–diffusion and discovery relations

People, whether as members of, or strangers to, a society, are interested in where power may be said to lie within it. At a simple level they want to know who must be obeyed and who may be safely ignored as they go about their own business. They are also interested in who is likely to make demands of them and of whom they may safely make demands. At a more complex level, they will also become interested in the understandings, conventions and rules that help shape the answers to such questions. The members of a society will generally obtain answers to these sorts of questions, whether or not they actually ask them, by socialization and education. Outsiders are more likely to have to find out for themselves by processes of discovery. Even in encounters between separate peoples, the request to "take me to your leader" or its equivalent not only assumes the existence of a Big Man or someone like him, it also betrays an interest in finding out who it is and what he's like. It is he (or she or they), who must be identified before relations can be properly opened. For reasons such as these, it is possible to identify a longstanding and ubiquitous tradition of interest and inquiry as to how other peoples live and are organized. It is driven initially by practical concerns of the sort above, and these never disappear. They are supplemented, however, by curiosity prompted by the identification of difference. Everyone is interested in travelers' tales, and this curiosity may lead to reflection on what, in general, can be said about how people organize their affairs and how it applies to us. Nearly everyone is interested in the lessons to be drawn from them, especially those that confirm the propriety and wisdom of our own arrangements.

The discovery of knowledge about others, however, poses an old problem in a new way. The problem is that of accounting for the sense of a gap existing between the ostensible or formal arrangements of one's world and what actually goes on. If people saw themselves as a family ruled by a god-king, then how was evidence of faction in the former and imperfection in the latter to be explained? It was so usually by asserting that something had gone wrong. It had been precipitated by either bad people or bad acts and might only be put right by someone good, either by restoring the old correspondence between "is" and "ought" or creating a new one. If this were so, however, then the Hebrew's old question arose. How did others manage to live and prosper under arrangements that were abominations in the eyes of God and, indeed, succeed in doing us harm? It helped immensely that they were others and could be reaffirmed as such, for this might lessen the pressure to set them straight. That they did live differently without the sky falling or the ground opening up, however, entailed that relations with them also had to fall outside the right ordering of such matters. Whatever held relations between different peoples together could not be viewed in the same terms as the sources of the right ordering which kept a people, our people, on the proper path.

No matter how troubling this state of affairs was, however, it did not go away and people – peoples – had no choice but to accommodate themselves and their sense of themselves to it. In this they were helped by the development of two related ideas: that of tolerance; and that of the ways peoples lived being particular expressions of general structures and functions which all human societies needed. The origins of both are conventionally associated in the Western world with its own scientific revolution in early modern Europe. By a series of discoveries, it is suggested, a number of important and longstanding beliefs formerly taken as axiomatic, and sometimes based upon observation, were demonstrated to be wrong. The lessons learned – trust not always to appearances and treat claims which cannot be substantiated with suspicion – raised people's tolerance levels, at least for certain kinds of ambiguity, if not always difference. It allowed them to think of the gap between appearances and reality as more than just something that had to be resolved quickly, and in favor of the former, at that.

However, this story oversimplifies at both its beginning and its end. At the beginning, it stretches the imagination inordinately to accept, for example, that god-kings, feudal monarchs, caliphs and sachems saw gaps between the supposed or right ordering of things and how they sometimes actually were only as evils to be vanquished and sicknesses to be cured. They, or their advisors at least, must have had some sense of a wider way in which things held together even if they dared not openly acknowledge it for fear of making things worse and hurting their own positions. Indeed, one of their major preoccupations must have been reconciling new discoveries and developments with the customary ways of seeing things. And we may point to the Greeks and the beginnings of Western political philosophy as evidence of this tolerance of ambiguity existing long before the scientific revolution. It also stretches our sense of generosity to suggest that the European scientific revolution brought with it only a new measure of tolerance with regard to older systems of thought about how people lived together. It also developed new certainties about what it was now believed had been discovered which led, in turn, to their own difficulties in relations between peoples. Where the scientific revolution deserves full credit, however, is for its part in the development of the second idea, that the ways people lived could be thought of as social arrangements enjoying, in some respects, a life of their own independent of the volition, and possibly even the consciousness, of their members. The societies of the godless and sinful, just like the societies of the God-fearing and good, succeeded or failed for broadly similar reasons. If societies had a life of their own, however, then it followed that so too did the broader international societies of which they might be regarded as members. Yet if it was already acknowledged that the rules which governed them could not be those that governed life within their righteous member, then what might these rules be?

We can see several early attempts to identify answers to this question. Some, like Ibn Kaldûn in North Africa, for example, looked to the basic identities of political communities and noted the different patterns of concerns and actions that distinguished simple agrarian and complex urban peoples from one another.[10] Elsewhere, in Europe, China and India, for example, others identified versions of what Wight called the pattern of power.[11] Irrespective of whether they were God-fearing, virtuous, agrarian, urban or otherwise, neighbors were likely to be enemies and thus friendships were likely to emerge between the neighbors of enemies, giving rise to a checkerboard pattern of international

---

[10] Watson, *The Evolution of International Society*, pp. 117–19.
[11] Wight, *Power Politics*, p. 168. See also the discussion of Kautilya in Watson, *The Evolution of International Society*, pp. 123–5.

relations. It was in the context of Europe's scientific revolution, however, that a far more developed version of thinking along these lines emerged. Theories of the balance of power suggested that in any system of states which value their independence, a tendency will exist for coalitions to form against any single member who becomes strong enough to threaten the independence of the rest. This can be viewed as happening automatically or as a contrivance of good men and women, who understand their circumstances, choosing to act wisely. A pattern of power resulting from the application of subjective and local conceptions of self-interest was transformed from a mere and apparent consequence into a governing system with its own properties and *telos* that bore down on its members whoever they might be.[12]

In both its automatic and contrived forms, the associations of the balance of power with seventeenth-century physics and its science of the motions of the planets are obvious. Notions of movements and orbits generated by forces which attracted and repelled were borrowed directly by theorists of the balance of power. In its more contrived form, however, it is particularly associated with diplomats, for the forces may be at work, but someone has to recognize that this is so and understand what has to be done as a consequence. Thus, this sense of a system which would take care of every state's – great or small – primary concern, securing its independence, provided its members were prepared to restrain others and act with self-restraint themselves, was widely presented as what diplomats discovered when they looked at the world. Indeed, working for an international society in which power was never concentrated enough to allow one member to dominate the rest, or think that it could dominate, was sometimes presented

---

[12] See Butterfield, "The Balance of Power" and Wight, "The Balance of Power," both in Butterfield and Wight, *Diplomatic Investigations*, pp. 132–48 and 149–75 respectively for this discussion. Butterfield favors the view of the balance of power as an effective product of conscious human contrivance which people are not always wise enough to establish. Wight leans towards both the automatic view of its operations and a general skepticism as to whether balances of power – whether automatic or contrived – have actually operated as presented. For a more contemporary consideration of the balance of power see John A. Vasquez and Colin Elman, *Realism and the Balance of Power: A New Debate* (Upper Saddle River: Prentice Hall/Pearson Education, 2003). See François Fénelon, *Adventures of Telemachus* (London: Meadows, Hitch and Hall, 1759) (first published 1694) for the claim that even a virtuous state achieving preponderance would be a danger to all.

as their primary occupation. The result is a powerful and attractive image of the work of diplomats and the business of diplomacy. As a consequence of dealing with the same problems, they can be presented as developing a shared culture given expression by the diplomatic corps in national capitals and the headquarters of international organizations. From their collaboration emerges a particular version of *la raison de système* referred to above by which the balance of power is sustained so that it can keep those they represent in line. A plausible account can be given of the emergence of the modern European diplomatic system in these terms, and a concern for this kind of balancing may be present to varying degrees in the operations of all diplomats. Indeed, the present neglect of the balance of power in world politics may be presented as a symptom of diplomacy's decline and a loss of respect for what it regards as important.

However, this close association of diplomats with maintaining balances of power presents an incomplete picture. It does so because it is based on a misunderstanding of the problems generated for diplomats by seeing international societies in terms of concentrations of power. To take an obvious example, diplomats represent emerging hegemons, as well as those disturbed by their rising power. Indeed, there is a sense in which all states aspire to be hegemons and, thus, it might be said, their general position on the balance of power is shaped by their prospects of success in this regard. China, for example, presently objects to hegemony in the international society as a whole and works with others to oppose it, but seeks to become a hegemon in its own neighborhood. Indeed, success in opposing hegemony at one level is very often intimately linked to the prospects for advancing it at another, and Chinese diplomats, like those of any rising power, must represent both dispositions.[13]

---

[13] See Xiaohong Liu, *Chinese Ambassadors: The Rise of Diplomatic Professionalism Since 1949* (Seattle: University of Washington Press, 2001) and Kishan S. Rana, *Asian Diplomacy: The Foreign Ministries of China, India, Japan, Singapore and Thailand* (Malta: Diplo, 2007). For objections to the notion of diplomats representing an international society in any way which is at odds with the interests of their states as these are articulated by their political masters see G. R. Berridge's "Review of Christer Jönsson and Martin Hall, *Essence of Diplomacy*" on G. R. Berridge's website at www.grberridge.co.uk/booknote.html. See also Dunne, *Inventing International Society*, p. 78 for similar skepticism.

Moreover, the discovery that power is becoming increasingly concentrated in some part of an international society is not necessarily a source of alarm for diplomats or those they represent. If the latter currently have no realistic hegemonic aspirations of their own, they may ask what benefits, in the form of public international goods and private gifts, such a development elsewhere is likely to bring their people, and what will be asked of them in return. No simple conception of independence conditions the answers that can be given to these questions at different times, in different circumstances by different actors. Britain's governments, for example, eventually regarded the prospect of America's assuming its former hegemonic role with a considerable degree of equanimity. Better this hegemony, than no hegemony at all or that of any other power. The reasons for this, although not entirely uncontroversial politically, are easily understood. In contrast, the question of whether Lebanese governments have, or should have, favored a Syrian hegemony over the last thirty years is unanswerable without taking a position on and settling many domestic political questions in the Lebanon first. Diplomats, however, have had to represent Britain and the Lebanon whether these sorts of questions were settled or not.

To complicate matters further, hegemonies have a way of just appearing, rather than growing in such a way as to give others time to worry and respond. Or, more accurately, the consensus that one exists has a way of being triggered by events, for example, the exercise of US military power in the Balkans during a four-year period in the final decade of the twentieth century. It was this, particularly the waging of a series of wars almost without casualties on the winning side, rather than the decline and fall of the Soviet Union, which allowed the idea that a new hegemony existed to develop in sufficient strength as to have some operational consequences for the conduct of international relations. Even when a hegemony appears, like Topsy apparently having "just growed," or its extent is suddenly revealed, the response may still proceed from asking what is in this new state of affairs for us.[14] And the historical record suggests that the answers to these questions vary widely and with important consequences for everyone else. Liberal empires and liberal hegemons, for example, seem nicer than other sorts to more people, but not everyone. Some people in south-eastern

---

[14] Harriet Beecher Stowe, *Uncle Tom's Cabin* (New York: Bantam Classics, 1982).

Europe still miss the days when Russia was able to exert a distinctly illiberal presence which contributed to the terms on which relations were conducted there, while most people in the Middle East appear to believe that they are suffering from a surfeit of America's liberal presence. Whatever their peoples and governments think of particular hegemons newly revealed, however, the response of their diplomats is more likely to be conditioned by the existence of a state of affairs which seems unalterable *pro tem* than by the insight from balance of power theory that the burdens imposed by even a virtuous hegemon will prove intolerable.[15]

In short, the injunction to seek a balance of power often provides diplomats with very little guidance as to what to do, even on the problem it purports to address, safeguarding the independence of states from the depredations engendered by their own egotism. It fails in this regard simply because it presents a general class of problems to which it provides a general solution. This may be attractive to those who think about international relations, and particularly for those who are interested in simplifying the theory and practice of statecraft. For diplomats, however, general problems always have a specific character and must always be managed from the specific positions the diplomats happen to occupy. This does not mean that the diplomatic tradition of international thought has no interest in generalizing and simplifying. What it does entail, however, is that a diplomatic understanding of what can be generally said about concentrations of power in international societies is quite different from the claims of the balance of power theory with which diplomacy has been closely linked. Rather, it is based on direct experience of the sort of shortcomings in this theory noted by International Relations academics, notably its assumptions about actors, interests and, above all, power. Instead of replacing one theory about the consequences of how power is concentrated in an international society with another, however, diplomats find themselves trying to manage the relations of people acting on the basis of different

---

[15] Herbert Butterfield, "Ideological Diplomacy Versus International Order," in Herbert Butterfield, *Christianity, Diplomacy and War* (London: Epworth Press, 1953), p. 117, Geoffrey Wiseman, "Pax Americana: Bumping Into Diplomatic Culture," *International Studies Perspectives*, 6, 4 (November 2005), pp. 409–30, and Paul Sharp, "Virtue Unrestrained: Herbert Butterfield and the Problem of American Power," *International Studies Perspectives*, 5, 3 (August 2004), pp. 300–15.

general theories and particular hunches about what the concentration and the distribution of power may imply at any given time. What then does the diplomatic tradition have to say about shifts in the balance of power and the problem of emerging (or disappearing) hegemons within an international society?

Diplomats and the discovery of shifts in the distribution of power

Through their relations with each other peoples may discover developments like the growth of Athenian power, the emergence of the Soviet threat, the decline of the British Empire, or the consolidation of American hegemony. They argue greatly among themselves and with others about both the facts and the consequences of such developments. The growth of Athenian power, for example, was classically supposed to have created fear in Sparta for its own survival and the survival of the world that sustained it. The Spartans then formed a league with others who shared this fear, or whom they had persuaded to share it, to restrain and reduce Athenian power by any and all means. Up to the point where one or both parties decided upon a war for existence, however, those who conducted diplomatic relations between them made representations to one another with something like the following structure. "This is how our people see the world. This is how our people see your part in making it so. This is how we see the consequences of what you are doing. This is what we think you must do. This is what will happen, depending on how you respond."

Thus people acting diplomatically are simultaneously engaged in presenting the world, as it has been discovered by one side to the other, and doing their best to make the consequential parts of that representation true. In the example above, Spartans acting diplomatically presented the threat posed by Athens and worked for the alliances in which they said that threat would result. It is, however, the representational element in diplomatic action that distinguishes it from, for example, political or military action and provides its distinctive orientation to the conduct of relations of separateness. In our example, the primary concern of Spartans acting diplomatically is not with the existence of an Athenian threat, what to do about it, or how this is to be accomplished. It is with representing how these things are seen and what may follow as a consequence. Historical distance, aided by the formal recitations of rights and wrongs by *proxenois* before assemblies that characterized Greek diplomatic relations, allows us to think of the latter in simple terms.[16] Even as reconstructed above, however, we can see how the task of representation is complex and can be undertaken more or less effectively.

This point may be better illustrated by a brief consideration of the diplomatic consequences of the contemporary world's "discovery" that vast power is now concentrated at a single place within it, namely the United States. I say "world," because it is at this level that discussion most obviously takes place. What are the implications of US hegemony, not for France, Nigeria, China or Brazil, but for the world as a whole? People argue over how powerful the United States may properly be said to be. Does it possess the sort of overwhelming strength that would allow it to dominate the whole world, or is it merely the strongest country in the world? If the former, does it actually dominate the world? Does it even try and, if so, in what sense? Its emphasis on a world of sovereign states with free market and political democracies makes it difficult, by historical standards, to describe the US as an empire or even, given its current attitude to international law, as a conventional hegemon. And yet, there it is, enforcing rules selectively and establishing military bases around the world in an apparently internationalized version of the garrison state. However, people also argue about whether American power is declining (look at what has happened to its relative share of the world's economic activity over the last quarter-century) or in the ascendant (look at the military-technical gap which has developed between it and the rest of the world over the same period).[17] Is its present assertiveness based on desperation, confidence or some combination of both? And, of course, lurking behind these questions are arguments about whether power, in the sense in

---

[16] Nicolson, *The Evolution Of The Diplomatic Method*, pp. 1–16, Watson, *The Evolution of International Society*, pp. 47–76 and Wight, *Systems of States*, pp. 46–119.

[17] See, e.g., Paul Kennedy, *The Rise and Fall of the Great Powers* (London: Fontana, 1989), Henry R. Nau, *The Myth of America's Decline: Leading the World Economy Into the 1990s* (Oxford: Oxford University Press, 1992) and Joseph S. Nye, *Bound to Lead: The Changing Nature of American Power* (New York: Basic Books, 1991) for a representative section of the literature on this theme.

which it is being talked about here, is, or ought to be, as important as it used to be.[18]

At the international society level, as opposed to the world level, in contrast, the questions raised by the spectacle of American power are generally dealt with much more circumspectly by governments, politicians, soldiers, but by diplomats especially. For them, the question is not "what do we do about American power?" or, in the case of American diplomats, "how do we continue to build and maintain our power, and what shall we do with it today?" It is, "how do we manage our part of a world in which this development – the whole ensemble of discussions about American power – is occurring as one development among many in the relations of our peoples?" A multiplicity of answers exist to this question, but from among them diplomats are unlikely to pick those suggested by balance of power theory or by any one-dimensional theory which purports to offer a better account of what is going on. Thus, we see very little evidence of diplomats, even French diplomats, advising their governments to balance the US by building up the strength of their own countries or by entering into new alliances with each other negotiated for this purpose.[19] Nor do we see American diplomats seeking to restrain whatever hegemonic ambitions the United States may be said to have for the overall good of the international society of which it is a member and from which it benefits.

Instead, a diplomatic understanding leads them to focus upon how relations are best conducted and relationships maintained in the context of these developments. Is there, for example, a better or worse way, in terms of its impact on existing relations, in which actions widely understood to involve the expansion of American power and influence might be undertaken? Is there a better or worse way in which activities widely understood as securing cooperation against this development might be

---

[18] Joseph S. Nye, *Soft Power: The Means to Success in World Politics* (New York: Public Affairs, 2004) and *The Paradox of American Power: Why the World's Only Superpower Can't Go It Alone* (Oxford: Oxford University Press, 2002).

[19] Robert A. Pape, among others, has developed a distinction between "hard" and "soft" balancing. The former conveys the traditional notion of countering other states by building up one's own military strength or allying with others. The latter suggests a more general notion of making life more diplomatically difficult for the target state as, for example, Russia, Germany and France were said to have done for the US at the UN in the run-up to the second American-led war against Iraq. See Robert A. Pape, "Soft Balancing Against the United States," in *International Security*, 30, 1 (Summer 2005), pp. 7–45.

undertaken? As the widely noted shortcomings of the diplomacy leading up to the second US-led war against Iraq strongly suggest, in specific circumstances practical answers can be given to both questions. The Americans should have conveyed a stronger impression of caring about what their allies and friends maintained, and their allies and friends should have acted in ways that made it easier, not harder, for the Americans to listen to them. One can build up power and exercise it, just as one can object to and counter it, if one wants, in ways that put more or less stress on existing relationships.

It may be objected that this is to deal with important issues of international relations at the tactical or superficial level only. The substantive problem is Athenian or American power and what to do about it, or the substantive problem is the opposition of outlaws, rogues and opportunists to those who would uphold a decent international order and what to do about it. Clearly, the diplomats' response that life is lived more tactically and superficially than is generally supposed, does not always secure a sympathetic hearing from governments or people. If so, then the substantive aim – in our example above the drive to extend/counter Athenian/American power – can override the diplomatic preoccupation with relations and relationships. When substance, in this sense, prevails, however, then the challenge of managing the impact on existing relationships of the different discoveries about the extent to which power may be said to be concentrated in an international society begins to fade. Instead, it is replaced by the need to manage the increased distancing and stronger desire to hold one another at arm's length that occur as a result. What then does the diplomatic tradition have to tell us about those circumstances in which peoples discover concentrations of power which they dislike so much that, in their responses to them, they appear willing to put their existing relationships at risk?

Concentration–diffusion and re-encounter relations

It is conventionally assumed that such circumstances force issues and require difficult choices involving appeasement or confrontation. If the former course is successfully adopted, then relations resume on the terms of the new dispensation and presumably improve. If the latter course is adopted, then diplomacy yields to other ways of conducting relations of separateness, principally by force. Certainly, re-encounter relations in these circumstances are more difficult to conduct than the ones by which separateness is routinely reproduced. For a number of reasons, however, the conventional understanding again over-simplifies what can happen when concerns about the concentration of power in an international society surface as arguments about balance, hegemony and the conduct of particular states or other actors. It does so primarily because the situation is rarely so dire as is commonly assumed, even after the line between peace and war is actually crossed. As diplomatic histories reveal, where diplomacy is said to have failed, its failure is rarely as hard to avoid as it often appears after the fact. The inevitable march to war that remains in the collective postwar memory is often at odds with the reality of multiple possibilities which actual international crises hold. The outbreak of the Second Word War, for example, hinged on Hitler's last-minute agonizing over the Anglo-French guarantees to Poland. The 1914 crisis, in which far more civilized leaders than Hitler saw themselves on tragic collision courses of almost mechanical provenance, could be said to have turned on the British cabinet's indecisiveness about its Belgian commitment. And in both US-led wars against Iraq, all turned on whether Saddam Hussein would keep his nerve and refuse to give way.

When force is resorted to, diplomacy need not necessarily come to an end. In fact, in the heyday of modern or classical diplomacy, it was expected to continue. Only in a war for annihilation might diplomacy cease completely and there are few, if any, examples of these actually occurring. Even those avowedly intended as such rarely turn out that way. Franco had to talk to the Republicans, and the Nazis had to negotiate with the representatives of all sorts of peoples whom they were trying to annihilate, even if only about surrender terms (latterly their own). In the age of total war, diplomacy continued, with even the attacks on Hiroshima and Nagasaki having their communicative components spelled out by unofficial and third party contacts. And, of course, the trend in the last half-century has been towards wars of both a limited and unofficial character. Limiting wars has underlined their communicative significance while keeping them unofficial has made communications between the belligerents easier.[20] Bargaining

---

[20] Limited warfare is a difficult and controversial concept, however, and official wars have fallen out of fashion for a number of reasons including the identities of the parties to them and their desire to preserve a freedom of action which an official declaration would not permit. The second war against Iraq suggests that the trend to limits in objectives is being modified.

theories of the sort produced by Thomas Schelling, and following Clausewitz's insight about war as the continuation of politics by other means, encourage us to think of this phenomenon in terms of a seamless continuum existing between peaceful and violent means of obtaining what we want from others.[21] And even Clausewitz's aphorism does not suggest that "other means" are suspended because the course of war has been chosen. Within governments avowedly committed to placing their interests above relationships there are war parties and peace parties, and so-called hawks and doves are rarely unconditionally so. Indeed, as the prospects for conflict increase, so too may the volatility of their respective positions on what should be done. In short, there always exist multiple opportunities for talking, and thus for diplomacy, until someone actively, and completely, refuses to talk.

That diplomacy is distinguished by its emphasis on the opportunity for conversations which continue to exist in the worst possible situations is reasonably well-noted, especially by its critics.[22] Equally distinctive, but less noted, however, is the diplomatic tradition's understanding of what should be going on in those conversations if they are to have a prospect of success. They should depreciate power for all the reasons noted earlier. In particular, however, they should avoid direct references to the distribution of power or shifts within it, except perhaps in the aftermath of a war or trial of strength which one side has more-or-less clearly lost. Thus, for example, until it was defeated, Nazi Germany was discussed and presented by diplomats as a power among powers, albeit a criminal one from which unconditional surrender had to be obtained. Even as its military fortunes declined, it was not presented as anything less. After the Cuban missile crisis, the United States and the Soviet Union reached an agreement about missiles in Cuba and Turkey that only indirectly confirmed that a shift in the overall distribution of power in the world had not taken place. And neither the Soviet Union's eventual collapse nor the United States' resulting ascendancy was directly addressed by negotiations. Instead, they were dealt with obliquely and by reference to second-order specifics such as the new forms of government

---

[21] Thomas Schelling, *The Strategy of Conflict* (Cambridge, MA: Harvard University Press, 1960) and Klaus von Clausewitz (edited and translated by Michael Howard and Peter Paret), *On War* (Princeton: Princeton University Press, 1976).
[22] See for examples of this *genre*, Con Coughlan, "John Bolton thinks diplomats are dangerous" and "Doves are winning the war on Iran," both in *The Daily Telegraph*, November 30, 2007 and December 4, 2007 respectively.

and the new principles of relations between states in Europe made possible by the end of their rivalry.[23]

It is tempting to conclude, therefore, that diplomacy and diplomats never directly affect changes in the balance of power. They merely confirm what those they represent now believe it to be by discussing old issues on new terms. Thus, we do not see diplomats calling for the reduction or securing of America's position in the current international society by direct negotiations. Instead, they seek two other things: general settlements of outstanding issues of the sort designed to deliver what is presented as a just, prosperous and lasting peace; and negotiations about the way in which such settlements are to be negotiated. The calls for general settlements are premised on what may be termed "underlying causes" arguments that have a surprisingly similar structure. Remove the arrangements that leave people in general poor, oppressed and insecure and replace them with arrangements that allow them to be comfortable, free and safe. Everyone agrees that a more peaceful and, hence, more prosperous world will result. The only disagreements, and of course they are major ones, are over which set of arrangements currently pertains and, thus, which set of arrangements may be said to be the sources of our present discomfort and future happiness respectively. It is over these disagreements that negotiations about negotiations are generally conducted. If we can get the right sort of modifications to the arrangements by which the members of our international society conduct their relations with one another, these will either constrain and finesse the power that has been standing in the way of progress or emancipate the right sort of power from the constraints that have historically hindered it. What the right sort of modifications actually are, however (for example, more freedom for the weak and less for the strong or more power for the right and less for the wrong?) and the assumptions which underlie them are precisely what is at stake, or can be, if negotiations get out of hand.

Small wonder, therefore, that from most perspectives, most of the time, nothing much seems to happen in international negotiations. Instead, projects for reform and transformation are thwarted and final settlements postponed or frozen. Yet the collisions which logical analysis of the respective negotiating positions dictates must happen, and

---

[23] See the text of the *Treaty On Conventional Armed Forces In Europe* (November 19, 1990) available at www.fas.org/nuke/control/cfe/cfebook/appenda.html.

which the media often invites us to anticipate as a consequence of these failures, somehow neither occur nor are averted. This is so because, while the opportunities to talk, even on so fundamental an issue as how power is concentrated in an international society, are limited almost only by how willing people are to talk, their ability to talk about it in the way they want to is severely limited by the existence of the other party. Thus, even though, as relations worsen, people may no longer be constrained in what they say by their desire to maintain a relationship with one another, each other's existence in itself entails, not only that they cannot have their way, they also still cannot have their say, in the sense of saying what they want. Israel decries the existence of a Hamas government, for example, and Hamas decries the existence of Israel, and still the existence of both involves them in relations they maintain they will not have. For much of the time, all that varies is how effectively those relations are conducted (although, as a matter of policy, one or both parties may not be interested in effectively conducted relations).

So what do the members of an international society talk about or, more accurately, what is going on when their diplomats meet on big disputes that one or both parties have decided must be resolved on their own terms, yet nothing seems to happen? For the most part, these diplomats are seeking to stabilize re-encounter relations on new and more distant terms. This may be presented in terms of working towards a future, and mutually agreeable, state of affairs or in more incremental terms such as negotiating a "road map" for charting a course of step-by-step progress.[24] We cannot agree, they seem to say, but we are working/moving towards a future point at which we can agree or, more subjectively, at which the other fellow will be nudged around to our point of view. From a diplomatic, as opposed to a policy, perspective, however, such talks are better understood in terms of a version of the old image of mountaineers bound together. In this one, however, they are tumbling down the slope and reaching out for the branches they hope will be strong enough to arrest their mutual descent. Establishing new terms on which re-encounter relations can be conducted may be a drawn-out process, and its achievement may consist of

---

[24] The "road map" refers to a Middle East peace plan set out in 2002 by which a quartet of "powers" (the US, Russia, the EU and the UN) would supervise a sequenced series of moves and declarations by Israel and the Palestinians leading to the creation of a Palestinian state.

nothing more than an agreement to continue, or resume, talking. Reaching such an agreement, however, is a precondition for recovering a state of affairs in which a relationship can be characterized once again by relations of discovery, rather than relations of re-encounter.

Political power, diplomatic talk and other people's problems

We may see, therefore, that the diplomatic tradition of international thought offers no general preferences regarding the diffusion or concentration of power in an international society. Nor do diplomacy and diplomats enjoy a special relationship with the balance of power theory often associated with them in the other traditions of international thought. In a sense, they are pioneers of the idea that identity, as well as a host of other contingent factors, matters in shaping reactions to how power is concentrated or changes in that concentration.[25] Sometimes, people can face the prospect of being dominated, in these terms, by those who are like them with a degree of equanimity, when the prospect of being dominated by those whom they view as different is intolerable. Consider the European experience with the United States and the Soviet Union respectively, in this regard. Sometimes, the reverse is the case. Consider how imperial rule as the rule of superiors can seem more acceptable than rule by one's own kind as equals on occasions, or even how American pre-eminence was preferable to Europeans than that of one of their own, Germany or France, after the Second World War. Therefore, diplomats are less concerned with the distribution of power than they are with how the preferences about it of those they represent may best be expressed if peaceful relations are to be maintained. Usually, this is not as difficult as it sounds. These preferences are buried in a host of other concerns with which the members of an international society engage in relations with one another.

The moment at which a sufficient number of members comes to regard the concentration of power, as they understand it, to be unhealthy remains the moment of danger, of course. Again, however, it need not be as dangerous as external observers often assume. The diplomatic challenge is to find and stabilize a new basis for relations that, while possibly characterized by more distance, will not require that

---

[25] See Buzan, *From International Society to World Society?* and *The United States and the Great Powers* for extensive treatments of these themes.

arguments about the concentration of power be definitively settled. Even talking about a new basis for relations may, itself, constitute a new basis for relations more stable than is commonly supposed. Keeping talking may prove difficult, especially if it is understood to confer a form of recognition on those one does not wish to recognize as such, or recognize at all. The injunction of the diplomatic tradition remains clear, however, to keep talking if this is at all possible. Why is it so important and valuable to keep talking, however? As a skeptical colleague noted, of course diplomats stress the importance of keeping talking, because this is what diplomats do.[26] We all have our favorite examples of diplomatic talks that were, or are, futile. The UN Military Staff Committee met for some thirty years merely to record itself meeting, and progress in talks to end the wars in Korea and Vietnam was, infamously, delayed by disagreements over the size of flags and the shape of a table, respectively. Today, talks on genocide, the status of women, climatic degradation and environmental destruction run on while, in Marysia Zalewski's vivid phrase, "still the bodies keep piling up."[27]

This is certainly an incendiary, and possibly a powerful, challenge. A diplomatic tradition of international thought may provide us with new and valuable insights into how quickly international societies come into being when peoples who are separate, and regard themselves as such, enter into relations with one another. It may provide us with insights into how relations of separateness might be best conducted, if they are not themselves to become another source of human misery. But how can such a tradition help us address the claim that terrible things go on despite the successful conduct of relations of separateness and that, indeed, their successful conduct may be a contributing factor? It does so by showing how, if we view international societies as arising out of relations of separateness, as the diplomatic tradition suggests we

---

[26] Eugene Goltz, private conversation.
[27] Marysia Zalewski, "'All These Theories Yet the Bodies Keep Piling Up': Theorists, Theories and Theorizing," in Steve Smith, Ken Booth and Marysia Zalewski, *International Theory: Positivism and Beyond* (Cambridge: Cambridge University Press, 1996), pp. 340–53. The size-of-flags argument, associated with the negotiations to end the Korean War, surfaced briefly during US Secretary of State James Baker's talks with Tariq Aziz, his Iraqi counterpart, in their Geneva talks just prior to the first US-led war on Iraq. See James A. Baker (with Thomas M. Defrank), *The Politics of Diplomacy: Revolution, War and Peace, 1989–1992* (New York: G. P. Putnam's Sons, 1995), p. 356.

should, these problems acquire a second-order character. If one wants to put a stop to terrible things, then what matters is not the integration, expansion and concentration of international societies *per se*. Indeed, worrying and arguing about these in an insistent way can itself be a source of terrible things. What matters is how relations are to be maintained in the midst of these and other processes, and in the midst of the arguments to which they give rise.

As noted above, the reformulation of the relationship between diplomacy and international societies suggested by a diplomatic understanding suggests that the terms in which most people think about the conduct of international relations are, in a sense, misguided. This may seem a solitary and slender gain for an approach touted by practitioners and those who study them alike, for its closeness to what actually happens in real international relations. It may also be seen as a dangerous one if it is purchased at the expense of saying that most people do not understand international relations and that the terrible predicaments in which they find themselves are in some sense second-order problems. No wonder all diplomats have to say when things go seriously wrong is that it is not their fault, and no wonder that the fact that this is usually the case does so little to redeem their reputations. What, therefore, does the tradition tell us besides the general observation that people often think about relations of separateness in terms which are unhelpful to their effective conduct, the general injunction to stop worrying about how international societies are configured, and the general advice to keep talking? To answer these questions, we must shift our focus from what the diplomatic tradition of international thought can tell us about international societies and consider how these general observations might contribute to our theorizing about how specific international issues are, and might be, handled.

PART IV

Thinking diplomatically about international issues

Mountolive was swayed by the dangerous illusion that now at last he was free to conceive and act, the one misjudgment which decides the fate of a diplomat.

Lawrence Durrell, *Balthazar*

10 Rogue state diplomacy

The diplomatic tradition of international thought suggests that how international societies are configured and might best be configured matters less than how relations are conducted in the midst of the arguments to which these questions give rise. This seems at once to be a big claim that relegates a great deal of international theorizing to the background, and one that does not seem to let us say a great deal. Relations of separateness require special skills. Peoples absorbed and driven by the content of those relations will be unlikely to exercise those skills. Hence, diplomacy and diplomats, or at least people equipped with a diplomatic understanding, are needed to make the world, any plural world, run more smoothly. Often, it will do so if peoples, or their representatives, keep talking and do not worry if the talks do not seem to be getting anywhere. Anyone who has read this far might be forgiven for thinking these insights dearly purchased and not particularly useful. They may seem at best platitudinous, mere exhortations for people to be good and wise in unspecified ways. And at worst, they may seem harmful, promoting a complacent and unwarranted quietism that aggravates those who see the existing order of things as threatening and those who see it threatened in equal measure.

Accordingly, in this final section of the book, my argument shifts from what a *diplomatic understanding* can tell us about international societies and how we might live in them, to what *diplomatic thinking* can tell us about particular international problems and issues that worry people. In making this shift, I want to accomplish two things. The first is to demonstrate that diplomatic thinking can, indeed, say useful and interesting things about contemporary issues. The second is to demonstrate that it does so by focusing on international relations, as opposed to what they are about, and by treating them as distinct and different from other sorts of human relations. The insights and understandings generated by this approach are very hard to see once you have been drawn into arguing about content and accepting that international relations are better viewed in terms of their similarities with other human relations rather than their differences.

What follows then are four "issue" chapters on: rogue state diplomacy; greedy company diplomacy; crazy religion diplomacy and dumb public diplomacy. I have selected them for their general topicality. Most attentive people in most places around the world agree that each of them presents a significant development with problems, even if they might not agree on the specific identities of those who pose the problem in each case. Thus, for example, there may be several rogues or one great rogue depending on one's point of view. Companies may be too greedy, but some may be more than others and greed may not be necessarily bad. Christian crusaders might be said to vie with radical Islamicists as manifestations of crazy religion. And, while it is generally agreed that the public keeps getting the wrong end of the stick on international issues, the questions of which public, which stick and why they get it wrong remain hotly contested. I have also deliberately framed the issues in "undiplomatic" terms to reflect the extent to which diplomacy is generally expected either not to handle them well or not to handle them at all. In their different ways, each issue can be seen to involve people to whom there is, or ought to be, "just no talking" and thus who have to be dealt with by other means. In addition, although this was not one of my original selection criteria, three of them may be said to emanate from the "awkward squad" of international institutions as far as international societies of states are concerned: nationalism; the market; and transcendent religious faith, and as malign emanations at that, while the fourth, the public, potentially poses the most extensive solidarist challenge conceivable to the plural condition of humanity on which the argument in this book is premised.[1]

History, International Relations and the idea of rogue states

At various times in the course of international history, certain states have been identified as rogues or outlaws by other states and, sometimes, by nearly all the members of an international society.[2] They are

---

[1] This last observation was prompted by remarks made by Barry Buzan at the ISA Convention in San Diego, 2006. His comments were restricted to nationalism and the market, however.

[2] Gerry Simpson, *Great Powers and Outlaw States: Unequal Sovereigns in the International Legal Order* (Cambridge: Cambridge University Press, 2004). See also

said to be rogues because of a combination of internal characteristics they possess and external actions they undertake which violate the conventions, understandings and rules that currently prevail about good international conduct. There is often said to be a relationship between the internal political arrangements of such states and their external actions. Bad arrangements at home may lead to bad behavior abroad, although this is not necessarily so. Whether states which have bad arrangements at home but which are well behaved abroad may be termed rogues is often a matter of considerable controversy, as is the reverse phenomenon, naming well-ordered states as rogues because of their bad international behavior.[3] Naming states as rogues within an international society serves much the same purpose as naming individuals as such within a society. Once so named, the offenders are on warning that their membership of society – with its attendant rights and protections – has been called into question and that something may be done about them. The major difference, of course, is that within a society such measures are widely seen as being authoritatively undertaken, whereas in an international society this reservoir of authority is regarded as being much shallower. Even when an international organization is mobilized for this purpose, therefore, it retains a highly political character in which the right and motives of the namers can be as much an issue as the conduct and character of the named.

It is important to emphasize that the phenomenon of rogue states is not new, because it is often presented as such as a way of amplifying the effects of identifying a state as a rogue.[4] Not only is it bad, its accusers want to say, it is so in a way which is unprecedented and, thus, unprecedentedly worrying. Nonetheless, regimes sustained, either directly or indirectly, by banditry and piracy have been variously regarded as rogues or outlaws in the past. Charges of roguery have permeated the

---

Gentili, A., "Three Books on Embassies," in Berridge, G. (ed.), *Diplomatic Classics*, pp. 57–74 for a reference to an "Embassy of Criminals."

[3] The complexities of the relationship between internal arrangements and external conduct of those currently identified as rogues is effectively explored in Mary Caprioli and Peter F. Trumbore, "Ethnic Discrimination and Interstate Violence: Testing the International Impact of Domestic Behavior," *Journal of Peace Research*, 40: (2003), pp. 5–23. The political character of the process of naming rogue states, especially well-ordered states on the basis of their external conduct, is well captured by William Blum, *Rogue State: A Guide to the World's Only Superpower* (Monroe: Common Courage Press, 2005) and T. D. Allman, *Rogue State: America At War With the World* (New York: Nation Books, 2004).

[4] Simpson, *Great Powers and Outlaw States*.

arguments surrounding both the rise of revisionist great powers and the efforts of status-quo ones to maintain their own places in the scheme of things. An obvious example of a state accused of roguery in all these terms would be England, and few of the great powers, indeed probably no state which has wielded power to thwart others, has escaped such charges on occasions. Certainly, the use and significance of the term have greatly increased since the end of the Cold War with the United States and its allies identifying a small number of middle and minor powers as rogues and outlaws because of the way they treat their own populations, their support for international terrorist movements and their pursuit of weapons of mass destruction together with the means to deliver them around the world.[5] This latter development, particularly, is said to give an old phenomenon a new and terrible significance. Unless they were great powers themselves, rogue states in the past were no more than local nuisances for particular great powers who presented them as an offence to general moral sensibilities. Now, by developing nuclear, chemical and biological WMD, they are said to pose a potential threat to great powers in general, everyone else and the order sustaining international life.

As such, the phenomenon of rogue states poses challenges to theorists laboring in all of the established traditions of international thought. It does so by creating a tension between their respective first principles and the basic terms on which they like to consider international relations, on the one hand, and the terms of the debates about foreign policy into which they are invariably drawn, on the other. Realist first principles, for example, ascribe a general character to all states. They are interest-driven power-seekers, differentiated primarily by the amount of power they possess and, to a lesser extent, by their status-quo or radical orientation to the existing distribution of power and the order sustained by it.[6] In such a scheme, questions of roguery should not arise or, at least, not be important, for all states will do what they can and suffer what they must. If we shift from first principles to the practical history of realist traditions, however, we can see how the practice of identifying rogues is longstanding within them. Indeed, the call to arms by which classical realists attempted to alert the populations of liberal

---

[5] Robert S. Litwak, *Rogue States and US Foreign Policy: Containment After the Cold War* (Baltimore: Johns Hopkins University Press, 2000), pp. 74–5.
[6] Morgenthau, *Politics Among Nations*, pp. 36–68.

democracies to the realities, as they understood them, of power politics was premised on the identification of wicked and ruthless regimes like Nazi Germany and the Soviet Union who would win unless others started to take these realities seriously. These rogues, however, were indisputably great powers capable of posing great threats to everyone else. Whether contemporary rogues pose threats of similar magnitude is a matter of considerable controversy for realists as much as everyone else, as evidenced by the arguments between those who see them as mortal threats and those who see greater dangers in the consequences of acting as if they are.[7]

Rationalist first principles, too, do little to suggest that the phenomenon of rogue states is interesting or important. Even if the rational tradition offers a richer set of interests than those suggested by realists, within it states themselves remain all of a type. They are interest-maximizers undertaking cost-benefit analyses of different courses of action in environments which may be shaped to encourage certain types of behavior and to discourage others. They vary only in how sensibly they are organized to go after what they and those who live in them want. This lack of anything distinctive to say about rogues may appear as something of a surprise, given the interest of the rational tradition in the possibility and desirability of mitigating political anarchy by rule-constrained or even rule-governed international societies and regimes. Those who flaunt the rules and break their promises, however, are still assumed to be actors susceptible to sanctions and incentives, who vary along a continuum in this regard between smart and dumb, not good and evil. Even in its more humanistic and liberal iterations, the rational tradition seems to follow the old Christian injunction to hate the sin and not the sinner, a position that, while laudable, leaves little to be said about rogue states other than to reject completely the way they are presented in contemporary political discourse. We may speak of them as rogues, but they are merely states and leaders for whom the right mix of incentives and sanctions has yet to be achieved. The right mix may not be achievable, but then the target is regarded as mad, rather than bad.

The rational tradition, no less than the realist one, has little to say about the idea of rogue states based upon first principles. Not so the radical tradition. From within the latter, rogues or, at least, the naming

---

[7] See, e.g., John J. Meirsheimer and Stephen M. Walt, "An Unnecessary War," in *Foreign Policy*, 134 (January/February, 2003), pp. 50–9.

of them as such, is taken very seriously, and the moral challenge implicit in the use of terms like rogue and outlaw is embraced and engaged. In the more overtly political versions, however, a mirror image of the conventional arguments about who are rogues and why is presented. It is the great powers and those they serve, in these views, who make rules, impose them on everyone else, yet hold themselves exempt. Since these rules maintain the dominance of the powerful and rich over the weak and poor and support the process by which the latter are exploited by the former, it is the rule-makers and enforcers who may properly be regarded as rogues.[8] The usual suspects are viewed in the more political versions of the radical tradition as either lesser rogues, some of whom have earned the enmity of their former patrons, or not as rogues at all, but as participants and leaders in processes of resistance to the prevailing state of affairs. More theoretically grounded expressions of the radical tradition, in contrast, present rogues, not in opposition to the prevailing state of affairs, but as in some sense produced by it and for it through discursive practices.[9] The production of rogues, in this sense, allows the boundaries of acceptable conduct, never clearly fixed in either time or space, to be specified as needed and facilitates their enforcement. The idea of identities by which an international society is constituted being produced is suggestive, but such accounts remain anchored in the same general emphasis on relations of dominance and exploitation informing their more political cousins. This leads them, albeit later rather than sooner, to the same mirror image and oppositional accounts of what is going on when the governments of great powers identify other states as rogues.

It may be seen, therefore, that the starting assumptions of all the major traditions of international thought cast doubt upon the existence and significance of rogue states as both of these are conventionally understood. They all suggest that nothing much is to be gained by the use of the term and much, in terms of sound policy and human happiness at home and abroad, may be lost. Nevertheless, proponents of all three traditions find themselves drawn into a public debate about rogue states whose core assumptions to a great extent reflect the foreign policy

---

[8] See, e.g., Blum, *Rogue State*, Noam Chomsky (with Edward W. Said), *Acts of Aggression: Policing Rogue States* (New York: Seven Stories Press, 1999) and Noam Chomsky, *Rogue States: The Rule of Force in World Affairs* (Cambridge, MA: South End Press, 2000).

[9] Simpson, *Great Powers and Outlaw States*.

priorities of governments and whose terms are very much framed by mass media's need to secure the attention of its audiences. In difficult times this is not so much a debate as a highly polarized and politicized argument in which the protagonists move along predictable and parallel lines. Thus the basic question this argument revolves around is not "are there rogue states?" but "who are they and what is to be done about them?" Their own first principles notwithstanding, therefore, many international theorists engage enthusiastically in what are actually arguments about foreign policy. They can do so usefully at times, highlighting, for example, the part which naming rogues as such can play in mobilizing domestic and foreign support for doing something about them.[10] Does it work to give people something "clearer" than the truth?[11] If so, may there be consequences in terms of one's subsequent freedom of action in dealing with parties you have made into personalized and demonized opponents? Indeed, at least one expert on rogue states investigates them in terms of whether they can be plausibly presented for US foreign policy purposes as replacements for the threat once said to be posed by the Soviet Union.[12] In such reflections, however, the question of whether or not there are rogues, an issue about which international relations theory might be expected to have something to say, merges into and is quickly overwhelmed by instrumental concerns given coherence only by a vulgar Machiavellian concern with what will work in terms of given foreign policy objectives.

The gravitational pull exercised by foreign policy concerns over international theorists and theory is no more in evidence than in their contributions to the arguments about whether to engage, contain or remove rogues. The consistency of their responses is no different from anyone else's in that it is based on dangerous combinations of political preferences, foreign policy priorities and threat assessments. Why is Cuba on America's list of terrorist states and Saudi Arabia not, and how can Syria be moved off the list while Libya stays on?[13] Is North

---

[10] See, e.g., Brigid Starkey, "Negotiating With Rogue States: What Can Theory and Practice Tell Us?" *DSPDP* (Leicester: Diplomatic Studies Programme, 56, May 2000).

[11] Warren Cohen on the need to "oversell" a threat to the public, cited in Robert S. Litwak, *Rogue States and US Foreign Policy*, p. 88.

[12] For the explanation of rogues in terms of the US "needing" an enemy after the collapse of the Soviet Union see Raymond Tanter, *Rogue Regimes*.

[13] Robert S. Litwak, *Rogue States and US Foreign Policy*, pp. 75–9.

Korea peacefully engaged because the regime is strong and the threat it poses is great, and was Iraq destroyed for the same reasons or because its regime was weak and the threat it posed was small? What do both cases tell us about the prospects for foreign policy towards Iran? Questions such as these are interesting, important and, if we let them, touch the very core of our basic political and moral orientation towards our own countries and the world at large. They have to be answered, however, only in the sense that those with power believe they need answers to them on the basis of which they are going to act. And they can only be answered in terms of scripts about politics and social action deeply rooted in what is going on in each country. The answers are nearly always clear, but they are many, and the arguments that produce them are heated, predictable and make conversation very difficult.

Academics, especially international theorists, are aware of the difficulties of debating foreign policy in foreign policy terms. Robert Litwak and Alexander George, for example, note the lack of correspondence between the debate in the US about engagement, containment and roll back and the reality of how foreign policy is conducted. While they are discussed as alternative courses of action, in real life it is perfectly possible for a government to explore opportunities for better relations with a hostile regime while, at the same time, maintaining its guard against its further encroachments and plotting all along to destroy it if this is deemed necessary.[14] At any given time, multiple actors with multiple interests and agendas are contributing to the formulation of and execution of foreign policy. Governments find it very difficult to be rational actors in any straightforward sense or even satisficers, no matter how hard they try. They do try, however, and ought to, and George, in particular, is interested in how they might be helped to try harder and better. Foreign policy coherence must be imposed, to the extent that this is possible, by the clear and authoritative articulation of objectives with which means must be matched.

This may well be a wise way to attempt to proceed when actually making foreign policy. As anyone who has attempted to identify the center of gravity in the recent Bush administration's policy towards Iraq before the fall of Saddam will realize, however, George's advice to match ends to means is of little use in the analysis, as opposed to the

---

[14] Alexander L. George, *Bridging the Gap: Theory and Practice in Foreign Policy* (Washington DC: United States Institute of Peace Press, 1993), pp. 45–60.

formulation, of foreign policy. The question, "why was Iraq invaded?" is hard to answer because in practice, the flow of causation between ends, means and rationales for both is multi-directional.[15] The need to secure people and oil supplies required an invasion of Iraq to topple Saddam, but the need to topple Saddam also required an invasion to secure oil supplies and people. To complicate matters in the case of the Bush administration's Iraq policy, objectives, rationales and possibly even motives all shifted in response to unfolding events in a variety of political environments both at home and abroad. These can be mapped, but it is very hard to get closer to the main drivers of the government's policy – even to the thoroughly plausible conclusion that under pressure, it reduced to the idea that getting rid of Saddam would solve a number of problems – without arbitrarily assigning weight to one factor among many.

The difficulty with George's position for our purposes is that his quest for coherence leaves us squarely in the debate about how to accomplish foreign policy objectives and the objectives of particular foreign policies at that. Its strength, however, lies in its account of the complex processes in which policy-makers operate as these appear to the policymaker. In this, George follows the longstanding tradition of attempting, or purporting, to stand over the shoulder of the statesman, asking how the world looks to him and imagining what he must think and feel about it as a consequence. It is a fine tradition but in what follows, I modify it by replacing the statesman or statesmen with diplomats. We shall look over their shoulders positioning ourselves, not in national capitals between internal and external environments but, as the diplomatic tradition of international thought suggests, in the spaces between the states called rogues and the states identifying them as such. Standing there and thinking diplomatically, we see the questions "who are the rogues?" and "what should be done about them?" displaced by three very different questions. In what senses may rogue states be said to exist? Is it a good idea to identify them as such? And how are relations to be conducted between rogues and others once such identifications have been made? Since the answers provided by the diplomatic tradition to the second question at least begin on familiar territory, I shall begin by addressing

---

[15] David Hastings Dunn, "Myths, Motivations and 'Misunderestimations': The Bush Administration and Iraq," *International Affairs*, 79, 2 (March 2003), pp. 279–97.

what it has to say about that question. Is it a good idea to identify rogues as such, even if the names used may accurately depict those so identified?

Diplomats, civility and the identification of rogue states

Whilst it is largely diplomats who are left with the challenge of conducting relations once incantations have been uttered, names spoken and bones pointed, we actually hear very little from them on the subject of rogue states in particular contexts. This is partly a matter of professional reticence, as we shall see, but it is also a signal of the extent to which they are the servants of their masters rather than their profession. Indeed, in specific situations, when we hear diplomats address the issue of rogue states, they generally align themselves with their government's policy. If they represent the country identifying another as a rogue, for example, they will enumerate the reasons for why, in this case, the identification is a timely, courageous and refreshing exercise in honesty and facing difficult facts. If, on the other hand, they represent the identified, they will note the use of the term "rogue" as a further obstacle to the settlement of whatever outstanding difficulties occasioned it, as *prima face* evidence of where the balance of merit probably lies in the argument about them and, insofar as the use of such language contributes to the lowering of standards of international conduct generally, as a matter of deep and general regret.[16] The usual consequences of name-calling and the nature of diplomacy being what they are, diplomats may find themselves both engaging in, and expressing regret about, the practice in almost the same breath.

Of course, the identification of rogues is, in an important sense, no more than an instance of name-calling and, as such, we have a sense of diplomats traditionally taking a dim view of it. Their primary responsibility is said to be the conduct of peaceful, indeed friendly, relations between states.[17] This is a difficult business at the best of times and anything which might make it harder, such as calling one another and those they represent names in the midst of an argument, is to be avoided at all cost. This consideration was buttressed in the full flowering of

---

[16] Mahmood Sariolghalam, "Understanding Iran: Getting Past Stereotypes and Mythology," in Alexander T. J. Lennon and Camille Eiss (eds.), *Reshaping Rogue States: Preemption, Regime Change, and US Policy Towards Iran, Iraq and North Korea* (Cambridge, MA: MIT Press, 2004), pp. 283–99.

[17] Vienna Convention on Diplomatic Relations, Preamble, line 4.

Rogue state diplomacy 205

diplomacy's modern iteration as the relations of gentlemen by the sense that name-calling, at least in regard to one another, also indicated a lack of refinement and breeding. Thus, it was expected that professional diplomats should conduct their own relations with civility, constrain their masters' inclinations to do otherwise and dilute the consequences of any failure in this regard with more doses of civility in their own intercourse. Diplomats who did not hold to these standards were judged to be neither good diplomats nor good gentlemen. It is widely believed that the standard of civility achieved in modern diplomacy has now greatly declined, with the taboo on name-calling being one of the casualties of the more culturally divided, ideologically driven and popularly based international relations of today.[18] Whether one regards this as victory for honesty over hypocrisy or as a sign of the intimate relationship between populism and barbarism, the growth of the phenomenon of rogue states and the willingness of others to name them as such is taken as more evidence of both these changes plus the inability or unwillingness of diplomats to resist them.[19]

In fact, of course, the past was never so good, nor the present so bad, as we tend to assume in this respect. Diplomats were, and remain, concerned that a lack of civility can cause unwanted tension. If bad relations were an objective of policy, however, this consideration might weaken (although not entirely; civility was usually maintained against the day when better relations might be restored), and even gentlemen had their lapses. Thus, intentional discourtesy might be regarded with disfavor in the normal course of events, but, as the Ems telegram episode suggests, it was regarded as a move made understandable, if not quite justifiable, on momentous occasions by pressing reasons of state. Indeed, it was the prevailing norms of diplomatic civility that gave Bismarck's communication its meaning and effect, and everyone knew this.[20] It is by no means clear that contemporary diplomacy has greatly changed in this regard. The vast majority of diplomatic relations, even the most difficult and politically charged ones, are still conducted with great civility. Lapses,

---

[18] The decline of diplomatic standards, if such there has actually been, may be regarded as a manifestation of the vanishing shared international culture about which Bull, Wight and other members of the BCTIP worried.
[19] Frey and Frey, *The History of Diplomatic Immunity* provides an example of the declining standards argument focused on the embassy takeovers at the time of the Iranian revolution.
[20] See Kissinger, *Diplomacy*, p. 118 for a brief account of this episode.

when they occur, may be harder to conceal or re-bury in the glare of media attention. The consensus about what constitutes civility may be a little harder to achieve than it was in the smaller, more culturally narrow diplomatic society of the recent past.[21] Yet diplomatic civility remains important for much the same reasons as before. As the experience of Taliban diplomats in the Islamabad diplomatic corps suggests, even those apparently at war with the world are quick to learn its prevailing forms of civility and appreciate manifestations of it towards them when they are able to recognize them as such.[22] And, as the Baker-Aziz meeting before the second Gulf War illustrates, the notion of the calculated breach of diplomatic norms about civility still has a force which can be exploited to make, or score, a point.[23]

What we can say, therefore, is that both the popular image of a collapse in diplomatic standards and the professional self-image of diplomats as the guardians of civility, always trying to damp down the fires ignited by the political character of foreign policy, are over-simplifications. Sometimes diplomats contribute to the fire, inadvertently as a professional lapse or intentionally as a matter of policy. More often, they try to keep things cool, at least between themselves. And they do so because, as the diplomatic tradition suggests, they, unlike their respective governments and most of us, spend an important part of their time in each other's company. Together, they inhabit a third world between those of the peoples they represent to one another, whether it is at the UN and its affiliated bodies, in the diplomatic corps of national capitals or, increasingly, in provincial settings far from formal centers but close to the political action. And, since everybody, certainly every state, needs diplomacy, they do so as the representatives of the great and the good, the meek and the mild, rogues and outlaws, Satans and little Satans, all together.[24] Indeed, there is a sense in which the cocktail party with its prescribed forms for social intercourse

---

[21] Cohen, *Negotiating Across Cultures*.
[22] Sharp, "Mullah Zaeef and Taliban Diplomacy," pp. 481–98.
[23] Baker, *The Politics of Diplomacy*, pp. 355–63. Note the ambiguity of whether the US had used insulting language to communicate a threat or whether the Iraqis had used the claim that they had to reject the message.
[24] For examples of the Ayatollah Khomeini's use of the term "Great Satan" in regard to the US see Takeyh, R., *Hidden Iran: Paradox And Power In The Islamic Republic* (New York: Holt, 2006), pp. 97–8. The term "Little Satan" was used for American allies like Britain. For President Bush's use of the term "The Axis of Evil" see his *State of the Union Address*, January 29, 2002 at

between those in good relations, those in bad relations and those difficult triangles where two friends have diverging attitudes towards the third party, actually does capture the distinctive orientation in diplomatic thinking to the naming of rogues. It is something done from outside their collective world, and yet it is something with which they all must live. This being so, diplomatic thinking also offers an equally distinctive orientation to the vexed question of in what sense rogue states may be actually said to exist.

How do rogue states exist for diplomats and diplomacy?

Rogue states, despite the primitive character of social relations suggested by the term and name-calling in general, are not a phenomenon of encounter relations as I have defined the latter. One may encounter aliens, savages and sub-humans, but one does not encounter rogues. This is because the term applies to people, states or others, who knowingly refuse to conform to rules that might reasonably be expected to apply to them. Rogue states, then, are members of an international society which, according to some or all other states, have been discovered to have gone bad and, from a diplomatic point of view, must be re-encountered as such. One can see, therefore, a possible distinction between the US government identifying Iran as a rogue state – that is, a state not fulfilling its obligations and duties as a member of international society – and the Iranian government identifying the US as the Great Satan – the primary source of evil and, presumably, therefore, the evil way in which the world is presently configured. Whether such a distinction has policy implications – would it be easier for foreign policy purposes, for example, to rehabilitate a rogue than a Satan – is not clear. What is clear, however, is that rogue states do exist to the extent that the governments of other states discover them to be so, can convince others that their discovery is correct and are both willing and able to act on the basis of this discovery.

This may sound like a complex way of explicating the obvious. What it is intended to convey, however, is the provisional and conditional character of rogue states' existence as such, at least as far as diplomats are concerned. States are identified as rogues, accused of acting like

www.whitehouse.gov/news/releases/2002/01/20020129–11.html, accessed May 24, 2008.

rogues and judged to have ceased being rogues as a consequence of purposes and passions at home, the intensity of which their diplomats do not and cannot share if they are to maintain relations with each other. This is not to say that diplomats cannot identify rogues themselves and become exercised about them. Indeed, through their work, they may make major contributions to their government's discovery that a rogue exists.[25] They cannot, however, be decisive in this regard – witness the fate of those diplomats who seek to alert their governments to the roguery of hosts about which, for one reason or another, their own governments do not wish to know.[26] This is because the identification and naming of rogues is a political act rather than a diplomatic one, and the center of gravity for political acts remains firmly at home.

While rogue states exist, therefore, they do so for diplomats as if a pale and possibly translucent sheet has been thrown over them. Its pattern can be seen, but more faintly and less clearly than it appears at home, for the underlying characteristics of the state beneath it, its regime and its representatives remain strong, and the possibility of the sheet's removal is ever-present. Consider, for example, the relations of Austria and the Ottoman Empire with a variety of newly independent Balkan rogues and outlaws (as they saw them) at the turn of the last century, as well as similar fluctuations in US relations with Iraq and Iran after the Cold War. All bear testimony to the fact that the status of a rogue is usually unstable and always transient. Rogues may be states with which there is just no talking, but the possibility of an opening or breakthrough always seems to exist just around the corner, much to the shock of all and sundry when efforts in this direction are discovered and publicized by those who do not welcome them.[27]

---

[25] Through conventional diplomatic reporting, for example, and naming. Note the prominence in the US of the State Department as a provider of various lists of states in bad standing.

[26] Consider, for example, the fate of the British ambassador to Uzbekistan after he spoke out about local human rights violations in 2003 and 2004. He was withdrawn. See BBC news report, "Former British Envoy Suspended," October 17, 2004 at http://news.bbc.co.uk/1/hi/uk/3750370.stm.

[27] The Iran-Contra scandal of 1985–86 in which the US, with help from Israel, supplied Iran with military equipment in return for Iranian help in securing the release of hostages held by its allies or clients in the Lebanon. For an account see Trita Parsi, *Treacherous Alliance: The Secret Dealings Of Israel, Iran and the US* (New Haven: Yale University Press, 2007), p. 123.

Treating rogues as existing, but faintly, has a number of advantages. It reminds us of the extent to which all states exist but faintly in terms of identities and personalities. It alerts us to the dangers of the alternative, namely treating these identities as real and concrete both for analytic purposes and in public discourse.[28] This point is confirmed by the important, but scarcely surprising, finding of much analytical research that it is difficult to distinguish named rogue states from all the other states by objective criteria such as patterns of domestic arrangements or external behavior. To be sure, the problems of treating rogues as solid and real are mitigated somewhat by the distinction which governments and others like to make between states and their people, on the one hand, and governments or regimes, on the other. It is the latter, it is claimed, which both concretely exist and can be judged to be wicked. This distinction only takes us so far, however. By governments, it is made about the governments and peoples of other countries. We have no quarrel with the Iranian people, US governments maintain, only the Iranian government. Meanwhile their own link with their own people is presented as authentic and solid when often it is not. Further, by no means all governments or all peoples accept this distinction. Political and religious leaders in Iran, for example, present the government and people of the United States as the Great Satan, and there is considerable evidence to suggest that much of the citizenry shares this view. And, as Americans have become more frustrated with events in Iraq, the temptation to lump its leaders and its peoples together as, if not wicked exactly, then morally deficient in their unwillingness to make their country work, has grown. Finally, it is, of course, as countries – regimes and people together – that states suffer the consequences of being identified as rogues. Bombs and economic sanctions alike cannot easily be made to distinguish between bad governments and good peoples in the way that one might wish. This fact, alone, provides a powerful argument for importing the distance of the diplomats from the processes

---

[28] See, e.g., Miroslav Nincic, *Renegade Regimes: Confronting Deviant Behavior in World Politics* (New York: Columbia University Press, 2005) and Mary Caprioli and Peter Trumbore, "Rhetoric vs. Reality: Rogue States in International Conflict, 1980–2001," *Journal of Conflict Resolution*, 49, 5 (2005), pp. 770–91. Nincic presents rogue states as a given and focuses on rationality of strategies for dealing with them, while Caprioli and Trumbore seek to identify a link between external roguery and internal violence and human rights violations, in which the latter are presented as early symptoms of the former.

of name-calling and identifying states as rogues into wider public discourse.

Whatever its attractions, however, the diplomatic position of treating rogue states as existing, but faintly, has it own problems and difficulties. It may be claimed that no matter how governments use the term and no matter how diplomats regard it, there actually are some states whose status as rogues is indisputable. Hitler's Germany and Pol Pot's Kampuchea would seem to satisfy every reasonable person's criteria in these terms by their external and internal conduct. It seems clear that to ignore the fact of their roguishness would court worse dangers than to treat it as a politically generated veil. Further, it might also be argued that declaring a state a rogue, no matter how misguided or cynical the reasons for doing so might be, can have far more substantive roots than those suggested by the diplomatic orientation towards the practice of name-calling. The US policy of regarding and treating Cuba as a rogue since the latter's revolution, whatever its other shortcomings, has manifested the qualities of being consistent and sustained. It would be a foolish diplomat, therefore, who underestimated America's degree of commitment to this policy and assumed that the veil might be removed with little effort should something called the "political will" exist.

However, neither difficulty appears overwhelming. Even in extreme cases like Nazi Germany and Kampuchea, a genuine consensus about their rogue status, untrammeled by political or foreign policy considerations, cannot exist, not least because most of the population of the states so named, rightly or wrongly, does not agree (possibly out of political or foreign policy considerations, albeit). Even after the full horrors of the concentration camps were known, and certainly before, perfectly good people could argue that there was nothing to be gained, and much to be lost, by treating a state as bad as Nazi Germany as a criminal. It would make it harder to achieve a peace and, in the meantime, permit terrible things to be done to ordinary Germans who, even if not entirely innocent, continued, through multiple actions and relationships unconnected with the regime under which they lived, to produce goodness and to enrich personalities. And while the constancy with which the United States has maintained Cuba's identity as a rogue undermines the notion that there is anything faint or flimsy about a practice which has had long-term consequences for that particular country, it does nothing to undermine the notion that it remains a good idea for diplomats to treat the practice as such. Openings, should they be desired, are more likely to be identified and exploited if someone is not taking the idea of Cuba as a rogue state, or the United States as an imperialist state, for that matter, too seriously. However, therein lies the real problem of treating rogue states as real, but faintly. How are and when are those who see them in this way to be influential in the conduct of relations between rogue states and those who identify them as such?

How is rogue state diplomacy to be conducted?

Note that the focus here is not upon how to conduct diplomacy towards rogue states. Such a focus leads quickly back down the track to foreign policy, what to do about rogues and all the assumptions such a question takes for granted. Rather it is upon the men and women who are charged with talking with one another against a backdrop inscribed with rogues, Satans and other dubious identities, who do not act with total disregard for this backdrop, but for whom it is fainter and less defining than it is for those they represent. Indeed, in some sense, even those they represent may be fainter and less defining, or become so as the process of talking with each other provides them with another social reality in which to function. "Hitlers come and go," Stalin remarked, "but Germany and the German people remain."[29] The diplomatic tradition, however, alerts us to how not only governments, but also peoples in their specific iterations come and go, while only the relations of peoples persist. The challenge, therefore, is to maintain relations, once these have led to the discovery of rogues and the development of intense pressures to break them off or to conduct them by violence. Diplomats have to find a way in which ordinary, and extraordinary, business can be conducted in extraordinary times until the latter, possibly with diplomatic assistance, pass. In short, new terms on which the parties can re-encounter one another have to be established.

This argument points strongly towards the idea of insulation of the sort established at Dayton between the warring parties from the former Yugoslavia, at Oslo between Israeli and Palestinian representatives and in the Netherlands between the US and Iran in talks about each other's

---

[29] See Felix Morrow, "Stalin Blames the German Proletariat," review in *Fourth International*, New York, Vol. 3 No. 6, June 1942, pp. 186–91. Text of Stalin's Order of the Day on the 24th Anniversary of the Red Army, Moscow, February 23, 1942, accessed at www.ibiblio.org/pha/policy/1942/420223a.html.

economic assets.³⁰ The assumption seems to be that if you can somehow get the right sort of people in a room and protect them from the turbulence of international relations and their respective political worlds, then you will greatly improve the chances for better relations and more reasonable outcomes. This may be so, but the rarity of such set-piece encounters and the fate of some of them, both during and after, suggest two sets of problems. The first set stems from the fact that governments are not diplomats, but possess the power and authority upon which diplomats greatly depend to function effectively, to be insulated, for example. The second set revolves around the skepticism noted above about the value of keeping talks going and the fear that, on occasions, such a preoccupation can be harmful.

Governments and diplomats

Generally speaking, governments are not diplomats, although individual members may act diplomatically on occasions. While neither the preoccupations of a particular government nor its conception of the national interest are eternal, however, they are, for as long as the government remains in power, intense and authoritative. Thus, for example, if governments decide that their states should have no diplomatic relations with each other at all, then the scope for the diplomatic management of their relations is severely, though not entirely, circumscribed.³¹ Governments are also apt to take themselves and their way of seeing things like rogue states and Satans very seriously. As such, they rarely set up, or even assent to, insulated re-encounters like those above because they rarely share the view that governments need to be saved from themselves and their constituencies in the conduct of their foreign policies. Thus, even such insulated settings are often effectively dominated by the priorities and policies of one particular party. The Dayton meetings about the future of the Balkans, the Israeli-Egyptian peace

---

³⁰ See G. R. Berridge, *Talking to the Enemy: How States Without Diplomatic Relations Communicate* (Basingstoke: Palgrave Macmillan, 1994).

³¹ Of course, states with no formal diplomatic relations continue to have relations of diplomatic significance in which their diplomats continue to be involved. See, e.g., Berridge, *Talking to the Enemy*, David D. Newsom (ed.), *Diplomacy Under a Foreign Flag: When Nations Break Relations* (Washington DC: Institute For the Study of Diplomacy, 1990) and Alan James, "Diplomatic Relations and Contacts," *The British Year Book of International Law* (1991), pp. 347–87.

talks at Camp David and the conference over the future of Rhodesia-Zimbabwe at Lancaster House all provide examples in which insulation strengthened a particular political control over the free run of diplomatic creativity which might have otherwise occurred.

Indeed, the high regard governments and most people with power have for themselves entails that they are uneasy with any distance – philosophical, diplomatic or otherwise – from their priorities they may detect among those working for them. They worry that such distance will result in their policies being ineffectively implemented and sometimes even interpret it as opposition. The immediate recall of most of Iran's ambassadors after the elections of 2006 replaced a reformist government with a more radical conservative one, provides a drastic example of the propensity of governments to keep their diplomats on a tight leash. However, less drastic versions of this practice are followed in many countries when a change of government takes place.[32] This concern is also reflected in the kind of people they appoint to sensitive positions. Insecure and fearful regimes especially, like Iraq under Saddam Hussein, may appoint diplomats whom they know they can either trust or intimidate by personal threats. Governments driven by strong moral or ideological convictions may appoint people who share them and, of course, all governments are supposed to benefit from the processes of recruitment and subsequent socialization by which foreign services are maintained as the supple, but obedient, instruments of their respective wills.

It may be supposed, therefore, that there are many bad diplomats, in terms of diplomacy as it is being presented here, engaged in the conduct of rogue state diplomacy. We might expect the rogues to be represented by those fearful of, or personally loyal to, their political masters, people who barely understand the give-and-take of conventional diplomacy, let alone the profession's autonomous understanding of what is supposed to be going on. The representatives of those who name them as rogues we might expect to enjoy more tactical freedom (and personal security), but to be scarcely less flexible when it comes to insisting on the basic framing of the situations in which re-encounters are undertaken. You represent rogues, they say, while we represent, if not the only voice, then the authentic and right voice of the international society against

---

[32] See "Iran Sacks Diplomats in Purge of Reformers," *TimesOnline* (November 2, 2005), www.timesonline.co.uk/tol/news/world/middle_east/article585547.ece.

whose rules you have transgressed. And of course, even good diplomats, in the terms set out here, will be constrained, not only by fear and personal loyalty, but also by the professional value they place on being known to represent faithfully their political masters. Diplomats, no matter how personally empathetic, self-restrained or distanced from the narrow clash of national interests they may be, are not much use if they cannot be trusted by their opposite numbers or host governments to convey the will of their masters authoritatively and accurately.

Yet, as all these very real difficulties indicate, a measure of indeterminacy comes into existence as soon as governments allow their diplomats to enter into conversations with one another, even in highly structured and insulated re-encounters. Indeed, the measures adopted to keep their diplomats on tight leashes may be taken to reflect the worries and insecurities of governments in this regard. They need this indeterminacy to explore the opportunities that may exist, even if only to advance their own narrow interests, yet they fear it for what else may happen when the talking gets underway. No matter how training, instructions, career structures, threats to relatives and even the presence of "minders" may be designed to make sure it does not happen, once the diplomats are no longer under direct control, their conversations may acquire a dynamic of their own, even if it is only the shared desire of their participants, for one reason or another, to keep talking. Is the desire to keep talking, however, no matter how difficult the circumstances and how odious those represented by the other fellow may be, always a good idea?

Talking for talk's sake

As noted above, diplomats may over-value talk because this is what they do. Their time may be spent in committee meetings whose connection to anything happening in the world of international politics, as this is conventionally understood, is remote. The purpose of such committees may be to ensure that nothing appears to happen and to bear witness to the fact. Indeed, the success or failure of a diplomatic career may be measured in terms of a successful campaign to insert a sub-clause into a sentence, the significance of which no one can subsequently remember.[33] Diplomats may acquire a manner of talking in bland generalities they are unable to shake off even when it is unnecessary or when

[33] Neumann, "To Be A Diplomat," pp. 72–93.

something else is required.³⁴ And in rogue state diplomacy, especially, re-encounters may take on the qualities of a highly scripted pantomime or farce. Witness, as noted earlier, the presentations of Iraq's UN permanent representative and the American Secretary of State to the Security Council regarding Iraq's compliance with resolutions on arms inspections.³⁵

As Churchill's aphorism about "jaw, jaw" being better than "war, war" demonstrates, the reasons for valuing talk are well known but, as his practice suggests, often discounted. Even those who have served in a primarily diplomatic capacity often struggle to maintain the diplomatic distance which allows talk to be valued almost for its own sake in this sense. This is especially so if they aspire to careers in public life at a later date, or to remain politically and policy-relevant. Thus, for example, few of the people who worked extensively with the Serbian leader, Slobodan Milosovic, during the breakup of Yugoslavia took the opportunity of his death to underline the importance of supping with devils on occasions. Rather, all took the opportunity of interviews to underline what a devil they thought him to be.³⁶ The rewards for staying onside with policy, and the penalties for failing to do so, often overwhelm whatever impulse exists for stressing the importance of keeping lines of communication open. They do so because, rightly or wrongly, the latter argument undermines the image of the rogue or Satan as someone with whom there is just no talking.

In addition, insofar as talking "for talk's sake" puts other forms of action on hold, it can be accused of undermining policies, worsening situations and increasing problems in more substantive ways. Thus, for example, the United States maintained that the longer talks went on with Iraq, the longer that country had to develop and perfect its WMD. Subsequent events demonstrated the hollowness of this concern but, with regard to the erosion of the sanctions regime around Iraq, the

---

[34] One diplomatic trainer noted how this phenomenon reminded him of the advice from generations of parents not to pull faces because they might stay that way (private conversation).

[35] See "International Developments, November 15 2002–February 1 2003," *News Review Special Edition* at www.acronym.org.uk/textonly/dd/dd69/69nr01.htm#summ.

[36] See P. Ashdown, "Butcher of the Balkans Found Dead," *CNN.com* (March 12, 2006) for Holbrooke and Ashdown, www.cnn.com/2006/WORLD/europe/03/11/milosovic/.

argument about having to act retained considerable force, even though the Bush administration could not make it effectively because it was too embarrassed. Similar considerations always come into play when governments are actively considering the use of force. Then, a wide range of operational considerations about weather, climate and force-readiness pull against the idea of continuing to talk merely to postpone the fighting so people will not be killed, or in the hope that something, in terms of an unforeseen diplomatic solution, will turn up. The same arguments against talking "... for talk's sake ..." put forward before both US-led wars against Iraq appear more compelling in the case of Iran's refusal to abandon policies consistent with the development of nuclear weapons and the means to deliver them. They are so, however, for both sides. The United States and Israel fear that Iran uses talks to stall measures against it until it reaches the stage where it has acquired all it needs to develop its own nuclear weapons, at which point it will be much more difficult to take those measures. Some of Iran's leaders, by the same reasoning, believe that their country cannot afford merely to talk while American pressure builds all around it. The argument about not entering the conference chamber naked would appear to be just as valid for Shia clerics as its was once for parliamentary socialists.[37]

The objections to talking "for talk's sake" elicit no simple responses either for or against them. The historical record certainly does not speak for itself without interpretation in this regard, as even such big and well-documented events as the two world wars of the twentieth century demonstrate. The first, it can be argued, occurred because the great powers talked and trusted too little. Even as they saw the crisis slipping out of control and taking a direction no one wanted, they did not dare to talk with one another because they feared the consequences of showing a lack of resolve and determination to stay their respective courses. The second occurred, arguably, because governments, or some of them, trusted too much and talked too long.[38] An earlier demonstration or use of force by France and Britain might have removed the threat posed by Hitler. Perhaps, but the uncertainties of prevention and preemption outface most governments and often punish those prepared to take the

---

[37] Aneurin Bevan, Labour Party Conference (October 4, 1957) on the constraining impact of a position of unilateral nuclear disarmament on the ability of a foreign secretary to exert influence on others in disarmament negotiations at www.spartacus.schoolnet.co.uk/TUbevan.htm.

[38] Tanter, *Rogue Regimes*, p. 222.

risks involved. And, as A.J.P. Taylor controversially argued many years ago, more talk, that is to say the Munich agreement followed by a Polish settlement the following year, might have worked had the terms been acceptable to one side and had the government of the other been prepared to adhere to them.[39]

What the historical record does suggest, however, are three things. First, some arguments cannot be settled on the terms of either of their protagonists. Secondly, some arguments do not have to be settled – in the sense that life can go on and many people stay alive even without a settlement. In situations such as these, "talking for talk's sake" may represent a solution of sorts and the best attainable until a change of heart takes place or, more likely, the protagonists become tired of arguing with each other. Thirdly, and more controversially, it suggests that many disputes might possibly be settled on either party's terms without an international (as opposed to a domestic political) catastrophe ensuing. While, strictly speaking, not an example of rogue state diplomacy, but of states behaving roguishly, the dispute over the Falklands/Malvinas in 1982 is suggestive in this regard. Arguably, it could have been reasonably settled on either side's terms had their respective governments not nailed their own political survival to complete victory.[40] It is not impossible that a similar conclusion might be drawn at some point about the dispute between the great powers and Iran over the latter's nuclear energy policy on whatever terms it actually resolves itself. Iran without a bomb might, as the US maintains, continue to be secure and begin to re-emerge, at some point, as a responsible regional power. Iran with a bomb might do precisely the same. Germans could have lived with a Polish corridor and Poles without one. Palestinians can live without a Palestinian state and Israelis with one. Both Pakistan and India have lived without exclusive possession of Kashmir, and Britain and Ireland appear to be creeping towards the idea that they are both better off without exclusively possessing Northern Ireland. Perhaps, as Edward Grey is reputed to

---

[39] A.J.P. Taylor, *Origins of the Second World War* (Harmondsworth: Penguin, 1963). See the Conclusion for a further consideration of this theme.
[40] This episode, of course, points to other difficulties with the practice of identifying rogue states. Argentina plausibly, Britain much less so, could have been identified as rogue states but were not. Indeed, both cited core important international society principles – national self-determination, self-defense and the maintenance of order by punishing those who use force, to justify their policies.

have commented after 1914, the greatest weakness in diplomacy is a deficiency, not an excess, of trust,[41] and we should be more inclined to let the other fellows, rogues or not, have what they want.

Rogue state diplomacy as a holding operation

On the other hand, the historical record strongly suggests that people rarely find a sufficient incentive in "possibly" for taking the sorts of risks which trusting others often involves. Thus, diplomatic thinking does not encourage us to believe that all disputes are resolvable by the application of reason to positions maintained out of ignorance and fear, not even in principle. They may, in principle, be resolvable by the application of virtue, but men and women find it difficult to be good at the best of times, let alone in the extraordinary circumstances they impose upon themselves in international relations. It is very difficult to the point of impossible, for example, for Iran and Israel to display the sort of trust which would allow the former to forgo an opportunity to develop weapons which its leaders believe are within its reach, or for the latter to witness this development with equanimity. Diplomatic thinking, therefore, provides no formula by which we might determine who is right or wrong in particular episodes of rogue state diplomacy or prescriptions about who should do what in terms of foreign policy. What it does instead is alert us to the extent to which the terms in which foreign policy is played out are framed and fueled by arguments going on within states, or their foreign policy establishments at least, about national values, state interests and, increasingly, the shape of the world as a whole and what that ought to be. The term "domestication," not only of foreign policy, but of international relations as a whole, is suggestive here, if not in quite the terms suggested by its original use. Both have always been domesticated to a point, but historically only for domestic purposes. Foreign policy had to be "sold" at home and, hence, presented in domestic political terms. Now, domestic political terms play a much stronger part not only in shaping foreign policy, but also in framing what international relations are and ought to be about.

---

[41] Butterfield, "Power and Diplomacy," in *Christianity, Diplomacy and War*, p. 75. See also Nicolson, *The Evolution of the Diplomatic Method*, p. 93.

Thus, rogue states and Satans, great and small, may exist, sometimes faintly and sometimes more clearly, sometimes because the governments of other states need them to be so named, sometimes because other domestic forces insist upon it. As far as the United States is concerned, for example, Libya under its current regime can change but Cuba cannot. As far as Iran is concerned, Iraq may change, but Israel, certainly, and America, probably, cannot. The important question, therefore, is not, "do rogue states exist?" It is "how are we to live in a world where rogues and others will be so named?" Diplomatic thinking, as a consequence, approaches the whole issue of rogue state diplomacy in terms of maintaining a series of re-encounters on very difficult terrain. The terrain itself cannot always be avoided and, sometimes, it is right that this is so, but talking, sometimes "for talk's sake," can avoid the worse consequences of traversing this terrain, and it can also hold the door open to recognizing opportunities for escapes from it. In a sense, therefore, rogue state diplomacy may be viewed as an immense holding operation, maintaining the peace until passions have been spent and arguments have lost their force. There are no guarantees it will succeed in this regard but, even if it fails, at some point, relations will be re-established and the processes of re-encountering across the difficult terrain will begin again.

If this is what the diplomatic tradition has to say about rogue state diplomacy, however, the question remains "to whom does it have to say it?" We are presented with two conflicting images. The first is the reassuring historical account, referred to above, of diplomacy and diplomats insulated from domestic processes which have been injected by political viruses and which infect foreign policy processes in their turn. The "dear colleagues" of modern diplomacy could meet against a backdrop of insults, hypocrisy and self-righteousness – they might even engage in verbal rough-housing themselves on occasions – but they did so with their fingers putatively crossed behind their backs. If the domestic terms in which foreign policy was understood were taken seriously at all, in this reassuring view, then they were so only instrumentally, to the extent that they served or hindered *la raison d'état* and *la raison de système*. This is how diplomats understood what was going on when insults were flying and, more importantly, they knew that this is how their opposite numbers understood what was going on. In contrast to this comforting view, on the other hand, we have a sense in which not only is diplomacy no longer insulated, it is positively permeated by outsiders and their ideas to the point where the professional diplomats have been shunted aside.[42] Or, to express this idea in the terms of the diplomatic tradition of international thought, the "domestication" processes referred to above seem to be crowding out the conduct of international relations on the latter's own terms. Into the resulting debates everyone, including international relations theorists, seems drawn by foreign policy considerations which they either have to accept or oppose and, as the arguments about rogue states and those who name them demonstrate, people seem unable to carve out the space required for doing much else.

This second image is, perhaps, overdrawn. As I have argued above, diplomats still encounter each other, even on such vexing issues as rogue states, sympathetically, or soon establish the grounds for a measure of sympathy and shared understanding. On occasions, they are even acknowledged as working their "magic," for example, in achieving the framework agreement between the United States and its allies, on the one hand, and the North Koreans, on the other, regarding the latter's nuclear energy ambitions.[43] The story of the magic worked by diplomacy in bringing Libya back in from the cold remains to be told, and there may yet be stories of the similar part played by diplomatic magic in securing an American disengagement from Iraq and Iran's rehabilitation on terms which remain to be seen. Nevertheless, the space for working such magic in the traditional way has been reduced by the removal of much of the insulation which diplomacy traditionally enjoyed from public consideration and debate. There is no prospect of such insulation being restored in the near-to-middle future. Indeed, all the ideational trends and the technological developments which fuel them are in the opposite direction and this, on the whole, is a very good thing. If the insights of the diplomatic tradition can no longer be made effective by restoring the degree of insulation diplomats previously enjoyed, then the only, but not unattractive, alternative is to disseminate them more widely within societies. In fact, this may already be seen to be occurring. It is conventionally assumed that the domestication of international relations is a process characterized by the flow of change

---

[42] George F. Kennan, "Diplomacy Without Diplomats?" *Foreign Affairs*, 76 (September/October 1997), pp. 198–212.
[43] See Tanter, *Rogue Regimes*, pp. 205–48, Michael O'Hanlon, "Towards a Grand Bargain With North Korea," in Alexander T. J. Lennon and Camille Eiss (eds.), *Reshaping Rogue States*, pp. 157–70 and Litwak, *Rogue States and US Foreign Policy*, pp. 198–237.

primarily in one direction. It is at least partly matched by a flow the other way in which domestic relations are being internationalized. By this, I do not mean the usual battery of arguments about globalization and international competitiveness by which citizens in general, and introductory international relations students in particular, are told that they must pay attention because their lives and prospects are being increasingly affected by what happens abroad. Rather, I refer to the processes by which general publics and domestic political actors are being drawn into confronting more directly the dilemmas which international relations present for their countries, their governments and, increasingly, themselves.

The debates about humanitarian military intervention provide a clear example in this regard. "How can we possibly do it" collides with "how can we possibly not?" If difficult issues like these and rogue state diplomacy are to be handled effectively, then the distance of the diplomats from the content of international relations or, at least, a greater sensitivity to that distance and the reasons for it, needs to be more widely disseminated. Then, at a very minimum, we might see states continuing to call one another names without publics becoming so shocked and governments feeling so vulnerable when it is discovered that rogues and Satans continue to talk to one another. This reduced prospect of shock and vulnerability might permit them to talk to one another more effectively. If we were very fortunate, however, and a diplomatic understanding of what is going on when governments call one another names became more widespread, then whatever attractions the practice might have to governments looking to mobilize support for their policies in this manner could be reduced. They might be less tempted to call one another names and, if they succumbed to the temptation nevertheless, the consequences might be less dangerous and painful.

11 | *Greedy company diplomacy*

Rogue states, while arguably aberrant phenomena whose character is in great part generated by the demands and preoccupations of domestic politics, belong to a world closely associated with diplomacy. Greedy companies, in contrast, belong to a world from which diplomacy is conventionally understood to have been exiled, the world of economic production, distribution and exchange. What are we to do about companies which exploit people, damage the environment and use up the natural resources of the planet in order to get rich by presiding over the creation of a stock of wealth from which nearly everybody wants what they see as their fair share, and what might the diplomatic tradition of international thought have to tell us about the debates surrounding these questions? From just about every point of the intellectual compass including, until relatively recently, diplomats themselves and those who study them, the received opinion was "not a lot."[1] In their priorities, in their ways of understanding the world and in their characteristic modes of thought and inquiry, diplomacy and economics, indeed diplomats and economists, have been presented in opposition to one another. And they have been so in a way that reflects poorly on diplomacy. Thus, we see diplomacy existing because of human weaknesses and imperfections: the predisposition to sacrifice the dictates of reason to the cupidities of willfulness; the desire to obtain what has not been earned; the urge to use force when other means have failed or even before, and, above all, the need to fudge that all this is, in fact, the case in order to

---

[1] See David Hudson and Donna Lee, "The Old and New Significance of Political Economy in Diplomacy," *Review of International Studies*, 30, 3 (2004), pp. 343–60 for a review of these themes and an argument that diplomacy's exile from economic relations and issues has been empirically unjustified and had harmful practical and conceptual consequences. See also Strange, *The Retreat of the State* for a now-orthodox account of the marginalization of state diplomacy by new and increasingly important patterns of economic relations.

manage its consequences. Economics, in contrast, is said to embody the rationality and honesty of a powerful understanding of what human affairs are and ought to be about. We may worry that it is an overly narrow and narrowing conception, but we can take comfort from the fact that it presents individual human beings at their most rational and their most reasonable, if not necessarily their most good. If only people would conform to this narrowness, its adherents claim, then all might be happier and certainly would be richer.

Of course, I could have written a mirror-image paragraph to the one above in which the diplomatic virtues: tolerance of others; acceptance of ambiguity; and a pragmatic flexibility in the application of principles were contrasted favorably with the materialist egotism and unforgiving rigidities of economic thought. And I could have concluded that, if only people were prepared to accept diplomacy's albeit narrow logic, they might be happier and certainly would live more independently and peacefully. It is the first story that has dominated, however, to the extent that diplomats, even those in diplomacy's modern heyday, accepted the economic view of their respective domains. Diplomats and economists differed not on the truth of the latter's claims so much as on the scope of the difficulties which putting them into practice might involve. Thus, economic thought and practice might focus on optimal solutions to problems, but diplomatic thought saw the risks of attempting to put such solutions into practice and, indeed, the risks of formulating problems in such clear terms that solutions might be developed and attempted. After all, there is no point in being right if being so precipitates a breach in relations that you wish to maintain in good repair.

We can see, therefore, why diplomats were prepared to accept a subordinate place for their own way of knowing the world. They had no choice. Publicly, at least, they had to share their masters' and the prevailing views on this matter, namely that if governments and diplomats were doing their jobs properly and all was well in the world, then life in it for most people was, and ought to be, about getting and spending in an economic sense. They were comforted in their subordination, however, by the daily experience that made them privy to the huge tracts of human endeavor and relations in which the first principles upon which an economic science depends were not agreed upon and, thus, its narrow logic secured no purchase. There was no fear that they would be putting themselves out of work by accepting and, indeed, proclaiming that economics came first in the priorities of governments and people alike, and that it was a realm to which diplomacy and diplomats should ideally be subordinate and from which they should keep their proper distance. After all, there were plenty of other important things to keep them busy which could even, on occasions, suspend the dominance of economic considerations, even if only temporarily.

During the twentieth century, however, this distancing on the part of diplomats from economics became an exile from more and more of what people were coming to regard as important. Economic activity and economic thought began to dominate reflections and action on virtually every human problem, including the conduct of governments. As Sir George Graham was reported as saying by one of his subordinates at Brussels in 1926, "When I first came here it was the Ambassador's Conference, Fiume, Vilna, Rapallo, the Ruhr and now it's pig casings."[2] Iconic in this regard is the apocryphal refusal of certain British diplomats in the 1960s to engage in selling washing machines to foreigners.[3] They had not joined the Service to engage in trade. If diplomats would not participate in export promotion, however, then as diplomacy became more and more about facilitating exports, then clearly it was so much the worse for them. As modernization theorists argued, an increasingly interdependent and globalizing international system could not be managed effectively by a code of practice developed over three centuries earlier for a handful of territorial actors enjoying relatively hard borders and relatively little interdependence all in one locale. As modernization proceeded, increasingly on a global scale, then diplomacy would either fade into irrelevance or adapt to the point of becoming, as far as the unhappy gentlemen referred to above were concerned, unrecognizable.[4]

---

[2] Sir Hughe Knatchbull-Hugessen, *Diplomat In Peace and War* (London: John Murray, 1949), p. 232. Knatchbull-Hugessen, however, while sympathetic from a professional point of view, expresses the view that this return to "routine" should be welcome.

[3] Lorna Lloyd has noted the apocryphal character of many of the stories about British ambassadors objecting to their involvement in commercial activity (private correspondence).

[4] Edward L. Morse, *Modernization and the Transformation of International Relations* (New York: Free Press, 1976) and Raymond Saner and Lichia Yiu, "International Economic Diplomacy: Mutations in Post-modern Times," *DPD* (The Hague: NIIRC, 84, January 2003) p. 37. We must be careful here to distinguish between the sort of economic modernization in which Morse is interested and which is directly related to the phenomenon of globalization, on the one hand, and the use of the term "modern" when applied to diplomacy and

The trends discomforting traditionalists of the sort above deepened and accelerated as the twentieth century progressed. With the end of the Cold War and the collapse of the Soviet Union, the market capitalism of large corporations serviced and facilitated by liberal democratic governments triumphed both in theory and in practice over other principles of economic organization. Market capitalism outperformed its rivals, and the states adhering to its principles defeated the others with help from the latter's citizens. They did so because this system of political economy not only generated more economic growth; it did so while allowing, many would say by providing, high levels of political freedom, the two things which nearly everybody seems to want. The extent of this triumph is such that, for now, the only serious objections to this claim come from those who question the desirability and sustainability of economic growth, not from those who offer alternative ways of delivering it. Indeed, debates on how to organize the creation of wealth have largely been replaced by ones about into which other spheres of life the principles of market capitalism can be gainfully extended. Thus, whatever the differences which may lie between the Washington consensus, the Brussels consensus and, now, the Beijing consensus, all are agreed that at the economic core of their concerns and the good life in general are markets inhabited by profit-seeking private companies.[5] Like the states it was designed to serve, therefore, modern diplomacy has to change or fade and, unlike many other people who work for states, professional diplomats are said to have experienced great difficulty in making the necessary adjustments. Indeed, it may be argued that diplomacy has only changed by taking much of it out of the hands of the professionals.

Thus runs the conventional account of the differences between economics and diplomacy, the rise of the former and its inverse effect upon the significance and status of the latter. It is, of course, an oversimplification to which objections can be made. As the more traditional students of diplomacy are fond of pointing out, the origins of its modern version are at least partly to be found in commercial activity, especially among the states of northern Italy, and between them and the

---

the states which modern diplomacy served, on the other. There was nothing modern about the modern state system in Morse's view, and modernity as he understood it, in terms of liberal economic development, was superseding that system.

[5] Leonard, *Why Europe Will Run the 21st Century*.

Ottomans. Indeed, among the first modern diplomats were often merchants who sought political representation and support from their home governments. Instead of obtaining support, they were sometimes credentialed, in what must be one of the earliest examples of diplomatic outsourcing, to take care of themselves, other nationals and the interests of their respective sovereigns.[6] Nor were its commercial roots entirely removed as modern diplomacy matured and became professionalized. It is possible to trawl through the memoirs of some of the oldest exponents of "old" diplomacy and find triumphs in securing commercial concessions alongside memories of conversations with emperors, archdukes and presidents recorded with something approaching equal pride. And, of course, once the investigation is widened beyond the scope of modern diplomacy, the conventional understanding of the two is further undermined. As noted above, studies of the international relations of the ancient world, for example, reveal the way in which commercial contacts predated political ones and provided the platforms upon which diplomatic relations, such as they were, might be built.[7] It is possible to argue, therefore, that the great changes that have taken place in European diplomatic practice, for example, are prompted more by the changing character of particular states, in this case the shift of European great powers away from the preoccupations of traditional high politics and the balance of power towards the commercial opportunism of *hansa* focused on trading and investing while under the protection of others. And the phenomenon of states changing from traders to great powers and great powers to traders certainly predates the economic modernizing and globalizing processes said to have spawned it.

Nonetheless, as Hocking and Lee rightly note, the identification of instances of similar activity across the passage of time and space does not, of itself, confirm the essentially unchanging character of what is going on.[8] It is interesting to find an exponent of "old diplomacy" advancing the interests of the Dundee textile industry, but we only obtain a sense of its importance by finding out how much of his time

---

[6] Berridge, "The Origins of the Diplomatic Corps: Rome to Constantinople," pp. 15–30.
[7] Carlo Zaccagnini, "The Interdependence of the Great Powers," in Cohen and Westbrook (eds.), *Amarna Diplomacy*, pp. 141–53 and Buzan and Little, *International Systems in World History*.
[8] Hocking and Lee, "The Diplomacy of Proximity and Specialness," pp. 29–52.

was spent in this kind of work.[9] The answer, of course, is not much. The received distinction between economic thinking and practice, on the one hand, and diplomatic thinking and practice, on the other, while overdrawn to the disadvantage of the latter, does reflect real changes which have taken place in international relations and what people think is important about them which have had profound effects upon the conduct of diplomacy. In particular, we live at a time when powerful interests have been able to argue and secure an audience for the adoption of market principles for organizing, not only what have been conventionally understood as economic relations, but also relations which have historically been understood to lie outside the marketplace.

To an unprecedented extent, these arguments for the "economization" of social life have been successfully made and, where they have not, their implications have been realized by practices associated with the notion of "governmentality."[10] By this, I am not referring to traditional conceptions of how governments politically seek to control and regulate aspects of social and economic life. Rather, I mean the whole array of measures (often quite literally), presented as apolitical in character and established by private and public organizations alike to encourage the adoption or mimicry of what they take to be efficient behavior in a marketplace. Thus the metaphors of, for example, production, exchange, customers, value and efficiency are introduced into new spheres of life through directives, training and the assessment of performances by monitoring, measuring and surveillance. By so doing, advocates argue, we will not only discover the best ways, in terms of performance and results, of doing things. Through the application of steady pressure, we will also empower and, where necessary, nudge everyone else to try to do their best in these terms.[11]

Taken together, the processes of "economization" and ideas of "governmentality" further fuel the expectation that the contemporary world is a hostile place for diplomacy and diplomats. They do so

---

[9] Lord Hardinge of Penshurst, *Old Diplomacy*, p. 53.
[10] Iver B. Neumann (following Foucault), "The English School on Diplomacy: Scholarly Promise Unfulfilled," *International Relations*, 17, 3 (2003), pp. 341–69.
[11] Kishan S. Rana, "MFA Reform: Global Trends" and John Mathiason, "Linking Diplomatic Performance Assessment to International Results-Based Management" in Rana and Kurbalija (eds.), *Foreign Ministries: Managing Diplomatic Networks and Optimizing Value*, pp. 20–43 and 225–32 respectively.

because they both, in principle at least, pose challenges to the idea of peoples living separately and the consequences of their so doing. "Economization" posits the desirability of a single market in which efficiency can be encouraged by uniform conditions of competition enforced by a single regulator. Whatever the reasons for why many states with many governments exist in the world, there is no necessity for them in terms of economic logic. "Governmentality" posits the desirability of a single and enforceable standard of "best" practice established by rules or laws, in terms of which people's performances are to be assessed by common measures. Multiple jurisdictions of separate peoples again complicate this task and, worse, provide grounds for their claiming that they cannot be subjected to such a common standard. For those who seek an "economized" and "governmentalized" social life in which the goals and effectiveness of actors are established and assessed by common rules and measures, diplomats, like typesetters in a print shop, firemen in steam locomotives, or the conductors on old London buses, are both manifestations and symptoms of a world which continues to fall far short of their desired mark. We have a puzzle, therefore. Why, at a time when these two ideas and their practical consequences seem to enjoy great salience, and when diplomacy and diplomats are said to be undergoing an existential crisis as a consequence, do the latter continue to prosper? How, indeed, have they managed to invade the very heart of the territory from which they are customarily regarded as having endured a long exile?[12] To answer these questions, we need to examine two things: what the diplomatic tradition can tell us about how to understand international economic issues; and what diplomatic thinking can tell us about the consequences of economic actors being drawn into diplomatic activity.

International economic issues as diplomatic issues

It often appears as if international economic issues cannot be handled by the methods of diplomacy as this is traditionally conceived. In the latter, diplomats represent with simple and formal precision the ambiguous substance of their sovereigns' maneuvers in their international

---

[12] Rik Coolsaet, "Trade is War: Belgium's Economic Diplomacy In The Age Of Globalisation," *DSPDP* (Leicester: Diplomatic Studies Programme, 62, February 2000), p. 20. See also Ron Barston, *Modern Diplomacy* (London: Longman, 1988), p. 97.

political relations with one another. Everyone knows how this game is played. To what specific ends, however, other than the advantage of each, remains a secret or an unknown contingent on other developments. In international economic relations, the reverse appears to be the case. Simplicity and formality are replaced by the representation of positions that are comprehensive, complex and often of a highly technical character, while the avowed objective of all these efforts is reasonably straightforward. The metaphors of dancing or racing with one another in a game are replaced by those of building and constructing a standing order of rules and sanctions about which nearly everyone involved agrees in principle. Thus, even simple bilateral negotiations, of a trade agreement, for example, can be almost overwhelmed at times by the amount of detail specific to the production, distribution and exchange of the goods involved, yet even the most complex set of multilateral trading rounds is informed by a shared sense of where it is supposed to be going. Nearly everybody says they agree, for example, that the world should move towards more open markets. Disagreements are expressed only about how fast everybody or some should be expected to move in this direction, and about how big everybody's share of the transition costs and maintenance costs of the regime as a public good should be.[13]

In practice, however, the distinction is not so straightforward, for many of the qualities said to distinguish international economic relations apply to all forms of international relations. Security talks, for example, when they involve negotiations about the numbers and capacities of weapons systems, can be just as complex as economic issues, and they take place within a framework of assumptions about a stable, peaceful international order the participants claim to share. Negotiations over environmental issues would seem to be even more technical and more in need of multilateral management than their economic counterparts, even though the shared endpoint is a world developing equitably and in a sustainable way. And even talks about diplomatic representation and the forms it might take are now characterized by complex discussions about the technical capacities of a variety of new and evolving mediums

---

[13] See, e.g., Stephen Woodcock, "The ITO, the GATT and the WTO," in Nicholas Bayne and Stephen Woodcock (eds.), *The New Economic Diplomacy: Decision-Making and Negotiation in International Economic Relations* (Aldershot: Ashgate, 2003), pp. 103–20.

of communication. What these examples reveal is that it is not the specific character of economic issues that poses challenges to diplomacy. Rather, it is the increasing technical application of scientific discoveries to human affairs, to communication about them and, hence, to our understandings of what is going on which affects the conduct of diplomacy across all the dimensions and sectors in which international relations are undertaken. Just as the routines of watching television or undertaking office work have been changed and rendered more complex by such developments, so too has the conduct of all relations between states.

Why, then, do international economic relations stand out? In fact, they do so only in the sense that expectations about them are different. We see these expectations largely in terms of the widespread expression of frustration when economic negotiations fail or are perceived to be dragging on. Other talks on other sorts of issues can take years, even decades, or end in failure and deadlock without attracting either much surprise or frustration, despite what is actually or putatively at stake in them.[14] There seems to exist an expectation that the inertia engendered by relatively static state positions and interests will likely prevail and an embedded tolerance of, or resignation to, the fact that this is so. We expect little movement precisely because the stakes, in terms of state interests, are so high, even though the aspirations of whole peoples may be thwarted and bodies may continue to pile up. Not so with international economic issues. From all points of view, success in negotiating, for example, a temporary tariff mechanism for curbing imports in the Doha round, a bilateral trade liberalization agreement between the United States and one of its neighbors, or the completion of the single market within the European Union, is treated as something which *has* to be achieved and soon. Failure is presented as a real disaster and blamed not only upon governments and those who negotiate for them, but also upon the whole system of states and those whose interests they are said primarily to serve.

We can see here, perhaps, the "power of economics" at work in shaping expectations that economic issues ought to be resolved and the resulting impatience and impending sense of disaster when they are not. By this I mean, quite simply, that those economically powerful

---

[14] Consider, for example, negotiations on the control of conventional and nuclear weapons, territorial settlements, population re-locations and even environmental and population issues.

actors with an interest in resolving such issues, on whatever terms, have the ability to confer these expectations upon them. From within the diplomatic tradition, however, we can see how international economic issues are intrinsically neither more nor less soluble than other international issues and, as such, present diplomats and those thinking diplomatically with the same sort of problems presented by other international issues. Indeed, from this perspective, the world of international economic relations presents a picture both stable and relatively unchanging. In terms of an implied standard of economic wellbeing, there are developed countries, developing countries and so-called "basket cases" which appear to be either going nowhere or falling back. There are greedy, powerful companies and needy, powerless people. There are economic sectors that are prospering and growing, and there are those in trouble and declining. There are status-quo public and private actors which more or less support the existing terms on which economic transactions take place, and there are revisionists who favor changes in some or all these terms, although no general agreement about the direction of change exists among them.

The specific identities of these various actors may change, and there are always arguments over who belongs in the categories. Indeed, growing arguments over which countries should be classed as developing call into question the idea of a division between the developed few and the undeveloped/developing many.[15] Countries themselves, however, still seem content to accept these categories, albeit with the proviso that they reserve the right to present themselves developed or developing as the issue, context and their interests dictate. The recommended routes to prosperity and power may also change. The development of knowledge and services sectors, for example, has replaced the emphasis on industrialization as the road forward for some, just as industrialization replaced the quest for land, a developed agriculture and food self-sufficiency in the past. For others, merely finding something they can export to rich foreigners, be it cheap cars or out-of-season fruits and vegetables, is presented as the way forward and, of course, we now have the spectacle of some of the developed exporting raw materials to some of the developing. Nevertheless, and to paraphrase Martin Wight on international relations in general, negotiators from the early GATT

---

[15] For a review of these arguments see Brown and Ainley, *Understanding International Relations*, pp. 159–61.

rounds or the economic agreements surrounding the Versailles settlement, would soon recognize the arguments and the interests at play if they were somehow parachuted into contemporary economic negotiations. Only the latter's public salience, together with their tendency to seek solutions, not so much in terms of agreements, but in terms of institutionalized mechanisms for monitoring and enforcing agreements, would seem novel.

Indeed, it is very difficult to point to any international economic problem in the past sixty years, at least, which we no longer talk about because it has been comprehensively solved in the terms in which negotiations about it have been presented. Agreement on how to achieve development, for example, remains highly conditional at best – the old doubts lie just beneath the surface, so that even the dismantling of traditional protectionist measures seems to be matched by a constant effort on the part of governments to find new ways of privileging domestic economic activity and the jobs it provides for their own people. So it is too that years of negotiating codes for the regulation and good governance of transnational corporations, whatever actual improvements may have resulted, have done nothing to diminish the greedy company debate. We live in a world in which large and wealthy companies will be regarded as greedy by some, in which those who make such arguments are regarded as obstacles to prosperity by others and in which the greedy company argument will be deployed to advantage "our" companies over "theirs." As a class of actors, however, big companies, like great powers, seem very resilient, they have not gone away and show few signs of doing so. Indeed, it is hard to avoid the conclusion that they simply present diplomacy and diplomats with their own variation of the "same old melodramas" which Wight suggested we read into all international relations.

Does this mean that economic diplomacy and, indeed, the sphere of human action it aspires to manage, are directionless and impervious to any general understanding of what is going on? Not at all. We may wish to identify medium- or long-term secular trends in the world economy, for example, the increasing level of economic transactions that cross international boundaries as a proportion of all economic transactions or the reduction of the traditional methods of protecting and privileging domestic economic activity. We may wish to credit policy with doing more than merely responding to these trends – if not leading them exactly, then at least facilitating them. We may even wish to subscribe to bigger theories of the way in which mercantilist or class-based realities undercut liberal visions of how the international economy is supposed to work or how a liberal crusade is busily uprooting authentic national cultures and silencing equally authentic identities in terms of race, gender and class. However, it is beyond my purpose and my competence to discriminate between these claims. They all capture aspects of what is going on in international economic relations in the sense that they are believed and acted upon and, as such, they are all just parts of a world of economic relations of discovery and re-encounter which remains remarkably stable for long periods for those responsible for conducting them on a daily basis.

Thus every multilateral economic negotiation will involve a rounding up of the usual suspects who can be expected to say the usual things to, and about, one another. They may develop new techniques of collaboration and communication for doing both, and shifting externalities – price changes, technical developments and military interventions, for example – may give new force to some of the arguments and diminish the effectiveness of others.[16] The important questions, however, will remain as follows. Is there anything left to be said, once the basic positions have been stated and, if there is, is there any prospect that agreements reached will be effectively implemented? Both involve diplomacy, and the diplomats' prospects of success may depend on not just the policy decision to let them work their magic, but also the extent to which letting them do so is politically and technically possible. There is a political sense in which both the American and French governments, for example, cannot agree that their markets should be completely opened to agricultural products from elsewhere. And there is a technical sense in which agreements about reducing carbon emissions, for example, by trading permits to pollute could not have been reached until relatively recently. What the diplomats' prospects of success emphatically do not depend on, however, is settling the big arguments about how economic relations are and ought to be organized, and how economic actors behave, and ought to behave, as these are customarily

[16] See, e.g., Ronald Walker, *Multilateral Conferences: Purposeful International Negotiation* (Basingstoke: Palgrave Macmillan, 2004), James P. Muldoon Jr., JoAnn Fagot Aviel, Richard Reitano and Earl Sullivan (eds.), *Multilateral Diplomacy and the United Nations Today* (Boulder: Westview, 1999) and Johan Kaufmann, *Conference Diplomacy: An Introductory Analysis* (Leyden: Sijthoff, 1968).

presented by experts, governments and often their representatives alike. That this is so helps explain the continuing disappointment with economic diplomacy after decades of experimentation involving individuals and organizations from the world of business in trade policy and economic negotiations. The world they confront and with which they have to engage exerts a pressure on them to become, at least in part, diplomatic. And while we should be extremely cautious about ascribing direction, pace and permanence to the great changes associated with the "economization" of international relations, there is evidence to suggest that they increase this pressure. As economic actors become more powerful and thus more important in international relations, they take on something of the character of states or, at least, of diplomatic actors.

Economic actors as diplomatic actors

From the standpoints of economic theory and economic thought more generally, economic actors like companies, banks and, of course, individuals are presented as rational actors interested in efficiency and the maximization of values and interests seen largely in material terms. Of course real economic actors are acknowledged as falling short of this ideal to various degrees, just as diplomats do not always conform to the dictates of good diplomacy. Such lapses, however, are regarded as departures from a standard of behavior to which economic actors ought to conform, and would conform if they could see clearly and were allowed to act in accordance with their vision. These lapses are also usually assumed to be in means and methods rather than objectives and ends. Both efficient and inefficient firms wish to maximize profits, but the former have more information than the latter, plus the intelligence and will to act on it and, hence, are more effective in this regard. Thus little attention is given to economic actors that cease to behave rationally in terms of these specific ends. A company which no longer wants to make a profit, for example, quickly loses both its theoretical interest – it is no longer, properly speaking, a firm – and its practical interest – it will not exist for long. A company which breaks a contract, in contrast, will be very interesting, for doing so may secure a one-off gain, but only at the expense of a principle whose general violation would render the sort of commercial activity from which companies are set up to gain impossible.

The parallels with the arguments by which good conduct is urged upon both diplomats and those they represent is striking, and it strongly suggests that the structure of arguments about abiding by rules, and having rules about rules, is similar across domains of human action. It also suggests that the temptation to defect from these rules produces similar dilemmas, both theoretical and practical, across all fields. Companies, like states, depend upon the systems of rules within which they function, but would also like to be exempted from those rules when they directly impinge upon important interests. However, while the structure of arguments and dilemmas about rule keeping may be broadly similar, the content of those rules can vary considerably across domains. Firms have clear obligations to shareholders, for example, which suggest that they should not give assets away to other people described as poor, deserving or even as stakeholders. Yet we see firms giving some of their resources away. Companies will present themselves as members of the community engaging in charitable work or promoting educational activity, for example. Such activities are, of course, subordinated to the primary mission or core business of the company. Indeed, it is widely assumed that they are tailored to serve the core business although, if nearly everybody assumes that this is so, it is not exactly clear why anyone should regard good corporate citizenship activities as effective. Firms also have explicit and simple purposes for which they exist, and if they fail as instruments of those purposes, their reason for existing is supposed to be at an end. Yet we see firms failing in economic terms and continuing to exist.

What we are seeing, of course, when this sort of thing occurs is not just irrationality in economic terms. We are also seeing economic actors responding to the rules and expectations of other domains in which they operate. In the cases above, for example, they may be acting as members of communities and as communities themselves respectively. Thus, while companies are fond of saying that they are in business to make a profit by manufacturing, for example, automobiles, they also try to make a profit by manufacturing automobiles to stay in business, to stay in existence as social worlds which over time develop their own center of gravity which exerts its own pull on their activities. Mergers, takeovers, breakups and closures demonstrate the limits to this notion of companies as communities existing as ends in themselves, but in this regard, their difference from other communities, states for example, is a matter of degree, not kind. These changes may happen more easily and with far less likelihood of violence, but the breakups and mergers of particular companies and states do not undermine the respective general constitutive principles; that all the above occurs in worlds of companies and states.

It is possible, therefore, to see economic actors as manifesting some of the attributes and priorities of communities. Their specific identities may not be valued to the extent that peoples are, but those who control them will seek to maintain their freedom of action to do things their way, even as they engage in relations with other economic actors, with governments and with the people of the broader communities in which they are rooted. At home, they operate according to a dense network of conventions, rules and laws which together constitute shared understandings about everyone's status, rights and duties, and about how to conduct relations with one another. While they are not free riders, for they contribute a great deal of the money which makes both government policy and political activity possible, they are great beneficiaries of the broader sense of community and society which also makes government and politics possible. However, when they operate internationally, the relative absence of this shared sense of community or society may encourage firms not only to behave as communities, but communities with state-like characteristics.

In regard to this "statization" of companies, the experience of the great European merchant trading companies of the seventeenth and eighteenth centuries is instructive. They acquired armies, navies and foreign services, they exercised control of territories, and entered into relations, sometimes diplomatic, sometimes quasi-colonial, with their neighbors. The British East India Company, in particular, not only attempted to establish a state-like authority over the peoples and territory it directly controlled, and enter into diplomatic relations with its neighbors, it also sought to draw them into a regional system or society to which it imparted central direction.[17] It behaved not just like a state, but also like a great power both in bossing its neighbors and in "statizing" the terms on which they could have relations with it. All this it could attempt because of its advantages in wealth and power, but its

---

[17] See Antony Wild, *The East India Company: Trade and Conquest from 1600* (Guilford: Lyons Press, 2000) and Nick Robins, *The Corporation that Changed the World: How the East India Company Shaped the Modern Multinational* (London: Pluto Press, 2006).

efforts were circumscribed by its status as a private actor in its relations with the British government. This was a subordinate status the latter was prepared to enforce and the company had to accept if it wanted the government to underwrite its efforts and assent to its activities. Once the British government became unwilling to underwrite this status after the Indian Mutiny or First War of Indian Independence, the British East India Company was wound up.

This notion of the "statization" of economic actors must be treated with great caution. It may be objected, for example, that the merchant companies retained very close relations with their respective home governments, and that their ultimate fates underline what is essentially their aberrant quality. Further, while major corporations today may employ security services and international departments, none have acquired an international political status on the scale of the British or Dutch East India Companies.[18] It may also be objected that it is hard to recognize practical manifestations of the theoretical distinction between acting in an environment for advantage and seeking to shape that environment for advantage, on the one hand, and, on the other, taking responsibility for securing that environment in the broader sense of maintaining a public good (although this is a generic objection to viewing all power-holders in these terms). Nevertheless, the fact of such "statized" companies in the past demonstrates that their existence is more than a theoretical possibility. More importantly, a number of contemporary trends ranging from the increasing incidence of failed states to the increasing desire of states to outsource some of their traditional security and diplomatic functions, suggests an international environment which may be becoming more friendly to the re-emergence of "statized" companies.

For where governments are unable, or unwilling, to create and sustain the worlds in which life is to be lived someone, certainly from the point of view of economic actors, has to do it. Should the ability and inclination of economic actors to act like states continue to grow, however, what kind of international relations will they want? The diplomatic tradition of international thought strongly suggests that

---

[18] Although the late Senator Eugene McCarthy argued, somewhat tongue-in-cheek, that the US government should appoint ambassadors to big corporations and even some branches of its own government which seemed to operate as a law unto themselves. See Eugene McCarthy, "Ambassador to Microsoft," *Minnesota Law and Politics* (June/July 2000).

they will not necessarily support the domestication of world order as this is currently (and ineffectively, in their view) being undertaken by states, or their own subordinate status within it. Instead, economic actors which were wealthy, powerful, had a strong sense of their own identity and independence, and which undertook an increasingly broad range of activities beyond the production of wealth and the creation of profits, would likely be interested in a world in which they played at least a part in creating the rules by which it ran, and in which those rules did much to safeguard their independence and freedom of action. They would seek, in short, a world characterized by relations of separateness, the presence of diplomacy and, although they might not recognize it as such, the need for their own diplomats.

Mixed societies and the diplomacy of less greedy companies

Whether they would want such a world to have the same sort of homogenous membership principles as its predecessor – a world of states replaced by a world of firms – is unclear. Whether they wanted it or not, however, the entrenched power of many states would make such a world less likely than a mixed society of states, firms and others. Most attempts to imagine and describe such a world assume that the purposes and functions of international actors will remain relatively unchanged. Thus Strange's notion of "triangular diplomacy," for example, between countries which continue to be state-like, between companies which continue to be firm-like, and between countries and companies.[19] In her presentation, the character of the resulting international relations under such conditions would seem to be a matter of power. Who can insist on their priorities being reflected in the content of those relations certainly, and possibly even the way they are conducted. Beyond this, the framework remains indistinct. We simply have a sense of a world in which states can get less of what they want and have to accommodate firms that are increasingly capable of getting their way. However, if economic actors are acquiring (or recovering) some of the characteristics and functions historically associated with states, while states appear to be disaggregating into enterprise-like entities acquiring

---

[19] Susan Strange, "States, firms and diplomacy," *International Affairs*, 68, 1 (January 1992), pp. 1–15.

operating practices and performance criteria associated with private economic actors, then the picture becomes even more complicated.

The great practical and greater conceptual difficulties implied by this observation create a strong intellectual temptation to resolve them in the direction of one of the implied poles. We might wish to say, for example, that states are being displaced by an essentially rootless network of transnational interactions or, conversely, that, beneath this network, the old structures of state power remain unchanged, but depreciated as always. Lying behind such claims, as always, are vexing questions about the extent to which changes have actually taken place and to what extent our reflection upon what states and firms do only makes it appear as if this is so. It may be, for example, that a close historical investigation would reveal that the lines between states and economic actors in terms of identities and functions have always been blurred in some respects. It may also be the case, however, that this does not matter, and that a realization, even if in some sense an inaccurate one, produced by new reflections, is a change in itself which, as it secures agreement, is capable of generating further changes. After all, it was as Wight noted, a change in the way that men came to see things that spelt the end for Christendom, not the host of material and social facts that could be read in multiple ways until this change of mind marshaled them decisively in one direction.

The difficulties such concerns pose for asking where our present international society currently is in these terms, and where it is heading are, indeed, considerable. This will not prevent people from trying, however, and their answers becoming part of the world we seek to apprehend and understand. The diplomatic tradition, in contrast, invites us not to look at where the world may be going in these terms. Rather, it invites us to consider how states that are becoming more enterprise-like, and firms that are becoming more state-like, might act, and how relations of separateness might continue to be conducted between them. On questions like these, it might be supposed that diplomatic thinking would get us off to a very unpromising start. After all, its own development in the modern era is closely associated with the great homogenization of international societies around the principle that only states could be members and enjoy representation. Indeed, modern diplomatic theory justified such homogenization on the basis of it creating a simpler and, therefore, more stable and more peaceful international politics. And modern diplomatic practice has a history of resisting pressures to let other types of actors, especially economic actors with their low issues and lower priorities, back to the high table of power politics and statecraft. If one concentrates on the modern experience, therefore, one might expect a defense of the old dispensation by which homogeneity was achieved, followed by a dash to develop new principles for achieving the same end once this position became untenable.

However, the extent of this resistance to both new actors gaining diplomatic representation and new forms of representation can be exaggerated by focusing too narrowly on the modern experience. When one looks beyond it to elsewhere and other times, the aberrant quality of the modern period's insistence on homogeneity becomes apparent, as does the extent to which it is currently in retreat. Elsewhere and at other times, what we can call with increasing confidence a more "normal" understanding of diplomatic relations prevailed in which the possibilities for representation were far more open and untidy. From this more "normal" diplomatic thinking two by now familiar insights can be applied to making sense of the mixed international societies that appear to be re-emerging. The first shows in the reactions of professional diplomats to the sorts of debates this development engenders among academics. As noted above, a realist account in which states and their interests in terms of power continue to dominate all else simply does not correspond to the realities of the world in which contemporary diplomats work. To do their jobs properly and to accomplish what their governments expect of them, diplomats will tell you, they have to be fully engaged with and integrated into the world of production, distribution and exchange, for they are seekers of commercial opportunities. Yet, no matter how aware they are of the increasingly internationalized and transnational character of contemporary economic activity, they remain resolutely convinced that they are so engaged and integrated on behalf of the governments and peoples of the countries they represent. In short, they work in a world in which the arguments about what is going on and ought to be going on – in this case, what transnational relations are doing to the idea of separate peoples and states existing as countries – remain both present and unresolved.

Intellectually, this may seem a prescription for incoherence based on insufficient reflection. This is why diplomats, especially when conducting commercial diplomacy, often seem to be actively engaged in undermining the core premise of their own jobs, for example when they court foreign ownership of domestic sectors or negotiate agreements which will restrict the ability of their own governments to exercise sovereignty. Practically, however, success in either regard or the fact that diplomats seek it, may not matter in the way that popular opinion is assumed to think they do, that is, purchasing short-term and precise economic gains at a cost which is long-term and unclear. It may well be, for example, that jobs and a healthy tax base are the real sinews of power for the sort of trading state which most countries now aspire to become. However, if this is not so, then it is possible that diplomats are not engaged in re-tooling themselves and their states for the new terms on which old games are to be played by their masters. They may be engaged instead, and whether they know it or not, in shifting power to new holders. States, or some of them, may fade to be replaced by other states, regional entities and, possibly, even greedy companies as the participants in and members of a new, or greatly changed, international society. At this point, however, diplomats have to work in a world in which both these possibilities remain simply that. They do not know which outcome, if either, will come to pass, nor how quickly or slowly.

In even this indeterminate condition, however, the second insight provided by diplomatic thinking is apparent. If economic actors are becoming more powerful and influential relative to those who previously sustained the international environment in which they operate, they will likely take on more of the responsibility for securing that environment. As they do so, they will be seen, and see themselves, in more than simply instrumental and functional terms. Thus, even greedy companies may undergo considerable changes. Just as great powers learned, albeit imperfectly, to moderate their ambitions and methods in regard to the quest for absolute power and absolute security, diplomatic thinking suggests that greedy companies might discover the value of moderating their ambitions and methods with regard to their need for growth and quest for profits. The diplomatic tradition suggests that they certainly should be encouraged to do so. This argument, of course, rests on a measure of willful economic illiteracy on my part, and the adoption of such changes would result in costs in terms of efficiency, gross production and profits. These companies, however, would no longer be only economic actors. As their power grew beyond that of some of those who traditionally have set the rules within which they operated, then they might eventually become rule-setters themselves. I say "might" because, just as the development of a consciousness among the great powers that their appetites should be moderated was not preordained, but the product of sustained reflection and acting upon it by people trying to be enlightened and good, so too would be such a development among greedy companies. What kind of world would best secure their independence and liberties, if states were no longer able to undertake this alone, and what kinds of changes in greedy companies would be required if they were to assume at least some of the responsibility for maintaining it? Such a world is still hard to imagine, but if the shift in relative power between private and public actors is as has been widely presented, and if that shift continues, then *la raison* of statized companies, its corresponding *raison de système*, and the parts of diplomacy and diplomats in developing both will require serious and sustained attention.

12 | Crazy religion diplomacy

Whatever the problems posed by greedy companies and other economic actors for the effective conduct of diplomacy, it is easy to assume that they cannot be as bad as those posed by crazy religions, denominations and their members.[1] The idea of "crazy religion" flags an apparently new and pressing challenge to the conduct of contemporary international relations. Since the attacks of "9/11" and subsequent events, largely in the United States, Western Europe, South West Asia and the Middle East, insurgent sects have appeared among peoples like hot cinders falling upon forests which, for reasons that to educated received opinion remain shocking and unfathomable, are dry and ready to burn.[2] In a world rendered increasingly intelligible, controllable and exploitable by the application of scientific enquiry and technological discovery to human affairs, growing numbers of people are attracted to pre-scientific accounts of the world and their place within it. Not only that, they are prepared to be mobilized and to act on the basis of these understandings. What does this development tell us about people, the impact of modernization upon them and the prospects for peoples living peacefully together? The international relations of the Middle East often illustrate the problems posed by religion for diplomacy in their sharpest form. How does one negotiate with people who believe their title to a contested piece of land comes from God, and how do they negotiate with people directed by false gods or no gods at all?

These questions, of course, gain their force from a very Western set of expectations about how material development would result in the secularization of religious thought and the economization of secular

---

[1] Hereafter, I shall generally use "religion" to cover "denomination" as well.
[2] See Brigitte Gabriel, *Because They Hate US: A Survivor of Islamic Wars of Terror Warns America* (New York: St. Martin's, 2006). See also Ken Booth and Timothy Dunne (eds.), *Worlds in Collision: Terror and the Future of Global Order* (Basingstoke: Palgrave Macmillan, 2002).

thought about human affairs. The extent to which these expectations are still subscribed to by international and diplomatic elites provides impressive confirmation of the way a European international society did, in fact, spread around the world. Recent events, however, confirm suspicions noted earlier that the depth of that society's penetration has always been over-estimated. Beneath it, older, indigenous and different systems of thought about the world and people's places within it have persisted, even on the home territories of modernization, secularization and "economization." It is the shock of discovering that this is so which has given rise to fears about religion-driven movements and even civilizations posing unprecedented challenges to the idea of globalization steadily overwhelming the resistance of older, local or regional forms of social organization.[3] An image of growing global solidarity – benign or otherwise – has been replaced by one of a growing pluralism involving actors whose fundamental character will make it very difficult for them to engage in relations with one another. Indeed, even secularists become infected by the new militancy as formerly secure ground becomes inundated by the rising tide of what they regard as willful ignorance and human weakness exploited by crazy or wicked people.[4] While the "rise of religion," and crazy religions especially, is regarded as a pressing issue at the moment, however, the problems they pose for peaceful relations between believers, and between those who believe and those who do not, are neither new nor insurmountable. Much depends upon the kind of religion with which one is dealing and, as we shall see, all religious thought offers an opening, in principle at least, to diplomacy.

Westphalia, modern diplomatic thinking and the problem of religion

The current reasons for presenting the relationship between diplomacy and religion as antagonistic have a specific historical provenance. To see how they became "enemies" it is necessary to go back to the beginnings of the modern version of diplomacy and, some would say, to the

---

[3] Samuel Huntington, *The Clash of Civilizations and the Remaking of World Order* (New York: Simon and Shuster, 1996).
[4] Christopher Hitchens, *God Is Not Great: How Religion Poisons Everything* (New York: Twelve Books, 2007) and Richard Dawkins, *The God Delusion* (New York: Houghton Mifflin, 2006).

beginning of the end for religion in seventeenth-century Europe.[5] The problems posed by religion for international relations at that particular time and place were not those of insurgent evangelicals threatening to set the world alight. That phase had passed and the new Christian confessions were as closely linked to established power in those parts of Europe where they had been successful as Roman Catholicism was in the rest. Rather, the problems were posed by what appeared to be the final shattering of the integral religious myth of Christendom by which the various political communities of Europe had continued to regard themselves as one. While Christendom's ability to stand and act as a single political unit, whether under pope or emperor, had been in long decline, it had continued to exert a fading sense of togetherness for certain purposes, restraining ambitions, moderating conduct and providing its members with a common moral frame of reference by which to make sense of and evaluate their relations with one another. Thus, the diplomatic challenge posed by this shattering was one of maintaining stable re-encounter relations between established polities which were experiencing increasing levels of alienation both from one another and from the previous terms on which they had conducted relations with one another.

The challenge was made more difficult, however, by two factors. First, neither the surviving rump of the Catholic Church nor the various Protestant sects that together now constituted a plural religious environment had lost the solidarist assumptions and universalist habits of thought of the order they had replaced. They all thought of establishing peace and order by restoring the unity of the past, albeit on their own terms. Secondly, the new confessions quickly became linked, like the old faith before them, to the principal centers of secular power. Thus states were fueled by faiths that encouraged and, indeed, insisted that they take a strong interest in the internal affairs of their fellows, while faiths were provided with the material means – guns and money – for advancing their agendas. The result was a war, or series of wars, of exceptional

---

[5] See, for considerations of religion and contemporary international relations, Scott M. Thomas, *The Global Resurgence of Religion and the Transformation of International Relations: The Struggle for the Soul of the Twenty-First Century* (Basingstoke: Palgrave Macmillan, 2005) and Ralph Pettman, *Reason, Culture, Religion: The Metaphysics of World Politics* (Basingstoke: Palgrave Macmillan, 2004).

intensity and destructiveness fought to the point where exhaustion overtook, and collapse threatened, all the participants.[6]

Since religious faith was widely seen as having driven states and their peoples to such extremes for an end it failed to realize – the restoration of Christendom on new or old terms – it might be said that it was religion that lost the Thirty Years War. By a process of negotiations which had actually begun before the final rupture, the various claims of Christian denominations regarding how all people should live and worship God were, for the most part, gradually removed from the agenda of issues about which it was appropriate for states to negotiate among themselves.[7] Whatever the universal claims of faiths in theory, in practice and among European powers, they would apply henceforth only within states or when governments consented to external spiritual guidance, which was not often. Religion was effectively nationalized or, more accurately, "statized" to the general satisfaction of all except those who continued to believe that worldly suffering was a small price to pay for conforming to God's will and avoiding eternal damnation. States, their mastery of secular power confirmed, prospered, and religious denominations, their inability to make their universal claims stick, went into what was thought to be terminal decline as effective international political agents.

In all this, of course, diplomacy and diplomats played a central role. Modern sovereignty clarified and cemented the conditions of their work to an extent that was unprecedented. The direction of the current was so strong that even when ambassadors insisted on traditional privileges such as *droit de chapel*, now given radical significance by the existence of multiple roads to Christian salvation, the assertion of one universal claim against another merely underlined the limits to all of them.[8] Faith became an internal state matter and even, in places, a personal matter, a right of individuals to be safeguarded. Neither sovereigns nor their diplomats were supposed to worry about matters of religious faith within other states, and religious concerns were no longer held to provide acceptable grounds for making demands on others or even advancing a position in legitimate diplomatic discourse. A weak and pale ghost of Christian community might appear in general declarations concerning

---

[6] C. V. Wedgwood, *The Thirty Years War: New York Review of Books Classics* (New York: New York Review of Books, 2005) (London: Jonathan Cape, 1938).
[7] Wight, *Power Politics*, p. 37.
[8] Mattingly, *Renaissance Diplomacy* and Frey and Frey, *The History of Diplomatic Immunity*.

infidels and savages, and, in the nineteenth century, that great internal infidel, social revolution. By taking questions of faith, and denominational ones especially, out of relations between states, however, it was generally agreed that a source of one of the great banes of effective diplomacy had been removed.

It is this story that explains the trepidation among most diplomats and attentive publics, particularly in the West, about the current revival of interest in religious thought as a guide to political action around the world. Self-righteous, faith-based systems of moral certainty, worse, contending systems of such certainty, may be re-populating a domain of human affairs from which both they and the general faith principle itself have been profitably excluded for nearly 400 years. And if this is so, then they may be driving out diplomacy, as this is conventionally understood to have developed over the same period. There is a chance that this may be happening, although not in the simple sense of intolerance driving out tolerance presented above. And to the extent that established patterns of diplomatic practice are being changed, rather than driven out, by the current "rise of religion," there is more than a chance that this may not altogether be a bad thing. Religious modes of thinking and understanding are different from other modes of thinking and understanding, to be sure. Yet neither is so different that those who are captive to them can escape both the need and the desire for diplomacy, any more than those who insist on seeing the world in political or economic terms. To see why, however, it is necessary to examine in more detail what sorts of things the idea of religion and religious thought convey. By doing so, it will be possible to demonstrate the narrowness of the experience on which the Westphalian lessons about diplomacy and religion are based, and to see how the diplomatic tradition of international thought suggests other, more encouraging, ways of presenting the relationship.

Religion, religions and crazy religion

In considering religion and religions, crazy or otherwise, it is important from the outset to keep in mind an important distinction between trying to view them from the "outside," and seeking to understand them from within or on their "own terms."[9] From the former standpoint we can

---

[9] Herbert Butterfield, *Christianity and History* (New York: Charles Scribner's Sons, 1950) and *Christianity in European History* (London: Collins, 1952).

examine the idea of religion analytically and actual religions in terms of sociology and psychology. Thus we may say, for example, that the term religion suggests a system of ideas that purport to offer a true understanding of the world and our place within it. Such systems usually, but not necessarily, posit a divine first, or ongoing, cause of why things and people exist, and they usually, but not necessarily, posit a spiritual essence to life that is more important than, and transcends, the mundane world of temporary and physical appearances. Most also suggest a moral code of conduct by which believers should live, and most, but not all, suggest that everybody should be believers. Further, we may say that these systems of ideas exist in the sense that groups of people, exhibiting various degrees of social cohesion, seem to need them, adhere to them, act accordingly, and are aware of themselves as such. We speak, therefore, of religions as movements, organizations and institutions. In the latter sense, they are often manifestations of a religious aspect to human associations like bands, tribes, kingships and states that exist for a wide range of purposes. However, there is often no tidy fit between religious institutions and the political communities in which they are found. There are state and national religions, but even these tend to spill over political borders. There are also a number of world religions, but even these tend to have an identifiable core geographical base, from which they may or may not have spread.

Nothing in the above, however, quite captures the force, energy and sheer life their own religions acquire at various times in the course of their existence. The same can be said, of course, for all forms of social organization from nations and peoples down to football teams' supporters clubs. It is particularly important in the case of religions, however, because of the comprehensive and foundational character of the beliefs they embody and may make manifest. Viewed on its own terms, a religion may completely lose the aspectival and functional qualities suggested by looking at it from outside. Instead, it becomes central to a person's, or a people's, whole way of seeing the world and their place within it. Indeed, like Christendom and the Dar ul Islam, it may appear, for those who live in it, to constitute the world for which everything else is organized and serves a purpose. This comprehensive quality becomes particularly evident under two separate, but sometimes related, conditions.

The first is at times of great change. Thus, as Wight notes, while we can trace the emergence of the modern European states system through a series of wars, confrontations and conferences by which a new political dispensation replaced an old one, the real change occurs when people stop seeing Rome and the Pope as the center of God's authority in the world and look for that authority elsewhere.[10] They collectively experience a change of heart about how they see things, the arguments begin to flow in different directions, and the evidence (often the same evidence) is washed up in new places sustaining new views of the way things are and should be.[11] The second set of circumstances in which this comprehensive quality becomes clear is when a religious movement possesses an evangelical or missionary quality requiring that believers not only live according to the will of God or the gods, but also spread the word and seek to convert others to the faith. This is particularly so, but not only so, when their message extends beyond the personal and personal relations to how communities and societies as a whole should be organized. Religious faith may hold a world together, indeed constitute it, by providing answers to the most profound sorts of questions that seem to trouble all people. In the process of establishing it and replacing its predecessors, however, religious faith may also tear a social world apart both figuratively and literally.

It is at this point that we move onto the terrain suggested by the term "crazy religion." There is, of course, a sense in which all religion and religions are crazy. They rest on developed, specified and demanding premises, the existence of which cannot be independently verified. As I noted above, this property is by no means restricted to religious thought. It does not seem to pose a problem to most people when they want to believe something, whether it be about the gods, true love, or the prospects of their favorite sports team. It is a problem, however, for those who do not believe, especially when believers become insistent. It is also the case that the soubriquet of "crazy" attaches more easily to what may be termed revisionist faiths, even though they may be based on premises that are no more crazy than those which their believers are seeking to displace. Indeed, to the outsider or non-believer, it is striking how minor the doctrinal differences may be which generate such hostility, especially when they are compared to the shared leap of faith which makes religious belief possible and to the very similar avowed purposes for which faiths exist. Then, what seems crazy is neither the premises on which contending religions rest nor the respective beliefs which these premises generate, so

---

[10] Wight, *Power Politics*, pp. 25–6.
[11] Herbert Butterfield, *The Origins of Modern Science* (London: Bell, 1949).

250   Diplomatic Theory of International Relations

much as the gap between what the contenders claim to believe about right conduct and the way they actually conduct themselves in regard to one another. When at least one party makes non-negotiable, faith-based claims upon others, enjoys considerable capacity to affect them, and acts in a way which appears to bear no relation to the moral precepts of its own faith, the nightmare of the Westphalian story of religion and diplomacy is realized and crazy religion diplomacy is required.

Encounters and discoveries between faith-based powers: the diplomatic thinking of early Islam

It may seem surprising that any sort of diplomacy could occur under such unpromising conditions. How is one to maintain relations of separateness between peoples, at least one of which believes that everyone is, or should be, the same, which is to say, like us in their general orientation to life and what it ought to be about? The answer is, of course, that though it is difficult under such conditions, it is possible and for all the usual reasons. When people want something from one another and cannot, or do not wish to, take it by force they must talk, even if only at the archetypal base level for negotiations, talks between hostage-takers and those who would free their captives. Difficulty, in itself, does not make such talks impossible. Zealots and Romans, Anabaptists and German princes, Sikh militants and Indian policemen, not to mention Branch Davidians and the Federal Bureau of Firearms and Tobacco, for example, all managed to talk to each other at something like this level. Crude bargaining undertaken in highly unstable conditions may be thought barely to constitute diplomacy. However, it would be obtuse to say that it bears no resemblance to diplomacy and, the optimist might argue, such situations are always pregnant with the possibility of a more developed diplomacy breaking out.

In fact, crazy religion diplomacy quickly develops beyond the sparse exchanges of hostage negotiations, especially when the conversion of the other side is an objective of at least one of the parties. To see how this can happen in what may seem to be the most unpromising circumstances, it is instructive to look at accounts of Muhammad's diplomacy in the early years of Islam.[12] Muhammad and his followers began as a

---

[12] See Afzal Iqbal, *The Prophet's Diplomacy: The Art of Negotiation As Conceived and Developed By the Prophet of Islam* (Cape Cod: Claude Stark and Co.,

desert group bound by his leadership and faith in his teaching, and they sustained themselves initially by raiding the trading caravans between the cities in their locale. They established control in one of the cities, and this became a platform for expansion by a combination of armed force, political negotiation and religious conversion. At each stage in the Muslims' consolidation of power, first in Medina, then Mecca and finally the rest of the Arabian peninsula, a call to others to accept that there was no god but God and that Muhammad spoke with absolute authority as his disciple and prophet, lay at the heart of his communications with others. Indeed, even after his position in the region was secured, Muhammad used the same formula in his greetings to the leaders of the great powers at the time. The Roman emperor, the Persian king and the Ethiopian negus were all summoned "to the call of Islam." "Embrace Islam" they were told "and you will be preserved." The formula varied only in that some had the rewards of acceptance, in both earthly and heavenly terms, enumerated, but all were told their refusal would make them "the sin of the people." Upon learning that the Persian king had torn up his offer, for example, Muhammad is reputed to have said that his kingdom would be "torn to pieces."[13]

On first reading, this would seem to confirm all the Westphalian doubts about the ability of religious faith and good diplomacy to co-exist. The greeting formula employed by the early Muslims suggests not so much diplomacy as a declaration of policy – the intention to secure the submission of pagans, polytheists, Jews and Christians to God's will as this is interpreted by Muhammad. If it is diplomacy, then it would seem to be diplomacy of the weakest sort, communicating a non-negotiable demand with profound consequences for the interests and identities of others, backed by a threat which, for most of the time, the Muslims were in no position to carry out. Where, it might be asked, is the respect for others living in their own way and the measure of, if not doubt, then humility and restraint about one's own position which are said to permit the give-and-take of good diplomacy? It is as though Muhammad, or those who have interpreted the external relations of the early *Umma* under his guidance, had no understanding of what good diplomacy assumes, values, or seeks to achieve. In accounts of

1975) and Yasin Istanbuli, *Diplomacy and Diplomatic Practice In The Early Islamic Era* (Oxford: Oxford University Press, 2001).
[13] Suaib Alam Siddiqui, *The Role of Diplomacy in the Policy of the Prophet (PBUH)* (New Delhi: Kanishka Publishers, 2002), p. 47.

the diplomacy of the Prophet, the virtues are all there. Gentleness; truthfulness; clarity; patience; moderation; and loyalty are repeatedly enumerated as the qualities of the Prophet exhibited in his dealings with believers and non-believers alike. However, they appear to pertain only to form. On principle and substance, there can be no movement.[14] Being right trumps all.

However, the judgment that Muhammad's approach barely qualifies as diplomacy, and then only of the weakest sort, is harsh, for there is more to the story. Clearly, the overlap or blur between policy and diplomacy in evidence here is a widespread phenomenon often found elsewhere. More importantly, the claim to base one's position on core principles that cannot be compromised is also not a feature of faith-driven statecraft alone. All governments and their diplomatic services claim to have at least some irreducible principles in this sense (whether this is true or not). And, unsurprisingly, an investigation of the texts soon yields statements which offer some sort of balance to the formulae of core principles in Muhammad's opening *démarches* set out above. It may well be that all must find the right way to God or perish, and that Muslims must play a part in bringing them to this right way. This missionary impetus notwithstanding, however, the Koran states with regard to disagreements between the Faithful and others,

> Unto us our works, and unto you your works
> No argument between us and you
> Allah will bring us together
> And unto him is the journeying.[15]

There may only be one truth, but in principle, at least, each travels his own road towards it at God's pace.

More importantly, the judgment that there is little or no diplomacy in the stories of early Islamic statecraft is harsh because it takes the latter out of its historical/cultural context and assesses it only in terms of criteria borrowed from another time and place. In his own terms, the purpose of Muhammad's diplomacy was to communicate peacefully a message about the Truth from God to other people. The immediate context for understanding it is not our own conception of diplomacy as a process of give-and-take between restrained and self-

---

[14] Iqbal, *The Prophet's Diplomacy*, pp. 82–131.
[15] *The Quran*, iii, 134, cited in Iqbal, *The Prophet's Diplomacy*, p. 84.

restrained egotists who recognize the relative character of their own identities and interests. It is the intensely tribal international society of seventh-century Arabia in which the blood ties and kinship by which the internal orders of its members were secured prevailed over broader conceptions of both order and justice as a guide to right conduct. Under such conditions, merely to speak peacefully in terms that applied to all human beings, no matter what tribe they belonged to, and whether they were believers or unbelievers, could be construed as an act of considerable diplomacy in itself.

This favorable view appears to be borne out by the response of others to Muhammad's efforts. They might reject his call, indeed, most of them did at the initial encounter, but, with the possible exception of the Persian king, they did not do so in terms that suggest that offence had been taken at the scope of the request. Indeed, initial encounters were often characterized by moderation on both sides, as they discovered the position of the other's faith on questions of doctrine. The formula followed was to reach a statement which captured the ground on which both parties could agree, for example, about the Virgin Birth or the fact that Jesus was of God's nature, rather than to emphasize the differences, for example, over the divinity of Jesus and the status of his teachings. And it seems clear that the threats which accompanied Muhammad's invitations to heed the call of Islam were more of the order of observations about what God would do to those who spurned his offer, rather than commitments about what Muslim armies would do to the infidels on God's behalf.[16]

Thus Muslim accounts of the Prophet's diplomacy tell a story of progress by what might be regarded as tactical appeasement. He conceded on most of the details, even on vital questions of protocol, for example, about whose terms for referring to God should be used in agreements.[17] He insisted, on one occasion, that an ambassador who had expressed a desire to convert and remain at Medina return to his own masters, saying he was not free as a representative, a *rasul* or *safir*, to do as he liked.[18] The very spectacle of Muhammad's willingness to

---

[16] The same cannot be said about Muhammad's successors, of course.
[17] Negotiations with the Quraysh at Hudaybiya, Iqbal, *The Prophet's Diplomacy*, p. 26.
[18] Iqbal, *The Prophet's Diplomacy*, p. 55 and Siddiqui, *The Role of Diplomacy*, p. 9. The terms *rasul* and *safir* connote a person sent out or abroad with a specific mission.

make concessions in such intolerant times, these sources maintain, drew others to him. Only on the issue of apostasy, then as now, did there exist little scope for tolerance, a not insignificant omission on the part of a movement for which conversion in its own direction was so important.

The effectiveness of this early inclination to avoid arguments over details and to pursue the diplomacy of personal example may be questioned. It certainly did not provide a way of settling big doctrinal differences other than by renunciation and submission. However, as thinking diplomatically suggests, this is not particularly important. Big arguments, generally speaking, do not have to be completely settled, especially those that can only be settled by one party's complete submission or destruction. What is important is that, in issuing his call, Muhammad committed his people to talking to others, at least initially, as others. This is confirmed by the agreements, both internal and external, reached with other peoples. The *Dastur-i-Madinah* or Covenant of Medina, for example, which set out the terms on which Muslims, Jews and polytheists would relate to one another in the city, noted that each group was free and independent on internal and, particularly, religious matters but that they would constitute a single community for certain purposes, for example, defense against external enemies. The treaty of Hudabiya with the Quaraysh, a prominent external enemy at the time, acknowledged the latter's right to impose restrictions on the terms and frequency of Muslim pilgrimages to certain holy sites.[19]

Thus, whatever their original intentions, once he had issued his call, Muhammad and his followers were both drawn into the give-and-take of diplomacy and propelled into it by what the dictates of their faith had to say about right conduct towards other human beings. In so doing, and under far more difficult conditions than those of seventeenth-century Europe, they demonstrated that it is possible for even an intensely evangelizing religious movement to engage in and be engaged by others in diplomatic relations which go far beyond the level of truce talks between belligerents or hostage negotiations between criminals and the authorities. Even evangelicals can find in their faiths grounds for subordinating the dictates of doctrine to the requirements of effective encounters with their neighbors. Amongst the tribes and peoples of the Arabian Peninsula, of course, the universalist message of Islam had a powerful and transforming effect, calling to them as human beings in

---

[19] Siddiqui, *The Role of Diplomacy*, p. 34.

relation to God rather than as members of their respective communities. Yet with other great powers possessing their own universal visions, the discovery of deep differences that were then aired at length provided a way in which they and Islam might re-encounter each other while maintaining their separateness. Indeed, and paradoxically as far as conventional diplomatic wisdom is concerned, the experience of early Islam suggests that, under certain conditions, the tendency of all parties to think in terms of universals and absolutes may prepare them better for the representations of their fellows in these terms.[20] Neither the Christian Roman Emperor Heraclius nor the Christian Negus in Ethiopia, for example, were half as offended by Muhammad's invitation as one might expect a British prime minister or French president would be if they had been similarly propositioned by the leaders of the Taliban or al Qaeda.

Beyond discovery to re-encounters: the difficulties of diplomacy between faith-based powers

The experience of early Islam demonstrates that diplomacy between intense evangelists and others, and even with each other, is nearly always possible. It also demonstrates, however, that it is rarely easy, is usually undertaken in highly unstable conditions, and is always vulnerable to disruption from all the parties to it. A major problem in rogue state diplomacy, noted above, is the subsequent reluctance of those who have identified the rogues to talk with them. The rogues, in contrast, generally work assiduously for recognition by, and relationships with, their accusers or, at least, their accusers' friends. In crazy religion diplomacy, in contrast, the shoe is often on the other foot. There may be no talking to those identified as crazy because, for a number of reasons, they do not want to talk to you. Not all faiths have an evangelical component. Some, for example, believe in an elect whose duty is merely to do their best to live according to God's will in a world that makes this difficult. They wish, as a consequence, all contact with outsiders to be

---

[20] Contrast this with the orthodox view expressed by Mattingly that "As long as conflicts between states are about prestige or profit or power, grounds of agreement are always accessible to sane men. But the clash of ideological absolutes drives diplomacy from the field." Mattingly, *Renaissance Diplomacy*, p. 196. It is not the adherence to absolutes that is the problem so much as the need to translate what they suggest into practice.

kept to a minimum, and all diplomats to be treated with suspicion, their own, because they must learn to negotiate the outside world, and the other fellow's, because they bring the outside world into their midst.

Non-evangelical religious movements rarely pose great problems in these terms, provided, and this is an important and increasingly difficult proviso to satisfy, they are left alone. Evangelicals, in contrast, while, by definition, keen on talking, may simply not want to talk with those they regard as evil and irredeemable. They may prefer, like al Qaeda, to conduct a total war against them to the best of their abilities, both as a good in itself – reducing evil in the world one infidel at a time – and as an example to those whom they really wish to convert and lead. The targets of their violence may well not be the targets of their diplomacy, but merely the unfortunate victims of an attempt to attract a third party's attention. And these same targets may adopt what is essentially a very similar approach to dealing with such movements for very similar sorts of reasons – reducing evil in the world one terrorist at a time – and impressing potential followers with their ability to lead in this regard. When both sides adopt such a position, no longer seeking a peaceful encounter, then, in principle at least, they communicate only to discover that which will make it possible to destroy the other.

I say in principle, however, for in fact such a state of affairs rarely seems to be reached or, if reached, does not last for long. The pressure to talk, to find a way, if not to peace then to advantage, while not always effective is, nevertheless, a constant. Both sides are always tempted to talk, therefore, and "both" sides usually consist of many "sides," some of which are more willing to talk than others. When they do, arms-for-hostage talks can be smoothed by gifts of cakes and bibles and mutate into discussions of faith, and even the most ascetic and pure militants may find themselves, on the rare occasions when they succeed in representing themselves to the wider world, using the opportunity to offer cease-fires and truces so that the terms of re-encountering one another can be re-established.[21] If they are successful in this regard, however, then a second problem emerges. It is one thing to discuss the divinity of Jesus in a process of mutual discovery, where nothing more is at stake than having one another's curiosity satisfied. It is another, as the

---

[21] George P. Shultz, *Turmoil and Triumph: My Years as Secretary of State* (New York: Maxwell Macmillan, 1993), p. 784. See also Parsi, *Treacherous Alliance*.

inhabitants of Taif discovered once they had agreed in principle to submit to Mecca, to negotiate the modalities by which the images of your gods will be destroyed and how long your derogations from the duties of *zakat* and *jihad* might last.[22] When negotiations between faith-based missionaries and others, or among themselves, move onto the details and substance implied by general principles and promises, the full implications of the expansive character of missionary movements come into play. Between peoples, one or both of which have all-encompassing views of the world and the right place of everyone within it, discussions of details and substance quickly impinge upon core conceptions of faith and identity, ostensibly leaving little room for maneuver. Between such protagonists, a reconciliation of viewpoints seems achievable only if one or both parties make concessions that effectively destroy the heart of their positions.

These difficulties may be compounded by the circumstances in which issues of substance are likely to come to the fore. The pressure to talk may be constant, but the pressure to talk about issues of substance, or to talk in such a way as to produce substantive consequences is less so, and more easily resisted. At least it is so until one or both parties believe that necessity insists and that power allows them to push talks in this direction. Muhammad's diplomacy, for all its demands upon people's very souls, had largely a declaratory character. It relied in great part upon the novelty and content of his message, together with a conduct conspicuously framed in moral and exemplary terms, to achieve results. The same cannot be said of his successors once Muslim power had been consolidated. Then, faith was more likely to be exported on the points of swords. Similarly, the core of Christ's teaching set forth in the Sermon on the Mount, eschewing power and promising final victory to the meek, gave way to the Church militant which eventually emerged as a powerful instrument of conquest and more-or-less forceful conversion. The achievement and exercise of power appear to be constant temptations to religious movements and ones to which the major parts, at least, of all of them eventually succumb, losing their own souls in the process.

To regard such developments as puzzles, it might be argued, merely illustrates the dangers of taking religion and religions seriously on their

---

[22] Negotiations for the adherence of Taif to Islam, Iqbal, *The Prophet's Diplomacy*, p. 58.

own terms.[23] Power should not be viewed as a temptation but as a property of people, because people are only superficially, not profoundly, religious. The course of this argument is well traveled and the objections to it are well known. All the diplomatic tradition can add to it is that, insofar as people can be described as being profoundly anything beyond group-dwellers, sometimes they are profoundly religious and sometimes they are not. The puzzle posed by faith and power for diplomacy and diplomats remains the one that faced them at the time of Westphalia. How are relations of separateness to be stabilized and maintained once material power and secular means are placed in the service of religious movements with universalist goals and a transcendent understanding of what life is and ought to be about? While the question remains the same as that which confronted the diplomatists of seventeenth-century Europe, the answers permitted by contemporary world politics and suggested by diplomatic thinking appear to be considerably different.

From "boxing and taming" to "exile and promotion"

The seventeenth-century European solution to the problems posed by religion was to box it, tame it and, although this was probably unintended, kill it by the spread of reason through education. Once the claims of faith were restricted to the interior life, first of the state and then of the person, they would not, by definition, be causes of international conflict. Once religious or denominational movements were no longer actively seeking the salvation of all mankind on their own terms, but settling for life as one faith with universal pretensions among several such faiths, they would no longer be taken so seriously on their own terms. At least, this may have been how it was supposed to work. The reality, as always, was more complicated. As a source of state power, religious faith often proved a difficult atom to harness, and even as specifically religious faith declined in the more developed parts of the world, the strength of conviction and certainty of purpose associated with it were often transferred to secular projects. It was quite possible, for example, for people to believe in Scientific and National Socialism in much the same way others had believed in God, the Five Pillars and the

---

[23] Michael G. Cartwright, "Biblical Arguments in International Ethics," in Terry Nardin and David R. Mapel (eds.), *Traditions of International Ethics* (Cambridge: Cambridge University Press, 1992), pp. 270–96.

Way of the Cross. And, of course, there were vast tracts of the world from which the centrality of religious faith was never deleted, never mind expunged.[24] On the whole, however, the "box and tame" solution worked sufficiently well for a system of diplomacy from which questions of religious faith were excluded to function, for a general agreement to emerge among international elites that this state of affairs was how things ought to be, and for most of us to have a memory of the world being, in fact, like this and becoming more so.

Very little of this general sense remains. "Boxing and taming," in the sense of keeping religious issues, except for persecution, off the international agenda of states, is still the preferred official solution. However, the conditions that made it as successful as it was in the past have been greatly weakened, at least for now. They have so by the usual suspects, the popularization, domestication and expansion of international affairs made possible by revolutions in communications technology and political expectations. People may not have changed a great deal in their degree of religiosity, but the ability to reach them by multiple sources of influence and, more importantly, to present their concerns and terms of reference as influential have both greatly expanded. National coalitions, transnational networks and, latterly, international civilizational movements, all animated by religious faith, seek to participate in international life and to make claims upon the international society of states. As a consequence, a consensus that religion can cause problems in international affairs, let alone about how to deal with them, is no longer so easily mobilized. For now at least, no one seems able to exert even the imperfect control which states enjoyed over religious belief in the past, and the option of "boxing and taming" which was so central to the modern current in the diplomatic tradition of international thought no longer seems to be an option.

Other currents in the tradition, however, suggest alternative ways of dealing with religion, some more likely to succeed than others.[25] One, which the experience of early Islam and the ecumenical movement of the last century both suggest, is to avoid issues of substance, or with

---

[24] Charles Jones, "Christianity in the English School: deleted but not expunged," paper presented at ISA Chicago, February, 2001.
[25] John Stempel, "Faith, Diplomacy and the International System," *DSPDP* (Leicester: Diplomatic Studies Programme, 69, 2000), pp. 1–20 and Douglas Johnston and Cynthia Sampson (eds.), *Religion: The Missing Dimension of Statecraft* (Oxford: Oxford University Press, 1994).

substantive consequences, for as long as possible. This fits squarely with the tradition's emphasis on the value of talk for talk's sake, even if it is only, in Satow's phrase, to effect "postponement of the evil day" when the dam must surely break.[26] In diplomacy, each day of peace purchased is a victory, even if the price is one that flies in the face of righteousness, reason, or might. Although they are not always correct in this regard, it is with good reason that diplomats are generally among the last to be convinced by the argument that pain must be embraced now to forestall greater pain at some later date. Thus we associate ecumenical and inter-faith dialogues between religious leaders not with restoring old unities or achieving new ones so much as achieving and maintaining stable relations between faiths. When inter-faith relations are not good, as at present, the fact of such summits being held, together with the shared risk of participating in them, might be more significant than any substantive gains they might or might not achieve. One can imagine, for example, an extended interfaith conference focused not on particular international issues, but on discovering the points of agreement and disagreement, about belief, doctrine and right conduct for human beings.[27] It might culminate in a summit of religious leaders confirming what had been stated and suggesting a direction for future talks, but one in which no one made a single gain or concession on matters of doctrine and belief. Indeed, any such movement would be actively discouraged as negating the point of the process, to demonstrate the possibilities of mutually non-threatening co-existence even between missionary faiths.

Another diplomatic technique for handling difficulties generated by differences in religious beliefs in the past is the tactical appeasement I referred to above. By this, I mean discovering and accepting the terms of reference with which the other party views specific relations, as opposed to matters of more general doctrine and faith. Many cultures, for example, regarded gift giving and exchange as sacred, rather than mundane, activities. Thus American Indians might be condoled and appeased by European settlers who had murdered one of their number by a sequence of gifts; tobacco to bury the victim properly, a bolt of

---

[26] Satow, *An Austrian Diplomatist in the Fifties*, p. 57.
[27] See, e.g., Donna Abu-Nasr and Abdullah Shihri, "Saudi King Calls For Interfaith Dialogue," *ABC News*, March 25, 2008 accessed August 4, 2008 online at http://abcnews.go.com/International/wireStory?id=4518593.

cloth to wipe away the tears of the relatives and so on.[28] In this manner, what the settlers could do and wanted to do was reconciled with what the Indians believed to be right and fitting. Some of the settlers saw this exchange of goods for lives as evidence of how cheaply Indians valued the latter and, hence, evidence of their inferiority. Others, though much fewer, came to grasp the significance of the practice in the context of the Indians' understanding of the world and their place within it.

Such brief glimpses of cross-cultural understanding, however, particularly given the eventual destination of Indian-settler relations, do little to inspire confidence in this as a future direction for diplomacy. They seem to work best in the encounter phase and in the early stages of discovery. Once re-encounter relations have been established such attempts at understanding appear restricted to the realm of ceremony and the requirements of civility. Consider, for example, the narrowness of the scope for active appeasement which those who claim to speak for the Abrahamic faiths can offer one another when a mosque in Rome creates unease, a church or synagogue in Mecca remain impossibilities, and Jerusalem provides our best guide to what happens when all three, together with their satellites, exist in close proximity. Nor do the prospects for some contemporary equivalent of the European settlers' appeasement of American Indians' view of trade as exchange with potentially sacred qualities seem encouraging. It remains hard, but not impossible, to imagine how the international exchanges of goods, services and capital could be imbued with such a quality. What we can say is that, were it possible, then economic actors might behave with more restraint in narrowly economic terms and their actions be viewed with less hostility by others. We might add that, if religiosity is once again on the rise, then the prospects for a greatly expanded notion of what is sacred are, in principle at least, increasing proportionately. For the moment, however, the active and positive association of economic activity with religious faith remains both submerged and on the margins of international life, and the impatience with diplomacy of the people and movements engaged in such activity is notorious.[29]

---

[28] Merrell, *Into the American Woods*, pp. 247 and 310.
[29] Reychler, "Beyond Traditional Diplomacy," p. 11.

A more promising course of action involves reversing modern diplomacy's strategy of "boxing and taming" religions. Historically speaking, of course, boxing did not always result in taming. Not only did co-opted religions become the high-test fuel for state projects, they sometimes threatened to take over the state for projects of their own. Nevertheless, it was those religions – and other forms of social movements and groups – which became attached to the great slabs of power that many states remain, that prospered.[30] Those which did not have struggled to exert consistent influence on a broad range of issues over a period of time. The faith-driven movements such as al Qaeda and its satellites, that have attracted attention and created much pain and suffering in recent years, confirm this supposition. Al Qaeda did not wish to be co-opted, even by the Taliban's Islamic Emirate of Afghanistan, and states have been unable to co-opt other movements like it for any more than tactical purposes. Hence, in historical terms, these radical religious movements remain weak. There is, for example, little or no prospect of today's radical Islam sweeping across Arabia, North Africa and Southern Europe in the manner of its predecessor between the sixth and ninth centuries, merely of its adherents continuing to destabilize existing political structures with which they are unhappy. And there remains no prospect of evangelical Christianity or any other faith hijacking a great power, even the United States, merely of them exerting a disproportionate and, sometimes, distorting influence upon their foreign policy. This being so, boxing and taming of religions might usefully be replaced by exile and promotion.

By this I mean that the radical religious movements about which we worry might be kept at arm's length, and those already enjoying an intimate relationship with states pushed into exile, by being granted a measure of diplomatic recognition as members of our international society. The case of the Catholic Church with its secular foundation in a very weak state is instructive in this regard. The Lateran treaties provided the Catholic Church with a place within the international society of states without overly disrupting the principles by which that society is organized. In so doing, it accomplished two things. First, it burdened the Church with the responsibilities of a state within a world

---

[30] The phrase "colossal slabs of power" is Butterfield's in "Christianity and Human Problems," *Christianity, Diplomacy and War*, p. 10.

of states. Second, it provided a way by which religions might be let back into international politics should a shifting balance between power expressed in secular and sacred terms seem to require it.[31] A similar standing might be conceded to other world religions by recognizing a similarly weak secular foundation, for example, of a restored Caliphate in a sovereign state consisting of Mecca, Medina or both. Mullah Omar might have been wrong, to the point of preposterous, in claiming such a standing for his position in Kandahar, but the existence of an alternative, and widely recognized, site for such a claim would have greatly complicated the Taliban's attempts to secure international, and even local, sympathy from Muslims.[32]

Any attempt to implement a solution that mimics the product of centuries of historical evolution, both intended and accidental, faces huge problems. A restored Caliphate, for example, could not take on sovereign statehood as its primary or defining identity because this would be at odds with Islamic understandings of the proper relationship between what others see as religion and politics. It would, instead, be an aspect of that entity's identity, a means by which to connect to the way in which the world is currently organized. What is important, however, about a strategy of "exile and promotion" is not its endpoint. It is the change of direction implied by it from the co-option of "boxing and taming" to freeing, recognizing and, with any luck, burdening with new responsibilities, those who speak on behalf of the new religious certainties. Such an emancipatory approach to religion would not only be well suited to the increasingly de-centered and disaggregated character of contemporary international relations (and, indeed, social life in general). It would also be consistent with one of the core convictions informing all currents in the diplomatic tradition of international thought. The really big arguments between people, regarding what life is and ought to be about, rarely generate lasting answers on which nearly everyone agrees. Neither, however, do they go away. Life goes on amidst, and in spite of, the arguments. At best, it is the process of arguing, and not the conclusions to which it may or may not lead, which contributes to life. People will argue in terms of truths and claims with

---

[31] R. J. B. Bosworth, *Mussolini's Italy: Life Under the Fascist Dictatorship, 1915–45* (London: Penguin, 2007).
[32] Sharp, "Mullah Zaeef and Taliban Diplomacy," pp. 481–98.

universal application and, thus, it is the task of diplomats to keep the talks going between people who want to argue this way, not to drive all universals out, not to co-opt them and, especially, not to become accomplices in any attempt to drive one set of universals out in the name of another.

It follows that diplomacy and diplomats should, to the extent that this is possible, be separated and keep themselves separate from the great secular projects designed to counter faith, ignorance and tradition, with reason, science and market democracies. With the benefit of hindsight we can see that even when the current of history was flowing strongly although but briefly, as it sometimes now seems, in the latter's direction, it remained shallow and was unable to re-shape decisively the contours of the underlying bed that had taken thousands of years of sedimentation to form. Now, with those old contours re-emerging from beneath the flood, there is evidence that these great, secular projects are actually counterproductive and help drive people, even people in some of the most powerful secular positions in the world, in the direction of intolerant faiths to orient themselves in a world which appears increasingly mysterious to them.

Finally, in advocating a strategy of "exile and promotion," it should not be thought that I regard religious faiths and religious belief as sources only of unhappiness in international relations. Pushing religious movements to become "diplomatic" would provide a powerful reminder to both people in general, and diplomats in particular, of the extent to which the moral strengths of diplomacy rest on the teachings of the great faiths about how to live a good life and please the gods. Sympathy, empathy, humility and self-restraint, all cardinal virtues of diplomacy, not to mention the wisdom of maintaining a sense of intellectual and emotional distance from the turmoil of worldly affairs, all have their roots in essentially religious answers to the questions of how and, more importantly, why people should be good. People ought to be good, but enjoining them to be so is easily criticized as mistaking the problem for the answer. We may know that people should be good. We may even agree on why and of what being good consists. The problem is that, knowing all this, why, so often, we are not. Yet it sometimes seems that people become so engaged in the difficulties posed by getting themselves and (more often) others to be good, that they lose sight of what that good actually is. As the first crazy religion treaty, the Covenant of Medina, declared,

> The Jews of Banu 'Auf are a separate community (ummah) as the believers. To the Jews their religion (*din*) and to the Muslims their faith.[33]

A public acknowledgment of that principle by, for example, all the parties to the current dispute in Palestine would be a positive contribution in itself. By it, Muslims would re-recognize their commitment to a place for the Jews, and Israelis would acknowledge that Muslims recognize this. Life, and its moral dimension, get a lot more complicated than this to be sure. In international relations, however, it is reaching agreement on basic principles, not about their application to ever-more complex problems, which often poses the stumbling blocks. How are peoples who disagree on basic principles like the identity claims of the other party to conduct relations with one another? Sometimes, the answer may be the starting point for considering what to do; in this case both parties acknowledging that each other is who they say they are as a basis for re-encountering each other. Even if we start with answers rather than questions, challenges and objections, however, they still need disseminating. How are diplomats, governments and especially people to be reminded and informed of the virtues of diplomatic thinking as a way of seeing the world, and how are these virtues to be made more effective? For the rise of the idea of religion in international affairs has occurred hand-in-hand with the rise of the idea of people being international actors in their own right. It is people, in the guise of the public, rather than states, religions, social movements, groups or even peoples, who are said to be increasingly populating the international stage and, thus, requiring a diplomacy of their own.

---

[33] Iqbal, *The Prophet's Diplomacy*, p. 13.

13 | Dumb public diplomacy

It is an indicator of the great changes taking place in international relations that a general agreement is emerging that the problems posed by crazy religions, greedy firms and rogue states alike would be greatly alleviated by more and better public diplomacy.[1] What the democratic and nationalist revolutions of the nineteenth century made it possible to conceive – peoples directly involved in international political life – the twentieth-century revolutions in the technologies of transportation and communication, it is argued, have enacted. Simonds and Emeny's claim that "diplomacy has largely lost its importance ... as a consequence of the progressive march of people to political power, on the one hand, and the consequent growth of the system of international conference on the other" was clearly premature when they made it in 1935.[2] Such a claim if made today would not sound premature, but what it meant and what it entailed would be just as unclear as they were over seventy years ago. Now, as then, we remain unsure about what is meant by people, the people and, especially, the public when we talk about diplomacy and international relations. Who are the public in public diplomacy? Are they the people of a country and, if so, must it be all of them or can it be some of them? Is it the people of all the countries constituted as some international or global public and, again, if so, must

---

[1] See, e.g., Center for Strategic and International Studies, *Reinventing Diplomacy in the information Age* (Washington DC: Center for Strategic and International Studies, 1998), *Diplomacy: Profession in Peril?* (London: Wilton Park Conference, 1997) and Leonard and Alakeson, *Going Public*. Since the terrorist attacks of "9/11," of course, there has been a huge expansion of interest in all aspects of public diplomacy, especially in the United States. Wilton Park offered another conference entitled *The Future of Public Diplomacy* in March 2007. The US reorganized its system for delivering public diplomacy, placing it in the State Department under an Under Secretary for Public Diplomacy and Public Affairs, Karen P. Hughes, in 2005.

[2] Frank Simonds and Broks Emeny, *The Great Powers in World Politics: International Relations and Economic Nationalism* (New York: American Book Company, 1935), p. 117.

it be all of them or can it be some of them? And on whatever scale – global, national, or local – one conceives it, does the existence of a public presume a government, public and government somehow managing to constitute each other? These are all difficult questions to which there are no settled answers. However, the fact that this is so has proved to be no obstacle to the emergence of arguments in favor of public diplomacy which have been so successful that governments, international organizations and private actors have committed considerable resources to developing the idea and attempting to put it into practice.

Even diplomats have embraced the idea, with varying degrees of enthusiasm and a mix of motives to be sure, to the extent that we now have a conception of public diplomacy that seems as clear as our ideas about the public remain foggy. What diplomats ought to be doing, according to this concept, is creating a receptive environment in the countries to which they are posted for their own countries' foreign policy interests. They can accomplish this by working at all levels of their hosts' societies to promote positive images of their own countries and the values in which they believe. Working at all levels entails directing messages at, and forming relationships with, people – individuals, groups and the whole – who may be in a position to help and be helped. Promoting positive images refers to those which accord with the values of their hosts, while promoting values is actually shorthand for suggesting that diplomats should work to get the values of their own country accepted in their hosts. At the heart of this notion of public diplomacy are two key assumptions on which Joseph Nye's idea of "soft power" is based.[3] The first is that if other people like you and agree with your values, they are more likely to do what you want. The second is that you can do things that make it more likely that other people will come to like you and accept your values, and that people in general and particular people are worth approaching in these terms. They are so in the traditional sense that they may pressure their government to respond favorably to you, and in the contemporary sense that they have both power and value in their own right. The public, publics and members of both are regarded as both political players and moral agents in international life.

---

[3] Nye, *Soft Power*. See also Melissen (ed.), *The New Public Diplomacy*.

As such, the public diplomacy that attracts so much interest at the moment combines both old and new elements. Much of it, for example, seems to consist of no more than a supercharged version of the old diplomatic practice of talent spotting – finding out who the movers and shakers are in a particular society and developing relationships with them against the day when a diplomat might find them useful. However, the level of this activity, the methods by which it is pursued and, in particular, the ends to which it is directed all suggest novelty. The purpose, it is argued, is not merely to acquire leverage by developing friendly sources of influence on the host government. Relationships with the host's public or members of it are to be cultivated for their own sake, and possibly to facilitate the processes by which members of the public of both countries can enter into direct relations with one another.[4] In this sense, it is sometimes referred to as the "new public diplomacy," made possible by revolutions in information and communication technologies. It is also presented by some of its advocates as having transformational potentials. It may, for example, bring governments closer to publics, all publics and not just their own, and help to destabilize our settled ideas about how international relations are to be conducted and between whom by bringing publics of different countries closer to one another. In this latter sense, the advocates of public diplomacy can be seen to be reaching out to and mending fences with the supporters of an older new idea, that of citizen diplomacy.[5] The potential for a full détente between these two remains to be seen, however, for public diplomacy is, as yet, very much a creature of the governments which advocates of citizen diplomacy often regard as obstacles to good relations between the ordinary people of countries.

---

[4] See, e.g., Riordan, *The New Diplomacy* and Shawn Riordan, "Dialogue-based Diplomacy: A New Foreign Policy Paradigm," *DPD* (The Hague: NIIRC, 95, November 2004), p. 15. See also Kathy Fitzpatrick, "Advancing the New Public Diplomacy: A Public Relations Perspective," *The Hague Journal of Diplomacy*, 2, 3 (2007), pp. 187–211 and Rhonda S. Zaharna, "The Soft Power Differential: Network Communication and Mass Communication in Public Diplomacy," in *The Hague Journal of Diplomacy*, 2, 3 (2007), pp. 213–28.

[5] See, e.g., *Sister Cities International*, which describes itself as a non-profit citizen diplomacy network, at www.sister-cities.org/ and Paul Sharp, "Making Sense of Citizen Diplomacy: The Citizens of Duluth, Minnesota as International Actors," in *International Studies Perspectives*, 2 (2001), pp. 131–50.

Considerable attention has been given to both the techniques of this new public diplomacy and measuring their effectiveness.[6] In general terms, however, a world in which all governments are assiduously cultivating each other's domestic constituencies on all issues on all levels, produces changes in diplomatic practice along at least two lines. First, some blurring of diplomatic and domestic political techniques occurs, since the ways in which support for government policies from home and abroad can be mobilized increasingly overlap. Secondly, however, we might expect governments to be increasingly concerned by the attempts to cultivate elements of their own public made by other governments. We have considerable evidence that the first of these is already occurring. We see ambassadors, for example, acting more like the lobbyists and coalition-builders. Governments and advocates of public diplomacy are only just becoming aware of the second, however, considering, for example, to what extent the activities of other governments in their own jurisdictions should be regarded as opportunities for cooperation rather than as threats to be countered.[7]

While we can identify changes and much talk of changes, however, it is very difficult to identify the center of gravity, if any, of what is going on. For example, through one lens the activities of those engaged in the new public diplomacy provides further evidence of the further "domestication" of international relations in general and diplomacy in particular, while through another it provides evidence of the "internationalization" of all aspects of domestic life.[8] Hence, we find discussion of the need for governments to conduct "internal public diplomacy," importing the techniques they use abroad into their domestic policy.[9] This idea may seem to rob the term "diplomacy" of all its content. It may be warranted, however, for the changes that

---

[6] See, e.g., Pierre C. Pahlavi, "Evaluating Public Diplomacy Programmes: Lessons from Key G8 Member States," in *The Hague Journal of Diplomacy*, 2, 3 (2007), pp. 255–81.
[7] See, e.g., Brian Hocking, "Reconfiguring Public Diplomacy: From Competition to Collaboration," in Jolyn Welch and Daniel Fern (eds.), *Engagement: Public Diplomacy in a Globalised World* (London: British Foreign and Commonwealth Office, 2008), pp. 62–75.
[8] Alan Henrikson, "Diplomacy's Possible Futures," in *The Hague Journal of Diplomacy*, 1, 1 (2006), pp. 3–27.
[9] See, e.g., Ellen Huijgh, "Domestic Outreach," paper presented at *1st The Hague Diplomacy Conference: Crossroads of Diplomacy*, June 21–22, 2007 and Leonard and Alakeson, *Going Public*.

go some way towards domesticating elements of foreign publics are just as likely to estrange elements of a government's own. In what sense, for example, should the British government or members of the British government regard British Petroleum as "ours" in quite the way it used to be and, thus, to what extent should they identify its fortunes with their own? As one source has lightheartedly suggested, we might now begin to think in terms of "total diplomacy," echoing the old Dutch idea of "total football" in which all players attack and defend.[10] If so, in the new public diplomacy, domestic and foreign resources and allies alike are identified and mobilized into coalitions around common interests and projects in a world in which foreigners may be your friends, whilst fellow citizens may be your rivals and, now, in an era of transnational terrorism, even your enemies.

Modern diplomacy and the traditionalist critique of public diplomacy

This conception of the new public diplomacy and the international relations it services can be criticized. In particular, advocates for the more traditional conceptions of diplomacy associated with the modern state system treat all the claims above with skepticism and hostility. They maintain that the involvement of the public in diplomacy is not new, cannot be very significant and is usually a bad idea. Governments have always been tempted by the idea of contacting the people of another country, tribe or group directly. Siege stories from the Bible and Thucydides provide us with two archetypes of such encounters with one side attempting to undermine the resistance of another by appealing directly to its people.[11] Many treaties, even if negotiated in secret, are

---

[10] Brian Hocking in conversation. See also Chester Bowles for the use of this term cited in Warren Christopher, "Normalization of Diplomatic Relations," from Elmer Plishke (ed.), *Modern Diplomacy: The Art and the Artisans* (Washington: American Enterprise Institute, 1979), pp. 37–40, also cited in Hamilton and Langhorne, *The Practice of Diplomacy: Its Evolution, Theory and Administration*, pp. 183–227.

[11] See The Rabashakeh, on behalf of the Assyrian king, Sennacherib, to Eliakim and Hilkiah, on behalf of Hezekiah, the Hebrew King, calling on the citizens of Jerusalem to surrender (in their own tongue), 2 *Kings* l, 6: 7 and the Athenians to the Melians regarding the surrender of their city/colony in "The Melian Dialogue," Thucydides, *History of the Peloponnesian War* (Harmondsworth: Penguin, 1954).

signed and ratified on highly public occasions. And diplomats have always sought out individual citizens in their hosts to gain information and, sometimes, to initiate espionage. What is new, the traditionalists say, is the importance attached to public diplomacy by governments and the credence which they and other people who should know better give to claims, made generally by people who are not interested in diplomacy and know little about it, that its public variant, if allowed, may save us all from ourselves, each other and the various messes we are said to be making of the planet.

According to traditionalists, the public ought to occupy a position peripheral to the conduct of diplomacy. People with power and responsibility want to exercise them under as few constraints as possible for reasons that are always understandable and not necessarily sinister. Anyone who has acquired even minor administrative responsibilities will be aware of how considerations of efficiency and effectiveness suddenly loom larger under the pressure of getting the job done. At the same time, concerns about the participation and inclusion of people who now seem less engaged, poorly informed and irresponsible fade into the background. All these concerns, traditionalists say, are magnified in matters of state that are both highly complex and of supreme importance. Thus the public, when it comes to international affairs, are dumb in the sense of their lack of understanding of what is going on, and ought to be so, in the sense of their having little or no voice in what is going on. One may exploit publics on occasions, when opportunities arise and circumstances warrant the breach of normal practice. One should keep them informed in general terms by state ceremonies, press conferences and websites. On the whole, however, publics, both "ours" and "theirs," should be kept out of the detailed business of managing the relations of states and their peoples. People, peoples or the public, the traditionalists maintain, do not understand international relations and they will mess things up.

Thus, one authoritative source asserts, public diplomacy is a form of "propaganda."[12] That is all it can be, given who and what is involved. It may be a necessary evil of international life, and an ever-growing one since the demands for open, conference diplomacy took off at the start

---

[12] G. R. Berridge and Alan James, *A Dictionary of Diplomacy* (Basingstoke: Palgrave Macmillan, 2001), p. 197.

of the twentieth century.[13] Heaven help us all, however, if governments and others begin to mistake it for the real business of conducting international relations diplomatically. And, by and large, traditionalists conclude, Providence has been on their side, for the attempts to open up diplomacy, like so many other administrative and political processes, are always outflanked by new measures to move the real action and power of decision elsewhere. Indeed, the very mechanisms of mass engagement and popular involvement may be said to protect these processes for, while they give everybody the opportunity for "input," these opportunities and the responses generate masses of information which is so dense, tiresome and often useless that only the truly dedicated work their way through them.

Problems with the traditionalist critique

There are two major problems with the view that public diplomacy is a peripheral, exceptional and, on the whole, questionable activity recently and wrongly elevated. The common source of both, however, is thinking only in terms of the narrow slice of historical experience from which modern diplomacy emerged and helped to define.

The first is that the public's relationship to diplomacy in the past was not always and everywhere as the traditionalists have presented it. If we look further back and elsewhere, we can see different conceptions of diplomacy in which the involvement of peoples, even publics, was regarded as neither peripheral nor exceptional. Instead, it was taken for granted as both a fact and a good thing. The oratorical diplomacy of the Greeks, for example, not only let the public in. It depended on their presence for its effectiveness, for speeches were nothing if not broadly witnessed and deliberated upon.[14] The performative diplomacy of the North American Indians went even further in that it often actively involved the larger community, not only as witnesses and audiences, but also as participants in ceremonies that had to be conducted properly

---

[13] Nicolson, *Diplomacy*, develops this theme.
[14] See Thucydides, *History of the Peloponnesian War*, Watson, *Diplomacy*, pp. 85–6 and *The Evolution of International Society*, pp. 47–68. Harold Nicolson notes that the first permanent ambassadors in early modern Europe were known as "resident orators." Nicolson, *The Evolution of the Diplomatic Method*, p. 33.

if minds and spirits were to be purified so that real communication could occur.[15]

It may be objected that oratory and ceremony mattered no more for the Greeks and Indians respectively than they do for governments and their diplomats today. In this view, nothing of importance could have turned on what *proxenoi* had to say and how well they said it before an assembly of citizens, just as nothing turns on how well an American president makes his annual speech before the General Assembly. And a poorly executed dance in edge-of-the-forest ceremonies could no more affect the outcome of subsequent talks than a mistake in identifying the name of the guest's country or an outbreak of heckling can at a joint press conference today.[16] From within the more positivist conceptions of international theory, this would be an understandable line of attack, but it is less convincing from one within which the things that people say to each other and the ways they are said are all held to be important. Besides, the evidence from the historical examples suggests that, while oratory and ceremony may not have always ruled, the importance of the "solemn frivolities" as Jules Cambon called them, to what happened was far greater than it is generally assumed today.[17] Indeed, as arguments that contemporary diplomacy is being "Americanized" by becoming less formal, more direct and focused on problem-solving suggest, some contemporary societies underestimate the continued importance of a proper observation of the forms to others.[18]

It may also be objected that the notion of the public implied by public diplomacy today is quite different from that of the citizens and people before whom ancient Greeks made speeches and American Indians

---

[15] William N. Fenton, "Structure, Continuity and Change in the Process of Iroquois Treaty-Making," in Jennings, Fenton, Druke, and Miller (eds.), *The History and Culture of Iroquois Diplomacy*, pp. 3–36 and Warren, *History of the Ojibway People*, pp. 146–93 and 222–78.

[16] Chinese President Hu Jin Tao was heckled on the White House Lawn at his arrival ceremony by a journalist sympathetic to the Falun Gong movement. President Bush also experienced difficulties in giving the People's Republic of China its correct name in his remarks, *Northstateman* (May 2, 2006) at www.northstatesman.com:2005/northstatesman/archives/cat_international_issues.html.

[17] Jules Cambon, *Le Diplomat* (Paris: Chez Hachette,1926) cited in John R. Wood and Jean Serres, *Diplomatic Ceremonial and Protocol* (New York: Columbia University Press, 1970), p. 4.

[18] Alan Henrikson, "The Washington Diplomatic Corps, the Place, the Professionals and Their Performance," in Sharp and Wiseman (eds.), *The Diplomatic Corps as an Institution of International Society*, pp. 41–74.

danced and sang. The idea of the public is linked to conceptual and practical distinctions between government and people that neither of them may have had. The significance of public diplomacy, therefore, is said to lie in its being directed at the public instead of, or as opposed to, at the government of a country, a significance which is lost in the absence of such a government/people distinction. This observation loses much of its force, however, when it is recalled that this distinction provides only one way, and one circumscribed by its insistence on a political or governing division of labor, of giving expression to the idea of a people. Thus, it might be argued that the significance of the American Indian practice of involving the people in diplomacy is invalidated neither by its historical character, nor by the absence of a government/people distinction in their affairs. Rather, the experience of the Indians in this regard could be said to pose a question to those who insist upon the distinction being made, for it holds out the possibility that diplomacy and, indeed, government and politics can be arranged in such a way that the distinction is not needed.

That this is so brings us to the second problem with the traditionalist conception of public diplomacy and critique of its current elevation. It is clear that contemporary diplomacy is not achieving the sort of success enjoyed by its early twentieth century counterpart in absorbing and deflecting the demands of Wilsonian reformers and Bolshevik revolutionaries that it should change.[19] Yet the traditionalist critique offers no coherent explanation of the current rise of public diplomacy or even the mistaken belief, if such it is, that public diplomacy is on the rise. As a consequence, traditionalists are restricted to discounting evidence that contradicts their assessment of public diplomacy, and decrying those instances when something appears to go wrong in foreign policy because the public has been let in. Finally, when the weight of evidence for change begins to make discounting it too difficult, they suggest that the situation in question is ceasing to be a site for diplomacy and foreign policy. Keens Soper, for example, argues that both are giving way to a new domestic politics in the European Union.[20]

---

[19] James Mayall notes the resilience of diplomacy (especially diplomatic immunity) as an institution of international society in the face of the earlier challenges, *Nationalism and International Society* (Cambridge: Cambridge University Press, 1990), pp. 147–8.

[20] Maurice Keens-Soper, *Europe In the World: The Persistence of Power Politics* (Basingstoke: Palgrave Macmillan, 2001).

If an uncooperative history cannot be finessed, however, and an even less cooperative present threatens to overwhelm the traditionalist account of public diplomacy as peripheral and exceptional, the objection that it is, nevertheless, a bad idea remains. It is an objection worthy of serious consideration, for it has been argued here that diplomatic systems do not merely reflect the structures and priorities of those represented by them. They are also contrived and designed to deal effectively with a distinctive class of human relations, those between peoples who regard themselves as separate from one another and want to be so. If this is the case, then what does diplomatic thinking suggest be done when a particularly effective way of conducting these relations – the modern state system with its hard boundaries between peoples and its clear distinction between inside and outside relations, appears to be threatened and possibly breaking down? Surely, the traditionalists speak for the diplomatic tradition as a whole, if not in their critique of the intentions and aspirations of those who advocate more public diplomacy, then in their sense of the consequences when the public is allowed to have its say.

Diplomatic thinking and public diplomacy

In fact, there has been no call to arms (nor even to pens) on behalf of modern diplomacy from serving diplomats in response to rising pressures of public involvement. The dog has not barked for two reasons. First, although some advocates of the new public diplomacy, including some serving diplomats, talk and act as if the divide between government and various conceptions of the public is, and ought to be, breaking down, they, like everybody else, also continue to think, talk and act in older, more established ways too. While the dimensions along which separateness between peoples is currently mapped may be changing, hardly anyone is acknowledging it unambiguously. The British public and the French public, or segments of both, for example, may increasingly talk directly to one another, and the public, or segments of it, from one country may increasingly need to be mobilized to serve purposes of the other's government. All this is presented, however, as having little or no impact – other than better and closer Anglo-French relations – on the idea a British government and a British people, on the one hand, and a French government and a French people, on the other, constituting fundamental political facts of the European and global international society. Nor is this simply a matter of transitions and arguments about how far we have come in making them. We still think in terms of Britain and France and other countries not because they have faded insufficiently. We do so because they are there and because many of the processes we assume to be dissolving them are, in fact, insuring, either directly or indirectly, that they continue to exist.

The second reason for the silence is that neither diplomatic thinking nor the daily experiences of diplomats from which it is derived encourage a call to arms. Such a call and the threats that prompt it both emanate from a world which diplomats do not inhabit and whose form of thinking they do not share. It is a world that thinks in historical and, often, historicist terms about the forces shaping it and giving rise to phenomena like public diplomacy. In such thinking, it is generally agreed that public diplomacy is a symptom of the rise of the masses, the people and the public together with their entry into political and, latterly, international political life. The big questions revolve around whether they make their entry as the co-opted chattels of elites who now need them so engaged, or as agents of their own emancipation who, once allowed on the stage, may well change everything. The little questions revolve around the roles of governments in all this. They present themselves as enablers, of course, but of what – cooption or emancipation, or merely themselves? These are important questions. It is certainly possible to conceive of the emergence of a global civil society with liberal characteristics and a global governmental counterpart. It is also possible to imagine through both radical and realist lenses a de-governmentalized global network of shifting partnerships between peoples existing in a variety of groups for different purposes, both benign and malign, although this involves a greater exercise of imagination for most people. However, this is not how diplomatic thinking attempts to make sense of what is going on.

The diplomatic tradition of international thought suggests a different story and one without a particular historical trajectory. For diplomats, public diplomacy poses problems concerned with representation and, in particular, the old tension which exists in their craft between those who are engaged in the conduct of international relations and recognized as such, and those who are not, but who wish to be. Diplomacy and diplomats are primarily engaged in managing relations of separateness between peoples. To make their task possible, they are also deeply engaged in the processes by which it is determined who is to be represented and how. Thus, what usually appears as a world of stable identities existing in reasonably unchanging relation to one another and negotiating with each other on that basis is invariably the product of a second set of negotiations, sometimes ongoing, about those identities and the terms of their relations with one another. Sometimes, during the period of European decolonization, for example, this second set of negotiations may focus on questions like, what is it to be a state and who qualifies as one. There is agreement on the type of actor qualifying for membership and, thus, representation in an international society, and the arguments are about who qualifies as such an actor. At other times, such as the present, or over the period when the Empire and Papacy declined, the focus may shift to what type of actors – states and/or others, for example – are to enjoy membership and, hence, representation, and on what terms. These can be intensely political questions over which parties will argue and fight, but even in settled times when fights abate, they are always diplomatic questions. The boundaries between who is and who is not entitled to diplomatic representation have to be maintained and adjusted, no less than the boundaries and relations between those whose status as diplomatic personalities is a relatively settled matter.

This being so, the relationship between even traditionally conceived diplomacy and the new public diplomacy is not as fraught as either's advocates and detractors usually assumed it to be. Public diplomacy may pose a challenge to certain conceptions of diplomacy, and even certain types of diplomat, but it does not pose an existential challenge to diplomacy *per se*. We obtain glimpses of this from the accounts diplomats provide of their everyday life. They take great pleasure, for example, in shocking those with a more formal or official understanding of what their work entails by revealing how protocol and form can be jettisoned when they become a hindrance. They will work with anyone to get the job done and will accord respect, if not recognition, in proportion to people's usefulness in this regard. They may wholeheartedly resist conferring recognition on specific political actors, knowing full well that they may have to completely reverse themselves on this course of action in the near future. And they may withdraw recognition from old friends with whom they have had a long relationship. They do so at the behest of changes in policy to be sure, but the pursuit and assertion of claims to recognition as participants in international life, together with the fending off, accession in and fudging of the claims of others in this regard, is bound up with what diplomats are continually doing. Diplomats have always had to work with yesterday's barbarians, infidels and, latterly, terrorists, knowing that they might become today's newest members of an international society. And they invite today's successful businessmen into the heart of their ministries and embassies to participate in commercial policy-making, knowing that these private actors might similarly be promoted tomorrow.

As far as diplomatic thinking is concerned, the real challenge is not one of identifying the direction of history in terms of a state system being swamped and rendered incoherent by the advances of public diplomacy. Rather, it is one of managing the consequences of some relations becoming more diplomatic in a conventional sense while others become less so. Canada, for example, has long had to deal with the tendency for its relations with the United States to have less and less a diplomatic character. That is to say that the proportion of its relations with the United States that can be characterized by separateness has shrunk relative to the proportion for which the peoples of both countries are treated as one and the same. One might say that the diplomatic dimension to US–Canada relations has a residual character, although it is a residue that remains of vital importance to at least one of the parties' sense of itself. At the same time, however, the Canadian government finds itself in the midst of a set of relationships, with its own provinces, for example, with international humanitarian organizations, and with the peoples of other countries as potential targets for its goods and values, which arguably have a burgeoning diplomatic character.[21] A similar point might be made about relations between member governments of the European Union, their relations with the EU as a whole, and their relations with other publics both within and beyond the Union. Just as Canada faces a decline of diplomacy in its relations with the United States at the same time as a rise in diplomacy in its relations with the provinces, so too, it might be said, does Britain in its relations with the EU and Scotland respectively. Movements in neither direction, however, lie outside the remit of what diplomacy and diplomats typically handle. While public diplomacy invariably raises questions

---

[21] Evan H. Potter, "Information Technology and Canada's Public Diplomacy," in Evan H. Potter (ed.), *Cyber-Diplomacy: Managing Foreign Policy in the Twenty-First Century* (Montreal-Kingston: McGill-Queen's University Press, 2002), pp. 177–200.

about representation and new actors, therefore, such questions are bread and butter ones with which diplomats are used to dealing. This being so, diplomatic thinking is not focused on how public diplomacy is to be cordoned off and rendered safe. Rather, it addresses the problem of how it may be more or less well-executed.

The failures of public diplomacy

The present context of this latter concern is a pervading sense that public diplomacy, whilst it may be on the increase, has been poorly executed by professional diplomats and stands in urgent need of improvement.[22] It is important to realize the extent to which this sense of failure is a Western phenomenon. While the advocates of a new public diplomacy present their arguments as having general application, they are primarily interested in a very few, developed, post-industrial market democracies.[23] Not only that, their interest is generally restricted to the practice of public diplomacy in only two areas. The first of these is the pursuit of trade and investment opportunities for economies that the advocates of commercial public diplomacy steadfastly continue to frame in national terms. It is directed at securing foreign partnerships that will create jobs and boost the flow of income to both private and public beneficiaries at home. To these ends, diplomats are instructed to encourage these partnerships by promoting their countries as good places in which to conduct business, their companies as good partners with which to work, and themselves as people capable of identifying potential partnerships. Some countries' foreign services are said to be better at doing this than others, but none of them do it enough or well enough. It is suggested that they may not regard this sort of partnership promotion as their proper job. They may not like the sort of work it involves. They may not be very good at it. And they may be lazy.

---

[22] See, e.g., Peter van Ham, "Power, Public Diplomacy, and the *Pax Americana*," in Melissen (ed.), *The New Public Diplomacy*, pp. 47–66.
[23] Note, however, the emerging interest in the public diplomacy of other states. See, e.g., Ingrid d'Hooghe, "Public Diplomacy in the People's Republic of China," in Melissen (ed.), *The New Public Diplomacy*, pp. 88–105. See also Humayun Kabir, "Public Diplomacy at Bangladesh's Missions Abroad: A Practitioner's View," *The Hague Journal of Diplomacy*, 3, 3 (2008), 299–302.

What one needs, therefore, are people more adept at identifying commercial opportunities and, hence, the rising practice of importing people from the commercial world on short to medium term appointments in foreign services. Smart people, it is hoped, can make dumb commercial public diplomacy smart, or at least smarter.

The second area of foreign policy in which the increased application of better public diplomacy is advocated cannot be so succinctly stated. It involves getting a large segment of the world's population, which is generally perceived as hostile, to accept, if not the principles of market economics and political democracy, then, at least, the inherent goodness and good intentions of those who currently subscribe to them. This is, perhaps, more an American problem than a European one and, as a public diplomacy problem, it tends to reduce to getting the Muslim world, and younger people within it especially, to learn things which will encourage them to have more positive attitudes towards the United States.[24] I say the focus is on the Muslim world because there is, for example, little inclination to present shifts leftwards in South American politics in terms of a failure of public diplomacy, or a problem better public diplomacy might rectify. Not so with the Muslim world. Here the puzzle remains neatly, if inaccurately, summed up by the question "why do they hate us?" even, indeed especially, when the ordinary people of the region get a chance to express their views freely.[25]

The widely assumed answer is that "they" do not know enough to understand us properly, and for this state of affairs diplomats receive much of the blame.[26] They would sooner, it is argued, talk to corrupt and out-of-touch governments and their colleagues who represent them and even, when needs press, to dangerous extremists, rather than to the ordinary people of the societies caught between these two obstacles to progress. The upshot is that the hearts and minds of ordinary Muslims are being lost to Islamic extremists and their allies by what amounts to better public diplomacy and propaganda efforts conducted by them. If

---

[24] See, e.g., Mohan J. Dutta Bergman, "US Public Diplomacy in the Middle East: A Critical Cultural Approach," *Journal of Communication Inquiry*, 30, 2 (April, 2006), pp. 102–24 cited in Fitzpatrick, "Advancing the New Public Diplomacy," pp. 187–211.
[25] Gabriel, *Because They Hate US*.
[26] David D. Newsom, *Diplomacy and American Democracy* (Bloomington: Indiana University Press, 1988), p. 179.

the "Muslim street," as it is sometimes termed, is to be won over, then a campaign must be conducted at all levels in Islamic societies which employs diplomats, area experts and "our" ordinary people mediated by the latest techniques of information technology to couch and convey "our" message about who we are and what we want in "their" terms. As in the case of commercial public diplomacy, therefore, so too in the civilizational international relations of globalization, we have been caught with the wrong sort of people playing the wrong sort of game. In the case of commercial public diplomacy, the diplomats have to catch up with private actors who are already playing "smart." In the case of public diplomacy towards the Islamic world, however, the picture is more complex. The diplomats have been "dumb" while the Islamic radical and their allies have been "smart." Between them, however, is an Islamic public up for grabs that can be won if only the right kind of public diplomacy is attempted. What then can diplomatic thinking tell us about these critiques and the prospects for improving public diplomacy in both areas of policy or, perhaps more importantly, easing the problems which more and better public diplomacy is supposed to address?

Diplomatic thinking and commercial public diplomacy

Diplomatic thinking provides very little support for the idea that commercial public diplomacy has failed. The puzzle, of course, is that governments, experts and diplomats themselves have been saying for decades that commercial activity at all levels of society should be occupying more of the latter's time. Originally, the diplomats were said to have resisted, and now they "talk the talk" but still do not "walk the walk." Somehow, vested institutional interests have waged a rearguard action so effective that it has managed to preserve a now-vestigial diplomatic culture even after numerous attempts to disrupt it have been instituted and the old diplomats have passed on or been passed over. No matter how you train the diplomats, rearrange the institutions in which they work, or supplement them with new personnel from other branches of government or the private sector, very little changes. Thus, while it seems hard to imagine what else the British or Canadian foreign services, as examples, might do to open up themselves to winds of change, which are now themselves over half a century old, still they manage to disappoint in this regard.

Some exogenous factors play their part in creating this sense of disappointment. Stakeholders in national economies, for example, are often intrinsically doubtful about the effectiveness of public servants in activities related to commerce. The commercially unsuccessful are even more likely to speak loudly in this regard, much like the supporters of losing football clubs when asked to comment on the state of football as a whole. Thus, a whole range of activities associated with commercial public diplomacy – consular fishing expeditions into their respective areas or promotional exhibitions and fairs which deliver few measurable results, for example – may come under critical scrutiny in a way which similar activities undertaken by private actors never would.[27] Indeed, the working habits of public officials may come under criticism in a way in which those of private actors would not, since the latter are working (or not) on their own time and are said to face the consequences of how well they perform more directly than those working in the public sector. And these micro-concerns may be reinforced – neither logically nor consistently, as it happens, but politically and effectively – by the doubts of liberal economists concerning the desirability of commercial diplomacy in general and commercial public diplomacy in particular. The latter may be sold as improving market signals and information, thereby raising the productivity and efficiency level of the international economy as a whole. Given the *telos* of commercial public diplomacy, however – advancing economic interests conceived in national-state terms – it might be just as easily directed at advancing and protecting the interests of inefficient producers thereby imposing additional frictions on the operations of the international economy.

From within diplomatic thinking, however, these objections are unconvincing for, in principle, the development of a commercial public diplomacy should pose no insurmountable problems. It seems reasonable to suppose that the prospects for identifying commercial opportunities and creating successful commercial partnerships will be improved to some unspecified extent by the presence of people who are able to recognize such opportunities, possess the skills to help realize them, are prepared to work hard to this end, and all this in an environment which

---

[27] A trip undertaken by two British consuls-general in the upper Midwest attracted the criticism of local business people in my own town of Duluth in a way in which a similar expedition by private sales people would probably have not (personal observation following dinner with the consuls-general and local business people).

is constantly producing new ways of working. It might equally be supposed that while the abilities of individual foreign service personnel might vary in this regard, the effects of individual variation could be reduced by selection, training and clear statements of organizational priorities to which energies should be directed with a reward structure to match. All this might be difficult to achieve, no doubt, because the required skills are difficult to acquire, but not impossible. Success in this regard would certainly not betoken or require a major revolution in diplomatic practice, merely an incremental extension of the sorts of things which diplomats have been accepted as getting up to within the societies of their host states for years.[28]

This sort of incremental extension and shift of emphasis is, of course, what most governments attempt to get their foreign services to undertake. Therefore, the best contribution which diplomatic thinking can offer to the arguments about commercial public diplomacy is to suggest why it must always be under attack from both those who think it cannot be done, and those who think that diplomats cannot do it. Commercial public diplomacy will always disappoint for two reasons. First, its characteristic activities can be read as instances of a very traditional diplomatic preoccupation with exerting a presence. Just as the value of showing the flag has always been hard to assess, so too the value of commercial public diplomacy activities, and their added value, in terms with which their critics will be satisfied, is very hard to quantify.[29] Yet diplomats, the wrong sort and the right sort alike, will be asked to engage in such activities, because the diplomats are there, because the activities might work, and because both provide a means by which their governments can demonstrate that they are pitching in to the battle for the national economic survival and prosperity of their respective trading states. Secondly, if even diplomats of the right sort for commercial public diplomacy are appointed, diplomatic thinking reminds us of the consequences of appointing people to represent countries, nations and even national economies, as opposed to companies, organizations and even just ourselves. *En post* much of their time is not their own, still less their masters'. Even the best will be constrained, pushed and driven

---

[28] This could be summarized as anything but espionage and open intervention in electoral politics.
[29] Pahlavi, "Evaluating Public Diplomacy Programmes," pp. 255–81.

by a broader set of concerns than those who are asked to represent private interests only. Indeed, the "best practice" of the new public diplomacy beyond commercial activity, if followed, will make it even harder for diplomats to avoid disappointing their commercial constituencies, at least on commercial matters.

Diplomatic thinking and public diplomacy with the Muslim world

Difficult though commercial public diplomacy may be, however, the problems posed by promoting and exporting values through the public diplomacy of Western countries towards the Muslim world are of a different order entirely. Diplomatic thinking suggests that the pressing questions are not with regard to whether these efforts have failed to date. They are with how such efforts are at odds with what diplomacy should be trying to achieve, namely the establishment and maintenance of good relations between peoples. Public diplomacy, as this is presently conceived, towards the Muslim world should not be seen as the sort of activity governments will always feel constrained to attempt, even though its effectiveness may be hard to assess. Rather, it should be viewed as something they are tempted to do for all the wrong reasons that, in all probability, will make things worse.

How so? Axiomatic to the diplomatic tradition of international thought are the following three assumptions: peoples want to live separately, do so, and want to be acknowledged as such. The specific groupings may shift over time and, at any time, the identity and boundaries of a particular group may be contested from both inside and outside, but the general separation principle still holds. Thus, once they have encountered and discovered one another, peoples often seek to conduct their relations at arm's length, and diplomacy embodies the virtues and skills of doing this well, that is, while avoiding unnecessary or unwanted conflict. Commercial public diplomacy, done properly, is able to satisfy these requirements. It generally focuses on sectored activity, rather than life as a whole and, if successful, leads to dialogical and, indeed, transactional, activity between parties who retain their autonomy.[30]

---

[30] I am less sure about economic diplomacy *per se*, however, where micro transactions, particularly between unequal parties, can lead to macro transformations in the environment and identity of the weaker party.

Axiomatic to the promotion and export of values by diplomacy, in contrast, are three very different assumptions. The first is how nice it would be, from the standpoint of one's own interests, if everyone saw the world the way you do. Of course, most people are uneasy with the idea of their own interests providing the only grounds for getting other people to adopt your point of view. Even those who are not, however, realize that their interests usually provide insufficient grounds for actually getting others to change. Hence, the second assumption, a generalized sense that other people do not understand you and that, if they did, they would realize your values are attractive and right. Indeed, they would assume some of your values, and this would lead to a more peaceful, prosperous and cooperative world. Why do they not understand and realize already? This introduces the third assumption, namely that people are either ignorant or that, when they are no longer ignorant, they are prevented by the efforts of others from coming around. Either way, they can be helped to overcome both difficulties by your efforts.[31] These three assumptions can be honestly maintained. After all, there is a sense in which each of us must regard our own core beliefs as both true and right, rather than merely conventional and self-serving. They can also be willfully maintained, in the sense that one wants to impose a world organized by your values on other people, no matter what they think. However, most of us are uneasy about accepting this view of ourselves, even if we find it easy to ascribe it to others whom we see preventing people from knowing or living according to what we believe to be true and right. Most importantly, however, all three assumptions can be unselfconsciously maintained, in the sense that we underestimate the extent to which our own form of life is just one among several.[32] Rather, we are tempted to see our own as the default from which the others depart, if only in superficial ways.

These three assumptions help explain why value promotion by public diplomacy is so tempting, but they also explain why its intended recipients nearly always do not like its content, its method, or both. They are regarded as attacks by others on "who we are," and the processes by which we come to be so. The result is an activity that is non-dialogical, non-transactional and very poor diplomacy. It may fail in the sense of

---

[31] Hence the notion of value promotion.
[32] The term "Lebensform" is associated with Ludwig Wittgenstein, *Philosophical Investigations* (Upper Saddle River: Prentice Hall, 3rd edn., 1999).

making things no better. It may make things worse by creating resentment in the recipient and exasperation that can feed hubris and redoubled efforts on the part of the promoter. And, insofar as it succeeds, it does so by creating friendly pockets, closed off from and easily regarded as strange and subversive by the other members of their own societies. Even then, an emphasis on the assumed attractiveness of content may cause problems with people who may be sympathetic with what one wants to tell them. The Western world's efforts, for example, to present its sense of the relationships between science and reason, on the one hand, and politics, economics, faith and other aspects of culture, on the other, often enjoys much sympathy among, particularly, the younger people of countries like Iran and Egypt. Many of them, too, want to see the best forms of politics and economics as being derived from the applications of science and reason, while faith and culture are restricted to the private and communal spheres.

However, Western attempts to insist on their own schematization of these relationships, to say, for example, that economic reasoning leads ineluctably to the market and political reasoning to secular multi-party competition, pushes young sympathizers elsewhere into the arms of those who reject and resist these schemata. Similarly, and despite a widespread sympathy in the West towards re-emphasizing the spiritual dimension to human life and its attendant priorities, Islamic attempts to claim authority in this regard fall upon Western ears that quickly become all but deaf. People may be willing to let someone into their home to demonstrate a vacuum cleaner for, at the least, they may get a clean carpet out of it, and they may even decide to buy the machine, offering their old one in part-exchange. Letting someone in to share the good news about life and your life in particular, like door-to-door evangelists, however, is another matter entirely. Such people take up time, want you to change and are never really interested in what you have to say to them. And they become a real problem when they will not take "no" for an answer and you are unable to close the door on them.

Diplomatic thinking and improving public diplomacy

To the extent that the characterization of public diplomacy suggested by diplomatic thinking is accurate, it appears that the prospects for improving it are very dim indeed. One should avoid the sort of value promotion being attempted towards the Muslim world at all costs and advise those you represent to do likewise. Of course, such advice is useless, for all the current trends in international relations seem to work in favor of getting people involved in them. They are more accessible to governments than they have ever been before, and many of them seem to want to become involved, both singly and collectively, in international affairs on their own behalf. If governments can reach foreign publics and want to, and if people can become involved in international affairs and want to, then it is the resulting relations with which diplomacy and diplomats must work. The challenge for diplomatic thinking, therefore, is not to discourage attempts at value promotion through public diplomacy by governments and peoples. It is to make such efforts safer and, if not more effective in terms of their present objectives, then at least more useful both to the maintenance of peaceful relations and the promotion of better ones.

One approach is to shift the emphasis from the content, and especially the big content, of public diplomacy to the techniques by which it is practiced. Instead of trying to get "our message across more effectively" governments and others should use the multiple new channels which now exist for transferring information to new targets for projecting multiple small messages and images. Here is our life, our music, our young people, even our Muslims. Make of it what you will.[33] The danger with such an approach, however, is that it may begin to look and sound like a modern advertising or political campaign. That is to say, it may become absorbed by the many ways in which a target can be reached as many times as possible by techniques developed in the communication sciences for the purposes of marketing. It is not that the techniques by which cars are sold or votes obtained will not work – although they often do not – but that they do not work in the way that someone concerned with creating and maintaining relationships would want. Their effects are short-term and specific. They may allow one to build a temporary coalition on an issue on which campaigning interests and the policies of certain governments coincide. They provide no way, however, for peoples who are deeply divided by general outlook either to come closer together or, more importantly, to stabilize the terms on

---

[33] See, e.g., Marc B. Nathanson, "Popular Culture and US Public Diplomacy," address given to the Advisory Board of the University of Southern California Center for Public Diplomacy, November 15, 2006 accessed August 5, 2008 at http://uscpublicdiplomacy.com/pdfs/061115_nathanson.pdf.

which they keep apart from one another. Indeed, it might be argued that a public diplomacy of value promotion built around its sophisticated techniques of communication, rather than content, diminishes trust. The target may come to see such efforts as involving an inappropriately shallow and opportunistic *realpolitik* of maneuver in which the invitation to make what you will of what we show of ourselves, is inspired by the intention that you make what we will of it, nonetheless.

If serious content cannot be projected without causing offense, even among those well disposed to it, and form cannot be emphasized without incurring suspicion, then what is to be done? One recent suggestion (recent in that it is now being advocated by some former diplomats and entertained by some governments) is to replace the concern with "getting our message across more effectively" with attempts to facilitate "genuine dialogue" and "real conversations" directly between peoples with a view to establishing mutually beneficial relationships.[34] People-to-people public diplomacy holds out the promise of some improvement provided that three assumptions on which it rests and which are associated with the premises of citizen diplomacy can be effectively modified. The first is that governments and their diplomats are part of the problem and should be excluded from genuine dialogues. It is, of course, by no means clear that governments and their diplomats are always part of the problem and, even on those occasions when they clearly are, this by no means constitutes a self-evident argument for leaving them out. It is a key principle of both politics and diplomacy, although one which neither politicians or diplomats always honor, that those with the power to influence outcomes should not be left out of at least some of the conversations. The second assumption is that the people, and peoples, are as good as their governments are bad and are, hence, capable of open, or at least authentic, dialogues. Sometimes this is the case, as when peoples find themselves in a lengthy war from which their respective governments find it impossible to withdraw for reasons of their own. At other times it is not, for example when the shock of encountering that other people are human and like us after all, is followed by the second shock of discovering that they are also who they say they are and mean what they say. Drawn-out negotiations may follow between peoples whose direct contacts with one another were

---

[34] Fitzpatrick, "Advancing the New Public Diplomacy," pp. 187–211.

supposed to remove obstacles and bring about swift progress. And in so doing, they reveal the weakness of the third assumption on which people-to-people public diplomacy rests, the idea that a people can be authentically identified and, as such, be practically capable of conducting its own diplomacy.

Just as in politics and government, so too in diplomacy, any drawn-out relationship results in a division of labor by which one, smaller, group comes to represent the rest. Then, the old objection to letting the people decide – the problem of deciding who are the people – emerges. Who is to make the decisions about who is to be represented and who is to represent them in people-to-people diplomacy? For all its difficulties, nevertheless, the idea of peoples talking to one another is the starting point for diplomatic thinking about the problems posed by value-promoting public diplomacy, other forms of public diplomacy and, perhaps now, even diplomacy in general. It is the starting point in an ethical sense. No matter how mediated international relations are by governments, diplomats and others, and no matter how those represented are aggregated – diplomacy and diplomats ought to be concerned with effectively conducting the relations of people and peoples. States, governments, parties, organizations and enterprises ought to be the servants of people and peoples, and not the other way round. It is also increasingly the starting point in a practical sense. More and more people in different sorts of aggregates are engaging in, or are being mobilized to engage in, international relations, that is relations in which these aggregates, nevertheless, regard themselves as separate from one another. It is in this sense that contemporary diplomatic relations might be said to be going public, even that all diplomacy is becoming public diplomacy or has an important public dimension to it. Nevertheless, diplomatic thinking does not present the challenge posed by this development in the way in which it is usually understood. It is not to find a way of reaching people more effectively to mobilize them for foreign policy purposes, nor even to empower people as more effective international actors on their own behalf, in terms of getting what they want. Rather, its focus is and ought to be upon getting the people and peoples who now seek to participate in international life to think and act diplomatically themselves. At the risk of sounding pithy, the focus in public diplomacy should be more upon the diplomacy and not, as it has been up to now, upon the public.

Becoming diplomatic

In making this claim about what diplomatic thinking can tell us about the significance of public diplomacy, I intentionally mix the descriptive with the prescriptive because, of course, diplomats have always spent a great deal of time encouraging those they represent to think and act diplomatically. The modern term "handlers" is useful in this regard. One thinks of the great diplomatists from antiquity to modern times urging restraint upon their masters in accordance with a higher conception of their interests and, eventually, a conception of the interests of the whole system or society which made their relations with one another possible and effective. There also exists a sense, however, that diplomats and diplomacy have always been the weak force in this regard, struggling against the strong forces of power, interest and right. Now, this weakness is compounded by the arrival on the international stage of a host of actors who seek to represent themselves directly and for whom diplomacy, as an emanation of states, appears to be a big obstacle to what they want to achieve or a big part of the problem they want to address. Chief executives, bankers, campaigners, field workers and missionaries, as such, are as unlikely to make good diplomats, as did emperors, kings, politicians and soldiers before them. Like emperors, kings, politicians and soldiers, they can be good diplomats, but the skills, virtues and priorities of diplomacy often pull in different directions from those associated with their own particular calling. What these new actors require, therefore, is not just diplomatic representation. In effect, they improvise that already. They need good diplomatic representation, and that requires people whose primary responsibility and whose sense of themselves revolve around the idea of conducting effective diplomacy on behalf of those they represent.

Can we imagine, therefore, a new hyphenated diplomat, the "public-diplomat" operating at the putative elbows of all these new actors as they nudge themselves onto the international stage? If we can, then the challenges before them are clear: first, to spell out what thinking and acting diplomatically entails; second, to make the case for why thinking and acting diplomatically is not, and ought not to be, the exclusive preserve of states; and third, to transform diplomats from a weak force into, if not a strong force exactly, then a stronger force in international relations. The great success of the modern state system, from the standpoint of diplomacy and diplomats, was in providing definitive answers to who was, and who was not, entitled to diplomatic representation. States were, and everyone else was, notionally at least, driven from the field. Even notionally, however, that distinction is eroding, as the enthusiasm of states themselves for public diplomacy confirms. The field is already open and the challenge for public diplomacy is to go beyond creating friendly environments for interests and values by seeking out targets and partners. Having found them, it could pose two of the oldest questions that have concerned diplomats, together with those who send and receive them. Who represents these new targets and partners authoritatively and authentically, and how are we to know?[35] The answer from the modern past that they are represented and validated by states and their servants is becoming increasingly unsatisfactory. Yet, as in the past, it is reasonable to suppose that more satisfactory answers regarding the terms on which these new actors participate in international life will be preconditions – both politically and practically – of an international society characterized by stable relationships.

Quite what such an international society would look like, and on what terms these new actors would participate in it, will remain open questions for now, and might possibly remain so indefinitely. It is difficult to imagine, for example, Oxfam, Microsoft, or the Campaign To Ban Land Mines acquiring something like sovereign status, although not so difficult as might be supposed when one recalls some of the micro entities which enjoy this standing alongside China, India, Russia and the United States in the teeth of every form of logic except those of convenience and tidiness. It is much easier to imagine, however, a world in which such questions do not get resolved, and yet in which different types of actors enjoy some sort of diplomatic standing and representation. That, after all, has been the normal state of affairs for all but a relatively short period of international history. To an extent, the pre-modern past was a world of "diplomacy without diplomats," in Kennan's phrase, and the future may be one also.[36] The important point, however, is not the presence or the absence of diplomats, as these have been conventionally understood in the modern era, but the omnipresence of relations in need of diplomacy.

---

[35] Langhorne, *Diplomacy and Governance*.
[36] George F. Kennan, "Diplomacy Without Diplomats?," 198–212.

Public diplomacy, therefore, may provide a way to raise the questions of who should be members of the emerging international society and on what terms. It may also provide a way of acquainting new members with the habits of mind associated with thinking diplomatically and opportunities to act in accordance with them. Whatever its contributions in these regards to helping new actors "become diplomatic," however, the problem of transforming diplomacy into a strong force, or stronger force, in international affairs remains. The diplomatic tradition of international thought provides us with a way of understanding international relations on their own terms and a way of thinking about how to approach the issues and arguments to which they give rise. However, does it tell us anything about how it might secure a greater audience for itself and more influence for diplomacy and diplomats, public or otherwise, in shaping what happens in international relations? I will conclude, therefore, with a brief recapitulation of my argument and a consideration of some of the principal obstacles to its adoption.

Conclusion

I have argued that it is possible to identify a diplomatic tradition of international thought which is distinct from the other traditions as these are conventionally represented. This tradition is drawn from the experience of diplomats and those acting diplomatically when peoples encounter one another, begin to discover things about each other, and decide to remain in contact, though at arm's length, through a process of re-encounters which maintain their separate identities. There are two key elements to the tradition.

The first is its account of why we need diplomacy and diplomats built on claims about the plural condition in which human beings live. Whether we like it or not, we live in groups and mostly we seem to like it. The term "groups" covers polities, societies and communities which exist for many purposes and may be said to exist for themselves, but it can also cover associations and enterprises which are created, at least, for simpler, more instrumental and private purposes. The historical record suggests that the distinction between these two classes of actors need not be as firm as it is at present and so, wherever possible, I have used the terms "people" and "peoples" to reflect this breadth of meaning. We have a stronger sense of obligation to, and connectedness with, members of our own people than others. As a result, relations between peoples are different from relations within them. These relations of separateness, as I have called them, are difficult to maintain because they are vulnerable to misunderstandings and lack many of the customary restraints on using violence when things go wrong. Since relations between peoples are not only different and difficult, but also unavoidable and desired, however, we need a distinctive set of practices to handle them. Since the eighteenth century and originating in Europe, these practices have been called diplomacy, but archaeological evidence and historical records both suggest that similar practices emerge very quickly everywhere and at all times when peoples enter into relations with one another yet maintain their separate identities.

Those acting diplomatically see themselves, and are seen by those they represent, as occupying, and operating from within, spaces existing between separate peoples. The second key element of the diplomatic tradition of international thought, therefore, is its account of the distinctive understanding of the world and what is important in it obtained from these spaces in between. From them it is possible to see how, while we live in plural conditions, peoples habitually misidentify their worlds, how things are and how things might be in them as *the* world. Whatever the merits of treating partial world views as true/false and good/bad for a variety of important purposes and reasons, doing so greatly complicates the task of maintaining peaceful and stable relations between groups of people who also regard themselves as separate from one another. It does so by making differences seem resolvable on terms which have a universal character for one party but which appear partial to the other. Thus, our desire to get others to reconcile with us on our terms, already charged by considerations of interest and power, is further fueled by the conviction that, in so doing, they will also be reconciling themselves with truth, reality, God's will or right reason.

If we are interested in peaceful relations with others, as others, rather than destroying, conquering, or absorbing them, then this diplomatic understanding above suggests two prescriptions for guiding diplomatic thinking about international issues. The first is that we should accord the content of these worldviews, including our own, a provisional, tentative and relative character. The second, however, is that we should regard the existence of peoples holding such worldviews as a primary social fact of international relations. Between worldviews, therefore, one should not be seeking reconciliation, for this may lead to conflict or absorption on someone's terms. One should be seeking modes of co-existence. The idea of co-existence, of course, points to some well-traveled paths of international thought and practice.[1] These present it as a process of temporary accommodation to be maintained by diplomatic skill until big issues are resolved or the parties return to conflict. Within the diplomatic tradition, however, co-existence has a strategic character, rather than a tactical one, for the big issues generated by relations of separateness either never go away or become replaced by new ones. The

---

[1] For a useful discussion of co-existence see Buzan, *From International Society to World Society?*, pp. 143–46 and Robert Jackson, *The Global Covenant: Human Conduct in a World of States* (Oxford: Oxford University Press, 2000).

plural character of our social arrangements and our ideas about them are both permanently operating factors entailing that this is so.

Such then are the elements of a diplomatic tradition of international thought from which, I have argued, diplomatic theory or diplomatic theorizing can allow us to say interesting things and provide new insights about why international relations are the way they are and how they might be. It makes us aware, for example, of the possibility of multiple international societies existing in the vertical, as well as the horizontal plane and the idea of their having relations with one another. It helps us to understand the dialectical character of the processes by which international societies change and the complex role of diplomacy and diplomats themselves in managing and facilitating these changes. They do not merely defend existing identities, but neither do they merely subvert them according to the logic of new forms or constellations of power. And while such theorizing has little to say about specific foreign policies, it can suggest a great deal which we might regard as policy-relevant, for example, about what is going on when countries call each other names. Most importantly it provides powerful insights into what we should expect and want as actors other than states become newly powerful and influential in international relations. We should not expect religions and religious thought to be enemies of diplomacy and the relations it sustains. We should expect private enterprises, civil society organizations and possibly individual people to engage in more and more diplomacy as they become more influential in international relations. We should want them all to be good at it.

And here we come to the problem noted at the end of the last chapter. How are they and we and, indeed, governments and diplomats to be made better at diplomacy? This is, in part, a practical problem to which answers like "more diplomatic education" can make a contribution. It is also a political problem because diplomats represent those who often do not listen to them and cannot be compelled to do so. Sitting behind both difficulties, however, is a conceptual problem associated with the idea of diplomacy as a weak force in a domain where the strong forces of power, interests and ideas dominate. It is a weak force paradoxically because of its greatest strength, its insistence that we – practitioners, scholars and people alike – should always try to separate the content – in terms of our respective senses of particular problems and solutions – of international relations from the activity of conducting them. People and peoples care greatly about the terms on which they live together, even if the diplomatic tradition alerts us to how these terms shift over time and by place. What is a matter of life, death and honor at one point or place barely merits attention at another. What is seen as a great and pressing problem requiring immediate action at one point or place fades into insignificance at another. It is not that nothing really matters. Rather, in social worlds, constituted largely by what we make of them, the problem is that everything, even a simple and innocent effort to feed starving babies, for example, involves people who become a collective actor acquiring an identity and interests capable of generating differences with other collective actors and needing representation as such. And, time and again, the costs of seeking to resolve such differences seem to be so much worse than the costs of merely living with them or even letting the other fellow have his way.

This can be read as a modest claim suggesting that we are able to be certain about very little regarding the issues over which people conduct their international relations and, hence, that we should always proceed with caution. Since the diplomatic tradition's call for epistemological modesty has its own universal implications, however, it can also be seen as an arrogant one. It purports to cast its blanket of doubt over everyone, especially those who disagree with it and want to say something with sufficient certainty about international relations as to provide a basis of for action within them. It is because people do not like this and find it difficult to accept that diplomacy, diplomats and diplomatic thinking together remain a weak force in international relations. The magic of diplomatic distance comes at a high price in terms of peoples' aspirations for how they would like the world to be and what they want from it. This price is clearly visible in three injunctions with which anyone engaged in diplomatic theorizing or diplomatic practice has to follow: be slow to judge; be ready to appease; and doubt most universals. If diplomacy is to be a stronger force in international relations, then its advocates have to respond effectively to those who say these injunctions will lead down dark and dangerous roads to places where we do not want to be and keep us there.

Diplomatic theory and the balance of virtue and right

In most arguments, most people have some sort of interest in who is wrong, who is right or, if there is no clear answer in these terms, where the balance of virtue lies between the protagonists in terms of both their respective positions and who they are. The protagonists themselves share this interest, even if only for the instrumental reason that to be regarded as right and good may yield some sort of advantage. However, we probably underestimate the extent to which being right and good matter for their own sake to people. Most of those generally regarded as wicked, after all, inhabit the same worlds of justifications as the rest of us, even if some of them seek to justify what they have done and who they have become only to themselves. One of the more difficult recommendations suggested by diplomatic theory of international relations, therefore, is that this pressure to establish the balance of virtue and right in international disputes should be resisted and attempts to draw conclusions in these terms indefinitely postponed. It is not that diplomats have no interest in the moral dimension to international relations in general or the positions which are taken in particular disputes – quite the reverse. Their interest, however, is of a different sort to the one above. Diplomats want to obtain the best understanding they can of the positions taken by all the parties to a dispute. They are interested in this on prudential grounds, to be sure. Their masters expect them to know the enemy (or rival or partner for that matter). They are also interested in a better understanding for their own reasons, however. Why protagonists adopt the positions they do may have an impact on the prospects for maintaining relations and, indeed, maintaining the system of diplomacy which facilitates relations. A better understanding requires a capacity for sympathy, however, and sympathy requires the ability to tease out what is right in one's own terms about how other people have arrived at their respective positions.

It is this ability and the value they place on it that provides diplomats with a measure of distance from the terms in which international disputes are framed and conducted. As Butterfield, among others, has argued, with the benefit of distance one can come to see how disputes have rarely had the good lined up on one side and the bad on the other. Rather, we see them taking place between parties, "one half-right that was perhaps too willful, and another half-right which was perhaps too proud" trapped in the "terrible predicaments which have the effect of putting men so at cross-purposes with one another."[2] Diplomats, therefore, perform like diplomatic historians of the present. If they can identify the extent to which all international disputes are

---

[2] Butterfield, "The Tragic Element in Modern International Conflict," p. 9.

morally complex and ambiguous affairs and persuade their respective masters that this is so, the latter will not, like seventeenth-century Protestants and Catholics, have to fight one another for thirty years to discover it for themselves.

However, is it prudent or right for diplomats to act like diplomatic historians of the present, always pointing out ambiguities and complexities with a view to rendering assessments of the balance of virtue and right both hazardous and unhelpful? It is one thing for A. J. P. Taylor, for example, to seek out the sense in Hitler's statecraft and attempt a revised estimate of the contributions of others to the ensuing catastrophe from the safety of Oxford twenty years on. Fortunes, other than his own, no longer hang in the balance, and the argument can be pushed to see what insights it yields even though it may be wrong. Can one take such risks with real, live enemies, however, and can one say, after the horrors of National Socialism, Stalinist Communism, Rwandan genocides and the Serb massacres of Bosnian Muslims, that all fights involve the partly right against the partly wrong? Surely we can identify where the balance of right and wrong lies in at least some international conflicts and, when we do, surely power and virtue ought to march hand-in-hand to right wrongs, if this can be accomplished without creating greater evils?

Affirmative answers to this last question lie at the heart of a new post-Cold War consensus around the foreign policy of humanitarian intervention.[3] Moral judgments and the actions for which they call should no longer be subordinated to narrow conceptions of state interests or self-serving devices like the principle of non-intervention in domestic affairs. Instead, the wickedness of states, both at home and abroad, must be identified and dealt with because it is wrong and because it is a potential source of international disorder. Indeed, the arguments are no longer about who is wicked; that much is said to be clear. Among the western great powers and their allies, at least, they are about how forcefully the wicked should be dealt with and how they should be prioritized for treatment. Even many serving diplomats subscribe to the view that we live at a moment of opportunity for raising international and domestic

---

[3] See J. L. Holzgrefe and Robert O. Keohane (eds.), *Humanitarian Intervention: Ethical, Legal and Political Dilemmas* (Cambridge: Cambridge University Press, 2003), Wheeler, *Saving Strangers* and Terry Nardin and Melissa S. Williams (eds.), *Humanitarian Intervention* (New York: New York University Press, 2006).

standards of conduct for governments and peoples alike. We should not miss this opportunity, and we should not return to the days when thousands, indeed millions, might be murdered by wicked governments allowed to shelter behind their sovereign status by their more virtuous fellows under the advice of diplomats about avoiding precipitate actions based on moral judgments.

Difficult though it may be, however, diplomatic theory still encourages skepticism about this view and the new consensus that has emerged around it. It does so on empirical grounds. The arithmetic of death and suffering in Kosovo and Iraq before, during and after the respective interventions, for example, cannot provide clear evidence that the benefits of righting wrongs in each case outweighed the costs. Yet the salience of the notion of intervention to right wrongs provides cover for all sorts of interventions.[4] The tradition also suggests skepticism, by employing what may be best termed a historical logic of probabilities. Even when a strong international consensus exists on where the balance of virtue and right resides, it is never a complete consensus. A case can be always made for the "other side's" point of view and historical experience suggests that with the passage of time, this case strengthens and the consensus about who was right and who was wrong almost invariably weakens. It is also never a consensus that is beyond criticism in terms of proportionality. The passage of time sharpens doubts about, for example, whether Serb wrongs outweighed those perpetrated by Croats, and why Serb wrongs were equated with the scale of wickedness achieved by the Nazis to justify an intervention at the same time as no such intervention took place in Rwanda. And, of course, skepticism is suggested on grounds of prudence. No matter how wicked men and women may be in your judgment and even nearly everybody else's, it rarely helps to treat them as wicked in the course of diplomatic relations. Diplomats from both sides will find it easier to maintain relations between those they represent if they can be somehow insulated from such judgments and their consequences.

In a sense, therefore, the diplomatic tradition of international thought offers the morality of suspending judgment. One ought to resist the temptation and pressure to act otherwise if one wishes to resolve

---

[4] See, e.g., Vladimir Radyuhin, "Medvedev, Putin accuse Georgia of genocide," in *The Hindu*, August 11, 2008, at www.thehindu.com/2008/08/11/stories/2008081156011500.htm.

differences without damaging or ending relations, and if one cares about the sort of more considered assessments of the balance of merit which the passage of time permits. What the tradition does not do, however, is provide a basis for its own theorizing about when to make such judgments and when to refrain from making them, not even in extreme cases. Suppose, for example, Nazi Germany had combined the extermination of its Jewish population with a peaceful foreign policy. Even in such terrible circumstances, diplomatic theory would suggest caution about making judgments with the sort of substantive consequences that might have materially affected the Nazis' behavior. It would do so by pointing to the likely indeterminacy and unforeseen consequences of such actions (killing more people than you save, for example, and creating new monsters even as you slay the old one), and contrasting this danger with the disposition to believe that civilized conversation always holds the potential, at least, for finding a way out of a jam.

Diplomatic theory and appeasement

This latter disposition, of course, highlights the dangers of the second injunction, namely that we should be ready to appease. What if those with whom we negotiate are not interested in diplomacy and are prepared to obtain what they want at all costs by deception, bluff, threats and force? If this is so, then it may be claimed that neither diplomatic theory nor diplomats themselves may have much to tell us about how to deal with such people, and that what they do tell us can get us into a great deal of trouble. The archetypal figure in this regard, although he was not a diplomat, is Neville Chamberlain, and the archetypal episode involves his dealings with Hitler in the late 1930s.[5] Chamberlain's mistake is said to have been that he regarded Hitler as a gentleman and, thus, was predisposed to see his demands as rooted in a reasonableness that might be discovered and accommodated. Since Hitler was not a gentleman, his demands could not be accommodated, only countered, and attempts to accommodate him, therefore, merely increased his appetite. By the time that Hitler had been given every chance to demonstrate that he was genuinely interested in diplomacy, and by the time everyone else had discovered that he genuinely was not, the

[5] Robert C. Self, *Neville Chamberlain: A Biography* (Aldershot: Ashgate, 2006).

position of Nazi Germany had been greatly strengthened. As a consequence, and in the name of averting pain and suffering in the short term, greater pain and suffering were stored up for the medium to long term by the diplomatic desire to seek good relations and peace at almost any price.

Leaving aside problems with the historical accuracy and, more importantly, with the completeness of this account, it may be seen that diplomatic theory would challenge each element of the general characterization of international relations to which it gives expression. Hitler may not have been a gentleman, but he was quite capable of acting as a gentleman towards those he believed entitled to, or requiring, such treatment. He was also bound by a moral code of obligations in his relations with them which most of us would recognize, trying to keep his promises as he understood them, and trying to justify his actions and how his departures from this code in certain circumstances were warranted right down to the very end.[6] This claim is very hard to swallow unless one realizes that it is not as important as it sounds. It merely serves to underline that whatever mistakes the British prime minister did make, treating the German Chancellor as a gentleman was not one of them. Gentlemanliness, or whatever general notion of civilized humanity this term seeks to convey, is not a necessary condition for the ability to conduct diplomacy. Bounders, cads and even monsters may engage in it, although they may be more likely to defect, or more quickly defect, from its commitments if they judge this to be necessary than the rest of us. Nor, as other historical episodes demonstrate, is gentlemanliness a sufficient condition for conducting diplomacy. Many "gentlemen" have been deeply implicated in the sort of international relations that attract moral condemnation. Gentlemanliness, therefore, is best viewed, not as a personal quality, but as an expression of a moral code of action which becomes operational in certain circumstances, specifically when people are dealing with those whom they believe to be, are prepared to accept, or wish to regard, as their equals. Thus, the only people with whom a diplomatic relationship is impossible for certain are those with whom you do not attempt to conduct one because you do not want it, and those who do not want one with you. Until that point is reached, diplomatic relations of some sort, even with Hitlers, are always a possibility capable of generating other possibilities.

[6] Alan Bullock: *Adolf Hitler: A Study in Tyranny* (New York: Harper Brothers, 1958).

What then of the objection that some of these possibilities may be bad, specifically that by seeking to appease the ruthless you strengthen them and weaken yourself? Diplomatic theory highlights the extent to which certainty in this regard depends on hindsight and confidence about who is being appeased and who is doing the appeasing. The "guilty men" of the 1930s did not know for sure that Hitler could not be satisfied; he did not know himself until the eleventh hour of the Polish crisis. As noted above, all they knew on the morning after the Munich settlement had been reached was that many more people would remain alive over the next few months than would otherwise have been the case, and that the possibility of keeping them alive remained open.[7] One suspects that had they been privy to subsequent events – a total war involving the deaths of millions, the expansion of Soviet communism and the collapse of their own international positions, then the resolve of the Anglo-French governments to abandon the course of appeasement during the final Polish crisis would have been weaker rather than stronger. Even the Poles might have reconsidered their policy of refusing to transfer their corridor back to Germany for, as Taylor asks, by 1945 was it better to have been "a betrayed Czech or a saved Pole." The same question might be asked today of "saved" Kosovars, Iraqis and South Ossetians.[8] Regarding confidence about the identity of appeasers and appeased, diplomatic theory alerts us to what is happening on the other side of the hill. Hitler believed that Germany's position as a revisionist state in the 1930s resulted not just from defeat, but from being willing to be put upon by the victorious allies in the 1920s. He was by no means alone in Germany (or elsewhere) in this regard, and it might be argued that it was Germany under the Nazis which took the "lessons of appeasement" to heart long before his opponents did.

These are difficult arguments to make, and my intention is not to launch a specific defense of appeasement in the 1930s. If, however, they

---

[7] The term is from Michael Foot, *Guilty Men* (London: Victor Gollancz, 1940).
[8] By Taylor's figures, six and a half million Poles were killed compared to less than 100,000 "Czechs," *The Origins of the Second World War*, p. 26. The intensity and longevity of the debate around Taylor's general argument is usefully captured by the essays and fragments in W. M. Roger Louis (ed.), *The Origins of the Second World War: A. J. P. Taylor and His Critics* (New York: John Wiley, 1972), Gordon Martel (ed.), *The Origins of the Second World War Reconsidered* (Boston: Allen Unwin, 1986) and Peter Neville, *Hitler and Appeasement: The British Attempt to Prevent the Second World War* (London: Hambledon Continuum, 2007).

can at least be raised in so iconic and apparently straightforward a case as this, then their relevance to situations that are typically far more ambiguous becomes clear. In these, we can see how the very indeterminacy and possibility of creative situations which diplomatic theory suggests we should value and preserve by talking are often sources of fear for governments and peoples alike. For the possibility exists that even in negotiations with those we regard as unprincipled, ruthless and fanatic, we may be maneuvered, not by bullying and lies, but by reasonable diplomacy, towards concessions which we do not want to make. Fear of this sort is present on both sides in the dispute between the US and Iran over the latter's nuclear energy policy. President Bush's administration worries that it may be talked into accepting a situation in which Iran acquires the ability to produce nuclear weapons. President Ahmadinejad's administration worries that it will be talked into accepting one which rules out that possibility. Thus, the Americans offer talks providing the Iranians will first give up their research into the manufacture of nuclear fuels.[9] The Iranians, in their turn, offer talks that will return Americans to God's way under the guidance of Iran.

The dynamics in play are well illustrated by what happened when Ahmadinejad sent an open letter to Bush in May 2006.[10] In it, he acknowledges commonalities – a shared God and shared responsibilities of government, for example. He expresses a measure of sympathy with Americans for the attacks of "9/11" and the resulting concern with US security. Ahmadinejad also attempts to justify Iran's nuclear energy program. It only wants that to which all countries are entitled. However, these kernels of diplomatic understanding and diplomatic arguments are surrounded by a shell of criticism and doubt about US motives which extends to suggesting that the "9/11" attacks were staged to provide a pretext for waging war on America's enemies. Ahmadinejad asks how current US foreign policy can be reconciled with the teachings of Jesus both Christians and Muslims respect. It is on a mistaken course, and its only hope of salvation lies in changing its heart and changing its course to follow God's will, a will already divined by the President of Iran.

---

[9] Helen Cooper and Isabel Kershner, "Rice Calls Dialogue With Iran Pointless," *The New York Times*, June 4, 2008.

[10] Mahmoud Ahmadinejad sent George Bush an open letter, May 9, 2006 offering talks. Text at FinalCall.com News at www.finalcall.com/artman/publish/article_2607.shtml.

As an exercise in diplomacy, Ahmadinejad's letter presents a number of problems. The Americans noted that it did not address their core concern at all, that its offensive form suggested an appeal to Ahmadinejad's domestic constituencies rather than to them and that, as such, a reply in kind would not be forthcoming.[11] Talks with Iran until it agreed to stop its work on nuclear fuels would be, in Secretary Rice's word, "pointless" and those who advocated talks were accused of appeasement (although not by her), because talking would allow the Iranians to carry on their work and make it harder to stop them if this was decided upon at some point in the future. Diplomatic theory, in contrast, would suggest that Bush should have replied, and it would do so without taking issue with the Americans' characterization of Ahmadinejad's *démarche* as a stunt. Far more important than the Iranians' reasons for the letter being sent, it would suggest, might be the potential consequences of their having sent it. It involved an explicit attempt on the part of the Iranian president to talk to those with whom, in his view, there is just no talking, and to frame Iranian and American identities as distinctive from one another, but with common roots and common ground. It offered a basis for talking about how stable relations of separateness between the two countries might be established. Certainly, this took the form of a claim that the Iranians spoke for God and that the Americans should move towards them. As we have already seen, however, this declaratory approach has deep roots in Muslim diplomacy stretching back to the days of Muhammad, when it did not prove an obstacle to the development of stable, bilateral relations between Mecca and Medina, on the one hand, and other independent entities on the other. Replying, therefore, would have given the Americans the chance to offer their own framing of the basis on which stable relations might be achieved and, together, the two letters could conceivably have pushed the whole question of Iranian-American relations out of the realms of subjective foreign policies and into the world of diplomacy between the two states where the possibilities of a world with or without an Iranian bomb might be more freely reflected upon.

One has to feel either secure enough or desperate enough to be willing to take the risk of being outmaneuvered or simply led in unanticipated directions by the open-ended potentials of talks. Clearly in this case

---

[11] "Iran Letter to Bush a Welcome Sign: Kissinger," *Journal of Turkish Weekly* (May 13, 2006), online at www.turkishweekly.net/news.php?id=31784.

neither party felt itself secure. Diplomatic theory would suggest, however, that a shared determination to avoid appeasement on the part of both the US and Iran could very quickly provide the sense of desperation required to take a chance. Considerations of security and risk, however, apply not just to one's own people and interests but to others as well. It may be objected, for example, that when one talks with dictators, ayatollahs and Great Satans, one is recognizing them and, in so doing, one is telling the people who live under them to accept their lots, at least for now. Again, diplomatic theory would suggest that the recognition implied by talking is a small price to pay for the possibilities inherent in such talks. Behind the recognition theme, however, sits a much bigger problem, the idea that one can tell other peoples to put up with their lot under dictators, despots and Satans in the cause of international peace. Modern diplomacy especially has a long association with images of whole peoples being left to their suffering, or having new suffering inflicted upon them, in the cause of supposedly greater goods achieved by compromises with their respective oppressors. The partitions of Poland, Czechoslovakia and Europe after Yalta can be all cited as examples of diplomatic attempts to purchase peace at the expense of others, as can the present predicaments of the Palestinians and the Kurds. Most people feel uneasy about the propositions that the Czechoslovaks did the right thing by capitulating and resigning themselves to their fate on at least two occasions, and that the Poles made a mistake by fighting and accepting help in a disastrously unsuccessful attempt to maintain their freedom and independence, no matter what the arithmetic of deaths suggests. However, these concerns move us beyond the issue of diplomacy and appeasement *per se* and towards the broader set of problems generated by diplomatic theory's third injunction, namely, to doubt most universals. It is this injunction that provides sanction for acting as if peace is, indeed, divisible in the sense that the peace of some and even most can be purchased at the expense of others. In so doing, however, does it reveal diplomatic theory and the practice from which it is distilled as obstacles to the implementation of more solidarist conceptions of how human beings might live?

Diplomatic theory and human solidarity

The answer to this question has to be "yes." Diplomatic theory can work against the development of solidarist possibilities in the world. It cannot be maintained otherwise because it is no longer possible to claim that any theory about human relations simply takes and leaves the social world as it finds it. All theorists encounter the world with their presuppositions and, insofar as anyone listens to what they have to say and acts upon it, their theories help shape the world through their framings, implications and recommendations. Thus, people armed with diplomatic theory of international relations will respond to solidarist proposals about, for example, universal human rights and, perhaps more importantly, universal obligations to uphold and protect those rights, differently from people who are not. In this sense, however, there is no difference between diplomatic theory premised on the way in which people exist in groups with different collective understandings of internal and external relations, on the one hand, and a humanitarian theory premised on the sameness of individuals whose ability to sympathize with each other squeezes out the empirical and moral grounds for according some people – strangers – less favored treatment, on the other. They both make claims upon the reasoning faculties and moral sensibilities of emotional human beings in a world replete with evidence that supports, or can be rendered consistent with, what they have to say.

While social theories do not simply take the world as they find it, however, they do in some sense have to take in the world. Even the most formal social theorizing is not derived from first principles that are entirely internally derived. Thus, solidarists, pluralists and individualists see humanity, peoples and human beings, respectively, in the world and reason from there. Each emphasis gives them a distinctive place to stand "outside" the world from which to say things about what it is like and how it might be. In these terms, diplomatic theory presents a world of humanity, peoples and people arguing about, and trying to live according to, their different views of themselves. Assuming that they do not want to kill each other and cannot convert one another or are willing to forgo trying, how might they best live together? This is diplomatic theory's distinctive standpoint. What it may lack, therefore, when compared to the other theories in terms of the answers which can be derived from it to questions about what should we do in specific situations, is compensated for by the greater authenticity of its claim to grasp the world as it is at any given moment. What it grasps is that while humanity might come to know itself as such, while peoples can live in communities and social worlds of their own, and while individuals may, in the end, be all there is and all there ought to be, we actually do live in a world where people argue about these sorts of things and, as a consequence of these arguments being unresolved, enjoy a plural existence. On the basis of this insight, I have claimed privilege for diplomatic theory as an international relations theory *per se*. Other theories, in contrast, are driven by views of the content of international relations, what they are, and ought to be about.

Even if this insight can be sustained, however, ought we to be making the sort of arguments that can be derived from it? Is to do so akin to building theories of human action on the bad habits, self-indulgences and other sins into which all people are tempted at times? Having noted the tendency of peoples to treat differently those they regard as others, can we regard its consequences as anything other than a problem? Just like the claims of those who say they can identify empirically verifiable differences between members of different races, the claims of diplomatic theory might be put to bad use by the wrong sort of people, and the fact that this is so might suggest irresponsibility or worse on the part of the authors and promoters of such theory. Certainly, there is a great deal of international history which can be made to support the claim that bad things can follow when the differences between people are emphasized in certain ways. As noted earlier, one of the great impetuses to establishing the study of international politics and relations as a field in its own right was the sense that it was this precisely this sort of differentiation which allowed peoples to treat others far worse than they would treat their own. Domesticate international relations, extend the sense of solidarity that exists within communities to the whole human race, so the argument ran (and often still does), and things will improve.

Subsequent experience, observation and reflection, however, have indicated that the problem of war and the causes of peace are both more complex than those armed with the domestic analogy originally believed. In the last hundred years, international wars have remained terrible but become fewer, while the horrors within states and the communities they encompass have become worse and their numbers have proliferated. There has also developed a sense that the source of both international and domestic violence is to be found within particular states and how they are organized. Like cholesterol, so too with solidarity; there are good and bad, that is – exclusive and inclusive, liberating and oppressive, sorts. Thus, while the anarchy constituted by sovereign states is often seen as hardening and sanctifying the differentiation between peoples that makes terrible things possible, it is not the case that any old domestication of international relations can be regarded as an improvement. It has to be the right sort of domestication. The problem is, of course, that, while there exists a great deal of certainty about the need for the right sort of states or other collectives embedded in the right sort of international society, there exists no matching consensus of any depth as to what that right sort in both cases is. It might well be that a world of liberal states would be more peaceful and wealthy than anything that has gone before, and that a reconstituted *umma* would be more peaceful and pious, but the world we live in is populated by peoples who are organized, willingly or not, around both sets of beliefs as well as many others. And a defining feature of such beliefs appears to be the salience of the conviction with which they are promoted by the powerful and those who wish to be powerful. In this respect, science-based claims and faith-based claims, for example, function in remarkably similar ways when they are used to capture and secure adherents at a mass level, and they produce remarkably similar reactions on the part of those who are hostile to what is being promoted.

To concede these points – first, about the change in the ratio of domestic to interstate violence and second, that differences over what the right sort of state and international society might be have themselves become sources of conflict – should not make us nostalgic for modern diplomacy, only some of its consequences. There is nothing to suggest that a return to hard barriers policed by professionals who exercise a monopoly over the conduct of trans-boundary relations is either feasible or desirable now or in the foreseeable future. Nevertheless, the successes of modern diplomacy in its time point to the necessarily contextual character of any conclusions we may draw about the charge that diplomatic theory promotes divisions and hinders the emergence of a sense of human solidarity. At certain times and under certain conditions it might do both in a way in which most people would wish it did not. One thinks of extreme circumstances such as the eve of a projected massacre or genocide, for example. To insist upon the separateness of human groups and communities, and the consequential sense of lesser obligations to the members of other groups, in such circumstances would be irresponsible and wrong. Even in far more benign circumstances, however, where peoples themselves seem to be accepting a decline in the significance of certain identities and the emergence of new ones, a reasonable case could be made for keeping diplomatic theory of international relations in the background. To insist, for example, that the people of Britain and France could not merge into some new and larger shared identity, under present conditions, would be to make a claim which was more political than theoretical in its character. In such circumstances, therefore, diplomatic theory of international relations might serve as theory-in-waiting for explaining difficulties, should they emerge, and suggesting how to handle them.

However, many of the great conflicts that attract our attention and absorb our energies today do not arise in the course of relations between peoples who regard one another as different and, in some respects, less than human. They result, rather, from the collisions of solidarist projects whose proponents will not, and probably cannot, refrain from promoting their goals on a global scale. They cannot avoid doing this principally because the old solution of multiple worlds which could see themselves in universal terms while, at the same time, being spatially bounded and separate, is no longer sustainable. Through their actions and, increasingly, through their very existence, peoples keep getting in each other's ways and making demands on the core aspects of each other's identities, whether they mean to or not. In such a context, what diplomatic theory has to say about the necessarily partial roots of solidarist projects in a plural world is very valuable. Indeed, in such a context the burden of what it means to exercise responsible scholarship might be said to rest more heavily upon those who advocate conventional solidarist and pluralist understandings of what is and ought to be going on. Privileging either senses of a human solidarity which exist both weakly and intermittently, or unproblematized conceptions of state identities and interests, in an attempt to short-circuit contemporary international difficulties does not seem to provide much help. All one gets are claims, pushed with more or less conviction, to be the authentic voice of everyone against the few bad apples who, be they terrorists, dictators, capitalists, imperialists, infidels, racists or misogynists, are spoiling it for all the rest.

Diplomatic theory, in contrast, rests on traditions of practice and thought that emphasize the reality of peoples' differences and separateness, rather than their similarities and togetherness. On the basis of this emphasis, codes of conduct have been developed which do not require high levels of agreement or thick inter-subjective understandings as bases for relationships. Rather, they presume their absence. Some of the codes, particularly those of the modern state system, may no longer be as useful as they once were, at least for now, but the problems they were developed to address remain broadly the same. Difference may be dealt with by destructive conquest, assimilation or developing modes of co-existence. It may be that the differences in our present world may be dealt by the first two procedures although, at the time of writing, this seems less likely than it did a short time before. Even if this is so, however, we should still hope for conquest and assimilation by diplomatic methods, for these involve less pain and suffering. And if, after an unspecified period of inflicting misery and suffering on each other, we learned, once again, that co-existence is the only durable way of dealing with difference, then diplomacy would offer the only way forward.

State sovereignty and national identity provided the theorists of the modern state system in Europe with conceptually elegant, if at times practically costly, categories for addressing the problems posed by a plural world of separate identities. The challenge for all international theorists, possibly all political theorists, and certainly not merely those who are interested in diplomacy, is to develop ideas about how the multitude of identities which now populate contemporary world politics are to be represented without posing existential threats to one another. Diplomacy's contribution – the mystery I identified at the beginning of the book – is the recognition on the part of those who practice it that relations between groups of peoples are different from those within them and are best treated as such. Diplomatic theory's contribution is to explore the ways in which this understanding may be given practical expression in different sorts of international and world societies which, despite the differing and changing character of their membership, remain plural in character. Diplomatic education's contribution is to disseminate this understanding, together with the priorities and skills associated with it. In plural worlds where co-existence is a shared problem, even where it is a shared value, an end to conflict in general is unlikely to be achieved. Indeed, there are times when conflict cannot and ought not to be avoided. Diplomatic theory is not good at identifying these. All it says is to treat all claims to this effect with extreme caution and, indeed, skepticism. This, however, is a valuable contribution. To paraphrase Wight one last time, while conflict in general may not be ended, particular conflicts, even existential ones, are more likely to be avoided if those responsible for avoiding them are aided by a diplomatic understanding of what is going on and diplomatic thinking about the issues and arguments to which they give rise.[12]

[12] Wight, *Power Politics*, p. 137.

Bibliography

Abu-Nasr, Donna and Shihri, Abdullah, "Saudi King Calls For Interfaith Dialogue," *ABC News*, March 25, 2008 at http://abcnews.go.com/International/wireStory?id=4518593.
Acheson, Dean, *Present at the Creation: My Years in the State Department* (New York: W. W. Norton and Co., 1969).
Ahmadinejad, Mahmoud, "Letter to George Bush," May 9, 2006, FinalCall. com News at www.finalcall.com/artman/publish/article_/2607.shtml.
Allman, T. D., *Rogue State: America At War With the World* (New York: Nation Books, 2004).
Anderson, Kai and Hurrell, Andrew (eds.), *Hedley Bull on International Society* (Basingstoke: Macmillan, 2000).
Annan, Kofi, "Nobel Peace Prize Lecture" (December 10, 2001) at http://nobelprize.org/nobel_/prizes/peace/laureates/2001/annan-lecture.html
Armstrong, David, *Revolution and World Order: The Revolutionary State in International Society* (Oxford: Clarendon Press, 1993).
  "Revolutionary Diplomacy," *Diplomatic Studies Programme Discussion Paper (DSPDP)* (Leicester: Centre for the Study of Diplomacy, November 1996).
Artzi, Pinas, "The Diplomatic Service in Action: The Mittani File," in Cohen, Raymond and Westbrook, Raymond, *Amarna Diplomacy: The Beginnings of International Relations* (Baltimore: Johns Hopkins, 2000), pp. 205–11.
Ashdown, P., "Butcher of the Balkans Found Dead," CNN.com (March 12, 2006) at www.cnn.com/2006/WORLD/europe/03/11/milosovic/.
Bagson, Brian, *History of the Soviet Government Documents website*, www.marxist.org/archive/trotsky/works/1918/gov.htm.
Baker, James A. (with Defrank, Thomas M.), *The Politics of Diplomacy: Revolution, War and Peace, 1989–1992* (New York: Putnam, 1995).
Barston, R., *Modern Diplomacy* (London: Longman, 1988).
Bayne, Nicholas and Woodcock, Stephen (eds.), *The New Economic Diplomacy: Decision-Making and Negotiation in International Economic Relations* (Aldershot: Ashgate, 2003).

Bergamn, Mohan J. Dutta, "US Public Diplomacy in the Middle East: A Critical Cultural Approach," *Journal of Communication Inquiry*, 30, 2 (April, 2006), pp. 102–24.

Bernard, Montague, *Four Lectures On Subjects Connected With Diplomacy* (London: Macmillan, 1868).

Berridge, G. R., *Talking to The Enemy: How States Without Diplomatic Relations Communicate* (Basingstoke: Palgrave Macmillan, 1994).

Diplomacy: Theory and Practice (London: Prentice Hall/Wheatsheaf, 1995).

"Guicciardini," in Berridge, Keens Soper and Otte, *Diplomatic Theory from Machiavelli to Kissinger*, pp. 33–49.

"The Origins of the Diplomatic Corps: Rome to Constantinople," in Sharp and Wiseman (eds.), *The Diplomatic Corps as an Institution of International Society*, pp. 15–30.

"Review of Christer Jönsson and Martin Hall, *Essence of Diplomacy*," on G. R. Berridge's website at www.grberridge.co.uk/booknote.html.

Berridge, G. R. (ed.), *Diplomatic Classics: Selected Texts from Commynes to Vattel* (Basingstoke: Palgrave Macmillan, 2004).

Berridge, G. R. and James, Alan, *A Dictionary of Diplomacy* (Basingstoke: Palgrave Macmillan, 2001).

Berridge, G. R. Keens Soper, Maurice and Otte, T. G., *Diplomatic Theory from Machiavelli to Kissinger* (Basingstoke: Palgrave Macmillan, 2001).

Bevan, Aneurin, "Labour Party Conference" (October 4, 1957), www.spartacus.schoolnet.co.uk/TUbevan.htm.

Beverly, Tessa, "Diplomacy and Elites: Venetian Ambassadors, 1454–1494," *Diplomatic Studies Programme Discussion Paper* (Leicester: Diplomatic Studies Programme, **51**, March 1999).

Bickers, Robert A. (ed.), *Ritual and Diplomacy: The Macartney Mission to China 1792–1794* (Port Murray: Wellsweep, 1993).

Blum, William, *Rogue State: A Guide to the World's Only Superpower* (Monroe: Common Courage Press, 2005).

Booth, Ken and Dunne, Timothy (eds.), *Worlds in Collision: Terror and the Future of Global Order* (Basingstoke: Palgrave Macmillan, 2002).

Bosworth, R. J. B., *Mussolini's Italy: Life Under the Fascist Dictatorship, 1915–45* (London: Penguin, 2007).

Bosworth, Stephen, "Political Transition in the Philippines," in Hopkins Miller, Robert, *Inside an Embassy: The Political Role of Diplomats Abroad* (Washington: Institute for the Study of Diplomacy, 1992), pp. 66–72.

Bremer, L. Paul and McConnell, Malcolm, *My Year in Iraq: The Struggle to Build a Future of Hope* (New York: Simon and Schuster, 2006).

Brontë, Emily, "No Coward Soul Is Mine," *The Complete Poems of Emily Jane Brontë* (New York: Columbia University Press, 1995), p. 243.

Brown, Chris, *International Relations Theory: New Normative Approaches* (Hemel Hempstead: Harvester Wheatsheaf, 1992).
Brown, Chris and Ainley, Kirsten, *Understanding International Relations* (Basingstoke: Palgrave Macmillan, 3rd edn., 2005).
Buckley, Anthony D. and Kenny, Mary Catherine, *Negotiating Identity: Rhetoric, Metaphor and Social Drama in Northern Ireland* (Washington: Smithsonian Institute Press, 1995).
Bull, Hedley, *The Anarchical Society: A Study of Order in World Politics* (London: Macmillan, 1977).
 "The European International Order (1980)," in Anderson and Hurrell (eds.), *Hedley Bull On International Society*, pp. 170–89.
 "The Grotian Conception of International Society," in Butterfield and Wight (eds.), *Diplomatic Investigations*, pp. 51–73.
 "Society and Anarchy in International Relations," in Butterfield and Wight (eds.), *Diplomatic Investigations*, pp. 35–50.
 "Theory and Practice of International Relations, 1648–1789, Introduction," cited in Vigezzi, Brunello, *The British Committee on the Theory of International Politics (1954–1985)*.
Bull, Hedley and Watson, Adam (eds.), *The Expansion of International Society* (Oxford: Oxford University Press, 1984).
Bullock, Alan, *Adolf Hitler: A Study in Tyranny* (New York: Harper Brothers, 1958).
Bush, George, W., *State of the Union Address*, January 29, 2002 at www.whitehouse.gov/news/releases/2002/01/20020129-11.html.
Bush, George and Scowcroft, Brent, *A World Transformed* (New York: Vintage/Random House, 1998).
Butterfield, Herbert, *The Origins of Modern Science* (London: Bell, 1949).
 Christianity and History (New York: Charles Scribner's Sons, 1950).
 History and Human Relations (Collins: London, 1951).
 Christianity in European History (London: Collins, 1952).
 Christianity, Diplomacy and War (London: Epworth, 1953).
 "The Tragic Element in Modern International Conflict," in Butterfield, *History and Human Relations*, pp. 9–36.
 "Christianity and Human Problems," in Butterfield, *Christianity, Diplomacy and War*, pp. 1–14.
 "Power and Diplomacy," in Butterfield, *Christianity, Diplomacy and War*, pp. 66–78.
 "Ideological Diplomacy Versus International Order," in Butterfield, *Christianity, Diplomacy and War*, pp. 102–25.
 "Comments on Hedley Bull's Paper on the Grotian Conception of International Society," Butterfield Papers University Library Cambridge 1962, also in Schweizer, Karl W. and Sharp, Paul (eds.), *The International*

Thought of Herbert Butterfield (Basingstoke: Palgrave Macmillan, 2007), pp. 198–206.

"Notes for a Discussion on the Theory of International Politics," Butterfield Papers University Library Cambridge 335 (January 1964).

"The Balance of Power," in Butterfield and Wight (eds.), *Diplomatic Investigations*, pp. 132–48.

"The New Diplomacy and Historical Diplomacy," in Butterfield and Wight (eds.), *Diplomatic Investigations*, pp. 181–92.

"Diplomacy," in Hatton, Ragnhild and Anderson, M. S., *Studies in Diplomatic History: Essays in honour of David Bayne Horn* (London: Archon Books, 1970), pp. 357–73.

"Raison D'Etat," First Martin Wight Memorial Lecture, Butterfield Papers University Library Cambridge (Brighton: University of Sussex, April 23, 1975).

Butterfield, Herbert and Wight, Martin (eds.), *Diplomatic Investigations* (Cambridge: Cambridge University Press, 1966).

Buzan, Barry, *The United States and the Great Powers: World Politics in the Twenty-First Century* (Cambridge: Polity, 2004).

From International to World Society? English School Theory and the Social Structure of Globalization (Cambridge: Cambridge University Press, 2004).

Buzan, Barry and Little, Richard, *International Systems in World History* (Oxford: Oxford University Press, 2000).

De Callières, François, *De la manière de négocier avec les souverains, de l'utilité des négotiations, du choix des ambassadeurs et des envoys, et des qualitez nécessaires pou réussir dans ces employs* (Paris: Brunet, 1717).

On The Manner Of Negotiating With Princes (South Bend: University of Notre Dame Press, 1963).

Calvet De Magalhães, José, *The Pure Concept of Diplomacy* (New York: Greenwood Press, 1988).

Cambon, Jules, *Le Diplomat* (Paris: Chez Hachette, 1926).

Caprioli, Mary and Trumbore, Peter F., "Ethnic Discrimination and Interstate Violence: Testing the International Impact of Domestic Behavior," *Journal of Peace Research*, 40, 1 (2003), pp. 5–23.

"Rhetoric vs. Reality: Rogue States in International Conflict, 1980–2001," *Journal of Conflict Resolution*, 49: 5 (2005), pp. 770–91.

Cartwright, Michael G., "Biblical Arguments in International Ethics," in Terry Nardin and David R. Mapel (eds.), *Traditions of International Ethics* (Cambridge: Cambridge University Press, 1992), pp. 270–96.

Center for Strategic and International Studies, *Reinventing Diplomacy in the Information Age* (Washington DC: Center for Strategic and International Studies, 1998).

The Central Intelligence World Fact Book available at www.cia.gov/library/publications/the-world-factbook/.
Chamberlain, Neville, www.secondworldwarhistory.com/quotes_neville_chamberlain.asp.
Chomsky, Noam, *Rogue States: The Rule of Force in World Affairs* (Cambridge, MA: South End Press, 2000).
— *Hegemony or Survival: America's Quest for Global Dominance* (New York: Henry Holt and Company, 2004).
Chomsky, Noam (with Said, Edward W.), *Acts of Aggression: Policing Rogue States* (New York: Seven Stories Press, 1999).
Christopher, Warren, "Normalization of Diplomatic Relations" in Plishke, Elmer (ed.), *Modern Diplomacy: The Art and the Artisans*, pp. 37–40.
Churkin, Vitaly, "Moscow Central Television First Programme Network," November 28, 1991 cited in *Foreign Broadcast Information Service* (November 29, 1991), pp. 23–5.
Clark, Eric, *Diplomat: The World of International Diplomacy* (New York: Taplinger Publishing Company, 1974).
Clark, Ian, *Globalization and Fragmentation* (Oxford: Oxford University Press, 1997).
— *Globalization and International Relations Theory* (Oxford: Oxford University Press, 1999).
Clark, Ian and Neumann, Iver B. (eds.), *Classical Theories of International Relations* (Basingstoke: Macmillan, 1996).
Von Clausewitz, Klaus (edited and translated by Howard, Michael and Paret, Peter), *On War* (Princeton: Princeton University Press, 1976).
Cline, Ray S., *World Power Assessment: A Calculus of Strategic Drift* (Washington DC: Center for Strategic and International Studies, 1975).
Cohen, Raymond, *Negotiating Across Cultures: Communication Obstacles in International Diplomacy* (Washington: United States Institute of Peace Press, 1991).
— "Language and Negotiation: A Middle East Lexicon," in Kurbalija, Jovan and Slavik, Hannah (eds.), *Language and Diplomacy* (Malta: DiploProjects, 2001), pp. 67–92.
Cohen, Raymond and Westbrook, Raymond (eds.), *Amarna Diplomacy: The Beginnings of International Relations* (Baltimore, Johns Hopkins, 2000).
Collins, Neill (ed.), *Political Issues in Ireland Today* (Manchester: Manchester University Press, 1999).
Connolly, James, "Diplomacy," *The Workers' Republic*, November 6, 1915 at www.marxists.org/archive/connolly/1915/11/diplmacy.htm
Conrad, Joseph, *The Secret Agent* (London: Penguin, 1963, first published 1907).

Constantinou, Costas, *On the Way to Diplomacy* (Minneapolis: University of Minnesota Press, 1996).

"Diplomatic Representation ... Or Who Framed the Ambassadors?" *Millennium*, **23**, 1 (Spring 1994), p. 19.

"Human Diplomacy and Spirituality," *Clingendael Discussion Papers in Diplomacy*, Clingendael, Netherlands, No. 103 (April 2006).

Coolsaet, Rik, "Trade is War: Belgium's Economic Diplomacy In The Age Of Globalisation," *Diplomatic Studies Programme Discussion Paper* (Leicester: Diplomatic Studies Programme, **62**, February 2000).

Cooper, Helen and Kershner, Isabel, "Rice Calls Dialogue With Iran Pointless," *The New York Times*, June 4, 2008.

Coughlin, Con, "John Bolton thinks diplomats are dangerous," *The Daily Telegraph*, November 30, 2007 at www.telegraph.co.uk/opinion/main.jhtml?xml=/opinion/2007/11/30/do3002.xml

"Doves are winning the war on Iran," *The Daily Telegraph*, December 4, 2007 http://blogs.telegraph.co.uk/con_coughlin/blog/2007/12/04/doves_are_winning_the_war_on_iran.

Crocker, Chester A., Osler Hampson, Fen and Aall, Pamela, *Herding Cats: Multiparty Mediation in a Complex World* (Washington: United States Institute of Peace, 1999).

Davis Cross, Mai'a K., *The European Diplomatic Corps: Diplomats and International Cooperation from Westphalia to Maastricht* (Basingstoke: Palgrave Macmillan, 2007).

Dawkins, Richard, *The God Delusion* (New York: Houghton Mifflin, 2006).

Daws, Gavin, *Shoal of Time: A History of the Hawaiian Islands* (Honolulu: University of Hawaii Press, 1974).

Der Derian, James, *On Diplomacy* (Oxford: Blackwell, 1987).

DeWitt, David B. and Kirton, John W., *Canada as a Principal Power: A Study in Foreign Policy and International Relations* (Toronto: John Wiley and Sons, 1983).

Diamond, Jared, *Germs, Guns and Steel: The Fates of Human Societies* (New York: W. W. Norton, 1997).

Dinan, Desmond, *Europe Recast: A History of the European Union* (Boulder: Lynne Rienner, June 2004).

Diplomacy: Profession in Peril? (London: Wilton Park Conference, 1997).

Dobrescu, Caius, "Charismatic, Egg-Head and No-Nonsense Diplomacy: Conflicting Models Within the Work-In-Progress of Contemporary Central European Diplomacy," in "The Role of Diplomacy in Countries in Transition With Special Emphasis on Education and Training," *Diplomatic Academy Year Book*, **1**, 1 (Zagreb: 1999), pp. 35–9.

Dobrynin, Anatoly, *In Confidence: Moscow's Ambassador to America's Six Cold War Presidents* (New York: Times Books, 1995).

Doran, Charles, "Canada–US Relations: Personality, Pattern and Domestic Politics," in James, Patrick, Michaud, Nelson and O'Reilly, Marc, *Handbook of Canadian Foreign Policy* (Lanham: Lexington Books, 2006).

Dougherty, James E. and Pfaltzgraff, Robert L. Jr., *Contending Theories of International Relations: A Comprehensive Survey* (2nd edn.) (Cambridge, MA: Harper Row, 1981).

Duke, Simon, "Diplomacy Without a Corps: Training for EU External Representation?" *Diplomatic Studies Programme Discussion Paper* (Leicester: Diplomatic Studies Programme, **76**, April 2001).

Dunn, David Hastings, "'Myths, Motivations and 'Misunderestimations': The Bush Administration and Iraq," *International Affairs*, **79**, 2 (March 2003), pp. 279–97.

Dunne, Timothy, *Inventing International Society: A History of the English School* (Basingstoke: Palgrave Macmillan, 1998).

Durrell, Lawrence, (London: EP Dutton, 1957–1960).

Europa, Glossary, "Subsidiarity," at http://europa.eu/scadplus/glossary/subsidiarity_en.htm.

Fatemi, K. and Salvatore, D. (eds.), *The North American Free Trade Agreement* (London: Pergamon, 1994).

Fénelon, François, *Adventures of Telemachus* (London: Meadows, Hitch and Hall, 1759) (first published 1694).

Ferguson, Niall, *Colossus: The Price of America's Empire* (New York: Penguin Press, 2004).

Fisher, Roger, Schneider, Andrea Kupfer, Borgwardt, Elizabeth and Ganson, Brian, *Coping With International Conflict: A Systematic Approach to Influence in International Negotiation* (Upper Saddle River: Prentice Hall, 1997).

Fitzpatrick, Kathy, "Advancing the New Public Diplomacy: A Public Relations Perspective," *The Hague Journal of Diplomacy*, **2**, 3 (2007), pp. 187–211.

Foot, Michael, *Guilty Men* (London: Victor Gollancz, 1940).

"Former British Envoy Suspended," BBC News Report, October 17, 2004 at http://news.bbc.co.uk/1/hi/uk/3750370.stm.

Foster, Michael K., "Another Look At the Function of Wampum in Iroquois-White Councils," in Jennings, Fenton, Druke and Miller (eds.), *The History and Culture of Iroquois Diplomacy*, pp. 99–114.

Foucault, Michel, *The Order of Things: An Archaeology of Human Science* (New York: Random House, 1970).

Frey, Linda S. and Frey, Marsha L., *The History of Diplomatic Immunity* (Columbus: Ohio State University Press, 1999).

Gabriel, Brigitte, *Because They Hate US: A Survivor of Islamic Wars of Terror Warns America* (New York: St. Martin's, 2006).

Galbraith, Kenneth, *A Life in Our Times: Memoirs of John Kenneth Galbraith* (Boston: Houghton Mifflin, 1981).

Gamble, Anthony, *Between Europe and America: The Future of British Politics* (Basingstoke: Palgrave Macmillan, 2003).

Garfinkel, Harold, *Studies in Ethnomethodology* (Englewood Cliffs: Prentice Hall, 1967).

George, Alexander L., *Bridging the Gap: Theory and Practice* in Foreign Policy (Washington DC: United States Institute of Peace Press, 1993).

Gentili, A., "Three Books on Embassies," in Berridge, G. R. (ed.), *Diplomatic Classics: Selected Texts from Commynes to Vattel*, pp. 57–74.

Gong, Gerrit W., "*China's Entry into International Society,*" in Bull and Watson (eds.), *The Expansion of International Society*, pp. 171–83.

Gibbon, Guy, *The Sioux: The Dakota and Lakota Nations* (Oxford: Blackwell, 2003).

Haig, Alexander M. Jr., *Caveat: Realism, Reagan and Foreign Policy* (New York: Scribner, 1984).

Halliday, Fred, *Soviet Policy in the Arc of Crisis* (Washington DC: Institute for Policy Studies, 1981).

  Rethinking International Relations (Vancouver: University of British Columbia Press, 1995).

Hamilton, Keith and Langhorne, Richard, *The Practice of Modern Diplomacy: Its Evolution, Theory and Administration* (London: Routledge, 1995).

Hardinge, Sir Arthur H., *Diplomacy in the East* (London: Jonathan Cape, 1928).

Hardinge of Penshurst, *Old Diplomacy* (London: John Murray, 1947).

Hatton, Ragnhild and Anderson, M. S.. (eds.), *Studies in Diplomatic History: Essays in Honour of David Bayne Horn* (London: Archon Books, 1970).

Henderson, Sir Neville, *Failure of a Mission: Berlin 1937–39* (London: Putnam, 1940).

Henderson, Nicholas, *Mandarin: The Diaries of Nicholas Henderson* (London: Weidenfeld and Nicolson, 1995).

  "Foreword" in McClanahan, Grant V., *Diplomatic Immunity: Principles, Practices, Problems* (New York: St. Martins Press, 1989).

Hill, David Jayne, *A History of Diplomacy in the International Development of Europe, Vol. 1: The Struggle for Universal Empire* (New York: Longmans, 1905).

Hitchens, Christopher, *God Is Not Great: How Religion Poisons Everything* (New York: Twelve Books, 2007).

  "The Persian Version," in *The Atlantic Online* (July/August 2006), at www.theatlantic.com/doc/prem/200607/hitchens-persian

Hoare, J. E., "Diplomacy in the East," in Sharp, Paul and Wiseman, Geoffrey (eds.), *The Diplomatic Corps as an Institution of International Society*, pp. 105–24.

Hocking, Brian, "Beyond 'Newness' and 'Decline': The Development of Catalytic Diplomacy," *Diplomatic Studies Programme Discussion Paper* (Leicester: Diplomatic Studies Programme, **10**, October 1995).

"Foreign Ministries: Redefining the Gatekeeper Role," in Hocking, Brian (ed.), *Foreign Ministries: Change and Adaptation* (Basingstoke: Macmillan, 1999), pp. 1–16.

"Introduction: Gatekeepers and Boundary-Spanners – Thinking About Foreign Ministries in the European Union," in Hocking, Brian and Spence, David (eds.), *Foreign Ministries in the European Union* (Basingstoke: Palgrave Macmillan, 2005), pp. 1–17.

"Reconfiguring Public Diplomacy: From Competition to Collaboration," in Welch, Jolyn and Fern, Daniel (eds.), *Engagement: Public Diplomacy in a Globalised World* (London: British Foreign and Commonwealth Office, 2008), pp. 62–75.

Hocking, Brian (ed.), *Foreign Ministries: Change and Adaptation* (Basingstoke, Macmillan, 1999).

Hocking, Brian and Lee, Donna, "The Diplomacy of Proximity and Specialness: Enhancing Canada's Representation in the United States," *The Hague Journal of Diplomacy*, **1**, 1 (2006), pp. 29–52.

Hocking, Brian and Spence, David, "Towards a European Diplomatic System?" *Discussion Papers in Diplomacy* (The Hague: Netherlands Institute of International Relations Clingendael), **98**, May 2005.

Hocking, Brian and Spence, David (eds.), *Foreign Ministries in the European Union* (Basingstoke: Palgrave Macmillan, 2005).

Holbrooke, Richard, *To End a War* (New York: Modern Library, 1999).

"Butcher of the Balkans Found Dead," *CNN.com* (March 12, 2006) at www.cnn.com/2006/WORLD/europe/03/11/milosovic/.

Holsti, K. J., *International Politics: A Framework for Analysis*, 1st edn. (Englewood Cliffs: Prentice Hall, 1967).

Holzgrefe, J. L. and Keohane, Robert O. (eds.), *Humanitarian Intervention: Ethical, Legal and Political Dilemmas* (Cambridge: Cambridge University Press, 2003).

Hudson, David and Lee, Donna, "The Old and New Significance of Political Economy in Diplomacy," *Review of International Studies*, **30**, 3 (2004), pp. 343–60.

Huijgh, Ellen, "Domestic Outreach," paper presented at 1st The Hague Diplomacy Conference: Crossroads of Diplomacy, June 21–22, 2007.

Huntington, Samuel, *The Clash of Civilizations and the Remaking of World Order* (New York: Simon and Shuster, 1996).

Hurd, Douglas, *Memoirs* (London: Abacus, 2004).
  Chatham House Lecture reported as "UK's World Role: Punching above our weight," BBC News, Open University, *Open Politics*, http://news.bbc.co.uk/hi/english/static/in_depth/uk_politics/2001/open_politics/foreign_policy/uks_world_role.stm.
Iqbal, Afzal, *The Prophet's Diplomacy: The Art of Negotiation As Conceived and Developed By the Prophet of Islam* (Cape Cod: Claude Stark and Co., 1975).
Istanbuli, Yasin, *Diplomacy and Diplomatic Practice In The Early Islamic Era* (Oxford: Oxford University Press, 2001).
Jackson, Robert, *The Global Covenant: Human Conduct in a World of States* (Oxford: Oxford University Press, 2000).
James, Alan, "Diplomatic Relations and Contacts," *The British Year Book of International Law* (1991), pp. 347–87.
  "Diplomacy and Foreign Policy," *Review of International Studies*, **19**, 1 (1993), pp. 94–9.
  "System or Society," *Review of International Studies*, **19**, 3 (1993), pp. 269–88.
Jennings, Francis, "Iroquois Alliances in American History," in Jennings, Francis, Fenton, William N., Druke, Mary A., and Miller, David R. (eds.), *The History and Culture of Iroquois Diplomacy: An Interdisciplinary Guide to the Treaties of the Six Nations and Their League* (Syracuse: Syracuse University Press, 1985), pp. 37–65.
Jennings, Francis, Fenton, William N., Druke, Mary A., and Miller, David R. (eds.), *The History and Culture of Iroquois Diplomacy: An Interdisciplinary Guide to the Treaties of the Six Nations and Their League* (Syracuse: Syracuse University Press, 1985).
Johnson, Chalmers, *The Sorrows of Empire: Militarism, Secrecy and the End of the Republic* (New York: Henry Holt and Company, 2004).
Johnston, Douglas and Sampson, Cynthia (eds.), *Religion: The Missing Dimension of Statecraft* (Oxford: Oxford University Press, 1994).
Jones, Charles, "Christianity in the English School: Deleted but not Expunged," paper presented at ISA Chicago, February, 2001.
Jönsson, Christer and Hall, Martin, *Essence of Diplomacy* (Basingstoke: Palgrave Macmillan, 2005).
Josephy, Alvin M. Jr., *America in 1492: The World of the Indian Peoples Before the Arrival of Columbus* (New York: Vintage Books, 1993).
Kabir, Humayun, "The Kathmandu Diplomatic Corps in Search of a Role in Times of Transformation" in Sharp and Wiseman (eds.), *The Diplomatic Corps*, pp. 145–67.
  "Public Diplomacy at Bangladesh's Missions Abroad: A Practitioner's View," *The Hague Journal of Diplomacy*, 3, 3 (2008), pp. 299–302.

Kaplan, Morton, *System and Process in International Politics* (New York: Wiley, 1957).

Kaufmann, Johan, *Conference Diplomacy: An Introductory Analysis* (Leyden: Sijthoff, 1968).

Keatinge, Patrick, *A Place Among the Nations: Issues of Irish Foreign Policy* (Dublin: Institute of Public Administration, 1978).

Keens-Soper, Maurice, *Europe In the World: The Persistence of Power Politics* (Basingstoke: Palgrave Macmillan, 2001).

"The Liberal Pedigree of Diplomacy" Butterfield Papers, University Library Cambridge, Box 332, paper for the British Committee on the Theory of International Politics (BCTIP) 1974.

"Abraham de Wicquefort and Diplomatic Theory," *Diplomatic Studies Programme Discussion Paper* (Leicester: Diplomatic Studies Programme, **14**, February 1996).

Keens-Soper, Maurice and Schweizer, Karl W. (eds.), *The Art of Diplomacy: François de Callières* (New York: University Press of America, 1983).

Kennan, George F., "Diplomacy Without Diplomats?" *Foreign Affairs*, **76** (September/October 1997), pp. 198–212.

Kennedy, Paul, *The Rise and Fall of the Great Powers* (London: Fontana, 1989).

Keohane, Robert O. and Nye, James S., *Power and Interdependence: World Politics in Transition* (Boston: Little, Brown, 1979).

Killgore, Andrew I., "Tales of the Foreign Service: In Defense of April Glaspie," *Washington Report on Middle East Affairs*, digital document from the American Education Trust (August 1, 2002), at www.wrmea.com/archives/august2002/0208049.html.

Kinross, Lord, *The Ottoman Centuries* (New York, First Morrow Quill Paperback, 1979).

Kissinger, Henry A., *A World Restored: Metternich, Castlereagh and the Problems of Peace 1812–1822* (Boston: Houghton Mifflin, 1957).

The White House Years (New York: Little, Brown and Co., 1979).

Years of Renewal (New York: Simon and Schuster, 2000).

"Iran Letter to Bush a Welcome Sign: Kissinger," *Journal of Turkish Weekly* (May 13, 2006), online at www.turkishweekly.net/news.php?id=31784.

Knatchbull-Hugessen, Hughe, *Diplomat In Peace and War* (London: John Murray, 1949).

Laffan, Brigid, "The European Union and Ireland," in Collins, Neill (ed.), *Political Issues in Ireland Today*, pp. 89–105.

Lane-Poole, Stanley, *The Life of Lord Stratford de Redcliffe* (Whitefish, Montana: Kessinger, 2006).

Langhorne, Richard, *The Coming of Globalization: Its Evolution and Contemporary Consequences* (Basingstoke: Palgrave Macmillan, 2001).
Diplomacy and Governance (Moscow: MGIMO-University, 2004).
"The Development of International Conferences, 1648–1830," *Studies in History and Politics/Etudes d'Histoire et de Politique: Special Issue, Diplomatic Thought 1648–1815*, 2 (1981/1982), pp. 61–91.
Larson, Lars-Göran, "Modernizing Foreign Services – Facing the Internal Challenge," in Rana, Kishan S. and Kurbalija, Jovan (eds.), *Foreign Ministries: Managing Diplomatic Networks and Optimizing Value* (Malta: Diplo, 2007), pp. 67–74.
Lenin, V. I., *Imperialism: The Highest Stage of Capitalism: A Popular Outline* (Peking: Foreign Languages Press, 1970).
"Primary Documents: Lenin's Decree on Peace, 26 October 1917," on *First World War.com*, www.firstworldwar.com/source/decreeonpeace.htm.
Lennon, Alexander, T. J. and Eiss, Camille (eds.), *Reshaping Rogue States: Preemption, Regime Change, and US Policy Towards Iran, Iraq and North Korea* (Cambridge, MA: MIT Press, 2004).
Leonard, Mark, *Why Europe Will Run the 21st Century* (London: Fourth Estate, 2005).
Leonard, Mark and Alakeson, Vidhya, *Going Public: Diplomacy for the Information Society* (London: The Foreign Policy Centre, 2000).
Lerche, Charles O. and Said, Abdul A., "Diplomacy-Political Technique for Implementing Foreign Policy," in Plischke, Elmer (ed.), *Modern Diplomacy: The Art and the Artisans*, pp. 19–23.
Lewin, Howard, "A Frontier Diplomat: Andrew Montour," *Pennsylvania History*, 23 (1966), pp. 153–86.
Lewin, Thomas, *The Invasion of Britain by Julius Caesar* (Whitefish: Kessinger Publishing, 2005) (first published 1859).
Little, Richard, "The English School's Contribution to the Study of International Relations," *European Journal of International Relations*, 6, 3 (2000), pp. 395–422.
Litwak, Robert S., *Rogue States and US Foreign Policy: Containment After the Cold War* (Baltimore: Johns Hopkins University Press, 2000).
Liu, Xiaohong, *Chinese Ambassadors: The Rise of Diplomatic Professionalism Since 1949* (Seattle: University of Washington Press, 2001).
Liverani, Mario, *International Relations in the Ancient Near East, 1600–1100 BC* (Basingstoke: Palgrave Macmillan, 2007).
Lloyd, Lorna, *Diplomacy With A Difference: The Commonwealth Office of High Commissioner 1880–2006* (Leiden: Martinus Nijhoff, 2007).
Long, David and Wilson, Peter (eds.), *Thinkers of the Twenty Years' Crisis: Interwar Idealism Reassessed* (Oxford: Clarendon Press, 1995).

Louis, W. M. Roger (ed.), *The Origins of the Second World War: A. J. P. Taylor and His Critics* (New York: John Wiley, 1972).
McCarthy, Eugene, "Ambassador to Microsoft," *Minnesota Law and Politics* (June/July 2000).
McClanahan, Grant V., *Diplomatic Immunity: Principles, Practices, Problems* (New York: St. Martin's Press, 1989).
Magstadt, Thomas M., *An Empire if You Can Keep It: Power and Principle in American Foreign Policy* (Washington DC: Congressional Quarterly Press, 2004).
Malcolm, Noel, *Bosnia: A Short History* (New York: New York University Press, 1994).
Malinowski, Bronislav, *Magic, Science and Other Essays* (Westport: Greenwood Press, 1992).
Martel, Gordon (ed.), *The Origins of the Second World War Reconsidered* (Boston: Allen Unwin, 1986).
Mathiason, John, "Linking Diplomatic Performance Assessment to International Results-Based Management" in Rana and Kurbalija (eds.), *Foreign Ministries: Managing Diplomatic Networks and Optimizing Value*, pp. 225–32.
Mattingly, Garret, *Renaissance Diplomacy* (London: Jonathan Cape, 1955).
Maus, Marcel (translated by Hallis, W. D.), *The Gift: The Form and Reason for Exchange in Archaic Societies* (London: Routledge, 1990).
Mayall, James, *Nationalism and International Society* (Cambridge: Cambridge University Press, 1990).
Mediate.com: The World's Dispute Resolution Channel at www.mediate.com/index.cfm.
Meirsheimer, John J. and Walt, Stephen M., "An Unnecessary War," in *Foreign Policy*, **134** (January/February, 2003), pp. 50–9.
Melissen, Jan (ed.), *The New Public Diplomacy: Soft Power in International Relations* (Basingstoke: Palgrave Macmillan, 2005).
Menzies, Gavin, *1421: The Year China Discovered America* (New York: Harper Collins, 2003).
Merrell, James H., *Into the American Woods: Negotiators on the Pennsylvania Frontier* (New York: W. W. Norton and Company, 1999).
Miller, Robert Hopkins, *Inside an Embassy: The Political Role of Diplomats Abroad* (Washington: Institute for the Study of Diplomacy, 1992).
Momaday, N. Scott, "The Becoming of the Native: Man in America Before Columbus," in Josephy, *America in 1492: The World of the Indian Peoples Before the Arrival of Columbus*, pp. 13–19.
Morgenthau, Hans. J., *Politics Among Nations* (New York: Alfred A. Knopf, 1948).

Morrow, Felix, "Stalin Blames the German Proletariat," review in *Fourth International*, New York, 3, (1942), pp. 186–91.
Morse, Edward L., *Modernization and the Transformation of International Relations* (New York: Free Press, 1976).
Muldoon, James P. Jr., Aviel, JoAnn Fagot, Reitano, Richard and Sullivan, Earl (eds.), *Multilateral Diplomacy and the United Nations Today* (Boulder: Westview, 1999).
Naff, Thomas, "The Ottoman Empire and the European States," in Bull and Watson (eds.), *The Expansion of International Society*, pp. 143–69.
Nardin, Terry and Mapel, David R. (eds.), *Traditions of International Ethics* (Cambridge: Cambridge University Press, 1992).
Nardin, Terry and Williams, Melissa S. (eds.), *Humanitarian Intervention* (New York: New York University Press, 2006).
Nathanson, Marc B., "Popular Culture and US Public Diplomacy," address given to the Advisory Board of the University of Southern California Center for Public Diplomacy, November 15, 2006 at http://uscpublicdiplomacy.com/pdfs/061115_nathanson.pdf.
Nau, Henry R., *The Myth of America's Decline: Leading the World Economy Into the 1990s* (Oxford: Oxford University Press, 1992).
Netanyahu, Benjamin, *A Place Among the Nations: Israel and the World* (New York: Bantam, 1993).
Neumann, Iver B., "The English School On Diplomacy," *Discussion Papers in Diplomacy* (The Hague: Netherlands Institute of International Relations Clingendael, March 2002).
  "The English School on Diplomacy: Scholarly Promise Unfulfilled," *International Relations*, 17, 3 (2003), pp. 341–69.
  "To Be a Diplomat," *International Studies Perspectives*, 6, 1 (2005), pp. 72–93.
Neville, Peter, *Hitler and Appeasement: The British Attempt to Prevent the Second World War* (London: Hambledon Continuum, 2007).
  Appeasing Hitler: The Diplomacy of Sir Neville Henderson 1937–1939 (Basingstoke: Palgrave Macmillan, 1999).
Newsom, David D., *Diplomacy and American Democracy* (Bloomington: Indiana University Press, 1988).
Newson, David D. (ed.), *Diplomacy Under a Foreign Flag: When Nations Break Relations* (Washington DC: Institute For the Study of Diplomacy, 1990).
Nicolson, Harold, *Sir Arthur Nicolson, Bart. First Lord Carnock: A Study in the Old Diplomacy* (London: Constable and Co., 1930).
  The Meaning of Prestige (Cambridge: Cambridge University Press, 1937).
  Diplomacy (Oxford: Oxford University Press, 1969).

The Evolution of the Diplomatic Method (Leicester: Diplomatic Studies Programme, University of Leicester, 1998).

Nincic, Miroslav, *Renegade Regimes: Confronting Deviant Behavior in World Politics* (New York: Columbia University Press, 2005).

Norwich, John Julius, *A History of Venice* (New York: Random House, 1989).

Numelin, Ragnar, *The Beginnings of Diplomacy: A Sociological Study of Intertribal and International Relations* (London: Oxford University Press and Copenhagen: Ejnar Munksgaard, 1950).

Nye, Joseph S., *Bound to Lead: The Changing Nature of American Power* (New York: Basic Books, 1991).

The Paradox of American Power: Why the World's Only Superpower Can't Go It Alone (Oxford: Oxford University Press, 2002).

Soft Power: The Means to Success in World Politics (New York: Public Affairs, 2004).

O'Hanlon, Michael, "Towards a Grand Bargain With North Korea," in Lennon and Eiss (eds.), *Reshaping Rogue States*, pp. 157–70.

Ortega, Martin C., "Vitoria and the Universalist Conception of International Relations," in Clark, Ian and Neumann, Iver B. (eds.), *Classical Theories of International Relations* (Basingstoke: Macmillan, 1996), pp. 99–119.

Osiander, Andreas, *The States System of Europe, 1640–1990* (Oxford: Clarendon Press, 1994).

Otte, T. G., "Satow," in Berridge, Keens-Soper and Otte, *Diplomatic Theory From Machiavelli to Kissinger* (Basingstoke: Palgrave Macmillan, 2001), pp. 149–50.

Pahlavi, Pierre, "Evaluating Public Diplomacy Programmes: Lessons from Key G8 Member States," in *The Hague Journal of Diplomacy*, **2**, 3 (2007), pp. 255–81.

Pape, Robert A., "Soft Balancing Against the United States," in *International Security*, **30**, 1 (Summer 2005), pp. 7–45.

Parsi, Trita, *Treacherous Alliance: The Secret Dealings Of Israel, Iran and the US* (New Haven: Yale University Press, 2007).

Peacock, Thomas and Wisuri, Marlene, *Ojibwe Wasa Inaabidaa: We Look In All Directions* (Afton: Afton Historical Society Press, 2002).

Pecquet, Antoine (Gruzinska, Aleksandra and Sirkis, Murray D., translators), *Discours sur L'Art de Négocier* (Paris: Nyon, 1737) (Currents in Comparative Romance Languages and Literatures, Bern: Peter Lang, 2004).

Pentland, Charles, *International Theory and European Integration* (New York: Free Press, 1973).

Pettman, Ralph, *Reason, Culture, Religion: The Metaphysics of World Politics* (Basingstoke: Palgrave Macmillan, 2004).

Plischke, Elmer (ed.), *Modern Diplomacy: The Art and the Artisans* (Washington: American Enterprise Institute for Public Policy, 1979).

Portilla, Miguel León, "Men of Maize," in Josephy, *America in 1492: The World of the Indian Peoples Before the Arrival of Columbus*, p. 175.

Potter, Evan H. (ed.), *Cyber-Diplomacy: Managing Foreign Policy in the Twenty-First Century* (Montreal-Kingston: McGill-Queen's University Press, 2002).

"Information Technology and Canada's Public Diplomacy" in Potter (ed.), *Cyber-Diplomacy: Managing Foreign Policy in the Twenty-First Century*, pp. 177–200.

Radyuhin, Vladimir, "Medvedev, Putin accuse Georgia of genocide," in *The Hindu*, August 11, 2008, at www.thehindu.com/2008/08/11/stories/2008081156011500.htm.

Rana, Kishan S., *Inside Diplomacy* (New Delhi: Manas Publications, 2000).

Asian Diplomacy: The Foreign Ministries of China, India, Japan, Singapore and Thailand (Malta: Diplo, 2007).

"MFA Reform: Global Trends," in Rana and Kurbalija (eds.), *Foreign Ministries: Managing Diplomatic Networks and Optimizing Value*, pp. 20–43.

"Representing India in the Diplomatic Corps" in Sharp and Wiseman (eds.), *The Diplomatic Corps as an Institution of International Society*, pp. 125–41.

Rana, Kishan S. and Kurbalija, Jovan (eds.), *Foreign Ministries: Managing Diplomatic Networks and Optimizing Value* (Malta: Diplo, 2007).

Ray, James Lee and Kaarbo, Juliet, *Global Politics* (Boston: Houghton Mifflin Company, 2005).

Redwood, John, *Superpower Struggles: Mighty America, Faltering Europe, Rising China*, (Basingstoke: Palgrave Macmillan, 2005).

Reychler, Luc, "Beyond Traditional Diplomacy," *Diplomatic Studies Programme Discussion Paper* (Leicester: Diplomatic Studies Programme, 17, May 1996).

Rice, Condoleezza, *Transformational Diplomacy*, speech given at Georgetown University, January 18, 2006, www.state.gov/secretary/rm/2006/59306.htm

Richter, Daniel K., *The Ordeal of the Long-house: The Peoples of the Iroquois League in the Era of European Colonization* (Chapel Hill: University of North Carolina Press, 1992).

Riordan, Shawn S., *The New Diplomacy* (Cambridge: Polity, 2003).

"Dialogue-based Diplomacy: A New Foreign Policy Paradigm," *Discussion Papers in Diplomacy* (The Hague: Netherlands Institute of International Relations Clingendael, **95**, November 2004).

Robins, Nick, *The Corporation that Changed the World: How the East India Company Shaped the Modern Multinational* (London: Pluto Press, 2006).

Rosenau, James N., *Turbulence in World Politics: A Theory of Change and Continuity in World Politics* (Hemel Hempstead: Harvester Wheatsheaf, 1990).

Ross, Dennis, *The Missing Peace: The Inside Story of the Fight for Middle East Peace* (New York: Farrar, Strauss and Giroux, 2005).

Saner, Raymond and Yiu, Lichia, "International Economic Diplomacy: Mutations in Post-modern Times," *Diplomatic Papers in Diplomacy* (The Hague: Netherlands Institute of International Relations, 84, January 2003).

Sariolghalam, Mahmood, "Understanding Iran: Getting Past Stereotypes and Mythology," in Lennon and Eiss (eds.), *Reshaping Rogue States: Preemption, Regime Change, and US Policy Towards Iran, Iraq and North Korea*, pp. 283–99.

Satow, Earnest, *An Austrian Diplomatist in the Fifties* (Cambridge: Cambridge University Press, 1908).

Guide to Diplomatic Practice, 2 vols. (London: Longman, 1979).

Schelling, Thomas C., *The Strategy of Conflict* (Cambridge, MA: Harvard University Press, 1960).

Schneider, Cynthia P., "Culture Communicates: US Diplomacy That Works" in Melissen (ed.), *The New Public Diplomacy*, pp. 147–68.

Schulzinger, Robert D., *The Making of the Diplomatic Mind: The Training, Outlook, and Style of United States Foreign Service Officers: 1908–1931* (Middletown: Wesleyan University Press, 1975).

Schweizer, Karl W. and Sharp, Paul (eds.), *The International Thought of Herbert Butterfield* (Basingstoke: Palgrave Macmillan, 2007), pp. 198–206.

Self, Robert C., *Neville Chamberlain: A Biography* (Aldershot: Ashgate, 2006).

Senn, Alfred Erich, *Diplomacy and Revolution: The Soviet Mission to Switzerland, 1918* (Notre Dame: University of Notre Dame Press, 1974).

Shakespeare, William, *The Tragedy of Hamlet, Prince of Denmark* (Fairfield: First World Library-Literary Society, 2005).

Sharp, Paul, "Making Sense of Citizen Diplomacy: The Citizens of Duluth, Minnesota as International Actors," in *International Studies Perspectives*, 2 (2001), pp. 131–50.

"Mullah Zaeef and Taliban Diplomacy," *Review of International Studies*, 29, October (2003), pp. 481–98.

"Virtue Unrestrained: Herbert Butterfield and the Problem of American Power," *International Studies Perspectives*, 5, 3 (August 2004), pp. 300–15.

"The Skopje Diplomatic Corps and the Macedonian Political Crisis of 2001," in Sharp and Wiseman (eds.), *The Diplomatic Corps as an Institution of International Society*, pp. 197–219.

Sharp, Paul and Wiseman, Geoffrey (eds.), *The Diplomatic Corps as an Institution of International Society* Basingstoke: Palgrave Macmillan, 2007).

Shultz, George P., *Turmoil and Triumph: My Years as Secretary of State* (New York: Maxwell Macmillan, 1993).

Siddiqui, Suaib Alam, *The Role of Diplomacy in the Policy of the Prophet (PBUH)* (New Delhi: Kanishka Publishers, 2002).

Simonds, Frank and Emeny, Broks, *The Great Powers in World Politics: International Relations and Economic Nationalism* (New York: American Book Company, 1935).

Simpson, Gerry, *Great Powers and Outlaw States: Unequal Sovereigns in the International Legal Order* (Cambridge: Cambridge University Press, 2004).

Smith, Steve, Booth, Ken and Zalewski, Marysia (eds.), *International Theory: Positivism and Beyond* (Cambridge: Cambridge University Press, 1996).

Sofer, Sasson, "The Diplomat as Stranger," *Diplomacy and Statecraft*, 8, 3 (November 1997), pp. 179–86.

Starkey, Brigid, "Negotiating With Rogue States: What Can Theory and Practice Tell Us?" *Diplomatic Studies Programme Discussion Paper* (Leicester: Diplomatic Studies Programme, **56**, May 2000).

Stempel, John, "Faith, Diplomacy and the International System," *Diplomatic Studies Programme Discussion Paper* (Leicester: Diplomatic Studies Programme, **69**, 2000).

Stowe, Harriet Beecher, *Uncle Tom's Cabin* (New York: Bantam Classics, 1982).

Strange, Susan, *The Retreat of the State: The Diffusion of Power in the World Economy* (Cambridge: Cambridge University Press, 1996).

"States, firms and diplomacy," International Affairs, **68**, 1 (January 1992), pp. 1–15.

Suganami, Hidemi, "Japan's Entry into International Society," in Bull and Watson (eds.), *The Expansion of International Society*, pp. 185–99.

Takeyh, R., *Hidden Iran: Paradox And Power In The Islamic Republic* (New York: Holt, 2006).

Tanter, Raymond, *Rogue Regimes: Terrorism and Proliferation* (New York: St. Martin's Griffin, 1999).

Taylor, A. J. P., *Origins of the Second World War* (Harmondsworth: Penguin, 1963).

The Struggle for Mastery In Europe: 1848–1914 (Oxford: Oxford University Press, 1954, paperback 1971).

Thomas, Scott M., *The Global Resurgence of Religion and the Transformation of International Relations: The Struggle for the Soul of the Twenty-First Century* (Basingstoke: Palgrave Macmillan, 2005).

Thucydides, *History of the Peloponnesian War* (Harmondsworth: Penguin, 1954).

Thwaites, Reuben Gold (ed.), *The Jesuit Relations and Allied Documents*, 73 vols. (Cleveland: Burrows Brothers Co., 1896–1901).

Tonra, Ben, *Global Citizen and European Republic: Irish Foreign Policy in Transitions (Reappraising the Political)* (Manchester: Manchester University Press, 2007).

Toynbee, Arnold, *A Study of History* (edited, revised and abridged by Toynbee, Arnold and Caplan, Jane) (Oxford: Oxford University Press 1972, Barnes and Noble, 1995).

Treaty On Conventional Armed Forces In Europe (November 19, 1990) available at www.fas.org/nuke/control/cfe/cfebook/appenda.html.

Trotsky, Leon, "Official Government Documents for the People's Commissar for Foreign Affairs," November 1917 to March 1918, Brian Bagson, *History of the Soviet Government Documents website*, www.marxist.org/archive/trotsky/works/1918/gov.htm.

Twigge, Stephen and Scott, Len, "The Other Missiles of October: The Thor IRBMs and the Cuban Missile Crisis," *Electronic Journal of History* (June 2000) at www.history.ac.uk/ejournal/art3.html.

"Twisting in the wind? Ambassador April Glaspie and the Persian Gulf Crisis (update)," Kennedy School of Government Case Program (Cambridge, MA: Harvard University Press, 1992).

Urban, G. R., *Diplomacy and Disillusion at the Court of Margaret Thatcher: An Insider's View* (London: I. B. Taurus, 1996).

Van Ham, Peter, "Power, Public Diplomacy, and the *Pax Americana*," in Melissen (ed.), *The New Public Diplomacy: Soft Power in International Relations*, pp. 47–66.

Vankovska, Biljana, *Current Perspectives on Macedonia*: No. 1, "The Path From 'Oasis of Peace' to 'Powder Keg' of the Balkans," Heinrich Böll Foundation (undated).

Vansittart, Robert, *The Lessons of My Life* (London: Hutchinson, 1943).

Vasquez, John A. and Elman, Colin, *Realism and the Balance of Power: A New Debate* (Upper Saddle River: Prentice Hall/Pearson Education, 2003).

Vienna Convention on Diplomatic Relations (April 14, 1961), available at http://untreaty.un.org/ilc/texts/instruments/english/conventions/9_1_1961.pdf.

Vienna Convention on Consular Relations (April 24, 1963), available at http://untreaty.un.org/ilc/texts/instruments/english/conventions/9_2_1963.pdf.

Vigezzi, Brunello, *The British Committee on the Theory of International Politics* (1954–1985) (Milan: Unicopli, 2005).

Vimont, Barthelemy, "The proceedings recorded by Father Barthelemy Vimont S. J., of the 'Treaty of Brotherhood Between the French, the Iroquois and the Other Nations'," in Reuben Gold Thwaites (ed.), *The Jesuit Relations and Allied Documents*, 73 vols. (Cleveland: Burrows Brothers Co., 1896–1901), reproduced in Jennings, Fenton, Druke and Miller (eds.), *The History and Culture of Iroquois Diplomacy*, pp. 137–53.

Viotti, Paul R. and Kauppi, Mark V., *International Relations Theory: Realism, Pluralism, Globalism* (2nd edn.) (New York: Macmillan, 1993).

Walker, Ronald, *Multilateral Conferences: Purposeful International Negotiation* (Basingstoke: Palgrave Macmillan, 2004).

Wallace, Paul A. W., *Conrad Weiser: Friend of Colonist and Mohawk* (Lewisburg: Wennawoods Publishing, 1996).

Walton, Joseph S., *Conrad Weiser and the Indian Policy of Colonial Pennsylvania* (Philadelphia: George W. Jacobs, 1900).

Waltz, Kenneth, *Theory of International Politics* (Reading: Addison Wesley, 1979).

Warren, William W., *History of the Ojibway People* (St. Paul: Minnesota Historical Society Press, 1984).

Watson, Adam, *Diplomacy: The Dialogue Between the States* (New York: McGraw Hill/New Press, 1983).

 The Evolution of International Society: A Comparative and Historical Analysis (London: Routledge, 1992).

Watts, Duncan and Pilkington, Colin, *Britain in the European Union Today* (Manchester: Manchester University Press, 2005).

Wedgwood, C. V., *The Thirty Years War: New York Review of Books Classics* (New York: New York Review of Books, 2005) (London: Jonathan Cape, 1938).

Weitz, John, *Hitler's Diplomat: The Life and Times of Joachim von Ribbentrop* (New York: Ticknor and Fields, 1992).

Welch, Jolyn and Fern, Daniel (eds.), *Engagement: Public Diplomacy in a Globalised World* (London: British Foreign and Commonwealth Office, 2008).

Wendt, Alexander, *Social Theory of International Politics* (Cambridge: Cambridge University Press, 1999).

West, Rebecca, *Black Lamb and Grey Falcon: A Journey Through Yugoslavia* (Harmondsworth: Penguin, 1994) (first published 1941).

Wheeler, Harvey, *Democracy in a Revolutionary Era* (New York: Praeger, 1968).
Wheeler, Nicholas J., *Saving Strangers: Humanitarian Intervention in International Societies* (Oxford: Oxford University Press, 2001).
Wheeler, Nicholas J. and Dunne, Timothy, "Hedley Bull's Pluralism of the Intellect and Solidarism of the Will," *International Affairs*, **72**, 1 (1996), pp. 91–107.
Wheeler-Bennett, John W., *Brest Litovsk – The Forgotten Peace, March 1919* (London: Macmillan, 1966).
White, Richard, *The Middle Ground: Indians, Empires, and Republics in the Great Lakes Region 1650–1815* (Cambridge: Cambridge University Press, 1991).
De Wicquefort, Abraham, *L'Ambassadeur et ses Fonctions* (The Hague, two volumes, 1680–1681).
Wight, Martin (Bull, Hedley ed.), *Systems of States* (Leicester: Leicester University Press, 1977).
Wight, Martin (Bull, Hedley and Holbraad, Carsten eds.), *Power Politics* (Harmondsworth: Penguin, 1979).
Wight, Martin (Porter, Brian and Wright, Gabriele, eds.), *International Theory: The Three Traditions* (Leicester: Leicester University Press/ Royal Institute of International Affairs, 1991).
Wight, Martin, "Why Is There No International Relations Theory," in Butterfield and Wight, *Diplomatic Investigations*, pp. 17–34.
  "*The Balance of Power,*" in Herbert Butterfield and Wight, Martin (eds.), *Diplomatic Investigations*, pp. 149–75.
  "*Western Values in International Relations,*" in Butterfield and Wight (eds.), *Diplomatic Investigations*, pp. 89–131.
  "The States-System of Hellas," in Wight, *System of States*, p. 53.
Wild, Antony, *The East India Company: Trade and Conquest from 1600* (Guilford: Lyons Press, 2000).
Williams, John, "Pluralism, Solidarism and the Emergence of World Society in English School Theory," *International Relations*, **19**, 1 (2005), pp. 19–38.
Wiseman, Geoffrey, "Polylateralism and New Modes of Global Dialogue," *Diplomatic Studies Programme Discussion Paper* (Leicester: Diplomatic Studies Programme, **59**, November 1999).
  "Pax Americana: Bumping Into Diplomatic Culture," *International Studies Perspectives*, **6**, 4 (November 2005), pp. 409–30.
Wittgenstein, Ludwig, *Philosophical Investigations* (Upper Saddle River: Prentice Hall, 3rd edn., 1999).

Wolfe, Robert, "Still Lying Abroad? On the Institution of the Resident Ambassador," *Diplomatic Studies Programme Discussion Paper* (Leicester, Diplomatic Studies Programme, **33**, September 1997).

Wood, John and Serres, Jean, *Diplomatic Ceremonial and Protocol: Principles, Procedures and Practices* (New York: Columbia University Press, 1970).

Woodcock, Stephen, "The ITO, the GATT and the WTO," in Bayne and Woodcock (eds.), *The New Economic Diplomacy: Decision-Making and Negotiation in International Economic Relations* (Aldershot: Ashgate, 2003), pp. 103–20.

Zalewski, Marysia, "'All These Theories Yet the Bodies Keep Piling Up': Theorists, Theories and Theorizing," in Smith, Booth and Zalewski, *International Theory: Positivism and Beyond* (Cambridge: Cambridge University Press, 1996), pp. 340–53.

Zhang, Song Nan, *The Great Voyages of Zheng He* (Union City: Pan-Asian Publications, 2005).

Zwass, Adam, *The Council for Mutual Economic Assistance: The Thorny Path from Political to Economic Integration* (Armonk, NY: M. E. Sharpe, 1989).

Index

Acheson, Dean, 3
Aerenthal, Aloys Lexa von, 63
Afghanistan, 31, 166, 262
Ahmadinejad, Mahmoud, 303, 304
alienation, 77, 245
Amarna archive, 62
ambassadors, 1, 20, 23, 28, 55, 58, 59, 60, 62, 65, 67, 76, 78, 79, 97, 101, 142, 213, 246, 269
American Indians, 127, 129, 133, 161, 260, 272, 273
Anabaptists, 250
anarchy, 48, 118, 199, 307
appeasement, 42, 70, 104, 185, 186, 253, 260, 261, 296, 300–305
Arabia, 31, 150, 154, 162, 173, 251, 253, 254, 262
Assyrian Empire, 151
Athens, 138, 182, 185
Austria, 208
Aziz, Tariq, 206
Aztec Empire, 151, 162

Babylon, 151
Baker, James, 206
balance of power, 44, 55, 118, 139, 149, 154, 175, 184, 188, 190, 226
bargaining, 3, 22, 43, 54, 57, 186, 250
Basque country, 141
Bavaria, 141
Beijing consensus, 225
Bell, Tinker, 45
Berridge, G. R., 42
Bible, 256, 270
bilateral negotiations, 229, 230, 304
Bismarck, Otto von, 69, 205
Bligh, William, 129
Bolshevik diplomacy, 25, 26–27, 31, 274
Bosnia, 144, 298

Branch Davidians, 250
Brest Litovsk, Treaty of, 31
Britain, 56, 68, 82, 139, 216, 278, 309
British East India Company, 236
British Empire, 116, 182
British Petroleum, 270
Brussels Consensus, 225
Bull, Hedley, 6, 114, 149, 150
Bush, George Herbert Walker, 56
Bush, George W., 56, 202, 216, 303–304
Butterfield, Herbert, 34, 297
Byzantine Empire, 125, 137

Caesar, Gaius Julius, 143
Caliphate, 162, 163, 164, 263
Callières, François de, 132, 169
Cambon, Jules, 273
Camp David Conference (1977–78), 213
Campaign to Ban Land Mines, 291
Canada, 56, 138, 278, 281
Chamberlain, Neville, 83, 300–302
China, People's Republic of, 25, 31, 34, 106, 136, 291
Chinese Empire, 84, 117, 118, 119, 120, 143, 151, 152, 153, 155, 159, 162, 177
Christendom, 36, 134, 159, 239, 245–247, 248
Christianity, 155, 262
citizen diplomacy, 140, 288
civil society, 37, 47, 125, 165, 166, 276, 295
civility, 204–206, 261
civilization, 27, 119, 151, 153, 162, 163, 173, 244, 259, 281
Clausewitz, Karl von, 187
Cohen, Raymond, 162

334

Index 335

Cold War, 35, 68, 198, 208, 225, 298
commercial diplomacy, 240, 282
commercial public diplomacy, 279, 280, 281–284
conditions of separateness, 10, 81–84, 87
Connolly, James, 19, 20
Constantinou, Costas, 79–81
consuls, 1
Cook, James, 129
Cortez, Hernando (Hernán), 151
Council For Mutual Economic Assistance, 116
court politics, 20, 58, 60, 62–64, 67–69
Croatia, 299
Cuba, 210, 219
Cuban Missile Crisis, 68
Cyprus, 106
Czechoslovakia, 305

Dar ul Islam, 248
Daustur-i-Madinah, 254
Davis Cross, Mai'a K., 36
Dayton Conference, 211, 212
decolonization, 144, 277
Der Derian, 77, 79
dialogue diplomacy, 44, 97
diplomatic community, 104
diplomatic corps, 32, 36, 62, 104, 179, 206
diplomatic history, 134, 141
diplomatic theory, 4, 6–7, 10, 11, 71, 174, 239, 295, 297, 299, 300, 302, 303, 304, 305, 306, 307, 309, 310
diplomatic tradition, 39, 71, 75, 78, 79, 81, 88, 89, 91, 95, 97, 103, 104, 107, 108, 109, 113, 122, 124, 128, 130, 131, 132, 133, 136, 141, 145, 147, 151, 152, 154, 157, 160, 162, 165, 168, 173, 181, 187, 190, 191, 195, 203, 206, 211, 219, 222, 228, 237, 239, 247, 258, 263, 275, 284, 292, 293–295, 296, 299
diplomatic understanding, 10, 12, 109, 146, 151, 157, 181, 184, 192, 195, 221, 294, 311
diplomats, 2, 9, 10, 11, 12, 19, 21, 22, 24, 29, 32, 34, 36, 38, 39, 42, 43, 45, 46, 50, 51, 52, 54, 57, 58, 60, 64, 65, 68, 70, 71, 76, 81, 88, 96, 146, 147, 148, 154, 157, 158, 159, 162, 166, 167, 169, 172, 173, 178, 179, 181, 184, 188, 189, 190, 191, 195, 204, 207, 208, 213, 214, 219, 222, 223, 224, 227, 228, 238, 240, 246, 256, 264, 275, 276, 277, 280, 281, 288, 290, 291, 297, 298
discovery relations, 10, 89, 131, 143, 153, 175
Dobrynin, Anatoly, 26, 68
Doha Round (trade talks), 230
Douri, Mohammed al, 28, 30
droit de chapel, 246
Dutch East India Company, 237

economization, 227, 234, 243
Egypt, 212, 286
Egyptian Empire, 151
embassies, 1, 26, 31, 32, 35, 36, 80, 278
Ems telegram, 205
encounter relations, 10, 89, 127, 143, 151, 173, 207
England, 152, 198
English School, 7, 9, 11
epistemic communities, 36
estrangement, 77, 78, 91, 104
European Union, 33, 35, 84, 108, 116, 134, 139, 140, 142, 230, 274, 278

Federal Bureau of Firearms and Tobacco, 250
Flanders, 140
France, 60, 135, 152, 154, 183, 190, 216, 276, 309
Franco, Francisco, 186

Galbraith, John Kenneth, 58
gentlemanliness, 301
George, Alexander, 202
Germany, 26, 30, 55, 152, 187, 190, 199, 210, 300, 301, 302
Glaspie, April, 55
globalization, 34, 163, 221, 244, 281
Gorbachev, Mikhail, 27
governmentality, 227
Graham, George, 224

great powers, 20, 32, 44, 49, 118, 136, 149, 198, 199, 200, 216, 217, 226, 232, 241, 251, 255, 298
Great Satan, 207, 209, 305
Greece, 97
Grey, Edward, 217
Guicciardini, Francesco, 63
Gun, Ben, 83

Hall, Martin, 77
Halliday, Fred, 119
Hamas, 189
hard power, 58
Hardinge, Charles, 68
Hatti, 100
Hawaii, 129, 136
hegemony, 53, 91, 120, 121, 179, 180, 182, 183, 186
Henderson, Neville, 55
Heraclius, Constantine, 255
heralds, 17, 93, 97, 99, 152
Hitler, Adolf, 57, 186, 210, 211, 216, 298, 300, 302
Hocking, Brian, 76, 78, 79, 226
Holy Roman Empire, 116, 120, 125, 143
horizontal relations, 82, 116, 119, 150, 162, 166, 168, 295
Hudabiya, Treaty of, 254
humanitarian intervention, 298
Huron, 157
Hussein, Saddam, 28, 30, 186, 213

identity, 12, 27, 41, 62, 83, 100, 116, 119, 122, 130, 136, 138, 163, 190, 210, 238, 257, 263, 265, 284, 296, 302, 309, 310
immunity, 17, 32, 34, 96, 97, 100, 107
Inca Empire, 151
India, 161, 237
information technology, 133, 281
interaction capacity, 55, 163
international relations theory, 4, 6, 7, 201, 307
international societies, mixed, 240
international society, 11, 12, 18, 22, 23, 24, 27, 28, 30, 31, 32, 33, 43–45, 84, 109, 113–118, 136, 137, 143, 148, 152, 159, 161, 162, 164, 165, 168, 170, 172, 178, 182, 188, 196, 200, 207, 213, 239, 241, 244, 253, 259, 262, 275, 291, 308
international thought, traditions of, 8, 9, 17, 19, 21, 70, 79, 106, 133, 142, 145, 153, 190, 198, 200, 294
internationalization, 269
Iran, 29, 31, 207, 209, 304
Iraq, 55, 56, 67, 106, 185, 186, 202, 208, 209, 213, 215, 219, 220, 299, 302
Ireland, 19, 24, 56, 138, 139, 217
Iroquois, 116, 117, 133, 157
Islam, 31, 117, 150, 154, 155, 156, 262, 263, 286
Islam, early, 250–255
Islamic extremists, 280
Islamic Jihad, 29
Islamicists, 196
Italy, 62, 97, 225

Japan, 117, 125, 127, 137
jihad, 257
Jönsson, Christer, 77, 78
Judaism, 156

Kaldûn, Ibn, 177
Kampuchea, 210
Kashmir, 217
Kennan, George F., 291
Kennedy, John F., 58, 68
ketman, 34
Khomeini, Ruhollah, 31
Kingdom of the Serbs and Croats, 144
Kissinger, H. A. K., 67, 68
Kollontai, Alexandra, 26
Koran, 252
Korea, North, 137, 201, 220
Kosovo, 299

Lancaster House, 213
Lateran treaties, 262
Lebanon, 31, 180
Lee, Donna, 226
Lenin, V. I., 121
liberal, 38, 79, 158, 180, 181, 198, 199, 233, 276, 282, 308
Libya, 29, 201, 219, 220

Little, Richard, 9
Litwak, Robert, 202
Lombardy, 140

Macedonia, 145
Machiavelli, Nicolò, 8
Machiavellianism, 54
Malayia, 161
Manchester, 106
Mazarin, Jules, 69
Mecca, 251, 257, 261, 263, 304
mediation, 76–79
Medina, 251, 253, 263, 304
Medina, Covenant of, 264
Mercosur, 163
Mesquita, Bruce Bueno de, 6
message strings, 133
Metternich, Klemens Wenzel von, 69
Mexico, 82, 139
Microsoft, 291
Milosovic, Slobodan, 215
modern diplomacy, 25, 62, 75, 97, 109, 205, 219, 225, 226, 262, 272, 275, 305, 308
modernization, 224, 243, 244
Mohammed, 156
Mongol Empire, 156
Montezuma, 151
Morgenthau, H. J., 53, 59
multilateral negotiations, 229, 233
Munich conference, 104, 217, 302

name-calling, 204, 207, 210
Napoleon, 125
Netherlands, 82, 211
Neumann, Iver B., 11, 51, 81
Nicolson, Harold, 17
Nigeria, 183
non-intervention, 32, 298
North American Free Trade Area, 116, 139
Nye, Joseph S., 267

Omar, Muhammed, 263
oratorical diplomacy, 272
Organization of South East Asian States, 163
Ormsby-Gore, David, 68

Ottoman Empire, 117, 127, 159, 208, 225
Oxfam, 291

Pakistan, 166, 217
Palestine, 265
Palestinian Authority, 24
Papacy, 136, 277
Parsons, Anthony, 66
people-to-people public diplomacy, 288, 289
performative diplomacy, 272
pluralism, 6, 37, 159, 244
Pol Pot, 210
Poland, 186, 305
Polish corridor, 217
Portugal, 158
Powell, Charles, 66
power, 67, 68, 69, 70, 79, 91, 98, 114, 117, 155, 168, 169–172, 175, 182, 212, 230, 238, 240, 257, 258, 267, 295, 298
power politics, 54, 199, 240
propaganda, 26, 31, 271, 280
protectorates, 115, 171
proxenoi, 97, 183, 273
Prussia, 141
public diplomacy, 47, 166, 167, 196, 266–270, 271, 274, 275, 276, 277, 278, 284–286, 289, 291, 292
public diplomat, 290

Qaeda, al, 29, 255, 256, 262
Quaraysh, 254

Radek, Karl, 26
radical tradition, 17, 19, 21, 24, 25, 28, 29, 33, 34, 36, 38, 79, 199
raison d'état, 219
raison de système, 22, 44, 45, 168, 179, 219, 242
rasul, 253
rationalist tradition, 8, 23, 53, 57
realist tradition, 8, 52, 53, 56, 57, 59, 61, 64, 69, 198
realpolitik, 288
reasonableness, 8, 40, 41, 43, 44, 46, 49, 51, 300

recognition, 1, 2, 21, 22, 139, 157, 166, 191, 255, 262, 277, 305, 310
re-encounter relations, 11, 90, 136, 147, 160, 163, 185
relations of separateness, 90, 91, 93, 96, 108, 109, 122, 127, 131, 134, 142, 146, 152, 159, 161, 166, 173, 182, 191, 195, 238, 246, 250, 258, 276, 293, 294, 304
religion, 12, 196, 243–244, 247, 248, 257, 263
representation, 1, 25, 26, 33, 35, 54, 59, 63, 75, 80, 101, 136, 141, 142, 182, 226, 229, 239, 240, 255, 279, 290, 296
revolution, 13, 20, 21, 25, 34–36, 38, 70, 176, 247, 266, 268, 283
revolutionary diplomats, 21, 22, 29, 33, 37
Rhodesia, 213
Richelieu, Armand Jean, 69
Rogue State diplomacy, 211
Roman Empire, 84, 97, 118, 119, 142, 151, 153
Rome, 120, 249, 261
Russia, 25, 27, 34, 143, 181, 291
Rwanda, 298, 299

sachems, 176
safir, 253
Satan, 206, 211, 212
Satow, Earnest Mason, 102, 260
Saudi Arabia, 201
Schelling, Thomas C., 187
Scotland, 141, 278
secularization, 243
security, 31, 90, 101, 132, 145, 166, 213, 237, 241, 303, 305
Serbia, 145
Sierra Leone, 125
Sikhs, 250
Silvers, Phil, 57
Slovenia, 145
Sofer, Sasson, 99
soft power, 267
solidarism, 34, 37, 45, 47, 108, 163, 196, 245, 305, 306, 309
South Ossetia, 302

sovereignty, 37, 51, 69, 124, 146, 147, 164, 165, 241, 246, 310
Soviet Union, 126, 145, 187, 190, 199
Spain, 155, 158
Sparta, 138, 182
Stalin, J. V., 211
stateization, 236, 237
Strange, Susan, 167
strangers, 78, 85, 86, 87, 90, 93, 96, 99–101, 173, 175, 306
subversion, 12, 29–33
suzerainties, 135, 146, 171
Syria, 180, 201

Taliban, 28, 29, 206, 255, 262, 263
talk, 208, 211, 212, 214, 215, 216, 217, 219, 221, 232, 250, 255, 256, 257, 260, 266, 275, 280, 281, 304
Talleyrand, Charles Maurice de, 51
Taylor, A. J. P., 217, 298
tension, 9, 26, 45, 78, 198, 205, 276
terrorism, 13, 31, 166, 270
Thatcher, Margaret, 66
theory, 4–7
thinking diplomatically, 10, 12, 95, 193, 203, 231, 254, 292
Thirty Years War, 246
Thucydides, 134, 270
Topsy, 180
total diplomacy, 270
total football, 270
Toynbee, Arnold, 121
transnational networks, 76, 259
triangular diplomacy, 238
Tuscaroras, 117

Umma, 159, 251, 265, 308
United Nations, 120
United States, 67, 68, 118, 125, 139, 171, 183, 184, 187, 190, 198, 209, 210, 215, 219, 230, 243, 262, 278, 280, 291

vassalages, 135
Venetian *relatzione*, 132
vertical diplomacy, 167
vertical relations, 164, 165

Vienna Convention on Consular Relations, 124
Vienna Convention on Diplomatic Relations, 31, 124
violence, 20, 86, 103, 125, 168, 211, 236, 256, 293, 307, 308

Waltz, Kenneth, 53
wampum, 133
war, 1, 38, 44, 45, 46, 56, 93, 94, 103, 134, 149, 153, 154, 157, 180, 182, 185, 186, 187, 190, 191, 206, 215, 216, 237, 245, 248, 256, 288, 302, 303, 307
War, First World, 45
War, Second Gulf, 206
War, Second World, 190

Washington consensus, 225
Watson, Adam, 12, 44, 91, 97, 118, 122, 149, 150, 170
weapons of mass destruction, 198
Weiser, Conrad, 134
West, Rebecca, 144
Westphalia, Treaty of, 35, 36, 37, 247, 250, 251, 258
Wight, Martin, 8, 9, 17, 38, 39, 42, 52, 54, 71, 79, 106, 150, 177, 231, 232, 239, 248, 310
world society, 45, 46, 108

zakat, 257
Zalewski, Marysia, 191
Zealots, 250
Zimbabwe, 213

Cambridge Studies in International Relations

98 Michael Barnett and Raymond Duvall
   Power in global governance
97 Yale H. Ferguson and Richard W. Mansbach
   Remapping global politics
   History's revenge and future shock
96 Christian Reus-Smit
   The politics of international law
95 Barry Buzan
   From international to world society?
   English School theory and the social structure of globalisation
94 K. J. Holsti
   Taming the sovereigns
   Institutional change in international politics
93 Bruce Cronin
   Institutions for the common good
   International protection regimes in international security
92 Paul Keal
   European conquest and the rights of indigenous peoples
   The moral backwardness of international society
91 Barry Buzan and Ole Wæver
   Regions and powers
   The structure of international security
90 A. Claire Cutler
   Private power and global authority
   Transnational merchant law in the global political economy
89 Patrick M. Morgan
   Deterrence now
88 Susan Sell
   Private power, public law
   The globalization of intellectual property rights
87 Nina Tannenwald
   The nuclear taboo
   The United States and the non-use of nuclear weapons since 1945
86 Linda Weiss
   States in the global economy
   Bringing domestic institutions back in

85 Rodney Bruce Hall and Thomas J. Biersteker (eds.)
    The emergence of private authority in global governance
84 Heather Rae
    State identities and the homogenisation of peoples
83 Maja Zehfuss
    Constructivism in international relations
    The politics of reality
82 Paul K. Ruth and Todd Allee
    The democratic peace and territorial conflict in the twentieth century
81 Neta C. Crawford
    Argument and change in world politics
    Ethics, decolonization and humanitarian intervention
80 Douglas Lemke
    Regions of war and peace
79 Richard Shapcott
    Justice, community and dialogue in international relations
78 Phil Steinberg
    The social construction of the ocean
77 Christine Sylvester
    Feminist international relations
    An unfinished journey
76 Kenneth A. Schultz
    Democracy and coercive diplomacy
75 David Houghton
    US foreign policy and the Iran hostage crisis
74 Cecilia Albin
    Justice and fairness in international negotiation
73 Martin Shaw
    Theory of the global state
    Globality as an unfinished revolution
72 Frank C. Zagare and D. Marc Kilgour
    Perfect deterrence
71 Robert O'Brien, Anne Marie Goetz, Jan Aart Scholte and Marc Williams
    Contesting global governance
    Multilateral economic institutions and global social movements
70 Roland Bleiker
    Popular dissent, human agency and global politics
69 Bill McSweeney
    Security, identity and interests
    A sociology of international relations
68 Molly Cochran
    Normative theory in international relations
    A pragmatic approach
67 Alexander Wendt
    Social theory of international politics

66 Thomas Risse, Stephen C. Ropp and Kathryn Sikkink (eds.)
   The power of human rights
   International norms and domestic change
65 Daniel W. Drezner
   The sanctions paradox
   Economic statecraft and international relations
64 Viva Ona Bartkus
   The dynamic of secession
63 John A. Vasquez
   The power of power politics
   From classical realism to neotraditionalism
62 Emanuel Adler and Michael Barnett (eds.)
   Security communities
61 Charles Jones
   E. H. Carr and international relations
   A duty to lie
60 Jeffrey W. Knopf
   Domestic society and international cooperation
   The impact of protest on US arms control policy
59 Nicholas Greenwood Onuf
   The republican legacy in international thought
58 Daniel S. Geller and J. David Singer
   Nations at war
   A scientific study of international conflict
57 Randall D. Germain
   The international organization of credit
   States and global finance in the world economy
56 N. Piers Ludlow
   Dealing with Britain
   The Six and the first UK application to the EEC
55 Andreas Hasenclever, Peter Mayer and Volker Rittberger
   Theories of international regimes
54 Miranda A. Schreurs and Elizabeth C. Economy (eds.)
   The internationalization of environmental protection
53 James N. Rosenau
   Along the domestic-foreign frontier
   Exploring governance in a turbulent world
52 John M. Hobson
   The wealth of states
   A comparative sociology of international economic and political change
51 Kalevi J. Holsti
   The state, war, and the state of war
50 Christopher Clapham
   Africa and the international system
   The politics of state survival

49 Susan Strange
The retreat of the state
The diffusion of power in the world economy

48 William I. Robinson
Promoting polyarchy
Globalization, US intervention, and hegemony

47 Roger Spegele
Political realism in international theory

46 Thomas J. Biersteker and Cynthia Weber (eds.)
State sovereignty as social construct

45 Mervyn Frost
Ethics in international relations
A constitutive theory

44 Mark W. Zacher with Brent A. Sutton
Governing global networks
International regimes for transportation and communications

43 Mark Neufeld
The restructuring of international relations theory

42 Thomas Risse-Kappen (ed.)
Bringing transnational relations back in
Non-state actors, domestic structures and international institutions

41 Hayward R. Alker
Rediscoveries and reformulations
Humanistic methodologies for international studies

40 Robert W. Cox with Timothy J. Sinclair
Approaches to world order

39 Jens Bartelson
A genealogy of sovereignty

38 Mark Rupert
Producing hegemony
The politics of mass production and American global power

37 Cynthia Weber
Simulating sovereignty
Intervention, the state and symbolic exchange

36 Gary Goertz
Contexts of international politics

35 James L. Richardson
Crisis diplomacy
The Great Powers since the mid-nineteenth century

34 Bradley S. Klein
Strategic studies and world order
The global politics of deterrence

33 T. V. Paul
Asymmetric conflicts: war initiation by weaker powers

32 Christine Sylvester
Feminist theory and international relations in a postmodern era

31 Peter J. Schraeder
    US foreign policy toward Africa
    Incrementalism, crisis and change
30 Graham Spinardi
    From Polaris to Trident: the development of US Fleet
       Ballistic Missile technology
29 David A. Welch
    Justice and the genesis of war
28 Russell J. Leng
    Interstate crisis behavior, 1816–1980: realism versus reciprocity
27 John A. Vasquez
    The war puzzle
26 Stephen Gill (ed.)
    Gramsci, historical materialism and international relations
25 Mike Bowker and Robin Brown (eds.)
    From cold war to collapse: theory and world politics in the 1980s
24 R. B. J. Walker
    Inside/outside: international relations as political theory
23 Edward Reiss
    The strategic defense initiative
22 Keith Krause
    Arms and the state: patterns of military production and trade
21 Roger Buckley
    US-Japan alliance diplomacy 1945–1990
20 James N. Rosenau and Ernst-Otto Czempiel (eds.)
    **Governance without government: order and change
       in world politics**
19 Michael Nicholson
    Rationality and the analysis of international conflict
18 John Stopford and Susan Strange
    Rival states, rival firms
    Competition for world market shares
17 Terry Nardin and David R. Mapel (eds.)
    Traditions of international ethics
16 Charles F. Doran
    Systems in crisis
    New imperatives of high politics at century's end
15 Deon Geldenhuys
    Isolated states: a comparative analysis
14 Kalevi J. Holsti
    **Peace and war: armed conflicts and international order
       1648–1989**
13 Saki Dockrill
    Britain's policy for West German rearmament 1950–1955
12 Robert H. Jackson
    Quasi-states: sovereignty, international relations and the third world

11 James Barber and John Barratt
   South Africa's foreign policy
   The search for status and security 1945–1988
10 James Mayall
   Nationalism and international society
9 William Bloom
   Personal identity, national identity and international relations
8 Zeev Maoz
   National choices and international processes
7 Ian Clark
   The hierarchy of states
   Reform and resistance in the international order
6 Hidemi Suganami
   The domestic analogy and world order proposals
5 Stephen Gill
   American hegemony and the Trilateral Commission
4 Michael C. Pugh
   The ANZUS crisis, nuclear visiting and deterrence
3 Michael Nicholson
   Formal theories in international relations
2 Friedrich V. Kratochwil
   Rules, norms, and decisions
   On the conditions of practical and legal reasoning in international relations and domestic affairs
1 Myles L. C. Robertson
   Soviet policy towards Japan
   An analysis of trends in the 1970s and 1980s